The Bread Book

The Bread Book

More than
200 recipes and
techniques for
baking and shaping
perfect breads,
sweet and savory
muffins, rolls, buns,
biscuits, and pizzas

BETSY OPPENNEER

HarperCollins*Publishers*

HarperCollins books may be purchased for educational,
business, or sales promotional use. For information, please
write: Special Markets Department, HarperCollins
Publishers, Inc., 10 East 53rd Street, New York, NY
10022.

FIRST EDITION

Designed by Joel Avirom
Illustrations by Jim Cozza

Library of Congress Cataloging-in-Publication Data

Oppenneer, Betsy.
    The bread book / Betsy Oppenneer. — 1st ed.
        p.   cm.
    Includes index.
    ISBN 0-06-016716-5
    1. Bread.   I. Title.
    TX769.068   1994
    641.8'15—dc20   93-33472

94   95   96   97   98   DT/RRD
10   9   8   7   6   5   4   3   2   1

Contents

Acknowledgments

Because cookbooks with recipes that do not work have always infuriated me, I wanted to make sure the recipes in this book really work. To ensure this, I enlisted family, friends, students, and colleagues to test the recipes. I even found two "bread virgins"—willing friends who had never baked before. All deserve a giant thank you.

These eager, enthusiastic testers baked and baked and baked. They filled out a questionnaire for each recipe, grading it on taste, ease of preparation, how attractive the bread was, and whether they would make it again. Without doubt, their comments helped me immeasurably.

I list the testers according to how many recipes they tested. Al Larson, a student of mine from Washington State, tested the most, coming in with sixty-one. Barb Knepper, a fellow military wife who took my bread class when we both lived in Fürth, Germany, tested nearly as many. I don't think either has bought a loaf of bread since they took the classes. Both Chick Terrell, from Miami, Florida, and Paul Meuse, from Jeffersonville, Vermont, are telephone friends from the days when I published the *Breadbasket,* a mail-order catalogue for home bread bakers. These devoted bakers tested numerous recipes, too.

I love to say I taught my father, Jim Wright, from Macon, Georgia, everything he knows (about bread baking!). His testing results taught me a lot, too, and I have included one of Dad's recipes in the book. My mother, Alice Wright, who tested many of the quick bread recipes, taught me a lot as well.

I also want to thank my former tennis partner, Sissel Tangen, who is from Norway and now lives in Redmond, Washington, for all the help she gave me with the recipes. Tracy Flynn-Scott, from Lyme, New Hampshire, one of the so-called bread virgins, happily fell in love with bread baking. Tracy also assisted me with my second video. My niece Mary Ann Bakker, from Shelby, North Carolina, is an avid baker who took time from work and caring for her husband and son to give me help when I needed it most.

Thanks go also to Nancy Eichler, of Mundelein, Illinois, a fellow cooking teacher, and to my sister, Martha Franks, from Kennesaw, Georgia, who says she could test muffin recipes forever. I met Billie Jo Johnstone, of Lebanon, New Hampshire, at a dinner party and am grateful for her offer to test recipes. I also want to thank Sandy Simester, from Issaquah, Washington, for her help. Sandy traveled with me to California to help with the first video, too.

I owe thanks to my niece Laura Pound, from Atlanta, Georgia, who, with three children, still found time to bake "one more thing," as did Yolanda Campbell, of Conroe, Texas. Many thanks to my neighbor and friend, Alice Schori, from Canaan, New Hampshire, and to Richard Scott, of Berkeley, California. Richard was the cameraman for both my videos and became intrigued with bread baking as he viewed it from his side of the camera.

Betsy Murray, my current girl Friday, claims not to be much of a cook, but as my other bread virgin, she taught me a lot. For instance, she was surprised to learn that whole wheat flour is brown —a good reminder that I should not take for granted what people know about baking.

Finally, I want to thank Grant McLaughlin, from Bellevue, Washington, Mary Ann Waters, from Norwich, Vermont, Anna Littlewood, from Bellevue, and Fran Folsom, from Colorado Springs, Colorado.

People from all over the country have contributed generously to this book, and because of their help you should have an easy time baking the recipes.

My thanks and love also go to my agent, Judith Weber. She has become a close friend and has helped me beyond the call of duty with this project. Also, thanks to my son Mark and my friend Mary Goodbody, who helped make my writing more exciting and easier to read. And last but not least, I thank Susan Friedland, my editor, who has taught me so much.

Preface

Few tasks gratify me more than baking bread. A couple of times a week, I head for my warm, friendly kitchen, toss the ingredients together, knead the dough until it comes alive, and then leave it to rise. In a matter of hours, the bread is baking, filling the house with its intoxicating scent; soon afterward, I take my creation from the oven. The entire process feeds my soul as well as my body.

Bread is as close to a perfect food as there is. Both making it and eating it are joyous experiences, satisfying the basic human needs for nourishment, sensuality, and a sense of hearth and home. Bread recipes do not have to be "basic" to meet these requirements. Throughout the book you will find the fancy and the sweet, the braided and the spiced, alongside more rustic loaves. What is more, you will discover the ancient art of bread baking, updated for today's kitchens.

I have taught bread baking for more than thirty years and still revel in its simplicity and its diversity. With *The Bread Book,* I will share with you what I have learned. To help accomplish this, I have included in this book three baking classes—one on yeast breads, the second on sourdough and other natural yeast starters, and the last on quick breads. Please read the pages devoted to these classes carefully before setting out to follow the recipes. The classes will take you through the process step by step, explaining along the way the whys and wherefores of bread baking.

After reading the text and trying the recipes you will realize that bread recipes are not rigid formulas. On the contrary, they are guidelines that give you the creative freedom to personalize your bread with different sorts of flour, sweeteners, herbs, spices, fruits, and nuts.

We have all heard people say they wish they had Grandma's recipe for one thing or another. Chances are, Grandma did not have a recipe for the bread she baked. She probably added a bit of this and a little of that and trusted her instincts and the feel of the dough. I hope this book will enable you to develop similar instincts and learn the importance of the feel of the bread dough. Your fingers and your senses will, more than any recipe, teach you how to make perfect bread, so that someday your grandchildren will ask for your recipes.

1

One of the many pleasures of bread making is that you need neither hard-to-find, expensive ingredients nor complicated utensils. Right this minute, you most likely have everything you need in your kitchen to bake a delicious loaf of bread: flour, yeast, and a bread pan.

To make the task easier and more interesting, I have discovered ingredients and utensils over the years that make a significant difference in the taste and texture of the finished loaf as well as the ease with which it is prepared. None is particularly expensive and few are hard to find. Breads come alive with a handful of raisins or a spoonful of honey, and they bake most evenly in a well-seasoned, heavy dark loaf pan, but there is also a lot to be gained by understanding and using various sorts of flours and sweeteners and having, for instance, the right size sheet pans and ceramic bowls on hand in the kitchen.

In this chapter, first I discuss the various types of grain, then I list the other ingredients I rely on, and finally I describe the utensils I feel have the most value in a home kitchen devoted to bread baking. I hope the information that follows will serve as a useful introduction to the pleasures of baking perfect bread.

The Bread Baker's Kitchen: Ingredients and Utensils

The Grains

Most flour used in American kitchens is milled from wheat. In fact, hard wheat, with its high, strong gluten content (as opposed to the soft wheat preferred for more delicate pastries), is the star of bread baking. The pages that follow present first an alphabetical listing of the most commonly used wheat flours, and then a discussion of some grains and meals that are also based on wheat. But not all flour is made with wheat, and this section concludes with a glossary of the other seeds, berries, and grains that, ground into flour or not, can embellish our so aptly named staff of life.

WHEAT FLOURS

Wheat is processed into a number of different flours: whole wheat, bread flour, bleached and unbleached all-purpose, pastry, cake, and whole wheat pastry flour. The flour is produced by grinding grains of wheat, also called wheat berries. The type of wheat plus where and when it is grown and harvested determines the best uses for the milled flour. The classes of wheat produced are hard red winter, hard red spring, hard and soft white, soft red winter, and durum wheat.

Winter wheat is planted in the fall. It sprouts and then lies dormant until spring, when it begins to grow so that it is ready for an early summer harvest. Flour milled from hard wheat has higher gluten-forming capabilities and is best for yeast bread. Flour milled from soft wheat has weaker gluten-forming capabilities and is best for such baked goods as cookies, cakes, pastries, biscuits, and other quick breads. I add soft cake flour or pastry flour to St. Joseph's Day Bread on page 86 to lighten the loaf.

Spring wheat is planted in the spring and harvested in late summer. Hard spring wheat is high in protein and is milled into flour that forms a good gluten meshwork. Durum wheat is an ancient strain of hard spring wheat grown mostly for use in pasta (see Semolina Flour, below), although it often is found in breads baked in Europe.

Today, most of the wheat grown is milled into white flour, which means the vitamin- and mineral-rich germ and bran are removed, leaving only the starchy endosperm. The endosperm contains the most protein, which in wheat flour means high gluten-forming capabilities. Without the germ and the bran, the flour has a long shelf life, and so is preferred by the commercial food companies.

The Food and Drug Administration requires that iron, niacin, thiamin, and riboflavin be added back to the flour—the very nutrients that are stripped when the germ and bran are removed. Many flour manufacturers also add malted barley flour because it contains an enzyme that renders the natural sugars in wheat more available to yeast. Some companies also add potassium bromate to hard wheat flours as an oxidizing agent that gives bread an added lift during rising. Potassium bromate is somewhat controversial, and its use is restricted in California.

Most all-purpose white flour is blended so that it is a mixture of hard and soft wheats with a protein content of 11 to 13 grams. This amount of protein makes it fine for bread baking and also acceptable for such other baked goods as cakes, pies, and cookies. We can be fairly certain that the all-purpose flour used in Texas will react similarly to the flour used in California, Vermont, or Minnesota. However, in the days before widespread national distribution, home cooks used the flour milled from local wheat. This explains, to some degree, why cooks in the South developed a reputation for baking light biscuits and tender cakes: they had access to soft wheat flour. Hearty loaves were common in the north and west, where the wheat was harder.

It takes about a month for flour to age naturally and be useful for baking. Many flour companies speed up the aging process by using chemicals. They also sometimes add bleach to the flour. I use only *unbleached* all-purpose flour and also stay away from any flour containing potassium bromate. Read the labels carefully on the side of the flour sack. Without the benefit of chemical treatment the flour may cost a little more, but I feel the overall goodness of the baked bread is well worth it.

ALL-PURPOSE FLOUR. This may be either bleached or unbleached. It combines different types of wheat flour so that it can be used for everything from cakes to yeast breads. Each manufacturer has its own blend—read the side panel to determine the protein level. If the flour contains only 9 to 10 grams of protein, it is not strong enough to use for yeast breads. The major flour manufacturers make all-purpose flour with an average of 11 grams of protein, which is enough for yeast bread, although 12 grams is better and 13 grams best of all. Quick breads (leavened with baking powder or soda) may be made with any of these protein levels, although in making them I often substitute pastry flour or cornstarch for a quarter of the all-purpose flour containing more than 11 grams of protein.

BREAD FLOUR. A hard wheat flour, often with potassium bromate or vitamin C added, bread flour is designed to give the baker a higher loaf of bread than all-purpose flour. Because the average protein level for bread flour is 14 grams, it is not advisable for quick breads. Bread flour reacts differently from all-purpose flour. For instance, it requires more kneading to activate the gluten sufficiently and it absorbs more liquid. If you use bread flour, use your judgment and the feel of the dough to determine how much flour to add. All my recipes using white flour call for unbleached all-purpose flour.

CAKE FLOUR. Cake flour is ground from soft wheat that has little or no gluten-forming potential. Because of its high starch level, it produces light, airy, tender cakes but should not be used in other forms of baking.

DURUM FLOUR. Durum flour is made from durum wheat as a by-product of the manufacture of semolina flour; it's the bran and germ from durum wheat with a portion of the endosperm. This hearty and full-flavored flour is used in many of today's newer breads. However, it must be mixed with all-purpose flour, or the bread will be too heavy.

GLUTEN FLOUR. This is also known as vital wheat gluten and is processed from protein-rich hard wheat flour from which so much starch has been removed that it is about 50 percent gluten. It should be used in conjunction with other flours to give it extra strength—never by itself. Many bakers rely on gluten flour to give lift to whole-grain flours such as rye that benefit from the additional gluten.

Gluten flour is expensive, but it is not necessary to use very much. It is hard to digest, and some people with only mild gluten intolerance react strongly to it. I rarely use gluten flour because I believe a properly handled dough does fine without it. In addition, bread made with gluten flour dries out quickly.

INSTANT FLOUR. Technically called agglomerated flour, instant flour is designed for making gravy and sauces rather than for baking. It is a low-protein flour that has been moisturized and then ground into tiny uniform particles so that it flows like sugar or salt and does not lump.

PASTRY FLOUR. This is very finely milled soft wheat and is used for cookies, cakes, muffins, pie crusts, quick breads, biscuits, and pastries. Similar to cake flour, it has even less starch and is often available unbleached. Because of its lack of gluten-forming proteins, it is not usually used for yeast baking.

SELF-RISING FLOUR. Most common in the South, self-rising flour is a low-protein soft wheat flour with added baking powder and salt. The flour is designed to make light quick breads such as biscuits or muffins, but should never be used for yeast breads. Store self-rising flour in an airtight container in a cool place to preserve the leaveners.

SEMOLINA FLOUR. Semolina flour is made from the coarsely ground endosperm of durum wheat and is used mainly for pasta and some European-style breads. It is high in protein and has a wholesome, nutty flavor and rich golden color. Semolina may be used by itself or combined with other wheat flour for yeast breads. When using it, keep the dough as slack as possible, since too much semolina flour makes the bread heavy. Try semolina in quick breads, especially muffins and waffles.

WHOLE WHEAT FLOUR. This is ground from the whole berry of hard wheat. Baked goods made with 100 percent whole wheat flour are denser and heavier than those made with unbleached all-purpose flour owing to the presence of the bran and germ. The weight reduces the effectiveness of the gluten to some degree.

I have found that, for the average taste, a mixture of one third whole wheat to two thirds all-purpose flour is a good balance. The resulting bread is light, with a texture similar to that of white breads, and has the good, nutty flavor of whole wheat.

Whole wheat flour may be substituted in any recipe calling for unbleached flour. If substituting whole wheat for a portion of all-purpose flour in quick breads, remove 2 tablespoons from every cup of whole wheat flour used.

Whole wheat flour is sometimes stone-ground or water-ground, two processes that treat the flour a little more gently than it is treated in huge commercial mills. Stone-ground flour is made by grinding wheat between two round stones, one stationary, the other not. If the stone is turned by water, the flour is considered water-ground. Although these flours are usually available in health food stores, they're becoming more available in supermarkets.

WHOLE WHEAT GRAHAM FLOUR. Graham flour, also called whole meal, was formulated by the nineteenth-century health food crusader Sylvester Graham. The original formula was made by grinding the entire kernel of wheat. Today, graham flour is produced by different companies, each with its own formula, in some of which a portion of the bran, or outer coating, has been removed. Graham flour can be used in any recipe requiring whole wheat flour—or vice versa.

WHOLE WHEAT PASTRY FLOUR. Ground from the whole kernel of soft wheat, whole wheat pastry flour is low in protein and thus not used in wheat breads unless combined with another wheat flour. However, it makes flavorful quick breads, cookies, and cakes.

WHEAT GRAINS AND MEALS

BULGUR WHEAT. Bulgur is made from wheat berries that are cut into coarse pieces, parboiled, and toasted. Since it is precooked during processing, bulgur may be added to baked goods with no further treatment. But because it absorbs twice its volume in liquid, it should be soaked first or it will dry out the dough. It adds a rich, robust flavor and crunchy texture to all types of bread.

COUSCOUS. Couscous is made from polished durum wheat from which the bran and germ have been removed. It is found in pilaf, steamed as a side dish, or added to salads and casseroles. Cooked or uncooked, it adds a delightful flavor and texture to breads.

CRACKED WHEAT. Made from coarsely chopped wheat berries, cracked wheat can range from extremely coarse to fine. When I use very coarse cracked wheat, I prefer to soak it in the liquid called for in the recipe before adding the other ingredients—otherwise, it can play havoc with dental work! Cracked wheat may be added to casseroles, soups, and salads, and it adds a crunch and nutty flavor to baked goods.

Since I like texture in breads, I prefer to use coarse cracked wheat. I also keep finely cracked wheat on hand to coat dough before baking—it adds a nice coating to the finished breads. (Both medium and coarse cracked wheat get too hard during baking for this.) However, the problem with finely cracked wheat is that it is barely discernible if used in the bread itself.

FARINA. The coarsely ground endosperm of hard wheat, farina is used in breakfast cereals and pasta. Many recipes call for farina in quick breads, cookies, or as an additive to yeast breads.

SPELT. This is an ancient variety of wheat with small brown grains that adhere tightly to the chaff. It has been cultivated since Biblical times (there are references to it in the Bible) but early in the twentieth century cultivation declined as higher-yielding crops took precedence. Today, spelt is experiencing something of a renaissance because it is tolerated by people with wheat allergies and can be used in recipes calling for wheat flour. Cook spelt as you do rice, or add it to pilafs and breads.

WHEAT BRAN. A by-product of white flour, wheat bran is the outer layer of the wheat berry and is high in dietary fiber. I like to add a little bran to bread and other baked goods for its flavor and fiber.

WHEAT FLAKES. Similar to oatmeal, wheat flakes are wheat berries that have been steamed and then rolled flat. For baking, use them as you would rolled oats (see page 10).

WHEAT GERM. Another by-product of white flour, wheat germ is the embryo or germ (sprouting section) of the wheat berry. Its protein quality is comparable to that of milk, and many health-conscious people sprinkle the flaky substance on cereal and fruit. I like it mixed into bread dough; it conditions the dough so that the bread has good volume and even texture. Do not add too much wheat germ to bread—the oil coats the flour, making the dough heavier. For best results, substitute 2 tablespoons of germ for each cup of the total flour in the recipe.

Toasted wheat germ has a pleasant, nutty flavor and keeps for nearly six months in an airtight container in the refrigerator or freezer. If left untoasted, the oils in the germ turn rancid and bitter. Use toasted wheat germ in place of ground nuts in granola, cakes, muffins, and other preparations.

NONWHEAT FLOURS

Nonwheat flours include those milled from grains that may not be as familiar as wheat. Here is a glossary of the most commonly found of these grains and flours.

AMARANTH. A small seed grown in Mexico and Central America, amaranth is exceptionally high in protein and other nutrients and is sometimes called the supergrain. Use amaranth grain in breads, casseroles, and pilafs and substitute the flour for wheat flour in quick breads. Since amaranth lacks gluten, it should be combined with wheat flour for yeast breads.

BARLEY. Reputed to be the first cultivated grain, barley was once the grain used most often for breads. Today we rarely find it in bread, although malted barley frequently is mixed with commercial wheat flour as food for yeast.

The grain is encased in two tough outer layers, or husks, that make it inedible. When the husks are removed, the result is hulled barley. Much of the barley available in grocery stores is pearled, which means the bran and the germ have been removed from the hulled grain. This makes it easy to digest but also strips it of vitamins and minerals. While pearled barley is tasty in soups, stews, casseroles, and pilafs, it adds little flavor or texture to bread.

Barley flour, milled from hulled barley, gives baked goods a moist, sweet flavor and soft, chewy texture. Toasting the flour improves and intensifies the barley flavor. Because barley flour is low in gluten, it should be combined with wheat flour when making yeast breads. Quick breads made with 100 percent barley flour tend to be dense, so I suggest mixing barley flour with wheat flour. Barley flour is extremely perishable and should be stored in an airtight container in the freezer for no more than three months.

Barley flakes, produced by steaming barley kernels and then rolling them flat, may be substituted in any recipe calling for rolled oats or oatmeal. I particularly like them in chocolate chip cookies.

For extra moistness, cook rolled barley flakes into a porridge before adding them to yeast bread recipes, and for a chewy loaf, add dry (uncooked) flakes.

BUCKWHEAT. Also known as saracen corn, buckwheat is not a grain but the edible fruit of the buckwheat plant and a close cousin to rhubarb and sorrel. It has a nutritional value similar to that of wheat and it flourishes in cool climates. Buckwheat is a staple of middle and northern Europe as well as parts of Maine and Canada. Its strong, pungent flavor is enhanced when the flour or groat (the hulled seed) is toasted lightly, and it may, unless used with discretion, dominate other ingredients. Dark buckwheat tastes stronger than light-colored buckwheat.

Buckwheat groats are eaten as cereal or ground into flour, which is most commonly used for pancakes, crepes, and muffins. The groats may also be steamed, roasted until dry, and then cracked to produce kasha. Kasha, sold boxed in supermarkets, is cooked as a cereal or used as an ingredient in pilafs, casseroles, stews, and salads.

CORN. Indian corn, or maize, has more uses than any other grain. It is eaten as a vegetable, made into cereal, turned into hominy (by soaking in a lye solution to remove the hull and germ), ground into meal, flour, and grits (coarsely ground dried hominy). Masa harina, used for tortillas, is made from corn soaked in lime which is ground into a fine meal with a consistency almost as fine as flour. Corn is also processed into oil, brewed into whiskey, and made into cornstarch.

Cornmeal, ground from yellow or white corn, is available stone-ground or enriched-degerminated. Stone-ground cornmeal, the more nutritious of the two, is made from dried whole kernels of corn; it has a rich, intense sweet corn flavor and an oily quality. Because it still contains the germ, stone-ground cornmeal should be stored in an airtight container in the refrigerator or freezer for no longer than four months. Breads made with stone-ground cornmeal are naturally sweet and crunchy.

Enriched-degerminated cornmeal, also known as bolted cornmeal, is produced by drying whole kernels of corn and grinding them with steel rollers. To extend shelf life, the fiber and germ are removed and then replaced with enrichments—added vitamins and minerals. Enriched-degerminated or bolted cornmeal keeps for up to nine months in an airtight container at room temperature. Breads made with this kind of cornmeal tend to be dry and crumbly.

Cornmeal enhances the flavor of yeast breads but, because it contains no gluten, must be mixed with wheat flour. A good ratio is one part cornmeal to two parts wheat flour. Because cornmeal is highly absorbent, I recommend soaking any cornmeal destined for a yeast bread in the liquid required in the recipe before adding it to the dough.

Cornmeal is often used to dust baking sheets or bread pans to prevent the bread from sticking. Rolling kneaded, shaped yeast dough in cornmeal gives the baked bread a good, crunchy crust.

Cornstarch is made from the starchy endosperm of the corn, and is generally used as a thickener. It also neutralizes the gluten in all-purpose flour and so may be added to quick breads to lighten their texture.

GARBANZOS. Also known as chick-peas, garbanzos are legumes that can be dried and ground into the flour used to make Indian and Pakistani breads. Mixed with wheat flour, garbanzo flour produces a sweet-tasting, nutritious yeast bread. Quick breads made with silky garbanzo flour alone often fall during baking.

MILLET. The cereal grass millet is rich in minerals, easy to digest, and considered to have the most complete protein of all the grains. Nevertheless, Americans are most familiar with the tiny seeds as birdseed. Happily, millet is showing up with increasing frequency in bread and other recipes because it is soft and may be used whole in breads for wonderful crunch. It is also ground into meal or flour. Toasting millet seeds and millet flour brings out their sweet, nutty flavor.

OATS. Rich in minerals and protein, oats have a natural antioxidant that prevents the germ from turning rancid as quickly as it does in other grains. This means that oats may be stored for up to a year in an airtight container on the pantry shelf without losing nutrients. It also means that breads baked with oat flour or a good measure of rolled oats stay fresh longer than other breads.

Oat bran is sometimes added to bread dough to extend the bread's freshness and to provide nutrients. Oat groats, the hulled grain sold in many health food stores and some supermarkets, also make breads more nutritious. When the groats are soaked in warm liquid before they are kneaded into the dough, they swell and give the baked bread a pleasingly chewy texture.

Oat groats are naturally soft and cannot be milled in the same way as other grains. They must be ground with metal blades, not between stones. They also can be flattened between metal rollers after they have been steamed to produce the well-known rolled oats, or flakes, that are cooked into breakfast porridge. Quick-cooking oatmeal is made from groats that are cut into pieces after steaming and before rolling; instant oatmeal is made from pre-cooked oat groats that are rolled very thin. Scottish or Irish oatmeal is made by cutting oat groats into small pieces with steel cutters. The size of these pieces speeds up cooking. For my recipes, I recommend old-fashioned rolled oats or, as it is more widely known, uncooked oatmeal.

You can grind old-fashioned rolled oats into flour in a blender or food processor to add to breads, or you can buy oat flour in health food stores or large supermarkets. Oat flour does not form gluten, so, like other whole-grain flours, it must be combined with wheat flour for yeast breads. Oat flour is often substituted for wheat flour when making quick breads for people with wheat allergies.

QUINOA. A high-protein grain used by the ancient Incas, quinoa (pronounced KEEN-wah) is soft with a slight crunch and is extremely nutritious. The seeds are coated with a bitter substance and so, unless otherwise specified on the package, need to be rinsed in cold water before using. Quinoa flour is made from rinsed grains and needs no special treatment. Toasting the grain intensifies its flavor. Quinoa can be substituted for rice in many recipes.

RICE. Cooked rice may be added to quick or yeast breads to produce a moist, dense loaf.

The product called rice flour is a powdery substance made from white rice and is used primarily as a dusting for baked goods such as croissants to prevent them from sticking to the pan during baking. It is sometimes used as an ingredient in commercial bread mixes to keep the leaveners dry.

Ground rice flour, also called brown rice flour, is milled from the whole grain. It is grainy and pale beige in color. If you want to bake yeast bread with ground rice flour, mix it with wheat flour, since ground rice flour contains no gluten. Lightly toasting rice flour intensifies its flavor.

Sweet rice flour is made from short-grain rice, which is more glutenous than long-grain rice varieties. It is used mainly for pastries.

RYE. Its rich, earthy, sweet-and-sour flavor has made rye a favorite for centuries. This versatile grain can be cracked, made into meal, or rolled into flakes. It also is milled into light rye, medium rye, dark rye, and pumpernickel flour.

Cracked rye, or "chops," is whole grain that has been chopped into coarse pieces. If you can get hold of rye grains, you can easily make chops at home in a blender or food processor. For baking, I advise softening chops briefly in water to prevent them from absorbing too much moisture from the dough and producing a heavy loaf.

Rye meal is more finely ground than chops and gives bread a rugged, hearty texture so important for peasant breads. Unfortunately, rye meal is hard to find.

Rye flakes are made from kernels that, similar to oat flakes, are first steamed and then rolled flat. As with oatmeal, I generally cook them into porridge before I add them to yeast dough for a moist dense bread. When I add them dry, the bread is nice and chewy.

Rye flour is available as light (also called white), medium, dark, and pumpernickel. Light rye is finely ground, milled from the endosperm alone and so contains none of the vitamins, minerals, or oils of the germ and bran. It most often is used by commercial bakeries and as such is hard to find in consumer markets. If you grind your own rye, sift it through a tamis (nylon sieve) or extremely fine strainer to make light rye flour. Do not discard the bran and germ but save it for use in another recipe.

Medium rye flour, ground from the grain after the bran is removed, is the kind generally used by the home baker. Dark rye and pumpernickel flour are milled from the whole grain with the bran and germ intact. These flours produce hearty, bold-tasting, dark loaves favored in parts of Europe.

Because of its low gluten content, rye flour should be mixed with wheat flour for bread baking. Add it with a very light hand and make sure the dough stays somewhat sticky; too much rye flour results in bricklike loaves. To find out if you have added enough flour, round the dough into a ball: if it holds its shape without spreading, there is sufficient flour, even if the dough feels sticky. Rye dough should rise in a relatively cool spot for a slow, even rise or the bread may fall during baking.

SORGHUM. Also known as milo, sorghum is not common in America except as a sweetener, but it is a major cereal grain in Africa and India. The whole grain may be steamed and used in baking as you would cooked rice. Sorghum is also ground into flour for baking. For best results, combine it with wheat flour in yeast breads.

SOY. A legume rather than a grain, the soybean boasts the highest protein level of any plant food and consequently is relied upon by many people as a major component of their diet. Dried soybeans may be ground into flour. As a general rule, if the flour is labeled "soy flour," it is made from raw beans; if it is labeled "soya flour," the beans were toasted first. Both types work well in baking but should be used sparingly and mixed with wheat flour, because too much soy flour imparts a soapy taste.

Soy flour conditions dough, making it rise higher, and aids in browning the bread's crust. I often substitute 1 or 2 tablespoons of soy flour for an equal amount of wheat flour, especially if I am using a large percentage of whole wheat flour and need the extra lift provided by the soy flour. Soy flour's high oil content makes it go rancid quickly and so it should be stored in an airtight container in the refrigerator or freezer for no longer than a month or two.

TEFF. This African cereal grass is an ancient grain that is gaining new popularity. Sold as brown, white, or red teff, the seeds are so tiny that it takes almost one hundred to equal a single wheat kernel. Despite its size, teff is a nutritional powerhouse and is particularly high in iron. It is difficult to grind in a home mill, but you can buy teff flour in health food stores. Both the whole grain and the flour add an unmistakable flavor to all breads. I especially like it in sourdough breads.

TRITICALE. A modern hybrid of wheat and rye, triticale (pronounced trit-i-KAY-lee) was developed to combine the gluten-forming capabilities of wheat with the nutritiousness and strong flavor of rye. It is a boon for persons with a wheat intolerance, since it rarely affects them. Breads made with triticale flour are quite perishable and should be eaten soon after baking.

Triticale is one of the few flours with enough gluten to make a yeast-risen loaf without adding pure wheat flour. But without wheat, the dough needs careful handling to keep the bread from falling during baking. When making bread with 100 percent triticale flour, knead the dough very gently for 3 to 5 minutes and then let it rest for a full 5 minutes. Do not let it rise in a bowl; instead, immediately shape it into a loaf, cover it with a tightly woven kitchen towel, and let it rise in a warm place (about 80°F) for 45 minutes, or until almost but *not completely* doubled. Take care, however, that the temperature for rising is not much warmer than 80°. Bake the bread for about 5 minutes longer than normal.

A fifty-fifty combination of triticale and wheat flour makes a marvelous-tasting bread. If you want to make yeast bread quickly, handle the dough as described above for 100 percent triticale flour. Otherwise, treat the dough as you would any wheat-flour dough.

Triticale is sold as berries, flakes, or flour. Because the berries are hard, they are best cooked or else soaked in hot water before being used whole in breads. Flakes are the whole grains that have been steamed and rolled flat. They may be cooked and eaten as you would oatmeal or added to yeast breads (in any recipes calling for rolled oats) for a moist, tangy loaf. Using dry flakes produces a chewy loaf.

The Other Ingredients

Grains and water are the basic requirements for making a no-frills bread (a tortilla, for example). It's the other ingredients that can take a simple loaf to sublime heights. Here is an alphabetical listing of the most important of them.

ACIDS
Acid ingredients in bread dough soften its elasticity and therefore are especially beneficial in recipes that call for whole-grain flours

exclusively, such as 100 percent whole wheat bread. Whole-grain flours are heavier than all-purpose white flour and need all the help they can get during rising.

Lemon juice, vinegar, and ascorbic acid are all good sources, but beware of too much, since an overdose of acid inhibits yeast fermentation. A good measure is about 1 tablespoon of acid to 3 cups of flour. If using powdered ascorbic acid (you may substitute a crushed vitamin C tablet), dissolve it first in the liquid called for in the recipe (water, milk, etc.).

Other acidic agents used in baking include sour milk, buttermilk, yogurt, sour cream, orange juice, cocoa (not Dutch processed), molasses, and cream of tartar.

CREAM OF TARTAR. The solid salt of tartaric acid that forms on wine casks, cream of tartar is a major ingredient in baking powder and is also sold on its own. In baking powder, acidic cream of tartar is blended with alkaline baking soda to create a substance with a balanced acid-alkaline pH. If you substitute cream of tartar for baking powder in a recipe that includes acidic ingredients such as sour cream, yogurt, buttermilk, or citrus juice, you must add baking soda, too, to neutralize the acids.

EGGS

Eggs add color and fat to breads and rolls. They also act as a leavener, and as such improve the structure of baked goods. The fresher the eggs, the better they are for baking. To test eggs for freshness, put them in a bowl of cool water—fresh eggs sink to the bottom, older eggs float. Brown and white eggs reflect only the breed of hen that laid them; they produce identical results.

The size and grade of the egg make a difference in baking. I developed the recipes in this book using U.S. grade A large eggs. Jumbo and medium eggs are, for the most part, too large or too small for good results. Grade B eggs, which are sold mainly to large food companies and institutions, are hard to find in supermarkets or other consumer outlets.

Egg yolks contribute to a delicate dough, and stiffly beaten egg whites to a light, airy texture. If a recipe calls for separated eggs, perform the task when the eggs are cold. Yolks break more easily when warm. For good volume, it is important that not a speck of yolk or piece of shell invade the whites. Let the egg whites reach room temperature before beating them and, if possible, use a balloon whisk and a strong arm to beat them to billowy heights. But if you prefer, use a standing mixer or a hand-held electric mixer. If the yolks require beating too, beat the whites first and then the yolks so that you do not have to wash the beaters.

FATS

Fats improve the keeping quality, texture, and moistness of breads. In yeast breads, they lubricate the gluten meshwork of dough, so that it expands more easily and helps the bread to rise and develop its characteristic texture. On the other hand, too much fat impedes the action of leaveners, so it is important to follow a recipe carefully. While I cover the most commonly used fats here, egg yolks also count as fat, so please read that entry as well.

BUTTER. Besides being prized for its flavor, butter produces extremely tender baked goods. Most domestic butter is produced from cow's milk and will vary in color and quality depending on its cream content, which in turn depends on the season and the cow's diet. Other countries make butter from the milk of the water buffalo, yak, goat, and sheep as well as the cow, and may use it in baking, which is one reason why some breads you taste as you travel abroad are impossible to duplicate at home (the flour and water of a particular country make a significant difference too).

Old or improperly stored butter turns rancid and can ruin baked goods. Never use butter that has an off smell or taste—both intensify during baking. And keep in mind that butter has a high cholesterol and saturated fat content, and therefore should be used only occasionally by those who are concerned about cholesterol.

Butter is available unsalted, salted, and whipped. I suggest using only fresh unsalted butter for breads. It is churned from sweet cream and has a mild, pleasing flavor. It scorches easily in sautéing but performs beautifully in baking. Buy it often and store it in the refrigerator or freezer. Salted butter is a poor second. The salt, added to extend the shelf life of the butter, interferes with the salt in the recipe. It also tends to mask the off flavors of rancidity, which will be noticeable in the baked bread. Whipped butter is not recommended for baking; the air incorporated into it to make it spreadable works against it in the oven so that it does not perform properly.

Butter reacts to heat more readily than other fats. Yeast doughs containing a lot of butter should rise in a relatively cool place for the best texture. If the dough is left to rise in a warm corner of the kitchen, the butter may break down and cause the bread to fall in the oven.

LARD. Lard is rendered pork fat and yields the most tender baked goods of all. Many good cooks throughout the history of baking have relied on lard for their breads, pie crusts, and biscuits. Today it is seldom found in recipes because it is high in saturated fat (although in truth it has less than butter). If you want to substitute lard for butter in baking, reduce the amount by 20 to 25 percent.

MARGARINE. This venerable butter substitute is produced from hydrogenated vegetable oils. Usually a mixture of polyunsaturated and saturated oils, many margarines also contain a lot of water that evaporates during baking. Furthermore, different manufacturers use slightly different methods of producing margarine and consequently alter the taste and texture of the product. For these two reasons, I find margarine unacceptable as a substitute for butter or other shortening in baking. Many people mistakenly believe that margarine is lower in fat than butter. It is not; it is, however, lower in saturated fat.

If you choose to use margarine in baking, never use diet or whipped. The air incorporated into it for volume means that a half cup of whipped margarine may be equal to only a third or a quarter of a cup of butter rather than a full half cup. Margarine is often confused with products labeled "spreads." By law, butter and margarine must be 80 percent fat, but spreads may have less fat. The lower fat content of spreads is compensated for by added water, so that when they are used for baking the end result is not as tender, flavorful, or finely textured as when shortenings with more fat are used.

OILS. Oils can be made from nuts, grains, fruits, and vegetables. Essentially, they are either pure or refined. Pure oils are extracted from a single source, such as olives or sunflower seeds. They are not processed further after extraction and consequently have a relatively short shelf life. They have distinctive flavor and therefore are recommended in recipes where that flavor is desirable.

Refined oils are mixtures of extremely stable vegetable oils and are processed, or refined, to extend their shelf life to six to ten months. This makes them especially useful for institutional kitchens and for use in commercial products. Many home cooks like these oils, too, for everyday cooking. They have no flavor or odor and cannot be detected in the baked or cooked product. Rather than being labeled according to their food source, refined oils are given names such as Wesson or Crisco oil.

VEGETABLE SHORTENINGS. These are made from saturated and polyunsaturated oils and contain little or no cholesterol. These are the familiar solid white shortenings found in wide-mouthed cans. Hydrogen gas, forced into the oils under pressure, makes them solid and stable enough to be stored at room temperature for as long as a year after opening. Many home cooks prefer solid shortening for baked goods such as biscuits and pie crusts. Its composition makes it work similarly to lard so that the baked product is light and tender. Keep in mind that vegetable shortening is easier to cut into flour if it is refrigerated first.

LEAVENERS

Any agent that causes a dough or batter to rise is called a leavener. For my purposes, I focus on the three products most people think of when they consider leaveners: baking powder, baking soda, and yeast.

BAKING POWDER. Probably the most widely used leavener for general baking, baking powder is a mixture of baking soda, flour or cornstarch (to prevent caking), and an acid such as cream of tartar. Different brands of baking powder vary these ingredients, but all contain them in some measure to create an alkaline/acid balance. It is this balance that causes the baking powder to produce carbon dioxide gas bubbles when it is mixed with liquid, exposed to heat, or both. In turn, the expanding gas causes the baking cake, muffins, or quick bread to rise.

There are two types of baking powder: single acting and double acting. Single-acting baking powder requires only moisture to release carbon dioxide. Double-acting baking powder releases some gas when mixed with liquid, but needs heat to release the remaining gas. Most home cooks use double-acting baking powder, in part because single-acting baking powder is difficult to find. Double-acting baking powder is a post–World War II innovation that freed the cook from having to rush the mixing process, since most of the rising action takes place in the oven.

Use baking powder before the expiration date on the package or your baked goods will lack volume. To ensure that the baking powder is still potent, test it by combining 1 teaspoonful with ¼ cup of hot water. If the mixture bubbles and fizzes, the powder is still good. You can make your own single-acting baking powder by combining two parts cream of tartar with one part baking soda.

BAKING SODA. This alkaline leavener is used for quick breads and other preparations containing an acidic ingredient (see Acids, above). Baking soda balances the acid so that the batter releases an appropriate amount of carbon dioxide bubbles for maximum leavening. Baking soda is sometimes added to sourdough recipes to cut the acidity of the starter.

If you decide to substitute an acidic ingredient in a recipe for a nonacidic one, I suggest adding ½ teaspoon of baking soda to the batter for every cup of acidic ingredient. In other words, if you decide to use buttermilk rather than whole milk, add ½ teaspoon of baking soda for every cup of milk called for, along with any baking powder called for in the recipe.

YEAST. Like something out of science fiction, yeast is a living microorganism, stored in suspended animation and waiting to be brought back to life. Warm water restores its life; once revived, it requires nourishment. When mixed with flour, yeast feeds on its natural sugars and multiplies. In the process, it produces carbon dioxide that becomes trapped in the network of developing gluten strands and causes dough to rise.

Active dry yeast is the most commonly available and most widely used sort of yeast. You can buy it in most grocery stores in small foil packages holding ¼ ounce of granular powder. The packages are dated for freshness, and you should use the yeast before the expiration date. If you do not bake often, this is the most economical way to buy yeast. If you bake often, try to find active dry yeast in 4-ounce jars (available in many supermarkets and some health food stores). These jars are also dated, and ounce for ounce, the yeast costs less than when individually packaged. For avid bakers, I recommend buying yeast in bulk as it saves money. Many grocery stores have bulk food sections, and bulk yeast is sold in health food stores. There also are several good mail order sources for yeast (see page 411). If you use active dry yeast before its expiration date, it will still be alive. If you are unsure of its viability, proof it in warm water with a pinch of sugar. If it is alive, it will foam and swell in the water. For more on proofing, see page 54.

Store yeast in a cool place. The refrigerator or freezer is ideal. Yeast is dormant at temperatures lower than 50°F and dies at temperatures hotter than 120°F. It does not have to be brought back to room temperature before mixing it with the liquid or other bread ingredients.

A scant tablespoon of active dry yeast equals one ¼-ounce package. American yeast manufacturers recommend using 1 scant tablespoon or one ¼-ounce package of active dry yeast for each pound of flour (about 4 cups of all-purpose flour or 3½ cups of whole wheat flour). While less yeast can be used (see below), beware of adding too much. This will affect the flavor and texture of the finished bread and cause it to go stale more quickly than loaves baked with the correct amount.

When I bake for myself, I use 1 teaspoon of yeast for each pound (about 4 cups) of unbleached all-purpose flour. If using whole wheat or another whole-grain flour, I increase the amount of yeast to a *heaping* teaspoon for every pound of flour. Because I use less yeast, the dough needs more time to rise. The longer rise contributes to better flavor. I provide more specific measurements in my recipes, but you may find that they use slightly less yeast than other bread recipes with which you are familiar.

Fast-rising or quick-rising yeast is available in most supermarkets in ¼-ounce packages and may sometimes be found in 4-ounce jars. It is a different strain of yeast from active dry yeast, and when the expiration date passes, cannot be tested by traditional proofing —it may foam up regardless of its viability. When the date expires, I suggest discarding the yeast.

Fast-rising yeast and quick-rising yeasts are marketed by both Fleischmann's and Red Star—the two companies use the slightly differing terminology for similar products—to encourage bread baking; they were developed because the home cook demands speed. I feel that whenever you rush bread baking, you sacrifice something. The breads leavened by these fast-acting yeasts are good, but use them only when you are really pressed. The loaves have a soft texture that reminds me of store-bought breads.

For best results, follow the instructions on the packages or use the rapid-mix methods discussed in chapter 2, "Baking Class: Making Yeast Breads" (see page 62). You may substitute this type of yeast for active dry yeast or use it with sourdough starter in a recipe and the dough will rise in half the time—but, as I said, the results are not quite as tasty or satisfying.

Compressed cake yeast was the most commonly used yeast in America several generations ago. The cakes have a shorter shelf life than dry yeast granules and so have lost favor here, but remain the preferred leavener in Europe. I recommend trying it now and again because it produces an outstanding loaf of bread. A ⅝-ounce package (or one third of a 2-ounce cake) is equal to 1 package of active dry or fast-rising yeast.

When you buy compressed yeast cakes, you may wrap them in plastic and foil and freeze them for up to three months. Thaw them in the refrigerator before activating them for baking.

To activate the yeast, crumble the cake over tepid water (about 90°F) that has been combined with a teaspoon of sweetener and let the mixture sit for about 5 minutes without stirring. When the yeast swells and foams it is ready to be added to the other ingredients.

Brewers' yeast is sold in health food stores mainly as dry powder and should not be confused with bread-baking yeast. It is consumed for nutritional purposes and will not react with bread dough. If you have access to a brewery, you might be able to obtain another sort of brewers' yeast: the barm that forms on beer or ale during fermentation. This active brew produces incredible bread, but it is difficult to come by.

For more on yeast, see page 53.

LIQUIDS

Liquids are essential to all breads. In yeast breads, they stimulate gluten development and cause yeast to ferment, the process that produces carbon dioxide. In quick breads, they moisten the leavener so that it releases carbon dioxide. In both instances, the carbon dioxide bubbles cause the loaves to rise.

BEER. Beer adds zesty flavor to both quick and yeast breads. Darker beer imparts a stronger flavor. You can use flat beer for bread baking; the carbonation has little effect on the results.

BROTH OR STOCK. The addition of beef, chicken, or vegetable broth can give some breads a savory taste and even texture. Canned broth tends to be extremely salty and so may affect yeast fermentation. Cut the amount of salt in the recipe in half if adding canned broth.

BUTTERMILK. Buttermilk adds tang to breads as well as the soft, light texture provided by all dairy products. Some stores sell powdered buttermilk, which is convenient and tastes just as good in the baked product as fresh buttermilk. If you add buttermilk to quick breads leavened with baking powder, be sure to add ½ teaspoon of baking soda for each cup of buttermilk (see page 19 for more information).

EVAPORATED MILK. This staple is a fine substitute for regular milk. It should be diluted with an equal amount of water before being used in any recipe calling for fresh milk.

FRUIT JUICES AND PUREES. Fruit can add fresh flavors to breads. Use unsweetened juices for yeast breads, since excess sugar retards rising. For a piquant flavor in quick breads, substitute orange, cranberry, white grape, apple, pineapple, or prune juice for the milk or water in the recipe. Bear in mind that orange juice is extremely acidic and performs best if you add ½ teaspoon of baking soda for every cup used. Raisin juice, which can be found in some health food stores, acts as an antioxidant and extends the life of baked goods.

HEAVY CREAM. Also known as whipping cream, this produces extremely light batters. In most instances, its presence means all other fats can be eliminated from quick bread recipes.

MILK. Milk is often used in bread to strengthen gluten, add nutritional value, help the crust brown, and extend the keeping qualities of yeast breads. In quick breads, it ensures soft, tender texture. Whole milk, 2 percent, 1 percent, or skim milk all work equally well in recipes.

Nonfat dry milk or powdered milk may be reconstituted and used for the amount of milk required in a recipe with excellent results. You can also combine the milk powder with the flour and then use water as the liquid in the recipe. Use ⅓ cup of milk powder and 1 cup of water for every cup of milk in the recipe.

From time to time, you will run across old recipes that call for sour milk. Undoubtedly, these recipes were developed to make use of unpasteurized milk that had begun to turn. To make mock sour milk, add 1 tablespoon of lemon juice or vinegar to 1 cup of milk and let the mixture sit for 5 minutes until it curdles. The curdled milk is called clabber. Sour milk tenderizes gluten and produces a lighter texture.

Most cooks buy pasteurized milk, but if you have access to unpasteurized milk, be sure to scald and cool it before using it. It contains an enzyme that interferes with yeast development but which is neutralized by scalding—this explains why old-fashioned recipes call for scalded milk.

POTATO WATER. This is simply water in which peeled potatoes have been boiled. Do not add salt to the cooking water if you plan to use the potato water for baking. Potato water creates a moist, velvety bread with more volume than bread made with plain water. You can store potato water in the refrigerator for several days, but be sure to scald and cool it before using it in yeast breads. As it sits it develops an enzyme, like the enzyme in unpasteurized milk, that interferes with yeast development but which is neutralized by scalding.

VEGETABLE JUICES AND PUREES. These add wholesome flavor and color to both yeast and quick breads. If the puree is so thick it refuses to pour from a bowl or pitcher, thin it with liquid until it no longer "plops."

WATER. Water makes crusts crisp and never masks the earthy flavor of the flour. If your tap water tastes of chemicals, let it sit, loosely covered, overnight at room temperature before using it in yeast breads. Better yet, buy bottled spring water for baking.

YOGURT. This adds tang to both yeast and quick breads. In America, yogurt is generally made from cow's milk, although in other countries it is made from goat, reindeer, mare, ewe, or water buffalo milk. Each imparts its own flavor to breads. Yogurt relaxes the gluten so that yeast breads are especially tender. If you use yogurt in quick breads, be sure to add baking soda to neutralize the acids in the yogurt (see page 19 for more information).

NUTS

These are among my favorite ingredients. Whether coarsely chopped or finely ground, nuts impart a variety of flavors and give breads interesting texture. Because of their high fat content, they tend to turn rancid quickly, so I suggest storing them in airtight containers in the refrigerator or freezer. It is also advisable, whenever possible, to buy them in the shell, because they tend to be fresher than the shelled, packaged kind. If you prefer to buy shelled nuts, try to buy them whole for the best flavor and freshness. Like seeds or grains, nuts taste better and keep longer when toasted.

ALMONDS. This widely grown nut is a member of the rose family and closely related to peaches and apricots. There are two types: the familiar sweet almond and bitter almonds. The former is the sort we use in baking and cooking; the latter, which is practically inedible, is used to make almond extract and some cosmetics.

The inner skin of almonds slides off easily when the nut is blanched (submerged in boiling water for a few seconds). Almonds are sold whole (plain or blanched), sliced, slivered, or chopped. Almond paste, made from ground almonds, sugar, and sometimes eggs, adds intense, sweet flavor to breads. I either spread the paste on the dough or break it up and incorporate it into the dough or batter. Marzipan, which like some almond paste is packaged in a log, is sweeter and should not be substituted for almond paste.

BRAZIL NUTS. One of the few available nuts that are not commercially cultivated, Brazil nuts grow wild in South America and are contained in coconutlike pods or capsules holding 12 to 30 nuts. Brazil nuts have a thick, hard shell that, once removed, reveals a dark brown skin that is easily pried off with the point of a knife. The skin can also be removed by blanching. Without their protective skins, the nuts perish quickly and so should be used very soon, or they may be frozen for up to a month.

CASHEWS. Originally from Brazil, cashews are now grown in many tropical countries and represent a significant export for many of these areas. They grow on evergreen trees that bear pear-shaped fruits called cashew apples. The nuts dangle just below the fruit, encased in a double shell separated by a toxic brown oil. The oil must be burned away during processing and so cashews are only sold shelled. In most cases they are toasted before packaging to render them digestible. Despite all these precautions, cashews are one of the most flavorful nuts to add to breads.

COCONUTS. The fruit of the coconut palm, coconuts are the largest of all nuts. They grow in tropical regions and have long been an indigenous dietary staple. They are the size of a softball or larger, with a hard, fibrous shell that must be cracked with a heavy instrument such as a hammer, large stone, or machete. When the outer shell is removed, you still must contend with a tough, inedible inner skin before reaching the crunchy, flavorful white flesh. The flesh is about ½ inch thick and is usually grated for use in baking. The hollow center of the nut holds a milky liquid that may be drunk or used in baking.

Coconut is most often sold already grated. Much of it is sweetened, and so if a recipe calls for unsweetened grated coconut, be sure to read the label carefully. How ever you use it, coconut adds moistness and unmistakable sweet flavor to baked goods. Its oil, used in a number of commercial products, is very high in saturated fat.

FILBERTS AND HAZELNUTS. Also known as cobnuts, these are so closely related that they are generally used interchangeably. Hazelnuts grow wild on shrublike plants, while filberts are cultivated on small trees. Both are sweet with a mild, distinctive flavor that intensifies when toasted.

HICKORY NUTS AND BUTTERNUTS. These nuts are native to America. Botanically they are close cousins to walnuts, although they taste more like pecans. The smooth-shelled nuts contain a sweet, oily nutmeat that is highly perishable. Use these soon after shelling or keep them in the freezer for a month or so. I particularly like using hickory nuts for baking, as the oil in the nut conditions the dough and gives good volume to the finished loaf.

MACADAMIA NUTS. Demand for macadamias often exceeds supply, and these nuts, grown in Hawaii and Australia, tend to be as pricy as they are delicious and highly caloric. Because macadamia nuts are among the hardest nuts to crack, they are almost always sold shelled. The chunky, cream-colored nutmeats have a wonderful mild, buttery flavor and, since they are so rich with oil, are highly perishable. They keep best when roasted and salted, although for many baking purposes I prefer them unsalted.

PEANUTS. These are not really nuts but legumes—similar to beans and peas in that they grow in pods that split along both sides. In the South, peanuts are called goober peas and have been a staple of Southern cooking for generations. They are an exceptionally good source of protein, although they are also very high in fat. Because of their fat content, they are usually roasted and salted to prevent their turning rancid. Peanuts tend to lose their flavor in yeast breads and become rubbery—though they keep their crunch and flavor in quick breads.

PECANS. After peanuts, pecans are the most popular nut in America. Native to this hemisphere, they grow all through the deep South and into Texas. The oblong nut has a hard, thin brown shell and the nutmeat is sweet, becoming even more assertive when roasted. Pecans are used in all types of baking and often may be substituted for English walnuts. As with most nuts, they are oily and should be stored in an airtight container in the freezer to delay rancidity.

PINE NUTS, PIÑON, PIGNOLI, PIGNOLIA, AND PIG-NOLO. All in the same family, these little nuts are, simply, the seeds of various pine cones. They generally come from the Mediterranean, China, or the southwestern United States. Small, off-white, and oval, pine nuts are sun-dried and then shelled by hand, which explains their high price tag. They have a delicate piny flavor that subtly perfumes breads and a soft texture that makes them amenable to many uses. They taste bolder when toasted. Pine nuts keep best when stored in an airtight container in the freezer.

PISTACHIOS. These are the seeds of an evergreen tree that originated in Syria more than five thousand years ago. The pistachio's natural gray-beige color is considered unappetizing by many, so the shells are dyed red or blanched until cream colored. Their hard shell is precracked to allow easy access to the pale green meat. For extended shelf life, pistachios are roasted and usually salted.

WALNUTS. Walnuts were once a symbol of fertility and tossed at the just married couple at a wedding, much as we today throw rice or birdseed. English walnuts are the most familiar sort. Their rich, bold flavor is heightened when they are roasted. Black walnuts, native to America, have a strong and somewhat bitter taste. Once their extremely hard outer shell is removed, the inside of the black walnut reveals a network of nutmeat and shell from which small pieces of nutmeat must be laboriously picked out. The outer covering exudes a dark oil that stains everything with which it comes into contact. Shelled walnuts should be stored in an airtight container in the refrigerator or freezer.

POTATOES

Often used in baking to add bulk and moistness, potatoes also act as a natural preservative and extend keeping qualities. Although they usually are cooked and mashed before being incorporated into the dough, in some cases the raw tuber is grated and added. Potato flour is used to bind soups and sauces and to dust loaves of bread before baking. Added in small amounts to bread dough, the flour gives bread marvelous moistness. I recommend about 1 tablespoon for every cup of wheat (or other) flour. Too much potato flour results in a gummy bread that falls during baking.

SEASONINGS

FRUIT PEEL. The peel from citrus fruits adds pungent, zesty flavor to baked goods. The thicker the skin on the fruit, the easier it is to peel. However, if you are relying on the fruit for its juice too, bear in mind that thin-skinned fruits yield more juice. When a recipe calls for grated peel, or zest, use only the colored outer portion of peel, being careful to avoid the bitter white pith beneath. Use a zester or stripper (see page 47) for removing the peel.

GINGER. Commonly available and familiar, ginger is sometimes used in yeast breads to lighten their texture without adding any gingery flavor. Called a "friend of yeast," ginger reacts chemically with both commercial and wild yeast to create extra fermentation, which in turn makes the texture of the baked loaf pleasantly light and airy. Other friends of yeast include soy flour, scallions, caraway, and cinnamon. Depending on how much is added to the dough, these ingredients will always lighten the bread and sometimes flavor it.

HERBS. Herbs add a tremendous amount of flavor to breads. Because they lose their flavor after a year or less, I suggest you buy the smallest quantity of dried herbs possible, write the date of purchase on the label, and replace them regularly. Store herbs in a cool, dark cupboard. Adding dried herbs to breads is a great way to use them before they lose their potency.

SALT. Salt enhances the flavor of the other ingredients in a loaf of bread and helps the complex carbohydrates convert into natural sugars that caramelize and brown the bread's crust. In yeast breads, salt controls fermentation, slows rising, and therefore strengthens the gluten; however, because it inhibits the yeast's growth during its early phases of development, it is best not to add salt to the liquid used to soften yeast. I recommend adding a scant teaspoon of salt to the dry ingredients for each scant tablespoon or package of yeast. Table salt contains anticaking agents that I feel interfere with rising and baking, so I recommend using kosher or sea salt.

SPICES. Spices have a limited shelf life and begin to lose their potency soon after they are ground. Whole spices, such as cinnamon sticks and whole nutmegs, keep twice as long as ground spices. I particularly urge you to try Chinese cinnamon, which is darker and more robust than the cinnamon sold in grocery stores and is especially good for baking. Look for it in specialty stores or order it by mail (see page 411). As is true with herbs, breads and other baked products are excellent ways to use up the spices in your cupboard that may be reaching the end of their shelf life.

SEEDS

A good source of nutrition, seeds can add taste and texture to baked goods. Some have extremely bold flavor while others are bland. Among my favorites are anise seeds (or aniseeds), caraway, cardamom, celery, dill, fennel, flax, poppy, pumpkin, sesame, and sunflower. All of these may, depending on the recipe, be incorporated in the dough or sprinkled on top of the loaf just before baking. Toasting seeds intensifies their flavor.

SWEETENERS

When used in baking, sweeteners help activate yeast, aid in browning a bread's crust, and help retain moisture. They also enhance the flavors of other ingredients. In small quantities, they provide food for the yeast, although too much retards the dough's development and produces a heavy bread. Liquid sweeteners, such as honey, molasses, and syrups, are more concentrated than granulated sweeteners and consequently can be used in smaller quantities in breads.

HONEY. This is one of the best sweeteners for baked goods. The type of honey you use has little effect on the finished product, since honey's subtle flavors are lost during baking. So, as much as I love the robust taste of strong buckwheat honey and the gentle flavor of raspberry honey, I cannot discern these differences in bread. Honey crystallizes over time whether it is stored in the refrigerator or on the pantry shelf, but this solidity does not affect its sweetening power. If you wish to return honey to its liquid state, set the jar in a heavy saucepan filled with very hot water and stir it until it is smooth.

MALTED BARLEY, MALT EXTRACT, AND DIASTATIC MALT. All three malt products are sold as powder or syrup and are made from sprouted barley, although occasionally sprouted wheat berries are used as well. Malt mellows and softens gluten and so conditions dough. Use no more than ½ teaspoon for every 2 cups of flour in the recipe. Too much malt makes bread chewy, with a taffylike texture.

MOLASSES. A by-product of the sugar-making process, molasses is a bold-tasting sweetener used in all types of baking. Molasses is sold as light, dark, or blackstrap. Light molasses provides the most mellow flavor, while dark is richer and more robust. Blackstrap, the most distilled and thickest of all, is strong and bitter with a flavor that people either love or hate. I suggest buying unsulphured molasses for the best flavor and results. It is marked "unsulphured" or "unsulfured" right on the label.

SUGAR. Sugar is available as granulated, superfine, confectioners' (powdered), light brown, dark brown, brownulated, or raw. Once a package of brown or confectioners' sugar is opened, it dries out and clumps quickly. Zip-style, freezer-weight plastic bags are ideal for storing sugar, especially if you remove all the air. Even brown sugar will remain clump-free if carefully stored.

Beware of baking with sugar substitutes such as Sweet 'n Low or Equal, which are not designed for such uses. They do not hold up when heated to the high temperatures required for baking and will only result in bitter-tasting breads with unappetizing textures.

Pärlsocker is a coarse, bright white Scandinavian sugar. Each granule is just slightly larger than a sesame seed. It remains bright white and does not dissolve during baking, but it will melt in your mouth. It should not be confused with another Scandinavian sugar called krystal sugar. If Pärlsocker is unavailable, sugar cubes that have been coarsely chopped can be substituted. The end result will not be the same, but it adds a nice topping. Another alternative is coarse sugar, available in some baker's supply houses. Coarse sugar has granules that are larger than granulated sugar, but smaller than Pärlsocker. It is slightly translucent rather than white.

SYRUPS. These are made from a number of sources, the most popular being cane, corn, and maple.

Cane syrup is nothing more complicated than light molasses. Use it in recipes calling for either. Golden or Lyle's syrup, which is cane-based, is used extensively throughout Great Britain and consequently shows up in recipes that make their way from there to here. Substitute cane syrup (or light molasses) if a recipe calls for golden syrup and you cannot find it.

Corn syrup is made by processing cornstarch and is sold in light and dark forms. It is intensely sweet and in small amounts can be substituted for granulated sugar in many yeast breads.

Maple syrup has a thinner consistency than corn and cane syrup and a mild distinctive flavor that cannot be matched. It is made from the sap of sugar maple trees, and because it takes about 40 gallons of sap (depending on the sugar season) to produce a gallon of syrup, maple syrup is quite expensive. U.S. grades range from Fancy (light and mild flavored) through grades A, B, and C (progressively darker and more intensely flavored).

Rice syrup, available in health food stores, is extremely thick, and I like the way it performs in yeast breads, yielding a wonderfully moist and delightfully flavored bread. However, I have had less success with it in quick breads; it tends to leave them gummy.

I do not suggest that you rush out and buy a boxful of expensive and elaborate utensils, but there are some tools that I find especially useful for a bread baker's kitchen. Of the utensils described (in alphabetical order) in the pages that follow, here is a short list of the ones I feel are the most important:

Large ceramic bowl, for mixing and rising
Measuring cups for liquid and dry ingredients
Measuring spoons, preferably long-handled
Danish dough whisk
Plastic dough scraper
8-inch whisk
Wooden rolling pin
Dark bread pans (heavyweight)
Instant-read thermometer
Large wire rack, for cooling loaves.

BAKER'S PEELS

Baker's peels are large wooden paddles with a tapered front edge and a handle. (Some peels are made of metal.) They're used to slide pizza and large freestanding loaves in and out of the oven.

BAKING SHEETS

Good-quality baking sheets are important in any baker's kitchen. I use professional half-sheet pans that measure 13 x 18 inches and have a 1-inch rim. Sometimes they are called jelly roll pans. The best baking sheets are made of heavy aluminum with a dull finish, which encourages a nice brown crust, but not so dark as to burn cookies.

I also use professional half-sheet pans that are perforated. They give the bread a crisp crust. When the perforated pans are placed

The Utensils

directly on baking stones, the loaves get all the benefits of baking on a stone, but can still be easily lifted from the oven.

I suggest you avoid air-cushioned baking sheets for bread baking. They do not conduct heat properly, so you get neither a good crumb nor a nice crust.

BAKING STONES AND BAKING TILES

Stones and tiles create intense heat in the oven, which produces crisp crusts on yeast breads when the dough is set directly on the stones or with no more barrier between the dough and the stone than a perforated pan (see above). The stones and tiles are especially efficient for pizzas and a number of yeast and sourdough breads.

Baking stones and tiles can be made of any of several hard, porous materials. In addition to the products made specifically for baking purposes, consider using the quarry tiles used to line fireplaces or large flat stones hewn to withstand extremely high temperatures (these last are usually made by artisans). All these come in many sizes and thicknesses. The best choice is the largest stone or tile that fits in your oven with about 2 inches to spare on all 4 sides. My favorite is 14 x 16 inches and about ⅝ inch thick. This size enables me to bake either 1 large loaf; 2 traditional-size loaves; 1 large pizza; several small pizzas; or a dozen or more dinner rolls at one time. I have never had good luck with individual tiles; they shift in the oven when I try sliding a loaf of bread onto them. What is more, they do not conduct heat as effectively as thicker stones.

Before baking, the stones or tiles must be hot all the way through. To ensure this, preheat the oven and the stones or tiles for at least 30 minutes before you bake. A good stone, guaranteed against breakage, can be left in place and cleaned along with a self-cleaning oven.

BANNETONS

These baskets are used to shape decorative loaves before baking. They can be lined with a cloth or not, but nearly always are dusted with flour before the dough is put in the basket to rise. When the loaves are ready for baking, they are gently tipped from the baskets so that they slip top side down onto a heated baking stone or baking sheet. The imprint of the basket's weave remains on the loaves.

BENCH SCRAPERS

Also known as bench knives, these are flat-sided tools with a dull blade used by professional bakers to divide dough. They are also handy for scraping the countertop or bread board while working with dough and afterward for easy cleanup. The best ones have a stainless steel blade and a sturdy handle.

BISCUIT AND DOUGHNUT CUTTERS

These are cylinder-shaped tools with one sharp-edged end for cutting dough into rounds. Doughnut cutters have a smaller inner cylinder so the center of the dough can be removed. Try to find heavyweight cutters that cut evenly and cleanly. The standard size is 2 or 3 inches.

BOWLS

Common pieces of equipment in any kitchen, regardless of its focus, bowls have high priority in the bread baking kitchen. They create a friendly environment in which the dough can rise.

CERAMIC BREAD BOWLS. Because ceramic bowls hold heat longer than metal ones, I strongly advise every bread baker to invest in at least one ceramic bowl that holds 5 or 6 quarts. This is ample room for mixing the dough and then accommodating its expansion during rising. I prefer ceramic bowls with relatively straight sides that protect the maximum amount of surface from exposure to air.

I personally do not recommend metal or plastic bowls for rising. Metal cools quickly and the dough most likely will not rise evenly. Plastic may hold heat but it does so unevenly. The dough may absorb impurities or take on any unpleasant odors in the plastic.

DOUGH RISING BOWLS OR SWEDISH BOCCA BOWLS. Both exceptions to the "no plastic" rule, these hard plastic upright bowls are fitted with an airtight lid. When you put the kneaded dough into the bowl and snap the lid in place, you trap heat and moisture inside the container, creating the ideal atmosphere for rising. Dough rises in these bowls in about half the time it does in ceramic bowls.

MIXING BOWLS. These come in a variety of materials and sizes. My favorites are made of melamine and have rubber rings around the bottom to hold the bowls securely on the countertop, plus deep, pitched sides to prevent ingredients from splashing during stirring. Glass and metal bowls are good too, although I avoid any that are shallow and wide. Nests of mixing bowls in graduated sized are convenient and stack for easy storage.

BOWL SCRAPERS

These simple but useful items are made of flexible plastic; most of them are rounded on one side and flat on the other. The rounded side cleans the bowl while the flat side scrapes the work surface during kneading. I use a metal bench scraper (see above) to divide dough but a plastic bowl scraper during kneading. I use these also to clean work surfaces and to scrape pans, especially those with nonstick surfaces.

BREAD KNIVES

To prevent tearing and squashing the loaf during slicing, a high-quality bread knife is well worth the investment. A good bread knife has a serrated blade that is 8 to 10 inches long and cuts through the bread smoothly, like a saw.

BREAD MACHINES

These are becoming increasingly popular in American kitchens. While I believe you should put your hands into the dough and *feel* it, I believe even more strongly in the goodness and nutritiousness of freshly baked bread and concede that the bread machine is an extremely efficient way to have fresh bread on hand.

Bread machines are appliances that mix, knead, raise, and bake a loaf of bread with the push of a button. You put the ingredients in the bread pan, turn on the machine, and walk away, returning a few hours later to the pleasant aroma of freshly baked bread. Some bread machines are equipped with timers so that you can set them to begin the kneading, rising, and baking processes when it is most convenient for your schedule.

As a rule, most simple yeast bread recipes can be converted for the bread machine (see the instructions on page 67). Breads made with unbleached all-purpose flour are the most successful. Breads made with whole grains are heavy and some machines cannot handle their doughs efficiently. Bread machines are usually equipped with a "fruit and nut" setting, so that at the sound of a buzzer you can add extra ingredients to the dough.

BREAD PANS
See Pans, below.

LA CLOCHE
La Cloche is an ovenproof, unglazed ceramic baker with a high dome top that covers a round base with 1½- to 2-inch sides. It is used to produce a very thin, crisp, crackled crust by creating a hot, moist environment in which to bake bread. Using La Cloche is the closest a home baker can come to producing bread baked in a professional steam oven. Instructions on using La Cloche are on page 68.

DOUGH SCRAPERS
See Bench Scrapers, above.

DUTCH OVENS
These deep, heavy lidded pots can be used on top of the stove or in the oven for cooking or baking. I use them for everything from poaching bagels to frying doughnuts. I have also been known to bury a Dutch oven under the coals of a campfire to bake bread.

ELECTRIC MIXERS
See Heavy-duty Mixers, below.

FOOD PROCESSORS
These are familiar machines to most of us who like to cook and bake. They are designed to cut, shred, chop, and mix food, and they render a variety of kitchen tasks easy and quick. Most bread recipes can be converted for mixing in the food processor, and this can save time.

If you do not own a food processor and plan to purchase one, buy the best and most powerful one you can afford. You will not be sorry. Dough for any bread can be made in the food processor by following the instructions on pages 64–66.

GRAIN MILLS
Breads made from freshly ground grains are rich in vitamins and minerals, and they impart full, robust flavor unattainable otherwise. Grain mills, whether hand-operated or electric, are wonderful luxuries. The hand-operated mills are adequate for small amounts of grain and occasional grinding, but the electric-powered are preferable if you plan to grind grain in any quantity. Before investing in

a home grain mill, consider your needs realistically. Electric mills are far more expensive than hand-operated mills. In either case, look for a mill that grinds grain quickly and efficiently without heating the flour and destroying the nutrients, and be sure to consider how easy the mill is to clean and store.

GRIDDLES

Griddles are large flat pans designed to be used on the stovetop to bake crumpets, English muffins, pancakes, and similar breads quickly and evenly. They should be made of heavy metal that conducts heat to the edges of the pan.

HEAVY-DUTY MIXERS

A boon for bread bakers who haven't the inclination or time to knead dough by hand, these freestanding electric mixers have strong motors designed to tackle heavy doughs with no danger of overheating. When you master the technique of using a mixer, you can make bread that comes out exactly as if you made it by hand. See pages 66–67 for instructions on converting the recipes in this book for a heavy-duty mixer.

ICE CREAM SCOOPS

Scoops make it easy to ladle dough or batter into uniform shapes, whether for muffins, large cookies, pancakes, or waffles. For best results, choose a scoop with a spring handle that activates a piece of metal inside, sweeping the dough or batter from the scoop.

KITCHEN TIMERS

See Timers, below.

MARBLE SLABS

These are ideal for working with doughs with a high fat content, such as those for croissants, Danish pastry, and brioche. The cool surface of the marble keeps the fat from softening or melting as you work with the dough. The slab is most effective if chilled first, which can be accomplished by placing the marble in the refrigerator or freezer, setting it on a cool back porch if the weather is frigid, or cooling it with ice cubes and wet dish towels. Be sure it is completely dry before you begin work. Marble is not an especially good surface for yeast breads, which need warmth.

MEASURING CUPS

Many home cooks are unaware that there are two sorts of measuring cups, one for liquids and the other for dry ingredients. The cups designed for liquids have a spout for easy pouring and ample space above the measuring line; they are generally made of heat-resistant glass or plastic. The cups designed for dry ingredients have no space above the measuring line, so you can make an even sweep of flour, sugar, cornstarch, etc., using a kitchen knife, dough scraper, or other flat instrument. These cups are sold in nests measuring ¼ cup, ⅓ cup, ½ cup, and 1 full cup; they are usually made of metal or sturdy plastic.

MEASURING SPOONS

These nearly always come in sets of four that measure amounts from ¼ teaspoon to 1 full tablespoon. I advise buying measuring spoons with fairly long handles that enable you to reach into deep jars, cannisters, and large sacks.

MISTERS OR ATOMIZERS

Spraying a fine mist of water over unbaked bread just before it's placed in the oven helps the bread form a crisp crust. Use plant misters or any atomizers sold for various purposes. If you use a spray bottle that contained something else first, be sure to wash it thoroughly and soak it in white vinegar to remove any perfumy smells or flavors.

MORTARS AND PESTLES

Used since ancient times, these simple but efficient utensils are great for crushing small amounts of ingredients such as seeds into powders or pastes. They may be made of marble, wood, or any other hard, durable substance. The mortar is the bowl and the pestle is a fat stick with a rounded end honed to fit the curve of the mortar. To operate, rotate the pestle in a firm, circular motion around the mortar to pulverize or mash the ingredients.

OIL CONTAINERS

These can range from the elegant and expensive polished stainless steel olive oil can to any small receptacle or pitcher in which oil is stored for easy access. I use a small (completely clean) detergent bottle with a push-and-pull top that protects the oil from exposure to air. You will find these bottles handy for squirting oil into a bowl or pan or for lubricating the work surface when working with dough.

PARCHMENT PAPER

This heavy, opaque paper has a number of uses in the kitchen, especially as a liner for baking sheets. I use it whenever I bake sweet breads or anything with a sticky, sugary filling that could ooze out and burn onto the pan, for a number of reasons. The paper protects the pan and makes cleanup easy. Second, the filling or sugar is less likely to scorch on parchment paper than on the dark, metal surface of the pan. Finally, breads with high sugar contents are less liable to develop hard, caramelized crusts when baked in pans lined with parchment paper. Good-quality parchment paper can be used several times before it turns dark and must be discarded.

PASTRY BRUSHES

I use a goose-feather pastry brush as well as 1- and 2-inch natural-bristle brushes. Goose feathers brush very lightly and are therefore perfect for delicate doughs. The 1-inch brush is good for spreading glazes on dinner rolls and formed loaves of bread. The 2-inch brush is good for glazing large loaves and also makes a convenient mini-broom to brush excess flour from dough, or to push a light coating of flour under doughs for Danish pastries or croissants to prevent sticking.

PASTRY BLENDERS

These devices, made of clustered blades or wire loops attached to an easy-grip handle, are designed to cut fat into flour. Since I always chill fat before cutting it into flour, I find blades work better than wires, which tend to spread over large pieces of fat rather than cut through them.

PANS

While you can get by with only a few bread pans, having a selection makes bread baking more fun and encourages experimenting.

I recommend using well-seasoned pans for baking. This is important for quick release of the baked breads. A well-seasoned pan is one that you treat as you bake with it. The term refers to pans that have been coated with vegetable cooking sprays such as Pam, or with solid shortening or butter, to a point where they develop a natural coating after being used over and over again.

When you first use a new bread pan, begin the seasoning process by rubbing or spraying it liberally with fat every time you bake. After many uses, the coating hardens and develops the natural patina that makes the pan almost nonstick. When this happens, the fat is so well baked onto the pan that it will not turn rancid. You will know your pan is seasoned when the surface dulls and baked bread slips easily out of it.

Wipe well-seasoned bread pans clean with damp cloths—do not wash them with soap and water or you will remove the valuable patina. Bread pans coated with nonstick surfaces such as Teflon do not need to be seasoned.

BAGUETTE PANS. These look like two halves of a pipe that have been welded together side by side. These half-cylinders are used for baking the long, narrow loaves known as baguettes; they are usually about 16 inches long and 4 inches wide. The best have a dark finish to promote a nicely browned crust, or are made of perforated tinned steel to promote a crisp crust, especially when set on a baking stone.

BRIOCHE PANS. These are round, fluted pans used to shape and bake French brioche, a rich batter bread made with butter and eggs. Brioche pans are shiny to reflect heat and keep the rich dough from overbrowning. The pans range in size from large to individual-size loaves.

BUN PANS. Rectangular or square baking pans that are 2 to 3 inches deep are ideal for baking buns. The buns are placed about a finger's width apart and allowed to rise in the pan so that when fully risen they join together. Once baked, they are easy to pull apart. Bun pans come in all sizes, but the average size is 9 × 12 inches.

BUNDT PANS. Used to bake breads and cakes, Bundt pans have a tube in the center, which promotes even baking. Bundt pans are fluted or designed to give the baked bread a pretty shape.

CORN STICK OR CORN PONE PANS. These cast iron pans are shaped like small troughs resembling ears of corn. The pan is heated in the oven before cornmeal batter is poured into it. The baked cornbread looks like little ears of corn.

FLOWERPOTS. Terra cotta flowerpots enjoyed a vogue as vessels for bread baking, but have fallen out of fashion today. However, some enterprising companies have begun to make kitchen-safe, ovenproof flowerpots specifically for bread. Loaves baked in flowerpots have a distinctive shape as well as well-browned, crisp crusts.

FRENCH PLAQUES. The long loaf made in this sort of pan is known as the traditional French bread. It usually is sliced at an angle so that optimum bread surface is exposed, making it ideal for garlic toast. The bread pans are about 17 inches long, 1 inch deep, and 2 inches wide. The most desirable are made of black or blue steel; some brands are punched down the center with slots for extra air circulation.

LOAF PANS. This ubiquitous pan is familiar to most home cooks. Until a few years ago, the standard loaf pan was $9 \times 5 \times 3$ inches and held 6 cups (about 2 pounds) of dough. Since the average slice is about ½ inch thick, the yield per pan was about 18 large slices of bread. Today, it is extremely difficult to find this size pan because it has been replaced with an $8½ \times 4½ \times 2½$-inch pan; this holds 5 cups (about 1½ pounds) of dough and yields about 17 slices. My favorite pan measures $8 \times 3 \times 3$ inches, holds 1 pound of dough, and yields about 16 medium slices. For quick breads, I prefer a $5 \times 3 \times 2$-inch pan. This size holds ½ pound of dough and yields about 10 small slices. Mini-loaf pans are $4 \times 2 \times 1$ inch and make attractive individual loaves for dinner parties. Each pan holds 6 ounces of dough.

Heavyweight metal loaf pans with dark, dull finishes are best for bread baking. They conduct heat evenly and rapidly for a strong, well-browned crust. Shiny pans reflect heat and yield a soft, pale crust. Ceramic loaf pans produce good loaves of bread. Glass pans are preferable to inexpensive lightweight shiny pans, but if you use glass pans, lower the oven temperature 25 degrees below what is called for in the recipe.

MUFFIN PANS. These rectangular pans contain a series of small cups to form rolls and muffins. The cups range in diameter from 1 inch to the standard 2¾ inches. Jumbo, or Texas-size, cups may be 4 inches in diameter. The depth of the cup and the diameter of the base vary, too, which makes it difficult to give actual dimensions in recipes. Muffin pans may have as few as 6 cups or as many as 24, but the average pan has 12 cups. Muffin pans are also used to shape dinner rolls, popovers, and individual sticky buns.

PIZZA PANS. This versatile round pan can be used not only for pizzas but for baking free-form or shaped loaves of bread and rolls. Dark gray, heavy anodized aluminum pans attract heat for crisp brown crusts, while shiny pans reflect heat so that the crust is not nearly as good. The pans come in varying diameters ranging from 5 inches for individual pizzas to 16 inches for extra-large pies. They are flat for traditional pizza pies, or rimmed with a 1- or 2-inch side for deep-dish pies.

POPOVER PANS. Similar to muffin pans but with deeper cups, cast iron popover pans produce higher, lighter popovers than do ordinary muffin pans. For some mysterious reason, the traditional cast iron popover pans are made with 11 cups.

PULLMAN PANS. Pullman pans are loaf pans with a lid that slides across the top to seal the dough inside. The pans are usually 13 × 4 × 4 inches and make perfectly square slices. Since the tight-fitting lid prevents the bread from expanding beyond a certain point, the texture of the bread is very compact, making it easy to slice thin for sandwiches. The dough rises in the pan for about three-quarters of the usual time, but needs about 10 minutes longer in the oven. Pullman pans hold 2 pounds of dough and produce about 26 slices.

SKILLETS OR SPIDERS. These cast iron pans are used for stovetop cooking and oven baking. They come in various sizes, the average being about 10 inches in diameter and 2 to 3 inches deep. I use them on top of the stove to bake English muffins as well as in the oven to bake cornbread or batter breads with a firm, crisp crust. (If you decide to follow this practice, be sure the skillet does not have a wooden handle.)

SPRINGFORM PANS. These deep, round pans have removable bottoms; their sides are often expandable and are closed with a spring or snap device. I find springform pans especially useful for making filled or shaped breads that might be awkward to turn out of a pan. With a springform, you simply unclasp and open the sides of the pan and slip the bread from the base onto a cooling rack.

Loose-bottom cake pans, which can be round, square, or even heart-shaped, are also useful for fancy breads and equally easy to unmold.

STAR-, FLOWER-, OR HEART-SHAPED PANS. These are tube-shaped devices with caps to close each end. The pans are shiny, so the bread's crust stays light and soft. I use breads baked in these pans to make decorative sandwiches or melba toast. Each pan holds about 1 cup of dough. Cap both ends and stand the pan on end to let the dough rise; if not standing on end, the expanding dough pushes off the caps. The dough rises in about 30 minutes, a little less time than it does in conventional pans, and requires about 10 minutes more in the oven. When it is time to bake the bread, make sure the oven shelf is lowered so you can stand the pan on end in the oven; thus the caps will not pop off during baking. When the bread is done, remove it from the pan and cool it on a rack. To cut uniform, ultra-thin slices, slip the cooled loaf back into the pan and use the edge of the pan as a cutting guide.

SAVARIN PANS. Savarins are shallow pans with a large tube in the center that creates a space for fresh fruit or another filling after the bread is baked. The pans are shiny to reflect the heat so that the bread has a light-colored crust and soft, cakelike texture.

PEEL
See Baker's Peels, above.

PEGGY TUB
See page 63.

PIZZA CUTTERS
These are 2-, 2½-, 3- or 4-inch sharp-edged wheels attached to a handle. They are rolled over baked pizza to cut it. I find pizza cutters useful for cutting Danish pastries or other breads into shapes. Roll the dough to the required thickness, let it rest for about 5 minutes (otherwise it shrinks a little), and then use the roller to cut the dough into squares, rectangles, triangles, etc. This is easier than using a knife.

PIZZA SCREENS

Wire mesh screens that come in the same sizes as most pizza pans are ideal for reheating pizza or holding prebaked pizza crusts. They can be placed directly on baking stones but should not be confused with the pizza pans or warmers that have large holes in the bottom. When the pizza comes from the oven, it can sit on the screen until you are ready to serve it—the free-flowing air keeps the crust from becoming soggy.

PIZZA SCISSORS OR SHEARS

Knife-sharp and large-bladed, angled for cutting pizza, these scissors keep the cheese and toppings from sliding off the crust. The blades are flat so that you can use them to serve the wedges after cutting. Pizza scissors are also good for cutting dough when shaping it (such as the Orange Macadamia Swirl Loaf, page 242).

RACKS

See Wire Cooling Racks, below.

ROLLING PINS

Most rolling pins are made of wood but some are made of marble or plastic. My preference is a 20-inch, solid-cylinder, hardwood rolling pin without handles, often called a pasta pin. This type of pin has a large rolling surface and is easy to clean. The first time you use it, rub it heavily with vegetable oil and let it sit for 30 minutes. Rub off the excess oil with a paper towel. From this point on, use only oil and paper towels to clean it. Soap and water dry the wood and encourage sticking.

SHAKERS OR DREDGES

Containers with small holes in the top are useful for filling with flour, confectioners' sugar, cinnamon, cocoa, or anything else you wish to sprinkle thinly and evenly. Since they are not airtight, slip the whole container into a zip-style bag for storage.

SIFTERS

These are cuplike devices with a screen or series of screens in the bottom designed to lighten flour or confectioners' sugar. As the flour or sugar filters through the screen it becomes aerated and any lumps are removed. Nowadays most flour is presifted. I find using a whisk to aerate flour and other dry ingredients easier and more efficient.

SKIMMERS

Large, flat, perforated spoons about 4 inches in diameter, skimmers are useful for lifting bagels and doughnuts from the poaching water or frying oil. Wire mesh skimmers also work well.

SPATULAS AND SPOONULAS

I find these tools especially handy for working with light doughs or batter. Spatulas have a flat blade made of flexible rubber or plastic that conforms to the mixing bowl and makes it easy to scrape. Instead of a flat blade, spoonulas have a spoon-shaped end made of the same flexible rubber or plastic and function as a spoon and a spatula.

SPOONS

A variety of spoons is basic to any kitchen utensil collection, and many cooks prefer heavy-handled wooden or stainless steel spoons for mixing batter and dough, stirring delicate sauces, and any number of tasks in between. I don't like using wooden spoons at all, but if you do, invest in hardwood spoons such as beechwood, cherry, or maple instead of pine, which is too soft, splintery, and porous. Also, I hardly ever use spoons with doughs and batters anymore, preferring a Danish dough whisk (page 46), which works better and more efficiently.

STEAMERS AND STEAMING BASKETS

These utensils are available in either bamboo or metal. They measure from 8 to 12 inches in diameter. Steamers are designed to be set in or suspended over pots holding boiling water. Steam from the water rises through them and surrounds and cooks food placed in the basket. Bamboo steamers are stackable so that you can steam up to three layers of food at one time.

TAMIS

This is a round French sieve sided with a light, thin wooden rim about 4 inches deep. Fine nylon mesh is drawn taut across the bottom of this rim. A 9-inch tamis meets most sieving needs, such as those for sifting home-ground flour to remove the germ and the bran as well as any large particles, or creating a thin layer of flour or confectioners' sugar on the work surface or on a loaf of bread or a cake.

THERMOMETERS

These may tread the thin line between being a luxury and a necessity to some cooks, but I have come to depend on mine for bread baking, and I recommend that every baker have two types of thermometer: an oven thermometer and an instant-read thermometer.

Because all ovens hold heat differently, your oven should be calibrated several times a year. For this, you will need an accurate thermometer that indicates when the oven reaches and holds a specific temperature. This can vary as much as 25 or even 50 degrees from the setting outside the oven. If you discover that your oven is not accurate, adjust it as necessary, using the oven thermometer as a guide. For instance, set the oven to 350°F and after 15 minutes or so, check the oven thermometer. If it does not read 350°F, make a note of the temperature it does register. If it says, perhaps, 325°F, then you know that your oven is 25 degrees off and to maintain a temperature of 350°F you must set the oven at 375°F. To avoid this arithmetic, you can get an appliance repair shop to calibrate the oven for you. My favorite oven thermometer attaches to the side of the oven with a magnet; others, equally good, hang from or sit on the oven shelf.

An instant-read thermometer is a gadget with a round dial on one end and a 5-inch skewerlike wand on the other. When the wand is inserted into food, the dial almost instantly indicates the internal temperature. I like it for checking the temperature of liquids used to activate yeast. I also use it to test baked bread for doneness.

Using an instant-read thermometer is a foolproof way to determine if a loaf of bread is fully baked and one I use constantly. When the bread has baked for the suggested amount of time, quickly remove it from the oven, slip it from the pan, and pierce the underside in the center with the wand. If the thermometer reads 190°F, the bread is done to perfection. If it is under 190°, return it to the oven. If the temperature is higher than 190°F the bread will be overdone; although still usable, it will go stale more quickly. If find these thermometers particularly important when determining the doneness of breads with a high proportion of eggs and fat—these loaves brown quickly and can appear done long before they actually are.

TIMERS

Kitchen timers are important for anyone who might get distracted and lose track of the time while the bread is rising and baking. And who among us does not fall into that category? I prefer a triple timer that keeps track of three different timing chores at once. These timers are also capable of timing for up to 10 hours, whereas standard timers usually time for only 1 hour.

WHISKS

Whisks are among the most useful kitchen tools I know. They are long-handled instruments ending with a rounded network of looped wires.

SMALL WHISKS. Mini and small whisks are great for combining yeast and water; the yeast dissolves almost instantly with only a few stirs. These are also good for beating eggs, dissolving cornstarch or confectioners' sugar in liquid, and blending small quantities of dry ingredients such as cinnamon and sugar or flour and baking powder.

BALLOON WHISKS. These larger whisks are ideal for whipping egg whites or heavy cream, which I prefer to do by hand because it gives me total control over the final texture of the aerated ingredient. If the egg whites are at room temperature or the cream is very cold, whisking by hand takes no more time than using an electric mixer.

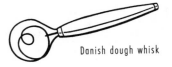

Danish dough whisk

DANISH DOUGH WHISKS. These resemble small, old-fashioned rug beaters. The sturdy metal whisks have thick wooden handles and are more effective for beating heavy doughs than wooden spoons. They are also wonderful for mixing muffins and quick bread batters, as their awkward-looking configuration makes overbeating difficult. For information on where to find them, see Sources, page 411.

WIRE COOLING RACKS

Cooling racks are essential equipment for the baker. The racks are usually made from a series of large metal wires shaped into a circle, square, or rectangle and have small feet to lift them about ½ inch above the countertop, so that air can circulate all around the cooling bread and keep it from turning soggy.

ZESTERS AND STRIPPERS

These are designed to remove thin slivers of rind from citrus fruits without also removing the bitter white pith. They are small tools fitted with metal blades attached to a small handle. Inexpensive zesters may be dull, so it is worthwhile to invest in a good one. You can buy zesters or strippers separately or, as I prefer, buy one tool designed to accomplish both tasks.

High Altitude Baking

As altitude increases, air pressure decreases, and so trying to bake at heights of 3,000 feet or more can be tricky. Because the air is thinner, less of it presses against the expanding gases and the bread rises higher than it should. At these heights, flour is drier and water evaporates more rapidly during baking. Fermentation is faster and bread rises faster, too, which is not good for flavor. When making bread at high altitudes, punch the dough down at least twice to give the flavors adequate time to develop.

There are ways to adapt recipes developed for sea-level baking to mountain cooking. None of these is absolute, because ingredients behave differently at different elevations, but they will help you achieve success.

First, if you are baking sweet breads remove about 2 tablespoons of sugar for every cup specified in the recipe. Sugar overtenderizes the gluten structure in yeast bread so that the loaf collapses in the middle. Second, be careful about adding flour. Learn to bake by feel rather than by measurement, because flour absorbs liquids quickly in the low humidity of high altitudes.

Third, decrease the amount of leavener. If a recipe calls for a scant tablespoon of yeast, add 1½ teaspoons instead. Substitute a scant teaspoon of baking powder or baking soda for a level teaspoon.

The higher you go, the more the dough needs extra moisture. The rarefied air at high altitudes is dry, and it is a good idea to add about 2 extra tablespoons per cup of liquid at heights of more than 5,000 feet. At these heights, cut the leavener in half and increase the oven temperature by 25 degrees. Otherwise the bread will fall or have a coarse, unpleasant texture—or both.

PART
ONE

2

To make perfect bread each and every time you bake, you must learn to trust your instincts and make the bread by feel. To illustrate how to achieve this, I will, on these pages, conduct a baking class, taking you through each step of making a classic loaf of white bread. I select white bread because nearly everyone is familiar with how it looks when baked and the dough is straightforward, making it easy to see the changes that take place during the kneading process.

When I teach, I begin every class by listing the four major steps on the road to perfect bread:

1. Activate the yeast.
2. Use the right amount of flour.
3. Knead the dough long enough.
4. Take care the bread does not burn.

Sound simple? It is!

Baking Class: Making Yeast Breads

A Word about Technique

Before we get started, I want to highlight a few techniques that make bread making foolproof. In the beginning, measure ingredients carefully. Admittedly, yeast breads are judged properly mixed by feel as much (or more!) as by measuring, and this determines the exact amount of flour used in any recipe. Use flour measurements as guidelines only. The more experienced you become, the easier it will be to know when the dough feels right under your fingertips, holds the right amount of flour, and is ready to rise. This is the most important lesson you will learn as you follow the recipes in this book: to trust your instincts and judge the correct amount of flour needed by *feel* rather than by measuring.

Never dip the measuring cup into the flour sack. Instead, fluff the flour a little with a whisk, fork, or the edge of the measuring cup before spooning it into the cup with a large kitchen spoon. All commercial flour is presifted, so there is no need to sift it before measuring. When the cup is full, level it with the sweep of a knife or pastry scraper. This way a cup of all-purpose white flour will weigh close to 4 ounces; if you scooped the flour directly into the measuring cup from the flour sack without fluffing it, the amount would be greater and could weigh as much as 5 or 5½ ounces. An extra ounce per cup can make a big difference in the outcome of the bread.

Depending on the type of flour, the humidity of the day, and the age of the flour, a cupful of flour may weigh slightly more or less than the standard 4 ounces. Because of this, all flour measurements for yeast breads are given as approximations. Take my word for it, when you begin making the breads, you will quickly learn to determine how much flour to knead into the dough by how it *feels* and will no longer need to measure the flour. The amounts given in recipes are estimates only.

Always read a recipe through before attempting it. Gather, measure, peel, and chop all ingredients and line them up in the order you will need them. This way, you are not apt to forget one should you become distracted.

Yeast is a living microorganism that is dormant at temperatures lower than 50°F and that begins to die at temperatures higher than 120°F. Between these two extremes, once it is activated by moisture, food, and warmth, yeast comes alive: its cells multiply and in the process produce carbon dioxide gas bubbles that are trapped in the meshwork of gluten in the bread and cause the dough to rise. The yeast and gluten work together during kneading, rising, and baking to produce bread that is light in texture and high in volume.

Yeast must be alive to work. Active dry yeast lies dormant for months when stored at room temperature, but I strongly recommend storing it in the refrigerator or freezer. If kept at room temperature, it should be used before the expiration date stamped on the package. Frozen, it keeps considerably longer. Compressed yeast, which is sold in moist cakes weighing either ½ ounce (equal to 1 envelope of active dry yeast) or 2 ounces, must be refrigerated and keeps for only about a week, although it may be frozen for several months. It is not as widely available as active dry yeast; it is stored in the refrigerated compartments of the supermarkets that stock it.

Compressed yeast should be activated in water that is between 80° and 90°F, while active dry yeast should be put in water between 105° and 115°F. I rely on an instant-read thermometer to gauge the temperature of the water. Yeast does not dissolve if mixed with fat, so do not use milk.

You may proof the yeast as a way to activate it, but nowadays active dry yeast is so reliable I find proofing unnecessary if the yeast is used before the expiration date stamped on the package. Three methods for activating the yeast are described below. Each achieves the same results; you will have to decide which you like best. My favorite is the method I call "standard." There is also proofing and "rapid-mix."

STANDARD METHOD OF ACTIVATING YEAST

Put the specified amount of water (at 105° to 115°F) in a bowl or glass measuring cup. Sprinkle the yeast granules on the water; try to scatter them over the surface so that each one comes into contact with the water. It is not necessary to stir as long as each granule is moistened. Add the water and softened yeast directly to the flour and begin mixing the dough.

PROOFING YEAST

Proofing is testing the yeast to find out if it is still alive. I proof yeast when making bread in a food processor, where everything happens so quickly I feel proofing gives the yeast a gentle boost, adds to the stability of the dough, and helps the final flavor of the bread. (For instructions on mixing the dough in these time-saving machines, turn to page 64.) I also proof if the expiration date has passed and I am not sure if the yeast is still good.

To proof the yeast, put the specified amount of water (at 105° to 115°F) in a bowl or glass measuring cup. Add ½ teaspoon of sweetener (sugar, honey, or syrup) for every scant tablespoon (or package) of active dry yeast. Whisk until the sweetener dissolves. Sprinkle the yeast granules over the surface of the water and whisk again. The yeast will feed on the sweetener and within about 5 minutes will begin to expand. The swelling foam indicates that the yeast is active and ready to use. Combine with the flour and proceed with the recipe.

RAPID-MIX YEAST

This is the method preferred by yeast manufacturers. Mix the yeast with two thirds of the dry ingredients called for in the recipe. Whisk well to combine. Heat the liquids in the recipe to 120° to 130°F (the instant-read thermometer is useful here) and pour them into the bowl with the dry ingredients. Mix the ingredients thoroughly. The flour and other dry ingredients insulate the yeast from the high heat just enough to activate it. The high temperature does not kill the yeast when it is so well insulated. Continue mixing and proceed with the recipe.

Mix the liquid ingredients with about one third of the flour and beat with a Danish dough whisk or a heavy-handled spoon to combine. Continue adding flour in ¼-cup amounts and beat well after each addition. Adding flour gradually gives the dough time to absorb it. When the dough forms a mass and pulls away from the side of the bowl, it is time to begin kneading.

USING THE RIGHT AMOUNT

The amount of flour added to bread dough varies according to the humidity, the age of the flour, the type of flour, and the kind of dough wanted (soft or firm). This is why I try to encourage people

Beating In the Flour

to make bread by feel rather than by the amount specified in the recipe. Flour is easy to incorporate into the dough; however, liquid is difficult. When you try to add liquid to a mass of dough, you end up with a slippery, gooey mass that requires extra kneading and squeezing. It isn't impossible to do, but is extremely messy, whereas adding flour is not. For these reasons, it is best to use a light hand with the flour.

Kneading the Dough

Kneading the dough properly is an important step for good bread. When the dough has been mixed, turn it out of the bowl onto a lightly floured work surface, sprinkle the dough with a little flour, and begin the rhythmic process of stretching and folding called kneading.

Using your fingertips, pull the far side of the dough toward you and fold it in half. Then, with the heels of your hands, lightly rock or push the dough away from you. When you push the dough away from you at the beginning of the kneading process, it should completely roll over—otherwise, it will stick to the work surface. Repeat this pulling and pushing motion two or three times until the dough forms a cylinder. Where flour from the work surface becomes absorbed by the dough, sprinkle lightly to replenish it. Rotate the dough a quarter turn and repeat the entire process, beginning with pulling and folding. Continue pulling, folding, pushing, and turning the dough a quarter of the way around, adding a bit of flour to the work surface as necessary.

I tend to be a one-handed kneader, working mainly with my right hand while my left hand turns the dough and is ready to sprinkle a little flour on the work surface. You may feel more comfortable using both hands for kneading. Either way is effective.

A common mistake novice bread bakers make is to push the dough down rather than away from them as they knead. The downward shove makes the dough stick to the work surface, and when this happens, your natural inclination is to add more flour. Too much flour produces a heavy loaf. If you have added so much flour that the dough is hard to handle, or if past experience tells you that you tend to be heavy-handed with the flour, turn the dough out onto a floured work surface, cover it with a kitchen towel, and let it rest for 5 to 15 minutes. This gives the dough time to absorb the excess flour and makes it easier to knead.

As you knead, several things are important. First, establish a good rhythm (count or sing—I suggest to my students to break into a rendition of "Row, Row, Row Your Boat"!). Second, keep the work surface clean by scraping it often with a plastic dough scraper. The dough puts a thin film on the countertop that causes sticking. Constant scraping and light sprinklings of flour alleviate this problem. Do both *before* the dough sticks, but beware of too much flour on the surface. You will develop a feel for when the dough is about to stick: it drags a little on the work surface. At this point, scrape the counter clean and dust it with a *little* flour. Once you establish a good kneading rhythm and the dough is moving well, add flour *only* when the dough drags on the work surface.

If the dough sticks, lift it off the countertop with one hand and use the other to spread flour over the counter. If any dough particles adhere to your hands or the work surface, knead them back into the dough. Do not toss them out—they represent bites of good bread!

Practice adding *as little flour* as possible during kneading. The better you become at kneading, the less flour you will use. You will know you have added enough when you can pinch the top of the dough and the raised portion holds its shape.

The best indication that the dough is well kneaded is the appearance after 8 to 10 minutes of blisters on the surface. They are easiest for the untrained eye to spot on white bread dough. When they appear, the dough is ready for rising. Even if the dough seems smooth and silken after 4 or 5 minutes of kneading, keep working if you cannot yet detect blisters.

Proper kneading is the secret of good bread. Do not take shortcuts. Fold, stretch, and push the dough until it feels smooth, forms blisters, is springy and slightly firm but still a bit tacky. The dough is what I call "slack." Remember that during rising the liquid continues to absorb flour and the dough will not be the least bit tacky after it has risen.

Letting the Dough Rise

Rising is necessary for strong gluten development. During this time, the kneaded dough takes on a life of its own, doubling in size in about an hour. Rising should not be rushed, but a warm environment is essential (with a few notable exceptions, such as the cool-rise method preferred for French bread, page 74). However, if the dough rises too quickly or is left too long before being shaped, the gases ferment and impart an off odor and flavor.

For most recipes, let the dough rise in a large bowl in a warm area, 65° to 80°F. I recommend using a deep ceramic bowl rather than a shallow wide bowl. The deep sides protect the dough from air, which will dry it. Before you begin kneading, fill the bowl with warm (not hot) water. When you've finished kneading, pour off the water and dry the bowl thoroughly. If you do not have a ceramic bowl and your kitchen is not especially warm, set the dough to rise in the oven with the door closed and the oven light switched on (do *not* turn on the oven!). Or place a pan of hot water on the oven shelf beneath the bowl containing the dough and shut the oven door. Both methods keep the oven sufficiently warm for good rising.

Oil the bowl lightly and place the kneaded dough into it, turning it over so that all sides are coated with oil. Cover the bowl with a tightly woven kitchen towel to protect it further from the drying qualities of the air. Terry cloth and loosely woven towels let in too much air to be effective. Plastic wrap works well as a covering, but it is more wasteful.

Most recipes, including mine, instruct you to leave the dough alone until it has doubled in bulk. Judging this is not as easy as it sounds, especially for the beginner. I suggest measuring the bulk of your kneaded dough in a large measuring cup (you may have to cut it into pieces and measure each one separately) to determine its volume. If the dough is approximately 7 cups, pour 7 cups of water into the bowl you plan to use for rising. Add another 7 cups of water to equal 14 cups altogether and note how high the water rises in the bowl. You may want to mark the place with a wax crayon or a small piece of tape. This is the height to which the dough should rise when it doubles. (Needless to say, this experiment does not have to be repeated each time you bake.)

Another method to determine if the dough has doubled in bulk is to poke two fingers about 1 inch deep into the center of the dough. If the indentations remain and the dough doesn't collapse, it has risen enough.

Take care the dough does not rise too quickly. If the dough has doubled in 30 to 40 minutes or less, turn it out onto a work surface, knead it just a little, and return it to the bowl, beginning the rising

Punching Down the Dough

Shaping into Loaves

process all over again. In fact, you can do this at least five times before the yeast gets tired. Some bakers like to let the bread rise three or more times, because it gives the flavor time to develop and the baked loaf has an especially fine texture.

Some recipes call for punching down the dough to deflate it. This is most necessary between risings when there is more than one preliminary rising. It is also done with dough that is going to be made into a free-form loaf, but rarely with dough that will be shaped. To punch down, gently push the risen dough to the bottom of the bowl with your palm, or push down several times with your fist. Turn it over to coat with oil, replace the cover, and permit to rise again.

After the first rising, the dough is ready for shaping and a second rise. While most recipes instruct you to punch down the dough and then turn it out onto a floured surface for kneading and shaping, I recommend a different procedure. Instead, lightly oil the work surface, using about 1 tablespoon of vegetable oil. Because risen dough does not accept flour readily, I find a lightly oiled surface is better for working the dough. If you use flour to prevent sticking, it may cause unsightly streaks in the dough, air pockets beneath the top crust, and gaps in the crumb. The oil simply will prevent sticking.

Punching down the dough at this stage makes the gluten elastic again; as a result, the dough is difficult to shape. Instead, turn the dough out of the bowl onto the oiled surface, letting it plop onto the counter. This one motion expels sufficient gas. Do not knead the dough unless you are making a freestanding loaf. Kneading also activates the gluten, so that when you roll or stretch the dough it creeps back like a piece of elastic. If the dough does this, cover it with a towel and let it rest for about 5 minutes on the work surface. Try shaping it again.

Many of the recipes in this book are for breads with unique shapes. Most shapes are interchangeable from recipe to recipe. I realize that there will be days when you want to shape the dough into standard loaves quickly rather than take time for fancy shaping. There are two standard shapes: freestanding round loaves and standard pan loaves. Here are shaping directions for both:

FREESTANDING LOAVES: To shape freestanding round loaves, turn the risen dough out onto a lightly oiled work surface. Divide it in half with a dough scraper or sharp knife and gently knead each piece in a circle to deflate it and to form a ball. Take care not to knead roughly or you will split the smooth outer skin that helps the bread hold its shape during baking. Place each ball on a parchment-lined or well-greased baking sheet and flatten the center slightly. If you don't flatten the center, the finished loaf will be round, like a bowling ball.

Cover with a tightly woven kitchen towel and allow the dough to rise for the second time according to the recipe directions. Just before putting the bread in the oven, slit the top of the loaves about ¼ inch deep and 2 inches apart with a sharp blade in two or three places. This controls where the gases escape so the loaves rise evenly. Should you forget to slit the tops, the inside of the loaves may burst through the outer crust, like a tire blowout, and the loaves won't rise fully.

STANDARD LOAVES: Standard pan loaves are the sandwich-style loaves familiar to most people. Turn the risen dough out onto a lightly oiled work surface and divide it in half. At this point you have a choice. First, you can flatten and shape the dough gently into a ball and roll it into a cylinder that fits a well-greased loaf pan. Put the dough in the pan, cover it with a tightly woven kitchen towel, and allow it to rise for the second time according to the recipe directions. The finished loaf will not have a picture-perfect shape and the texture will not be completely even.

Second, you can turn the dough out onto a lightly oiled work surface and divide it in half, as above, then use a rolling pin to roll each piece into a 10 × 14-inch rectangle. Using your hands, roll the dough loosely *toward* you to form a 10-inch cylinder, and pinch the edge to seal the cylinder along its length. If the dough is rolled too tightly, it will burst through the outer crust. Since your natural inclination when rolling dough *away* from you is to give it a slight tug back, I roll the dough toward me, which prevents it from being rolled too tightly.

Fold each end toward the center of the loaf and bring up the bottom edges of the dough, just as you would if you were wrapping a gift box. Pinch the dough to hold it in place—this tidies up the ends of the loaf. Fit the dough, seam-side down, into well-greased loaf pans, cover with a tightly woven kitchen towel, and allow to rise for a second time according to the recipe directions. This method—which requires a little extra work—produces a perfect-looking loaf that is evenly textured.

Note: I recommend you grease loaf pans with solid shortening or butter. A treated oil (such as Pam) will also do the job. However, if you merely lightly oil the loaf pan, the dough will frequently stick.

Take care the shaped loaf does not rise too much. Use your eye to determine when the bread is *almost* doubled. Over-risen dough may collapse in the oven. If you think yours has expanded too much, turn it out onto the oiled work surface again and reshape it, letting it rise a third time. I once found it necessary to do this with a loaf of cinnamon swirl bread. The procedure resulted in ¼-inch layers of dough sandwiching the sweet, rich cinnamon mixture rather than the originally desired ½-inch layers. What a delicious mistake that turned out to be!

Baking, Cooling, and Storing Yeast Bread

Unless otherwise instructed in a recipe, bake the bread in a pre-heated oven on a rack positioned so that the bread itself is in the middle of the oven. All ovens hold heat differently and so it's a good idea to test the bread for doneness about 5 minutes before the recipe indicates the bread should be done.

My preferred method of testing for doneness is to use an instant-read thermometer. To do this, remove a loaf from the oven, tip it out of its pan, and insert the wand into the bottom of the loaf. If the internal temperature is 190°F, the bread is done. For baguettes, I usually wait for the internal temperature to reach 200°. The higher temperature results in an especially crisp crust. If you stick the wand of the thermometer in the end of the loaf, a number of the bread slices will have a puncture in them. Putting it in the bottom causes the least damage. With the thermometer, there is no guesswork involved. Unlike cake, bread does not fall after it is taken from the oven, so if the loaf is not done, simply return it to the oven for a little longer. Check it at 5-minute intervals. (Work quickly so the loaves don't cool down.)

Testing can also be done by thumping the bottom of the loaf with your fingertips or knuckles and listening for a hollow sound.

This sound is difficult to describe but with practice you will come to recognize it.

Once you take the bread from the oven—warm, brown, and filling the kitchen with tantalizing aromas—resist the urge to cut right into it. Instead, immediately turn the loaf out of the pan and let it cool on a wire rack for at least 15 minutes. Setting the bread on a rack enables air to circulate all around it and keeps the crust from turning soggy and soft as it would if left in the hot pan to steam. Cooling also gives the bread a chance to complete the baking process and the crumb to set. If you cut it without waiting for at least 15 minutes, the interior crumb will be gummy.

Since bread has no preservatives, it doesn't last more than a couple of days stored at room temperature. (This time frame varies around the country—for instance, in warm, humid climates, bread molds quickly; and in high altitudes it dries out quickly.) Also, it is virtually impossible to see nutrients destroyed in food. Bread stored in the refrigerator goes stale. If bread won't be used during this time frame, freeze it to preserve the optimum flavor and nutrients (see instructions, below).

Store cooled bread at room temperature in airtight plastic bags or tightly wrapped in plastic wrap or foil. When wrapped airtight, the crust softens, which is fine if the bread is to be used for sandwiches or toast. However, breads with a chewy crust should be wrapped in a tightly woven towel for no longer than two days in order to preserve this crust.

As wonderful as freshly baked bread is, there are times when you will want to freeze a loaf or two to enjoy on those days you simply do not have time to bake. It is most important that the bread be completely cool before freezing it; otherwise, the center of the bread will turn into an ice cube in the freezer and its texture will be sodden when thawed. It takes about 5 hours (depending on the size of the loaf) for a loaf of bread to cool completely. Keep in mind that bread can also be sliced before freezing, so that it can later be taken out a few slices at a time (the slices don't take long to thaw).

Wrap the cooled loaf in at least 2 millimeters of protection. The plastic bags holding store-bought breads are about 1 millimeter thick, and if you use these for freezing, be sure to use two to wrap the bread. Wrap them so that the logo and other writing are facing outward. Otherwise, wrap the bread first in freezer paper or plastic wrap and then in aluminum foil. I like to use freezer-weight zip-style bags, instead of all the wrapping, I can reuse them several times and it's easy to remove the air which causes ice crystals to form on the bread, from the bag. Simply insert a straw in the corner of the almost-sealed bag and suck out the air. Remove the straw and seal the bag at once.

Properly wrapped bread freezes well for about six months, retaining all its nutrients and most of its freshly baked flavor. To defrost the bread, leave it in its original wrapping at room temperature for a few hours. You might choose to refresh the thawed loaf by wrapping it in foil and putting it in a 375°F oven for about 5 minutes, then opening the foil and returning the bread to the oven for another 5 minutes.

How to Rush or Delay Bread Making

It is said that you cannot rush bread, but it just isn't so. True, you cannot rush it and expect the same full flavor as when the bread has ample time to rise at least twice, but you can make delicious bread in about half the time normally required. On the other hand, you can slow down the entire process, which is useful for those cooks who like to plan ahead and for those who may start to bake only to be called away unexpectedly.

RUSHING THE RECIPE

Mix and knead the dough according to the recipe. Instead of putting it into an oiled bowl to rise, cover it with a tightly woven kitchen towel and let it rest on the work surface for 10 minutes to give the gluten time to relax. Shape the dough (as you would before the second rise), cover, and let rise until nearly doubled. Bake it at once.

Another way to speed up the process is to use one of the fast-acting yeasts available, such as SAF, Rapid-Rise or Quick-Rise. Use the rapid-mix method of activating yeast described on page 54. You will discover that the dough rises twice as quickly as ordinarily required.

DELAYING THE RECIPE

There are several ways to stall the process. First, you can add cool (70° to 80°F) water to the *already activated* yeast. Activate the yeast first, using ¼ cup of warm water for every package or scant tablespoon of yeast. The rest of the liquid required should be cool. Let the dough rise until doubled and then deflate it and let it rise two or three more times before shaping it, letting it rise a final time, and baking it. This produces a wonderfully textured and tasty bread.

PEGGY TUBS. Another way to slow down the bread making process is to employ what is called the peggy tub method, a peggy tub being a large basin used to wash clothes. Substitute a large bowl or the kitchen sink for the tub.

Begin by making the dough according to the recipe but adding an extra ½ cup of flour, so that the kneaded dough is firm and *not tacky.* Roll the dough in more flour and then wrap it loosely in a large, tightly woven kitchen towel that has been sprinkled with flour. Take care not to roll the towel too tightly—the dough will rise inside the towel and needs room for expansion.

Fill the tub, bowl, or sink with cool water and put the towel-wrapped dough in it so that the side of the bundle with the loose edges of towel is facing up (this prevents the dough from slipping out). The bundle sinks to the bottom of the tub, but as the dough rises, it floats to the top. When it reaches the top, the dough may be shaped, allowed a second rising (outside the tub!) and then baked. You may leave the wrapped, risen dough in the water for as long as 12 hours. When you unwrap the dough, it may be sticky and you will have to oil your hands to work it. This method yields a moist, flavorful loaf.

SPONGES. Making a sponge is another good way to prolong the bread making process. A sponge is a combination of ingredients that always includes flour, yeast, and liquid, has the consistency of cake batter, and may be left to rise for as short a time as 30 minutes or as long as 2 days. The sponge gives the liquid plenty of time to absorb the flour. Therefore, you use less flour during the final kneading and get a delightfully light loaf.

Sponge-risen breads have different textures from other breads. Bread plucked from the center of a loaf risen by the standard method of activating the yeast without making a sponge is tuftlike. Bread plucked from the center of a sponge-risen loaf pulls off in strips similar to string cheese. A sponge often means bread with better texture and fuller flavor than if the bread were made the standard way. Almost any recipe can be converted to the sponge method.

To make a sponge, activate the yeast according to your preference or the recipe. Add half the flour and all the liquid *but not the salt,* which would inhibit the yeast's development. Beat the mixture vigorously for 2 minutes, cover the bowl with a tightly woven kitchen towel, and let the sponge rise for 30 minutes or overnight. Depending on how long you leave it, the sponge will swell and fall during rising (do not be concerned if either happens). When you are ready to proceed, add the salt and beat in enough of the remaining flour until the dough begins to pull away from the side of the bowl. Turn the dough out onto a lightly floured surface and knead it as you ordinarily would. You can allow the sponge-based dough to rise until doubled before shaping, or you can simply cover it with a towel for 10 minutes and then shape it, relying on only one rising before baking.

COOL RISES. Finally, the dough can be refrigerated in a process developed by Fleischmann's Yeast called the cool rise method. For this, knead the dough, cover it with a kitchen towel, and let it rest on the work surface for 10 minutes. Shape the dough and brush it with oil. Cover it loosely first with plastic wrap (one of the purposes of the oil is to prevent sticking) and then with a towel to hold the plastic in place. Refrigerate the dough for 2 to 24 hours —depending on when you want to bake it. Fifteen minutes before baking, take the dough from the refrigerator and leave it covered while the oven heats. Bake the bread according to the recipe, although because of the chilling, the bread may take about 5 minutes longer to cook.

I particularly like this last method for cinnamon rolls. I make a batch on Friday or Saturday night and then plan on sleeping late the following morning. My husband, who rises early, pops them in the oven so that I awake to the delicious aroma of freshly baked breakfast rolls. What a luxury!

Converting Recipes for the Food Processor

The food processor has been said to have revolutionized home cooking, but when it comes to bread making, it is a temperamental genius. It mixes the dough easily and efficiently, but can also damage it in a flash if you are not careful. For more control and less friction, use the pulse button rather than the on button. Never turn your back on the food processor when it is on—it can overknead the dough before you can turn around. Learn to rely on an accurate timer when using it, since precision is important here.

My recipes are developed for the Cuisinart Professional 14 size, SuperPro 7, or Food Preparation Center. If your machine is smaller and less powerful, divide the recipe in half.

1. Make sure the processor can accommodate the amount of flour specified in the recipe. If not, cut the recipe in half.

2. I proof yeast for use in the processor. Everything happens so quickly, I feel this extra step gives the dough a flavor boost. Whisk ½ teaspoon of sugar for every scant tablespoon (¼-ounce package) of yeast into ¼ cup of warm (105° to 115°F) water. Whisk the yeast until it dissolves. Let it sit for about 5 minutes, until it foams and swells. (For more on proofing, see page 54.)

3. Set the plastic blade in the food processor. You can use the metal blade if you do not have plastic. Plastic produces less heat and treats the dough more gently.

4. Put all but ¼ cup of flour in the bowl of the processor. Add the remaining dry ingredients. Butter and other shortening are considered dry ingredients.

5. Add the proofed yeast and pulse 6 or 7 times.

6. Warm the liquid ingredients to 90° to 100°F. Eggs and oil are considered liquid ingredients. Do not heat the liquids any hotter or they will kill or damage the yeast. The processor's blade causes friction that heats the dough, too.

7. With the processor running (use the on button this time), pour the liquids through the feed tube. If you hear sputtering, pour the liquids more slowly to prevent the dough from creeping under the blade. When all the liquids are incorporated, turn off the machine immediately.

8. Pulse the machine 7 or 8 times. The dough should gather into a ball on top of the blade. If there are dry crumbs where the sides of the processor bowl meet the bottom, add a little more liquid, 1 tablespoon at a time. If the dough is too wet and sticky to gather together, add more flour, 1 tablespoon at a time. Be sure to pulse the machine to mix the dough. It causes less friction than turning the machine to on.

9. After the dough forms a ball, turn the processor on and knead for 60 seconds. Use a timer. If you are using a metal blade, knead for only 45 seconds and then turn the dough out onto a floured surface and knead the dough by hand for 5 minutes. This hand kneading is not necessary with the plastic blade.

10. Lift the dough from the bowl of the processor and put it into an oiled bowl. Turn the dough to coat it with oil and cover the bowl with a tightly woven kitchen towel. Proceed with the recipe, letting the dough rise as required.

Converting Recipes for the Heavy-duty Mixer

I have found that following the manufacturer's directions for kneading bread dough in mixers such as a KitchenAid or Kenwood does not produce the same good results as does following my technique. Put away the manuals, for I think you will find doing it my way easy and foolproof. The dough does not crawl up the dough hook, and the baked loaves are the same as if made by hand. Use this method for any yeast bread recipe in the book. It saves you the task of kneading the bread by hand on a work surface.

1. Soften the yeast in the liquid, as instructed in the recipe. This can be done right in the large bowl of the electric mixer. (You can also mix the ingredients together using the rapid-mix method described on page 54.)

2. Fit the mixer with the paddle attachment (not the dough hook).

3. Combine the remaining liquid ingredients with the yeast in the bowl. Add half the amount of flour required plus the rest of the dry ingredients. Eggs and oil are liquid ingredients; butter and shortening are considered dry ingredients.

4. Turn the mixer to medium speed (number 4 on some mixers) and beat for 2 minutes.

5. Reduce the speed to low (number 1, or stir, on some mixers). Add the remaining flour, ¼ cup at a time, while continuing to stir, until the dough gathers on the paddle but spreads back onto the sides of the bowl a few seconds later.

6. Remove the paddle attachment. Scrape any dough adhering to the paddle back into the bowl. Fit the mixer with the dough hook.

7. Scrape down the sides of the bowl and turn the mixer on to medium-low (number 2 on some mixers). Add more flour, 1 tablespoon at a time, until the dough gathers on the dough hook in a ball but spreads back onto the sides of the bowl a few seconds later. Do not add enough flour yet to clean the sides of the bowl or the dough will be too stiff.

8. Increase the speed to medium (number 4) and let the mixer knead the dough for 5 minutes. At the end of this time the dough should clean the sides of the bowl. If it does not, add more flour, 1 tablespoon at a time, until the dough cleans the sides of the bowl.

9. Remove the dough and put it into a clean, oiled bowl. Turn the dough to coat it with oil and cover the bowl with a tightly woven kitchen towel. Let the dough rise according to the recipe directions and proceed.

Converting Recipes for the Bread Machine

Most bread machines produce 1-pound or 1½-pound loaves. Any recipe calling for approximately 6 cups of flour (which can include some cracked wheat, old-fashioned rolled oats, etc.) can be converted for use in either size bread machine. Six cups is the magic number because it can easily be divided by 3 or by 2. Every cup of flour represents ½ pound of bread. The math is easy, although the formula does not apply to yeast. And the amount of yeast makes a significant difference in the outcome of the bread. Take my word for it—my calculations for the yeast conversions work.

FOR A 1-POUND LOAF: Divide all the ingredients in your 6-cup recipe by 3, except the yeast. Put the ingredients into the machine in the order specified in the manual (the liquid is added first in some machines, the flour in others). Use 1 teaspoon of yeast for white flour breads. For breads containing whole wheat flour, increase the yeast to 1½ teaspoons. If you find that the finished bread is dense, next time increase the yeast by ½ teaspoon.

FOR A 1½-POUND LOAF: Divide all the ingredients in half, except the yeast. Put the ingredients into the machine in the order specified in the manual. Use 2 teaspoons of yeast for white flour breads. For breads containing whole wheat flour, increase the yeast to 2½ teaspoons. If the baked bread is dense, next time increase the yeast by ½ teaspoon.

Follow the manufacturer's instructions for operating the bread machine.

Converting Recipes for the La Cloche

To use a La Cloche, prepare the dough and shape it into a round loaf that is a little smaller than the ceramic base. Sprinkle cornmeal on a baker's peel or rimless baking sheet. Put the shaped loaf on the peel and cover it loosely with a tightly woven kitchen towel. Let the dough rise until almost doubled in size.

While the dough is rising, fill the dome of the La Cloche with tap water and let it sit. Set the dome handle over the sink drain or in a saucepan so it will sit flat. Preheat the oven to 400°F. Grease the base of the La Cloche with solid vegetable shortening or vegetable cooking spray, such as Pam, and heat the base for 30 minutes in the preheated oven.

Use a very sharp knife to make a slit ½ inch deep across the length of the risen loaf and gently slide the loaf onto the heated base. Be careful not to plop the dough into the base or it will deflate. Spray the loaf with water or brush it with water or a glaze. Discard the water from the dome and immediately position it over the base. Do not dry the lid; it needs the moisture.

Bake the bread for about 40 minutes in the 400° oven. After 40 minutes, remove the dome and bake the bread for 5 to 10 minutes longer, or until it is golden brown and sounds hollow when tapped on the bottom (the internal temperature should reach 190°F). When the bread is done, lift it from the base and let it cool on a wire rack. As it cools, you will hear the thin, crisp crust crackle. When completely cool, the crust will look as though it is shattered.

3

The first recipe in this chapter is a basic loaf of white bread, the ideal loaf for you to practice your bread making skills. Once you feel confident with the bread, proceed through the chapter, selecting those loaves that appeal to you. You will quickly see that, whether you are making a focaccia redolent with herbs and cheese, braiding challah, or forming feta cheese–filled buns, the fundamentals of making yeast-raised bread dough apply.

All the recipes in this chapter use unbleached all-purpose white flour, easy to find in any market and totally reliable. Properly treated, it produces loaves with good rise, sturdy structure, and balanced flavor.

Here are recipes for dinner rolls, egg breads, breadsticks, and soft buns as well as for white bread, French bread, crusty Cuban bread, and more. I hope they all become trusted favorites in your household.

White-Flour Yeast Breads

Basic White Bread

2 scant tablespoons or
2 (¼-ounce) packages active
dry yeast

2½ cups warm water (105° to
115°F)

2 tablespoons vegetable oil

2 tablespoons sugar

2 teaspoons salt

5½ to 6½ cups unbleached
all-purpose flour

Makes 2 loaves

This loaf will help you master your bread baking abilities. It is easy and straightforward and during kneading blisters are readily discernible so you know right away when the dough is properly kneaded. Don't be discouraged if your first few attempts are not perfect—you will improve with each loaf. As long as you don't kill the yeast, it's hard to make a really bad loaf of bread.

1. In a large bowl, soften the yeast in the water.

2. Add the oil, sugar, salt, and 3 cups of the flour. Beat vigorously with a dough whisk or a heavy-handled spoon for 2 minutes.

3. Gradually stir in more of the remaining flour, ¼ cup at a time, until the dough forms a mass and begins to pull away from the side of the bowl. Turn the dough out onto a floured work surface.

4. Knead, adding more flour, a little at a time as necessary, for 8 to 10 minutes, or until you have a smooth, elastic dough and blisters begin to develop on the surface. You may not need to use all the flour.

5. Put the dough into an oiled bowl. Turn to coat the entire ball of dough with oil. Cover with a tightly woven kitchen towel and let rise for about 1 hour, or until doubled in size.

6. Turn the dough out onto a lightly oiled work surface. Divide the dough in half. Roll one piece into a 10 × 14-inch rectangle (diagram 1). This removes the excess gases and gives a more uniform texture to the finished loaves. Roll the dough into a 10-inch cylinder, and pinch the loose edge to the loaf (diagram 2). Fold the ends of the loaf by bringing each side into the center of the end then bringing the bottom layer of dough to the top and pinching it to the top (diagram 3)—the process is similar to wrapping paper over a package. Repeat with the other end of the dough.

7. Repeat the same procedure for the second half of the dough. Then place both loaves pinched-side down, into well-seasoned loaf pans.

(continued)

8. Cover with a towel and let rise until almost doubled, about 45 minutes.

9. Preheat the oven to 375°F.

10. Bake for 30 minutes, or until the internal temperature of the bread reaches 190°F.

11. Immediately remove bread from pans and cool on a rack to prevent the crust from becoming soggy.

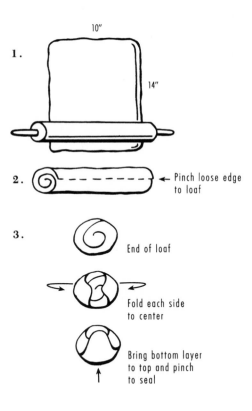

Tomato Basil Baguettes

1 cup finely chopped onion

3 cloves garlic, finely chopped

2 tablespoons olive oil

2 scant tablespoons or 2 (¼-ounce) packages active dry yeast

½ cup warm water (105° to 115°F)

¾ cup chopped fresh basil leaves or 3 tablespoons dried

2 teaspoons salt

1 cup fresh tomatoes, peeled, seeded, and chopped, combined with 1 cup tomato juice (or 2 cups canned tomatoes, undrained and chopped)

2 tablespoons sugar

5 to 6 cups unbleached all-purpose flour

2 ounces finely grated Parmesan cheese (about ½ cup)

Makes 2 baguettes

I usually put the tomatoes in my food processor rather than chop them by hand since it is quicker. But do not overprocess them. Small pieces of tomato in the dough add a bit of character to the baguettes.

1. Gently cook the onion and garlic in the olive oil for 3 to 5 minutes over medium-low heat until transparent. Set aside and cool to lukewarm.

2. In a large bowl, soften the yeast in the water.

3. Add the cooled onions and garlic, the basil, salt, tomatoes and juice, sugar, and 3 cups of the flour. Beat vigorously with a dough whisk or a heavy-handled spoon for 2 minutes.

4. Gradually add more of the remaining flour, ¼ cup at a time, until the dough forms a mass and begins to pull away from the side of the bowl. Turn the dough out onto a floured work surface.

5. Knead, adding more flour, a little at a time as necessary, about 8 to 10 minutes, or until you have a smooth, elastic dough and blisters begin to develop on the surface.

6. Put the dough into an oiled bowl. Turn to coat the entire ball of dough with oil. Cover with a tightly woven kitchen towel and let rise for about 1 hour, or until doubled in size.

7. Turn the dough out onto a lightly oiled work surface and divide it in half. Using your hands, roll each piece into a 15-inch rope. Fit the ropes into lightly oiled baguette pans or arrange about 3 inches apart on a well-greased baking sheet.

8. Cover the loaves with a towel and let rise for about 45 minutes, or until almost doubled in size.

9. About 15 minutes before the end of rising, preheat the oven to 375°F.

10. Just before baking, make three diagonal slits, about ¼ inch deep, in the top of each loaf and sprinkle with Parmesan cheese. Bake for 20 to 25 minutes, or until the loaves have pulled slightly from the pan and sound hollow when tapped on the bottom (the internal temperature should reach 190°F).

11. Immediately remove from the pans and cool on a rack.

French Bread

1 scant tablespoon or
1 (¼-ounce) package active
dry yeast

¼ cup warm water (105° to
115°F)

2 cups cool water (45° to
55°F)

5½ to 6½ cups unbleached
all-purpose flour

2 teaspoons salt

Cornmeal

Makes 4 baguettes

This bread should really be described as "French-style," because authentic French bread is made with French-milled flour, which produces a lighter loaf than we can achieve here with American-milled, unbleached all-purpose wheat flour. But the cool water and long rising time give this loaf great flavor and the airy texture and crisp crust we associate with traditional French bread. For this recipe, I form the loaves into the long narrow cylinders called baguettes.

1. In a large bowl, soften the yeast in the warm water.

2. Add the cool water, 3 cups of the flour, and the salt. Beat vigorously with a dough whisk or a heavy-handled spoon for 2 minutes.

3. Gradually beat in more of the remaining flour, ¼ cup at a time, until the dough forms a mass and begins to pull away from the side of the bowl. Turn the dough out onto a floured work surface.

4. Knead, adding more flour, a little at a time as necessary, for 8 to 10 minutes, or until you have a smooth, elastic dough and blisters begin to develop on the surface.

5. Put the dough into an oiled bowl. Turn to coat the entire ball of dough with oil. Cover with a tightly woven kitchen towel and let rise in a cool place (about 60°F) for about 3 hours, or until tripled in size. (In the winter, place the bowl on the floor of a closet or cabinet away from a heat source—this should be about the right temperature. In the summer, before putting the dough in a ceramic bowl, warm the bowl by putting 95° to 100°F water in the bowl; drain, then proceed as directed, and then place the slightly warmed bowl in the refrigerator—in this way, the dough will not get too cool during the 3 hours.)

6. Turn the dough out onto a lightly oiled work surface. Knead for 2 minutes to remove most of the air. Put the dough back into the bowl, turn to coat with oil, cover with a towel, and let rise again in a cool place for about 1½ hours, or until doubled in size.

7. Sprinkle four well-greased baguette pans or two baking sheets with cornmeal.

8. Turn the dough out onto a lightly oiled work surface and divide it into quarters. Roll one piece of dough into an 8 × 10-inch oval. Fold the oval lengthwise into thirds. Using the side of your hand, make a lengthwise crease down the center. Fold in half and pinch the seams, tapering the ends slightly. Starting in the center and working out to the ends, roll the dough back and forth with your hands to form a 14-inch cylinder. Repeat this process with the remaining pieces of dough. Put the loaves seam side down on the prepared pans or baking sheets. The folding and rolling are necessary to develop a skin on the outside of the dough, which is very important for the final crust.

9. Cover the dough with a towel and let rise at room temperature for 40 minutes.

10. About 15 minutes before the end of rising, preheat the oven to 425°F. Put a shallow pan on the lower shelf of the oven.

11. Shortly before baking, cut diagonal slashes in the loaves, about ¼ inch deep and 2 inches apart, using a sharp serrated knife. Lightly brush the loaves with cold water and let sit uncovered for 5 minutes. Brush with cold water again.

12. Put 1 cup of ice cubes in the heated pan on the lower shelf of the oven. Quickly put the loaves on the shelf above and close the door to hold the steam in the oven.

13. Bake the loaves for 20 to 25 minutes, or until they have pulled slightly from the pans and sound hollow when tapped on the bottom (the internal temperature should reach 200°F).

14. Immediately remove the bread and cool on racks.

Make sure to consult the information on flour and other ingredients and on utensils (chapter 1) and the baking class on making yeast breads (chapter 2).

County Fair Egg Bread

2 scant tablespoons or
2 (¼-ounce) packages active
dry yeast

½ cup warm water (105° to
115°F)

4 tablespoons (½ stick)
unsalted butter, at room
temperature

¼ cup sugar

3 large eggs, at room
temperature

1½ cups warm milk (105° to
115°F)

6 to 7 cups unbleached all-
purpose flour

2 teaspoons salt

1 large egg beaten with
1 tablespoon cold water, for
the egg wash

Poppy seeds or sesame seeds
(optional)

**Makes 1 large braided loaf or
3 medium unbraided loaves**

This bread is often entered in county fair bake-offs; hence the name. Its texture is velvety and the crust has a rich brown color. Before I braid the ropes of dough, I brush them with egg and then roll them completely in seeds so that there are seeds marbled throughout the loaf. This bread is similar to the Challah on page 96, but it has a softer texture.

1. In a small bowl or 1-cup measure, soften the yeast in the water.

2. In a large bowl, beat the butter and sugar together until fluffy. Add the eggs one at a time, continuing to beat until light. Add the softened yeast, milk, and 3 cups of the flour. Beat vigorously with a dough whisk or heavy-handled spoon for 2 minutes. The resulting sponge should have the consistency of a cake batter. Cover the bowl with plastic wrap and a tightly woven kitchen towel and let rise for 30 minutes, or until the sponge is light and full of bubbles.

3. Stir the sponge to deflate it. Add the salt and beat in additional flour, ¼ cup at a time, until the dough forms a mass and begins to pull away from the side of the bowl. Turn the dough out onto a floured work surface.

4. Knead, adding more flour, a little at a time as necessary, about 8 to 10 minutes, or until you have a smooth, elastic dough and blisters begin to develop on the surface.

5. Put the dough into an oiled bowl. Turn to coat the entire ball of dough with oil. Cover with a towel and let rise for about 40 minutes, until doubled in size.

6. Turn the dough out onto a lightly oiled work surface and divide it into thirds. Shape each piece of dough into a rope 20 inches long.

7. Lightly brush the dough ropes with the egg wash, coating them completely. Sprinkle the work surface with sesame or poppy seeds. Roll the dough ropes in the seeds so that they are coated on all sides. Lay the ropes side by side on a well-greased baking sheet (diagram 1). Starting in the center of the loaf for a more balanced braid, begin braiding as follows:

1.

2.

3.

4.

5.

8. Take the right rope over the center rope (diagram 2), then the left rope over the center (diagram 3), the right over the center, the left over the center, etc., continuing until the ropes are too short to braid. Pinch all three ends together and tuck them under (diagram 4).

9. To braid the other end of the loaf, turn it so that the braided portion is at the top and the loose ropes are at the bottom. Take the center rope over the right rope, the center rope over the left, the center over the right, and so on until the ends are too short to braid. Pinch all three ends together and tuck them under (diagram 5).

10. Cover the braid with a towel and let rise for 30 minutes.

11. About 15 minutes before the end of rising, preheat the oven to 375°F.

12. Bake for 45 to 50 minutes, or until the braid is golden brown and sounds hollow when tapped on the bottom (the internal temperature of the braid should reach 190°F).

13. Immediately remove the loaf from the baking sheet and cool on a rack.

VARIATION

Shape the dough into either 3 round freestanding loaves and place well apart on a well-greased baking sheet, or 3 standard pan loaves (for directions, see page 59) and place in 3 well-greased loaf pans. Cover the loaves with a towel and let rise for 45 minutes. Just before baking, score the tops of the freestanding loaves ¼ inch deep in two or three places. Bake the loaves 25 to 30 minutes.

Crescia

*1 scant tablespoon or
1 (¹/₄-ounce) package active
dry yeast*

*¹/₂ cup warm water (105° to
115°F)*

1 tablespoon sugar

*2¹/₂ to 3¹/₂ cups unbleached
all-purpose flour*

¹/₂ teaspoon salt

*1 teaspoon coarsely ground
black pepper*

*6 ounces Parmesan cheese,
shredded (about 1¹/₂ cups)*

4 large eggs, beaten

2 tablespoons olive oil

**Makes 1 large coiled loaf or
2 smaller loaves**

This savory egg bread is very much a part of the Easter celebration in northern Italy. The dough is speckled with coarsely ground black pepper and flavored with shards of aged Parmesan cheese. Four eggs provide most of the liquid and also contribute to the bread's rise—it doubles again in the oven! But the eggs also make the dough fragile, so handle it gently. As with most cheese breads, the flavor of the crescia intensifies if it is allowed to mellow for at least an hour before serving.

1. In a large bowl, soften the yeast in the water.

2. Add the sugar and 1 cup of the flour to the yeast. Beat vigorously with a dough whisk or heavy-handled spoon for 2 minutes. The sponge will have the consistency of cake batter. Cover the bowl with plastic wrap and a tightly woven kitchen towel and let stand at room temperature for 2 hours. The dough will be full of small bubbles and will rise and perhaps collapse—this is normal. It will rise again later after it has been kneaded.

3. Add the salt, pepper, 1 cup of the cheese, the eggs, and the oil to the sponge. Mix thoroughly.

4. Gradually add more of the remaining flour, ¹/₄ cup at a time, until the dough forms a mass and begins to pull away from the side of the bowl. Turn the dough out onto a floured work surface.

5. Knead, adding more flour, a little at a time as necessary, about 8 to 10 minutes, or until you have a smooth, elastic dough and blisters begin to develop on the surface.

6. Put the dough into an oiled bowl. Turn to coat the entire ball of dough with oil. Cover with a towel and let rise for about 1 hour, until doubled in size.

7. Turn the dough out onto a lightly oiled work surface. Punch the dough to deflate it, but do not knead it. Roll beneath the palms of your hands into a 36-inch rope. If the rope becomes too elastic and difficult to roll out, let it rest for 2 minutes before continuing. Form the rope into a loose coil on a well-greased 12-inch round pan (such as a pizza pan).

8. Cover with a towel and let rise for 45 minutes.

9. About 15 minutes before the end of rising, preheat the oven to 375°F.

10. Just before baking, sprinkle the top of the bread with the remaining Parmesan cheese.

11. Bake for 30 to 35 minutes, or until the bread is browned and sounds hollow when tapped (the internal temperature should reach 190°F).

12. Remove the bread from the pan and cool on a rack.

VARIATION

Shape the dough into either 2 round freestanding loaves and place well apart on a well-greased baking sheet, or 2 standard pan loaves (for directions, see page 59) and place in 2 well-greased loaf pans. Cover the loaves with a towel and let rise for 45 minutes. Just before baking, score the tops of the freestanding loaves ¼ inch deep in two or three places. Bake the loaves 25 to 30 minutes.

If you have a small oven or other limitations on your ability to bake on 2 or more baking sheets at the same time, see the Note on page 189.

Garlic Rosemary Focaccia

3 whole heads (not cloves) garlic

½ cup extra-virgin olive oil

2 scant tablespoons or 2 (¼-ounce) packages active dry yeast

2 teaspoons sugar

2 cups warm water (105° to 115°F)

4½ to 5½ cups unbleached all-purpose flour

1 cup whole wheat flour

2 teaspoons salt

Cornmeal, for pans

2 tablespoons crushed fresh rosemary leaves or 2 teaspoons dried

Coarse salt (optional)

Makes one 13 × 18-inch flat bread

Focaccia, an Italian flat bread, changes style and character in each village throughout Italy. This is my adaptation of one we tried near Portofino.

It's hard to imagine ever having leftover focaccia, but if you do, split it in half horizontally and sprinkle the exposed surfaces with olive oil. Lay fresh spinach leaves, salami, provolone cheese, mortadella, tomato slices, and another layer of spinach leaves on one of the bread layers. Top with the second layer and wrap the sandwich in foil. Bake in a preheated 375°F oven for 15 minutes. The warm sandwich makes a delectable lunch or, if cut into small pieces, is wonderful with cocktails.

1. Separate the garlic heads into cloves and peel. Put the olive oil in a small, heavy saucepan. Add the garlic, cover, and cook over very low heat for 30 minutes, or until softened but not browned. (Cooking the garlic very slowly caramelizes the natural sugars and makes it sweet.) Remove the garlic from the heat and strain. Set the oil aside to use later. When cool, cut the garlic cloves into lengthwise slivers.

2. In a large bowl, dissolve the yeast and sugar in the water. Add 1 cup of the all-purpose flour and stir thoroughly. Let sit for 15 minutes, or until the mixture is filled with tiny bubbles.

3. Add 2 tablespoons of the reserved garlic oil, 1 more cup of the all-purpose flour, all the whole wheat flour, and the salt to the yeast mixture. Beat vigorously with a dough whisk or a heavy-handled spoon for 2 minutes.

4. Gradually add more of the remaining flour, ¼ cup at a time, until the dough forms a mass and begins to pull away from the side of the bowl. Turn the dough out onto a floured work surface.

5. Knead, adding more flour, a little at a time as necessary, for 8 to 10 minutes, or until you have a smooth, elastic dough and blisters begin to develop on the surface.

6. Put the dough into an oiled bowl. Turn to coat the entire ball of dough with oil. Cover with a tightly woven kitchen towel and let rise for about 1 hour, or until doubled in size.

7. Sprinkle a well-greased 13 × 18 × 1-inch baking sheet with cornmeal.

8. Turn the dough out onto an oiled work surface. With the heel of your hand, flatten the dough into an 11 × 16-inch rectangle. Lift the dough onto the baking sheet. Using your hands, press the dough into the corners and edges of the baking sheet. Flattening the dough with your hands rather than a rolling pin will give it the irregular texture usually associated with focaccia. Cover the dough with a towel and let rise for 20 minutes.

9. Sprinkle the top of the dough with rosemary and the slivered garlic. Using your fingertips, make indentations in the dough, about ½ inch deep and 1 inch apart, to give a dimpled effect. As you do this, press the garlic slivers into the dough to keep them from falling off or overcooking. Cover the dough with a towel and let rise for another 20 minutes.

10. While the dough is rising, preheat the oven to 400°F. Put a shallow pan on the lower shelf of the oven.

11. Drizzle the remaining garlic oil over the top of the focaccia. Use a brush to pat the oil over the entire surface, allowing any excess oil to pool in the indentations. Sprinkle with 1 to 2 teaspoons of coarse salt, if desired.

12. Put 1 cup of ice cubes in the heated shallow pan in the oven. Immediately put the focaccia in the oven and bake for 30 to 35 minutes, or until the focaccia is pale gold (the internal temperature should reach 190°F).

13. Remove the focaccia from the pan and cool on a rack. To serve, cut or tear the bread into 3-inch squares. Focaccia is best eaten slightly warm or at room temperature.

The center of whatever you're baking should be as close to the vertical center of the oven as the racks will allow. This enhances more even baking.

Provolone Oregano Focaccia

4 cloves garlic, finely chopped

½ cup olive oil

1 scant tablespoon or 1 (¼-ounce) package active dry yeast

1½ cups warm water (105° to 115°F)

1 tablespoon sugar

1 teaspoon salt

1 cup whole wheat flour

1 cup semolina flour

6 ounces provolone cheese, cut into ¼-inch dice (1½ cups)

2 tablespoons fresh oregano leaves or 2 teaspoons dried

1 to 2 cups unbleached all-purpose flour

Makes one 14-inch-round flat loaf

Focaccia can range from being thin and crisp to being from 1 to 2 inches thick. Despite its lumpy-looking, uneven configuration, it is leavened with yeast and develops a light, hole-filled texture during rising and baking. Although it can be topped very simply with good olive oil and coarse salt, it takes to embellishment with such savory ingredients as cheese, herbs, and vegetables. Focaccia with savory seasonings is terrific any time of year, but it seems to taste best in the summertime, when the herbs and vegetables are freshest and most available. It is a perfect picnic bread.

1. Gently cook the garlic in the oil over medium heat for 3 to 5 minutes, or until the garlic begins to brown slightly. Be careful not to burn it; burned garlic is bitter. Remove from the heat and let cool.

2. In a large bowl, soften the yeast in the water.

3. Add the sugar, salt, 2 tablespoons of the cooled garlic–olive oil mixture, the whole wheat flour, semolina flour, provolone, and oregano. Beat vigorously with a dough whisk or a heavy-handled spoon for 2 minutes.

4. Gradually add the all-purpose flour, ¼ cup at a time, until the dough forms a mass and begins to pull away from the side of the bowl. Turn the dough out onto a floured work surface.

5. Knead, adding more flour, a little at a time as necessary, for 8 to 10 minutes, or until the dough is elastic and blisters begin to develop on the surface.

6. Put the dough into an oiled bowl. Turn to coat the entire ball of dough with oil. Cover with a tightly woven kitchen towel and let rise for about 1 hour, or until doubled in size.

7. Turn the dough out onto a lightly oiled work surface. Using your hands, press it into a 14-inch circle. Do not remove all the air, as the large holes make this bread interesting. Transfer the dough to a well-greased 14-inch round deep-dish pizza pan, pressing it to the edges of the pan.

8. Cover with a towel and let rise for 20 minutes.

9. Using your fingertips, dimple the dough by making indentations about 1 inch apart, pressing all the way to the bottom of the pan. Cover the dough with a towel and let rise for 20 minutes more.

10. About 15 minutes before the end of rising, preheat the oven to 400°F.

11. Just before baking, drizzle the top of the dough with the remaining garlic–olive oil mixture, using a brush to pat it over the entire surface and allowing it to puddle in the dimples.

12. Bake the focaccia for about 25 minutes, or until it is golden (the internal temperature should reach 190°F).

13. Immediately remove the bread from the pan and put it on a rack. Focaccia is best eaten slightly warm or at room temperature.

Make sure you have at least 1 inch between baking pans inside the oven, and that you have at least 1 inch between the pans and the sides of the oven. Good air circulation is vital to successful bread baking.

Fugassa

2 tablespoons olive oil

½ cup finely chopped onion
(1 medium onion)

1½ cups chopped bell pepper
(red, green, or yellow, or a
combination) (2 medium
peppers)

1 scant tablespoon or
1 (¼-ounce) package active
dry yeast

1¼ cups warm water (105° to
115°F)

1 teaspoon salt

1 tablespoon sugar

3½ to 4 cups unbleached all-
purpose flour

8 ounces sharp Cheddar
cheese (2 cups), shredded

1 egg white beaten with
1 tablespoon cold water, for
the egg wash

Coarse salt (optional)

Makes 1 large loaf

Fugassa is especially pretty when you use a combination of colorful peppers. As they cook, the peppers turn sweet and add excellent flavor to the bread. I do not suggest using dark purple peppers, as they turn a disappointing grayish color in the oven. This recipe works nicely for individual buns, too.

1. Combine the oil, onion, and pepper in a skillet over medium-low heat and sauté for about 20 minutes, stirring occasionally, until the onion is transparent. (Cooking onion and peppers slowly makes the natural sugars caramelize so that the vegetables become sweet.) Set aside and cool to lukewarm.

2. In a large bowl, soften the yeast in the water.

3. Add the salt, sugar, 2 cups of the flour, 1 cup of the cheese, and the cooled onions and peppers to the yeast. Beat vigorously with a dough whisk or heavy-handled spoon for 2 minutes.

4. Gradually add more of the remaining flour, ¼ cup at a time, until the dough forms a mass and begins to pull away from the side of the bowl. Turn the dough out onto a floured work surface.

5. Knead, adding more flour, a little at a time as necessary, about 8 to 10 minutes, or until the dough is elastic and blisters begin to develop on the surface.

6. Put the dough into an oiled bowl. Turn to coat the entire ball of dough with oil. Cover with a tightly woven kitchen towel and let rise for about 1 hour, or until doubled in size.

7. Turn the dough out onto a lightly oiled work surface. Knead in the remaining cup of cheese so that large streaks of cheese are visible. The streaks will toast for an attractive look and marvelous flavor.

8. Shape the dough into a ball and, since this is a rustic bread, form it into an irregular shape. Flatten the top slightly in several places with your fingertips so that the loaf is not smooth. Put the loaf on a well-greased baking sheet.

9. Cover with a towel and let rise for 45 minutes.

10. While the dough is rising, preheat the oven to 400°F. Put a shallow pan on the lower rack.

11. Just before baking, brush the top of the dough lightly with the egg wash and sprinkle with coarse salt, if desired. Make three slits, about ½ inch deep and 2 inches apart, in the top of the loaf.

12. Put 1 cup of ice cubes in the heated shallow pan. Put the baking sheet on the top shelf and close the oven door to trap the steam.

13. Bake for 30 to 35 minutes, or until the loaf begins to brown (the internal temperature should reach 190°F). Remove the bread from the baking sheet and cool on a rack.

VARIATION

Fugassa Buns: Follow the recipe through step 7. Divide the dough into 12 equal pieces and shape into balls. Put them about 3 inches apart on well-greased baking sheets. Flatten the tops with your fingertips to make them irregular. Cover with a towel and let the buns rise for about 45 minutes.

Just before baking, brush the tops with the egg wash and sprinkle with coarse salt, if desired. Make 2 slits, about ¼ inch deep, in top of each bun. Bake in a preheated 400°F oven for 18 to 20 minutes, or until they start to brown. These buns benefit from the steam mentioned in step 12, but it is not necessary.

Make loaves into one or two balls, then put them in a standard loaf pan. After they're baked you can pull the sections apart to use as short loaves. A good idea for those who are apt to let a loaf go stale before using it.

St. Joseph's Day Bread

PANE SCANATO PER
SAN GIUSEPPE

FOR THE SPONGE

1 teaspoon active dry yeast

½ cup warm water (105° to 115°F)

1½ cups unbleached all-purpose flour

FOR THE BREAD

1½ cups warm water (105° to 115°F)

2 teaspoons active dry yeast, or the yeast remaining in the ¼-ounce packet after the teaspoon for the sponge has been removed.

1 cup cold milk

1½ teaspoons salt

1 tablespoon sugar

2 cups pastry flour or cake flour

3½ to 4½ cups unbleached all-purpose flour

1 large egg beaten with 1 tablespoon fresh lemon juice, for the egg wash

Sesame seeds

Makes 1 extra-large, 2 large, 4 medium, or 32 individual loaves

If you have not heard of the March 19 celebration called St. Joseph's Day, I hope you are as charmed to discover it as I was. During a stint teaching baking in Buffalo, New York, I heard about the feast day and found my way to a wonderful family-run bakery called Balistreri's. Frank and Chris Balistreri graciously explained the feast-day traditions to me, and later, cookbook author and teacher Carlo Middione shared his knowledge, too.

When an Italian family decides to celebrate the St. Joseph's Day feast, they light a bonfire on their front lawn or position children at their doorway to recite religious poetry. The feasts are held to give thanks for a special blessing the family received during the past year, whether it is someone's recovery from illness, a visit from a long-lost relative, or the birth of a child. Family and friends are welcome at the meal—and I have heard that complete strangers are welcome.

St. Joseph's Day bread may be shaped into any fanciful design favored by the baker—a braid, a lily, a crown, a cross, or carpenter's tools—and it also may simply be shaped as a loaf. At home, the loaves are either individual size or slightly larger. Some St. Joseph's Day loaves are big and bold and are used to decorate the altar in the church where the celebrations are held.

The bread is made with a sponge that is started well in advance. For my version, I add pastry or cake flour because these flours, made with soft wheat, retard gluten development and the resulting bread is very soft and airy with a crisp crust.

1. Begin the sponge 8 to 24 hours before baking the bread. Stir the yeast into the water to soften. Gradually add the flour, ¼ cup at a time, beating until the sponge forms a mass and begins to pull away from the side of the bowl. Turn the sponge out onto a floured work surface and knead for about 5 minutes, gradually kneading in all the remaining flour.

2. Put the sponge into a large glass or pottery bowl. Cover lightly with plastic wrap and then with a tightly woven kitchen towel. Let the sponge sit at a cool room temperature for 8 to 24 hours. It will rise at first and then collapse after a few hours.

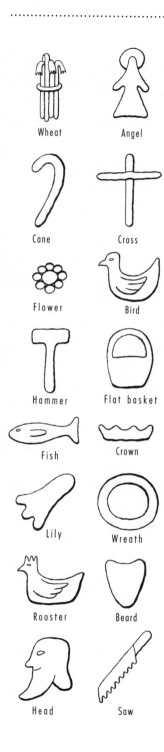

Wheat

Angel

Cane

Cross

Flower

Bird

Hammer

Flat basket

Fish

Crown

Lily

Wreath

Rooster

Beard

Head

Saw

3. When you are ready to begin making the bread, add the 1½ cups warm water to the sponge in the bowl. Squeeze your fingers through the sponge until it has dissolved in the water. Sprinkle the yeast over the mixture and let it sit for 5 minutes.

4. Add the milk, salt, sugar, pastry flour, and 1 cup of the unbleached flour to the yeast mixture. Beat vigorously for 2 minutes.

5. Gradually add more of the remaining flour, ¼ cup at a time, until the dough forms a mass and begins to pull away from the side of the bowl. Turn the dough out onto a floured work surface.

6. Knead, adding more flour, a little at a time as necessary, about 8 to 10 minutes, or until you have a smooth, elastic dough and blisters begin to develop on the surface.

7. Put the dough into an oiled bowl. Turn to coat the entire ball of dough with oil. Cover with a towel and let rise for about 1 hour, or until doubled in size.

8. Turn the dough out onto a lightly oiled work surface. Decide what size loaf you are going to make—individual, medium-size, large, or extra-large. Divide the dough according to the appropriate directions in steps 9 through 12. Then, regardless of their size, shape the loaves into one or more of the fanciful forms shown in the illustrations to this recipe. (Small individual breads are made for the St. Joseph's Day feast table, and the larger loaves are used to decorate the altar.)

9. For *individual* loaves, use a knife or bench knife to divide the dough into 32 pieces. (This is easily done by dividing the dough in half and then dividing each half in half again, and so on.) Shape each piece into a small loaf to match one of the shapes shown. If your oven isn't big enough to bake all 32 at once, see special instructions in step 13.

10. For *medium-size* loaves, divide the dough in half and then in half again for 4 loaves.

(continued)

11. For *large* loaves, divide the dough in half for 2 loaves. Instead of using the shapes shown, you can make either 2 round freestanding loaves or 2 standard pan loaves (for directions see page 59).

12. For an *extra-large* loaf, use all the dough. Shape the dough into a large loaf.

13. Put the loaves on parchment-lined or well-greased baking sheets. Cover with a towel and let rise for 45 minutes. (If you're making the individual loaves in 2 batches, set the first batch of shaped loaves aside to rise. Cover the remaining dough with a towel for 20 minutes before starting to shape. That way the second batch will not overproof while the first batch is baking.)

14. About 15 minutes before the end of rising, preheat the oven to 375°F. Put a shallow pan on the lower shelf of the oven.

15. Just before baking, brush the loaves with egg wash, taking care not to let it drip onto the pans, and sprinkle liberally with sesame seeds.

16. Put 1 cup of ice cubes in the heated pan on the lower shelf of the oven. Quickly place the loaves on the shelf above and close the door to hold in the steam.

17. Bake the extra-large loaf for 35 to 40 minutes, large loaves for 30 to 35 minutes, medium loaves for 20 to 25 minutes, and individual loaves for 15 to 18 minutes, or until golden brown (the internal temperature of the loaves should reach 190°F).

18. Immediately remove the loaves from the baking sheets and cool on a rack.

Cuban Bread

1 scant tablespoon or 1 (¼-ounce) package active dry yeast

2 cups warm water (105° to 115°F)

1 teaspoon salt

4½ to 5½ cups unbleached all-purpose flour

Makes 1 large round loaf

Although it is made with the same basic ingredients as French bread, the baking procedure for Cuban bread is different. The dough is put in a cold oven, set above a pan of boiling water, and left to rest for a few minutes before the oven is turned on. Because the bread continues to rise as the oven heats, its crust is very thin and crisp. It is made without fat, so it is best if eaten on the day it is baked as it will stale quickly. You can try this method with any yeast bread.

1. In a large bowl, soften the yeast in the water.

2. Add the salt and 3 cups of the flour. Beat vigorously with a dough whisk or a heavy-handled spoon for 2 minutes.

3. Gradually add more of the remaining flour, ¼ cup at a time, until the dough forms a mass and begins to pull away from the side of the bowl. Turn the dough out onto a floured work surface.

4. Knead, adding more flour, a little at a time as necessary, about 8 to 10 minutes, or until you have a smooth, elastic dough and blisters begin to develop on the surface.

5. Put the dough into an oiled bowl. Turn to coat the entire ball of dough with oil. Cover with a tightly woven kitchen towel and let rise for about 1 hour, or until doubled in size.

6. Turn the dough out onto a lightly oiled work surface and knead it into a ball. Put the dough on a well-greased baking sheet and flatten it slightly so that it is about 3 inches high. Make 3 slits in the top of the loaf, about ¼ inch deep and 2 inches apart.

7. Pour 1 cup of boiling water into a shallow pan and put the pan on the lower shelf of an unheated oven. Put the dough on the shelf above, wait 10 minutes, and turn the oven to 400°F. Bake the bread for 35 to 40 minutes, or until the internal temperature reaches 200°F.

8. Immediately remove from the baking sheet and cool on a rack.

Greek Olive and Sun-Dried Tomato Bread

2 scant tablespoons or
2 (¼-ounce) packages active
dry yeast

½ cup warm water (105° to
115°F)

1¼ cups warm milk (105° to
115°F)

2 tablespoons honey

1 large egg, beaten

2 teaspoons salt

1 cup pitted and coarsely
chopped kalamata olives

½ cup coarsely chopped sun-
dried tomatoes

¼ cup chopped fresh parsley

5½ to 6½ cups unbleached
all-purpose flour

8 ounces feta cheese,
crumbled (about 2 cups)

1 large egg beaten with
1 tablespoon cold water,
for the egg wash

Makes 1 large twisted braid

Regardless of who tested this bread while I was writing the book, it was always the favorite loaf. The olive oil, kalamata olives, and sun-dried tomatoes give it the heady, seductive flavor of classic Mediterranean food.

Small, black, robust kalamata olives are sold in the specialty section or deli section of many grocery stores, as well as being available in gourmet shops. Because bread dough absorbs oil, it really does not matter if you use sun-dried tomatoes packed in oil or those packed dry. Both taste good and provide their special chewy texture.

1. In a large bowl, soften the yeast in the water.

2. Add the milk, honey, egg, salt, olives, tomatoes, parsley, and 2 cups of the flour. Beat vigorously with a dough whisk or a heavy-handled spoon for 2 minutes.

3. Gradually add more of the remaining flour, ¼ cup at a time, until the dough forms a mass and begins to pull away from the side of the bowl. Turn the dough out onto a floured work surface.

4. Knead, adding more flour, a little at a time as necessary, for 8 to 10 minutes, or until you have an elastic dough and blisters begin to develop on the surface.

5. Put the dough into an oiled bowl. Turn to coat the entire ball of dough with oil. Cover with a tightly woven kitchen towel and let rise for about 1 hour, or until doubled in size.

6. Turn the dough out onto a lightly oiled work surface and flatten it into a 15-inch square. Sprinkle with the feta cheese. Using your hands, roll the dough toward you to form a cylinder. Cover with a towel and let rest for 10 minutes.

7. To make a braided loaf, cut the dough cylinder into three equal pieces. With the palms of your hands, roll each piece into a 30-inch rope. Lay the ropes side by side. Starting in the center, braid the dough (see illustrations on page 77). Turn the dough and braid the other end. Loosely coil the braid and tuck the end under to keep it from unwinding (diagram 1). Put the loaf on a well-greased baking sheet. Cover with a towel and let rise for 45 minutes.

1.

8. While the dough rises, preheat the oven to 375°F.

9. Just before baking, lightly brush the top and sides of the loaf with the egg wash, taking care not to let it drip onto the pan. Bake for 30 to 35 minutes, or until the braid is golden brown and sounds hollow when tapped (the internal temperature should reach 190°F).

10. Remove the bread from the baking sheet and cool on a rack.

VARIATION

Shape the dough into either 2 round freestanding loaves and place well apart on a well-greased baking sheet, or 2 standard pan loaves (for directions, see page 59) and place in 2 well-greased loaf pans. Cover the loaves with a towel and let rise for 45 minutes. Just before baking, score the tops of the freestanding loaves ¼ inch deep in two or three places. Bake the loaves 25 to 30 minutes.

Cranberry Apple Nut Bread

2 scant tablespoons or
2 (¼-ounce) packages active
dry yeast

2½ cups warm water (105° to
115°F)

½ cup firmly packed brown
sugar

2 teaspoons salt

2 tablespoons vegetable oil

1½ cups fresh or frozen
cranberries, washed and
coarsely chopped

2 cups pared and chopped
tart apples (3 medium
apples)

1 cup coarsely chopped
walnuts

1 teaspoon ground cinnamon

5½ to 6½ cups unbleached
all-purpose flour

1 large egg beaten with
1 tablespoon cold water, for
the egg wash

**Makes 2 loaves, or 1 loaf and
12 large dinner rolls**

Cranberries and apples give this bread a pleasing flavor; the nuts add texture. Dividing the dough in half produces a loaf for sandwiches and a pan of rolls for the dinner table.

1. In a large bowl, soften the yeast in the water.

2. Add the brown sugar, salt, oil, cranberries, apple, walnuts, cinnamon, and 3 cups of the flour to the yeast. Beat vigorously with a dough whisk or heavy-handled spoon for 2 minutes.

3. Gradually add more of the remaining flour, ¼ cup at a time, until the dough forms a mass and begins to pull away from the side of the bowl. Turn the dough out onto a floured work surface.

4. Knead, adding more flour, a little at a time as necessary, about 8 to 10 minutes, or until you have an elastic dough and blisters begin to develop on the surface.

5. Put the dough into an oiled bowl. Turn to coat the entire ball of dough with oil. Cover with a tightly woven kitchen towel and let rise for about 1 hour, or until doubled in size.

6. Turn the dough out onto a lightly oiled work surface. Divide it in half and shape both pieces into loaves. Fit the loaves into two well-greased loaf pans. Alternatively, shape one half of the dough into a loaf and divide the remaining dough into 12 equal pieces. Shape each piece into a ball and put into a well-greased muffin pan.

7. Cover with a towel and let rise for 45 minutes.

8. While the dough is rising, preheat the oven to 375°F.

9. Just before baking, lightly brush the egg wash over the top of each loaf or roll, taking care not to let it drip onto the pan or the bread will stick.

10. Bake the loaves for 30 to 35 minutes, the rolls for 20 to 25 minutes, or until the bread is brown and shrinks slightly from the sides of the pan (the internal temperature should reach 190°F).

11. Immediately remove from the pans and cool on a rack.

Cranberry Oatmeal Nut Bread

2 cups boiling water

1½ cups old-fashioned rolled oats (not instant), plus additional for sprinkling

1½ cups dried cranberries (see Note)

2 scant tablespoons or 2 (¼-ounce) packages active dry yeast

½ cup warm water (105° to 115°F)

½ cup firmly packed brown sugar

2 teaspoons salt

¼ cup vegetable oil

4½ to 5½ cups unbleached all-purpose flour

1 cup coarsely chopped walnuts

1 large egg beaten with 1 tablespoon cold water, for the egg wash

Makes 2 loaves

I love the taste of cranberries in bread and often use chewy, tart, and tasty dried cranberries.

1. Pour the boiling water over the rolled oats and dried cranberries. Stir, cover, and let cool for about 45 minutes.

2. In a large bowl, stir the yeast into the warm water.

3. Add the brown sugar, salt, oil, 2 cups of the flour, the walnuts, and the cooled oats and cranberries to the yeast. Beat vigorously with a dough whisk or heavy-handled spoon for 2 minutes.

4. Gradually add more of the remaining flour, ¼ cup at a time, until the dough forms a mass and begins to pull away from the side of the bowl. Turn the dough out onto a floured work surface.

5. Knead, adding more flour, a little at a time as necessary, until you have an elastic dough and blisters begin to develop on the surface.

6. Put the dough into an oiled bowl. Turn to coat the entire ball of dough with oil. Cover with a tightly woven kitchen towel and let rise for about 1 hour, or until doubled in size.

7. Turn the dough out onto a lightly oiled work surface and divide it in half. Shape into loaves following the instructions on page 71.

8. Fit the loaves, seam sides down, into well-greased loaf pans. Cover with a towel and let rise for 45 minutes.

9. About 15 minutes before the end of rising, preheat the oven to 375°F.

10. Just before baking, brush egg wash over the top of each loaf, taking care not to let it drip onto the pans, and sprinkle with rolled oats. Bake the loaves for 30 to 35 minutes or until they are browned and shrink slightly from the sides of the pan (the internal temperature should reach 190°F).

11. Immediately remove the bread from the pans and cool on a rack.

Note: An equal amount of raisins can be a less expensive substitute for the dried cranberries.

Swirled Orange Raisin Bread

*2 scant tablespoons or
2 (¼-ounce) packages active
dry yeast*

*½ cup warm water (105° to
115°F)*

*1 cup warm milk (105° to
115°F)*

*1 cup warm orange juice
(105° to 115°F)*

*¼ cup solid vegetable
shortening*

¼ cup sugar

*1 tablespoon grated orange
peel*

2 teaspoons salt

*5½ to 6½ cups unbleached
all-purpose flour*

1 cup raisins

2 teaspoons cinnamon

Makes 2 loaves

As delicious as this aromatic bread is when eaten soon after baking, it is almost better sliced and toasted or used for sandwiches. Toasting enhances the fragrance of cinnamon and reinforces the mingled flavors of orange and raisin. When shaping the dough, I brush it with water rather than oil or melted butter to keep the swirls from separating when they're rolled into a cylinder.

1. In a large bowl, soften the yeast in the water.

2. Add the milk, orange juice, shortening, sugar, orange peel, salt, 3 cups of the flour, and the raisins. Beat vigorously with a dough whisk or heavy-handled spoon for 2 minutes.

3. Gradually add more of the remaining flour, ¼ cup at a time, until the dough forms a mass and begins to pull away from the side of the bowl. Turn the dough out onto a floured work surface.

4. Knead, adding more flour, a little at a time as necessary, about 8 to 10 minutes, or until the dough becomes elastic and blisters begin to develop on the surface.

5. Put the dough into an oiled bowl. Turn to coat the entire ball of dough with oil. Cover with a tightly woven kitchen towel and let rise for about 1 hour, or until doubled in size.

6. Turn the dough out onto a lightly oiled work surface and divide it in half. Using a rolling pin, roll one piece of dough into an 8 × 18-inch rectangle. Brush lightly with water and sprinkle with cinnamon. Using your hands, roll the dough toward you to form an 8-inch cylinder. Pinch all along the seam to seal. Fit the dough, seam side down, into a well-greased loaf pan. Repeat with the second piece of dough.

7. Cover the loaves with a towel and let rise for 45 minutes.

8. About 15 minutes before the end of rising, preheat the oven to 375°F.

9. Bake for 30 to 35 minutes, or until the loaves are well browned and have shrunk slightly from the sides of the pans (the internal temperature should reach 190°F).

10. Immediately remove the bread from the pans and cool on a rack.

Egg Bagels

2 scant tablespoons or
2 (¼-ounce) packages active
dry yeast

2 cups warm water (105° to
115°F)

3 large eggs, at room
temperature

2 tablespoons vegetable oil

2 teaspoons salt

3 tablespoons sugar

5½ to 6½ cups unbleached
all-purpose flour

2 tablespoons milk

2 quarts boiling water

Poppy seeds, sesame seeds,
coarse salt, or caraway seeds
(optional)

Makes 32 bagels

Bagels were made famous in this country by Jewish immigrants who peddled them on the streets of New York City. The doughnut-shaped bread is poached in sugared water before baking, a process that gives it a wonderful texture and extremely chewy crust. For variety, bagels may be topped with seeds or onions.

1. In a large bowl, soften the yeast in the water.

2. Add 2 of the eggs, the oil, salt, 1 tablespoon of the sugar, and 3 cups of the flour to the yeast. Beat vigorously with a dough whisk or heavy-handled spoon for 2 minutes.

3. Gradually add more of the remaining flour, ¼ cup at a time, until the dough forms a mass and begins to pull away from the side of the bowl. Turn the dough out onto a floured work surface.

4. Knead, adding more flour, a little at a time as necessary, until you have a smooth, elastic dough and blisters begin to develop on the surface.

5. Put the dough into an oiled bowl. Turn to coat the entire ball of dough with oil. Cover with a tightly woven kitchen towel and let rise for about 1 hour, or until doubled in size.

6. Turn the dough out onto a lightly oiled work surface and use a knife or a dough scraper to divide it into 32 equal pieces. (This is easily done by dividing the dough in half, then dividing each half in half again and so on.) Shape each piece into a ball. Insert your finger or thumb through the center of each ball and stretch to make a 1½-inch hole. Cover the bagels with a towel and let rest on the work surface for 30 minutes.

7. Preheat the oven to 425°F. Beat the remaining egg with the milk to make a glaze; set aside.

8. In a 12-inch Dutch oven or large pan, dissolve the remaining 2 tablespoons of sugar in the boiling water. Keep the water at a slow boil.

9. Drop 3 or 4 bagels, one at a time, into the water. Do not crowd them. After 1 minute, turn the bagels and simmer for 3 more minutes. Remove them from the pan with a slotted spoon

(continued)

and put them upside down on a well-greased or parchment-lined baking sheet. Turning the bagels upside down gives a better crust.

10. When you have poached enough bagels to fill a baking sheet, brush the top of each bagel with the egg wash and sprinkle with seeds or salt, if desired.

11. Bake the bagels for 20 minutes, or until browned. Do not use an instant-read thermometer to check for doneness since this is less accurate with bagels than with other breads.

12. Immediately remove the bagels from the baking sheet and cool on a rack. Proceed with making bagels in batches until all the dough is used.

Challah

2 scant tablespoons or
2 (¼-ounce) packages active
dry yeast

2 cups warm water (105° to
115°F)

¼ cup sugar

¼ cup solid vegetable
shortening

3 large eggs, at room
temperature

6½ to 7½ cups unbleached
all-purpose flour

2 teaspoons salt

1 large egg beaten with
1 tablespoon cold water,
for the egg wash

Poppy seeds or sesame seeds
(optional)

Makes 1 large braided loaf

Challah (pronounced HALL-lah) is a traditional Jewish bread served on Friday nights for the Sabbath dinner and on holidays. The Friday-night challah is generally braided, but Rosh Hashanah's challah is always round and smooth. The bread may be braided or not on other holidays. The rich egg bread is usually made with white flour, although it is acceptable to use whole wheat instead, or a combination of whole wheat and white. Because of the eggs, the dough almost doubles in size before it goes into the oven and then doubles again during baking. This recipe can be divided in half for two smaller braids, or the dough can be formed into a round loaf or dinner rolls.

1. In a small bowl, soften the yeast in the water.

2. In a large bowl, beat the sugar and shortening together until fluffy. Add the eggs and continue to beat until light. Stir in the softened yeast and 3 cups of the flour. Beat vigorously with a dough whisk or a heavy-handled spoon for 2 minutes. The resulting sponge will have the consistency of a cake batter. Cover the bowl with plastic wrap and a tightly woven kitchen towel. Let rise for 30 minutes, or until the sponge is light and full of tiny bubbles.

3. Stir the sponge to deflate it. Add the salt and beat in more of the remaining flour, ¼ cup at a time, until the dough forms a mass and begins to pull away from the side of the bowl. Turn the dough out onto a floured work surface.

4. Knead, adding more flour, a little at a time as necessary, for 8 to 10 minutes, or until you have a smooth, elastic dough and blisters begin to develop on the surface.

5. Put the dough into an oiled bowl. Turn to coat the entire ball of dough with oil. Cover with a towel and let rise for about 40 minutes, or until doubled in size.

6. Turn the dough out onto a lightly oiled work surface and divide it into thirds. With the palms of your hands, roll each piece of dough into a rope 20 inches long. Lay the ropes side by side on a well-greased baking sheet.

7. Braid the dough, following the instructions on page 77.

8. Cover the braided dough loosely with a towel and let rise for 30 minutes.

9. About 15 minutes before the end of rising, preheat the oven to 375°F.

10. Just before baking, brush the egg wash lightly over the braid, brushing the top of the loaf first and then the sides. (If you start with the sides, the glaze will run onto the pan and seal the braid to the pan.) Sprinkle the top of the braid with poppy or sesame seeds, if desired.

11. Bake the challah for 40 to 45 minutes, or until it is golden brown and sounds hollow when tapped (the internal temperature should reach 190°F). Cool on a rack.

VARIATION

Shape the dough into either 2 round freestanding loaves and place well apart on a well-greased baking sheet, or 2 standard pan loaves (for directions, see page 59) and place in 2 well-greased loaf pans. Cover the loaves with a towel and let rise for 45 minutes. Just before baking, score the tops of the freestanding loaves ¼ inch deep in two or three places. Bake the loaves 25 to 30 minutes.

Classic Croissants

1 pound (4 sticks) unsalted butter, at room temperature

5½ to 6½ cups unbleached all-purpose flour

1 scant tablespoon or 1 (¼-ounce) package active dry yeast

¼ cup warm water (105° to 115°F)

2 cups warm milk (105° to 115°F)

¼ cup sugar

1 teaspoon salt

2 tablespoons lemon juice

2 eggs beaten with 2 tablespoons cold water, for glazing

Makes 36 croissants

The crescent-shaped croissant originated in Budapest in 1686, when Turks attempted to besiege the city in the dead of night by entering it through underground passages. Bakers, who worked through the night, heard the invaders and raised the alarm in time to save their city. Afterward, they fashioned pastries in the shape of the crescent on the Ottoman flag to celebrate the victory. Since then, the seductive, flaky breads have been perfected and elevated to a cherished status throughout Europe and the United States.

Few home bakers make croissants very often—they are time consuming. But as with many tasks demanding time, the effort is well worth it. Parchment paper is absolutely necessary for these buttery creations. If you do not line the baking sheets with it, the bottoms of the croissants will be hard and taste as though they were fried.

1. Cut a 36-inch-long piece from a 15-inch-wide roll of parchment paper. Lay the strip on the work surface with a long edge nearest you. Crease the long edges of the paper 3½ inches from the top and the bottom. On the sides, crease the paper 10 inches from the left and the right.

2. Combine the butter with ½ cup of the flour. Spread this mixture into the 8 × 16-inch rectangle in the center of the creased parchment paper (diagram 1). Fold in the sides of the paper at the creases (diagram 2), and then fold the top and bottom at the creases (diagram 3). Turn the packet over on the work surface. With a rolling pin, carefully roll the butter inside the packet to an even thickness. You can hold the packet up to the light to see if there are any thick or thin places.

3. Lay the butter packet flat on a refrigerator shelf to chill while working with the dough.

4. In a large bowl, soften the yeast in the water.

5. Add the milk, sugar, salt, lemon juice, and 2 cups of the remaining flour to the yeast. Beat vigorously with a dough whisk or a heavy-handled spoon for 2 minutes.

6. Gradually add more of the remaining flour, ¼ cup at a time, until the dough begins to pull away from the side of the bowl.

1.

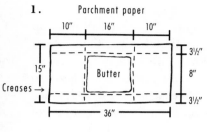

2.

3.

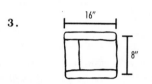

4.

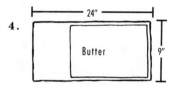

5.

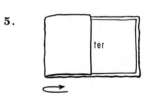

6.

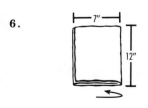

At this stage, the dough should be *very* soft. Flour your hands and pluck off a marble-size piece. If it rolls into a ball but then disintegrates into a sticky glob, it is the right consistency. Adding too much flour at this point will make it hard to roll the croissants later. Cover the bowl with plastic wrap and a tightly woven kitchen towel (both coverings are necessary to protect the dough in the refrigerator). Refrigerate for 30 minutes.

7. On a well-floured work surface, roll the dough into a 9 × 24-inch rectangle. Partially unwrap the chilled butter packet and position it, butter side down, over the dough so that one third of the dough remains uncovered (diagram 4). Make sure to leave a ½-inch border at the top, bottom, and one side. Peel off the paper and save it to line the baking sheets later. Fold the uncovered third of dough over the butter (diagram 5). Fold the resulting rectangle of dough in half (diagram 6). You now have three layers of dough and two layers of butter.

8. Give the dough a quarter turn so that the longer (12-inch) side is closest to you. Make sure the work surface is covered with flour, or the dough will tear and the butter will break through (should this happen, pat the tear with flour and continue). Using a rolling pin, press firmly on a short end of the dough (diagram 7). Lift the rolling pin and press down about 2 inches from the first press. Continue to do this across the dough (diagram 8). Press down on the dough, but do not roll it.

9. Lift the dough carefully to make sure there is still a good coating of flour underneath. Take the rolling pin and press as before, but all across the long side. The dough now has trenches in two directions (diagram 9). (I call this the waffling technique—it distributes the butter evenly without breaking the dough packet.) Now that the dough has been waffled in both directions, roll it into a 10 × 18-inch rectangle. Fold the dough into thirds. Cover with plastic wrap and a towel and refrigerate for 20 minutes.

10. On a well-floured work surface, waffle, roll, and fold the dough twice more, refrigerating for 20 minutes each time. After the third waffling, cover the dough with plastic wrap and a towel and refrigerate for 20 minutes or overnight.

(continued)

7.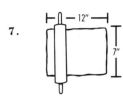

8.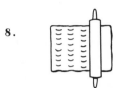

9.

10.

11.

11. When you are ready to shape and bake the croissants, turn the dough out onto a lightly oiled work surface and divide it in half. Refrigerate one piece of dough while working with the other. Line a baking sheet with parchment paper. Roll one piece of dough into a 20 × 20-inch square. Let it rest 5 minutes. Cut it into two 10 × 20-inch rectangles. Cut each rectangle into 4 × 10-inch triangles. Cut a 1-inch slit in the center of the 4-inch side (diagram 10). Open the slit to form a V by folding the edges back (diagram 11). Starting at the wide end, roll up the triangles and put them about 3 inches apart on the parchment-lined baking sheet with the pointed ends underneath. Bend the ends inward slightly to form a crescent shape. There will be two half-triangles left from each end of the 10 × 20-inch rectangle; pinch them together to make one croissant, and roll and form as above. Repeat with the remaining half of the dough.

12. Brush the glaze lightly over the top and sides of each croissant. Let rise uncovered for 30 minutes at cool room temperature. If the rising environment is warmer than 75°F, the butter will melt and the croissants will fall when baked. Alternatively, they can be covered with lightly oiled plastic wrap and a tightly woven kitchen towel and refrigerated up to 24 hours.

13. While the croissants are rising, preheat the oven to 400°F.

14. Just before baking, brush the croissants again with the glaze. Bake for about 20 minutes, or until golden brown. An instant-read thermometer is not a good test for croissants because of the amount of fat in the recipe. If you prefer extra-crispy croissants, return them to a 200°F oven for 10 minutes more.

15. Remove the croissants from the baking sheets and cool on a rack.

English Muffins

2 scant tablespoons or
2 (¼-ounce) packages active
dry yeast

½ cup warm water (105° to
115°F)

2 cups warm milk (105° to
115°F)

2 tablespoons sugar

2 teaspoons salt

2 tablespoons vegetable oil

1 large egg, at room
temperature, beaten

5½ to 6½ cups unbleached
all-purpose flour

Cornmeal

Makes about 36 muffins

These marvelous muffins are cooked on a griddle on top of the stove rather than baked in an oven. Their rough texture demands that they be pried apart with the tines of a fork. Cutting English muffins with a knife just won't do! Freshly baked and still warm, there's no need to toast them—just split them open and butter.

1. In a large bowl, soften the yeast in the water.

2. Add the milk, sugar, salt, oil, egg, and 2 cups of the flour to the yeast mixture. Beat vigorously with a dough whisk or a heavy-handled spoon for 2 minutes.

3. Gradually add more of the remaining flour, ¼ cup at a time, until the dough forms a mass and begins to pull away from the side of the bowl. Turn the dough out onto a floured work surface.

4. Knead, adding more flour, a little at a time as necessary, for 8 to 10 minutes, or until you have a smooth, elastic dough and blisters begin to develop on surface.

5. Put the dough into an oiled bowl. Turn to coat the entire ball of dough with oil. Cover with a tightly woven kitchen towel and let rise for about 1 hour, or until doubled in size.

6. Turn the dough out onto a lightly oiled work surface. Using a rolling pin, roll to a thickness of ¼ inch. Let the dough rest for 2 minutes—without this resting time, the muffins will shrink when cut. With a large round cutter, cut the dough into 3-inch rounds and put them about 1 inch apart on a work surface or on baking sheets sprinkled lightly with cornmeal. Gather the dough scraps together and knead into a smooth ball. Cover and let rest for 5 minutes to allow the gluten to relax before rerolling. Roll and cut as before.

7. Cover the dough rounds loosely with a towel and let rise for 45 minutes.

8. Meanwhile, heat a heavy griddle or skillet over medium heat until hot. I use a stove-top griddle and two 12-inch skillets at the same time. Brush the cooking surface lightly with oil and reduce the heat to low. Gently place the muffins on the griddle, cornmeal side down. Bake the muffins for 2 minutes on each side; then,

(continued)

continue to bake for 10 minutes more, turning them every 2 minutes for 14 minutes of total cooking time. Watch carefully to make sure they do not scorch.

9. Cool the muffins on a rack. If not serving immediately, store them in a plastic bag, and split apart before toasting.

VARIATIONS

Orange English Muffins: Substitute 1 cup orange juice for 1 cup of the milk. Add 1 tablespoon of grated orange peel to the first addition of flour.

Cheddar English Muffins: Knead 4 ounces (1 cup) shredded Cheddar cheese into the dough just before putting it into the oiled bowl to rise.

Spiced English Muffins: Add 2 teaspoons ground cinnamon and 1 teaspoon grated nutmeg along with the first addition of flour.

Raisin English Muffins: Knead 1 cup of raisins into the dough just before putting it into the oiled bowl to rise.

Honey Bran English Muffins: Substitute ¼ cup honey for the sugar and 1 cup unprocessed bran for 1 cup of the flour.

Herbed English Muffins: Add 2 tablespoons minced fresh herbs or 1 tablespoon crumbled dried herbs along with the first addition of flour. Use your favorite or try mine—oregano. Or combine different herbs. Remember, making herb breads is a great way to use herbs so they do not sit in the cupboard until stale.

Do-Ahead Rolls

1 scant tablespoon or
1 (¼-ounce) package active
dry yeast

½ cup warm water (105° to
115°F)

1 cup warm milk (105° to
115°F)

½ cup melted shortening

½ cup sugar

1 large egg, beaten

2 teaspoons salt

3½ to 4½ cups unbleached
all-purpose flour

2 tablespoons butter, melted

Makes 16 rolls

These rolls develop a lot of flavor during rising, which happens in large part in the refrigerator. All the work of making them takes place 12 to 24 hours in advance of baking, which makes them absolutely splendid for a party. Let them sit at room temperature for 30 minutes before you bake them.

1. In a large bowl, soften the yeast in the water.

2. Add the milk, shortening, sugar, egg, salt, and 2 cups of the flour to the yeast. Beat vigorously with a dough whisk or a heavy-handled spoon for 2 minutes.

3. Gradually add more of the remaining flour, ¼ cup at a time, until the dough forms a mass and begins to pull away from the side of the bowl. Turn the dough out onto a floured work surface.

4. Knead, adding more flour, a little at a time as necessary, for 8 to 10 minutes, or until you have a smooth, elastic dough and blisters begin to develop on the surface. You most likely will not need all the flour. For these rolls, add the least amount of flour possible for a soft but workable dough.

5. Divide the dough in half with a knife or a bench scraper. Divide each piece in half again and continue dividing until you have 16 equal-size pieces. Cover with a tightly woven kitchen towel and let rise on the work surface for 5 minutes.

6. With lightly oiled hands, shape each piece of dough into a ball. Put the dough balls, evenly spaced, into a well-greased 12-inch round baking pan with sides. Cover lightly with plastic wrap and a towel. Refrigerate for 12 to 24 hours.

7. About an hour before serving, remove the rolls from the refrigerator. Let sit for 30 minutes at room temperature.

8. Meanwhile, preheat the oven to 400°F.

9. Bake the rolls for 15 to 20 minutes, or until they begin to turn golden (the internal temperature should reach 190°F).

10. Brush the tops of the rolls with melted butter. Immediately remove them from the pan and serve warm, or else cool them on a rack.

Parker House Rolls

2 scant tablespoons or
2 (¼-ounce) packages active
dry yeast

½ cup warm water (105° to
115°F)

½ cup solid vegetable
shortening

2 cups warm milk (105° to
115°F)

2 tablespoons sugar

2 teaspoons salt

5 to 6 cups unbleached all-
purpose flour

Melted butter, for brushing
(optional)

Makes about 40 rolls

Parker House rolls were made famous during the late nineteenth century at the Parker House, a hotel in Boston. The classic folded shape sets them apart from all others. I have fashioned light, airy, soft rolls, just as I imagine the real McCoys were.

1. In a large bowl, soften the yeast in the water.

2. Add the shortening, milk, sugar, salt, and 3 cups of the flour to the yeast. Beat vigorously with a dough whisk or a heavy-handled spoon for 2 minutes.

3. Gradually add more of the remaining flour, ¼ cup at a time, until the dough forms a mass and begins to pull away from the side of the bowl. Turn the dough out onto a floured work surface.

4. Knead, adding more flour, a little at a time as necessary, about 8 to 10 minutes, or until you have a smooth, elastic dough and blisters begin to develop on the surface.

5. Put the dough into an oiled bowl. Turn to coat the entire ball of dough with oil. Cover with a tightly woven kitchen towel and let rise for about 1 hour, or until doubled in size.

6. Turn the dough out onto a lightly oiled work surface. Using a rolling pin, roll the dough out until it is about ½ inch thick. Cover and let rest for 5 minutes. Using a 3-inch round cutter, cut as many circles in the sheet of dough as possible. Gather up dough scraps surrounding the circles and knead into a smooth ball. Set the dough ball aside, covered with a towel.

7. Stretch one of the 3-inch circles into a 4-inch oval. Make a crease just off center by firmly pushing the blunt side of a knife about two-thirds of the way through the dough. Fold the larger half over the smaller half and press together. Repeat with the remaining circles. For soft-sided rolls, arrange them about ¼ inch apart on a well-greased baking sheet. For slightly crisper rolls, put them about 1 inch apart.

8. Cover the rolls with a towel and let rise for 45 minutes.

9. Meanwhile, reroll the dough scraps and repeat steps 6 through 8.

10. About 15 minutes before the end of rising, preheat the oven to 375°F.

11. Just before baking, brush the tops of the rolls with melted butter. Bake for 20 to 25 minutes, or until golden (the internal temperature of the rolls should reach 190°F).

12. Remove the rolls from the baking sheet and serve warm or cool on a rack. For softer tops brush again with melted butter while still warm.

Why do Americans measure ingredients while most other cultures weigh them? American pioneers traveled across the country in wagons or on horseback. Scales were too heavy and bulky to carry. However, every pioneer had a drinking cup and spoon handy. If a small amount of an ingredient was used, the spoon scooped it. If a large amount was used, the cup scooped it.

Overnight Beer Rolls

FOR THE SPONGE

2 scant tablespoons or
2 (¼-ounce) packages active
dry yeast

½ cup warm water (105° to
115°F)

2 tablespoons brown sugar

1½ cups (one 12-ounce
bottle) flat beer

3 cups unbleached all-
purpose flour

FOR THE DOUGH

1 teaspoon salt

4 eggs, separated

2½ to 3½ cups unbleached
all-purpose flour

1 large egg beaten with
1 tablespoon milk, for egg
wash

Sesame seeds, poppy seeds,
or both (optional)

Makes about 20 rolls

These light, airy rolls have a pleasing, slightly bitter flavor provided by the beer. For a full-bodied taste, use dark beer or stout. For an attractive presentation, I like to top the outside ring of rolls with sesame seeds, the middle ring with poppy seeds, and the center rolls with sesame seeds, but you may prefer one seed to the other and want to use only one kind.

1. At least 12 hours before baking, make a sponge: Combine the yeast, water, brown sugar, and beer in a large bowl. Whisk to dissolve the yeast and sugar. Add the flour and stir. The resulting sponge will have the consistency of a cake batter. Cover the bowl with plastic wrap and a tightly woven kitchen towel. Both coverings are necessary to protect the sponge. Let the sponge sit overnight at room temperature (65° to 80°F). The sponge may rise and then fall, but will gain strength again when the other ingredients are added.

2. For the dough: When you are ready to begin baking (at least 3 hours before serving time), mix the salt, egg yolks, and 1 cup of the flour into the sponge. Beat vigorously with a dough whisk or a heavy-handled spoon.

3. In a separate bowl, beat the egg whites until stiff but not dry. Fold the whites into the yeast mixture. Although this may be hard to do at first, the dough becomes soupier as you fold in the whites.

4. Gradually add more of the remaining flour, ¼ cup at a time, until the dough forms a mass and begins to pull away from the side of the bowl. Turn the dough out onto a floured work surface.

5. Knead, adding more flour, a little at a time as necessary, for 8 to 10 minutes, or until you have a smooth, elastic dough and blisters begin to develop on the surface.

6. Put the dough into an oiled bowl. Turn to coat the entire ball of dough with oil. Cover with a tightly woven kitchen towel and let rise for about 1½ hours, or until doubled in size.

7. Turn the dough out onto a lightly oiled work surface. Divide the dough into 20 equal pieces and shape each piece into a ball. Place a saucer containing the egg wash next to a saucer of sesame seeds and one of poppy seeds if you are using them.

8. Dip the top of each ball into the egg wash and roll the dipped part into the seeds. Arrange the rolls, seed side up, ½ inch apart in a well-greased 14-inch round pan (deep-dish pizza pans are perfect, but baking sheets or a pair of 8-inch cake pans can be used).

9. Cover the rolls with a towel and let rise for 45 minutes.

10. About 15 minutes before the end of rising, preheat the oven to 400°F.

11. Bake the rolls for 15 to 20 minutes, or until golden (the internal temperature should reach 190°F).

12. Remove from the baking sheets and serve warm. If you are not serving immediately, let them cool on a rack.

Slightly undercook rolls and croissants. When you reheat them, you can brown them.

German-Style Kaiser Rolls, Brötchen, or Weck Rolls

2 scant tablespoons or
2 (¼-ounce) packages active
dry yeast

2½ cups warm water (105° to
115°F)

2 tablespoons solid vegetable
shortening

1 tablespoon sugar

2 teaspoons salt

6 to 7 cups unbleached all-
purpose flour

3 egg whites, stiffly beaten

1 egg white beaten with
1 tablespoon cold milk, for
the egg wash

Poppy seeds, caraway seeds,
coarse salt, or sesame seeds,
for sprinkling tops (optional)

**Makes 18 kaiser or weck rolls,
or 24 brötchen**

The kaiser roll and brötchen are German staples. Soft on the inside with a crisp crust, both are made from the same dough but shaped differently. Kaiser rolls are large round buns with a five-sided pinwheel design on top, while brötchen are smaller and oval-shaped. In Buffalo, New York, they make kaiser rolls that are lightly glazed and sprinkled with coarse salt and sometimes caraway seeds. Called weck rolls, they are extremely good for roast-beef sandwiches.

1. In a large bowl, soften the yeast in the water.

2. Add the shortening, sugar, salt, and 3 cups of the flour to the yeast. Beat vigorously with a dough whisk or a heavy-handled spoon for 2 minutes.

3. Fold the egg whites into the yeast mixture. Gradually add more of the remaining flour, ¼ cup at a time, until the dough forms a mass and begins to pull away from the side of the bowl. Turn the dough onto a floured work surface.

4. Knead, adding more flour, a little at a time as necessary, for 8 to 10 minutes, or until you have a smooth, elastic dough and blisters begin to develop on the surface.

5. Put the dough into an oiled bowl. Turn to coat the entire ball of dough with oil. Cover with a tightly woven kitchen towel and let rise for about 1 hour, or until doubled in size.

6. Punch the dough down. Cover and let rise again for about 45 minutes, until doubled in size.

7. Turn the dough out onto a lightly oiled work surface.

8. For *kaiser* or *weck rolls:* Divide the dough into 18 equal pieces. Using a rolling pin, flatten each piece into a 7-inch circle (diagram 1). Fold the left side to the center to form a flap (diagram 2). Starting about halfway along the folded side, fold the dough to the center to form another flap (diagram 3). Repeat the folding all around the circle to make overlapping folds. When forming the fifth and last flap, lift the edge of the first flap and ease the edge of the last underneath it to make a continuous design. Press firmly in the center to seal the dough. This design takes a little practice, but

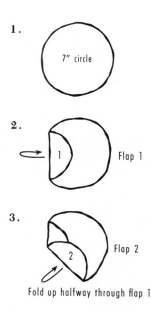

1.

7" circle

2.

Flap 1

3.

Flap 2

Fold up halfway through flap 1

it is quite easy once you get the hang of it. Be patient! As the rolls are made, place them upside down on a well-greased baking sheet, 3 inches apart. This helps the rolls keep their shape better.

9. For *brötchen:* Divide the dough into 24 equal pieces. Shape each piece into an oval about 3½ inches long and place on a well-greased baking sheet.

10. If your oven will not fit all the rolls or brötchen at once, prepare only half the dough at this time, covering the rest on the work surface for 15 minutes. Flatten the tops of the rolls slightly. Cover with a towel and let rise for 45 minutes.

11. About 15 minutes before the end of rising of the first batch, turn the rolls right side up. Then preheat the oven to 425°F. Put a shallow pan on the lower shelf of the oven.

12. Lightly brush the rolls or brötchen with the egg wash, taking care not to let it drip onto the pan. Sprinkle with seeds or coarse salt, if desired.

13. Put 1 cup of ice cubes in the heated pan on the lower shelf of the oven. Immediately put the rolls in the oven and bake for 15 to 20 minutes, or until golden (the internal temperature should reach 190°F).

14. Remove from the baking sheets to cool on racks.

Greek Feta Buns

3 cloves garlic, chopped fine

½ cup olive oil

1 scant tablespoon or
1 (¼-ounce) package active
dry yeast

¼ cup warm water (105° to
115°F)

½ cup warm milk (105° to
115°F)

3 large eggs, beaten

1 tablespoon sugar

1 teaspoon salt

3½ to 4½ cups unbleached
all-purpose flour

8 ounces feta cheese (2 cups)

Makes 12 buns

When my husband, Keith, and I visited the Greek island of Ídhra (Hydra), we returned every day to the waterfront, where a small bakery made these outstanding buns. We savored them as we sat in the warm sunshine on the water's edge, eating the buns with fresh tomato and basil salad and washing our lunch down with cold beer.

Feta cheese is usually packed in brine. If you find the salty flavor objectionable, rinse the cheese with cool tap water and let it drain before crumbling it for the buns. Serve these buns fresh from the oven, or freeze them and refresh the thawed buns in a preheated 350°F oven for about 10 minutes. For freezer information, see page 61.

1. In a small skillet, gently cook the garlic in the olive oil over medium-low heat for 3 to 5 minutes, until it is soft but not brown. Take care not to burn it; burned garlic is bitter. Set aside to cool.

2. In a large bowl, soften the yeast in the water.

3. Add the milk, eggs, sugar, salt, and 2 cups of the flour to the yeast. Beat vigorously with a dough whisk or a heavy-handled spoon for 2 minutes.

4. Measure 3 tablespoons of the olive oil and strain out any small pieces of garlic. Set aside.

5. Pour the remaining oil and garlic into the yeast mixture and stir to combine.

6. Gradually add more of the remaining flour, ¼ cup at a time, until the dough forms a mass and begins to pull away from the side of the bowl. Turn the dough out onto a floured work surface.

7. Knead, adding more flour, a little at a time as necessary, for 8 to 10 minutes, or until you have a smooth, elastic dough and blisters begin to develop on the surface.

8. Put the dough into an oiled bowl. Turn to coat the entire ball of dough with oil. Cover with a tightly woven kitchen towel and let rise for about 1 hour, or until doubled in size.

9. Crumble the feta cheese and divide it into 12 equal portions.

1.

Pinch to seal

2.

Pinch to taper

3.

Pierce with
toothpick

10. Turn the dough out onto a lightly oiled work surface and divide it into 12 equal pieces. Pat each piece into a 5-inch round. Put one portion of cheese in the center of each round, bring the edges to the center, and pinch firmly to seal the cheese inside (diagram 1). Arrange the buns, seam side down, 3 inches apart on a parchment-lined baking sheet. Pinch to taper the ends of the buns (diagram 2).

11. Cover with a towel and let rise 45 minutes.

12. About 15 minutes before the end of rising, preheat the oven to 400°F.

13. Just before baking, prick each bun six times with a toothpick (diagram 3), to allow air to escape during baking. Brush lightly with the reserved olive oil.

14. Bake for 20 to 25 minutes, or until golden brown. Do not rely on an instant-read thermometer because the buns are filled with cheese, which gets very hot.

15. Immediately remove the buns from the baking sheet and serve warm or cool on a rack.

Multi-Seed Hamburger Buns

½ cup sesame seeds

¼ cup poppy seeds

¼ cup flax seeds (see Note)

2 tablespoons caraway seeds

1 scant tablespoon or
1 (¼-ounce) package active
dry yeast

2 cups warm water (105° to
115°F)

2 tablespoons honey

1½ teaspoons salt

2 tablespoons solid vegetable
shortening

4½ to 5½ cups unbleached
all-purpose flour

Vegetable oil

Makes 12 buns

These buns are mixed, shaped, and then left to rise in the refrigerator for 12 to 24 hours. The cool rise not only gives them great flavor but makes baking them easy to fit into your schedule. For intense flavor, I toast the seeds before adding them to the dough. If you cannot find all the varieties of seeds in your local markets, just increase the amount of those you can find to equal 1 cup.

1. Put the sesame seeds, poppy seeds, flax seeds, and caraway seeds in a skillet. Toast over medium-low heat for about 5 to 8 minutes, stirring often, until the sesame seeds have turned golden brown. Remove from the heat and cool.

2. In a large bowl, soften the yeast in the water.

3. Add the honey, salt, shortening, the cooled seeds, and 2 cups of the all-purpose flour. Beat vigorously with a dough whisk or a heavy-handled spoon for 2 minutes.

4. Gradually add more of the remaining flour, ¼ cup at a time, until the dough forms a mass and begins to pull away from the side of the bowl. Turn the dough out onto a floured work surface.

5. Knead, adding more flour, a little at a time as necessary, for 8 to 10 minutes, or until you have a smooth, elastic dough and blisters begin to develop on the surface. Let the dough rest on the work surface, covered with a tightly woven kitchen towel, for 10 minutes.

6. Divide the dough into 12 equal pieces. Shape each piece into a ball. Cover and let rest for 5 minutes.

7. Pat each ball to flatten into a 3½-inch round. Since bread tends to rise higher in the center, the buns will have a better shape if you make them slightly concave. Arrange the buns ½ inch apart on a well-greased baking sheet and brush the tops with vegetable oil. Lay a piece of plastic wrap over the buns and cover the plastic wrap with a towel (the oil prevents the plastic wrap from sticking to the buns). Refrigerate for 12 to 24 hours.

8. About 20 minutes before baking, remove the buns from the refrigerator and let sit, covered, at room temperature.

9. Preheat the oven to 375°F.

10. Bake the buns for 20 to 25 minutes, or until golden (the internal temperature should reach 190°F).

11. Remove from the baking sheets and cool on a rack.

Note: Flax seeds are usually available in health food stores. An equal amount of the other seeds may be substituted—or you may omit them.

Anise, caraway, cardamom, celery, dill, and fennel are strong-flavored seeds and should be used sparingly. Individual taste dictates how much you should use. Try 1 teaspoon for approximately 6 cups of flour for a hint of flavor. A tablespoon for the same amount of flour gives a bold flavor. Add 3 tablespoons and you really know it's there!

Angel Biscuits

1 scant tablespoon or
1 (¼-ounce) package active
dry yeast

2 tablespoons warm water
(105° to 115°F)

5 cups unbleached all-
purpose flour

½ cup sugar

3 tablespoons baking powder

1 teaspoon baking soda

1 teaspoon salt

1 cup (8 ounces) solid
vegetable shortening, chilled

2 cups chilled buttermilk

Makes about 40 biscuits

These light biscuits earn their name because they rise to celestial heights and taste heavenly besides. The yeast demands time to develop, which is why angel biscuits are more flavorful than their baking powder biscuit relatives. They really do require 3 tablespoons of baking powder—that's the way we make them in the South.

1. Stir the yeast into the warm water. Set aside for 5 minutes to soften.

2. In a medium bowl, whisk together the flour, sugar, baking powder, baking soda, and salt until well combined.

3. Using a pastry blender or two knives, cut the shortening into the dry ingredients until it forms pieces the size of corn kernels (slightly coarser than for ordinary biscuits).

4. Stir the buttermilk and yeast into the flour mixture just until it holds together and forms a ball. Do not overmix.

5. Turn the dough out onto a lightly floured work surface and roll it into a square about ½ inch thick. Fold the dough in half and then in half again. Roll and fold the dough again, as before. Small pieces of shortening should remain visible in the dough.

6. Lay a piece of plastic wrap over the dough and cover with a tightly woven kitchen towel. Let rest on the work surface for 30 minutes.

7. Sprinkle more flour on the work surface as necessary to keep the dough from sticking. Roll the dough out until it is ¾ inch thick. Let rest for 5 minutes before cutting.

8. Using a 2½-inch biscuit cutter, cut out as many biscuits as possible. Cut straight down without twisting the cutter. Lightly knead the dough scraps together and let rest for 5 minutes before rerolling.

9. Place the cut biscuits ¼ inch apart on ungreased baking sheets. Cover with a towel and let rest for 30 minutes.

10. About 15 minutes before the end of rising, preheat the oven to 400°F.

11. Bake the biscuits for 12 to 15 minutes, or until golden brown. Serve at once.

Grissini

2 scant tablespoons or 2 (¼-ounce) packages active dry yeast

2½ cups warm water (about 105° to 115°F)

2 tablespoons olive oil

2 tablespoons honey

2 teaspoons salt

5½ to 6½ cups unbleached all-purpose flour

Sesame seeds, poppy seeds, caraway seeds, coarse salt, or a combination, for topping

Makes 48 thick or 72 thin breadsticks

Grissini are classic Italian breadsticks, coated with tiny seeds. They make a wonderful addition to a party or a picnic basket. Eat grissini freshly baked, or freeze them and reheat in a 375°F oven for about 10 minutes until crisp.

1. In a large bowl, soften the yeast in the water.

2. Add the oil, honey, salt, and 2 cups of the flour. Beat vigorously with a dough whisk or a heavy-handled spoon for 2 minutes.

3. Gradually add more of the remaining flour, ¼ cup at a time, until the dough forms a mass and begins to pull away from the side of the bowl. Turn the dough out onto a floured work surface.

4. Knead, adding more flour, a little at a time as necessary, for 8 to 10 minutes, or until you have a smooth, elastic dough and blisters begin to develop on the surface.

5. Put the dough into an oiled bowl. Turn to coat the entire ball of dough with oil. Cover with a tightly woven kitchen towel and let rise for about 1 hour, until doubled in size.

6. Turn the dough out onto a lightly oiled work surface. Divide it into 48 pieces for thick breadsticks (about the size of an adult thumb) or 72 pieces if you prefer them thinner (just slightly larger than a pencil). Remember that the breadsticks will double in diameter. Roll each piece under your palms into a 10-inch rope. Scatter one of the toppings over the work surface. Lightly roll the rope in the topping so that the seeds or salt crystals are slightly embedded in the dough. Put the breadsticks 1 inch apart on well-greased baking sheets. Cover with a towel and let rise for 30 minutes.

7. About 15 minutes before the end of rising, preheat the oven to 400°F.

8. Bake the thicker breadsticks for 20 minutes, the thin ones for 10 minutes. Immediately remove the breadsticks from the baking sheets to a rack. For extra-crisp breadsticks, cool the oven to 200°F. Put the breadsticks back in the oven for 20 minutes more. There is no need to space the breadsticks out on the baking sheets this time.

Buttery Cheese Breadsticks

½ pound (2 sticks) unsalted butter, at room temperature

3 to 4 cups unbleached all-purpose flour

1 scant tablespoon or 1 (¼-ounce) package active dry yeast

¼ cup warm water (105° to 115°F)

1 large egg, beaten

1 cup warm milk (105° to 115°F)

¼ cup sugar

1½ teaspoons salt

8 ounces Parmesan cheese, grated (2 cups)

Makes 48 breadsticks

These breadsticks are made using the same method as for croissants. Because they are made with butter, they are flaky, crisp, and full of flavor. If you prefer vegetable shortening, use it—but do not expect the breadsticks to be as flavorful. The breadsticks are best served fresh but can be frozen and then heated in a 400°F oven for 5 minutes without thawing.

1. Cut a 36-inch-long piece from a 15-inch-wide roll of parchment paper. Lay the strip on the work surface with a long edge nearest you. On the long edges, crease the paper 3½ inches from the top and the bottom. On the sides, crease the paper 10 inches from the left and the right.

2. Combine the butter with ½ cup of the flour. Spread this mixture into the 8 × 16-inch rectangle in the center of the prepared parchment paper (see illustrations on page 99). Fold in the sides of the paper at the creases and then fold the top and bottom at the creases. Turn the packet over. With a rolling pin, carefully roll the butter inside the packet to an even thickness. You can hold the packet up to the light to see if there are any thick or thin places.

3. Lay the butter packet flat on a refrigerator shelf to chill while you work with the dough.

4. In a large bowl, soften the yeast in the water.

5. Add the egg, milk, sugar, salt, 2 cups of the flour, and 1 cup of the cheese to the yeast. Beat vigorously with a dough whisk or heavy-handled spoon for 2 minutes.

6. Gradually add more flour, ¼ cup at a time, until the dough begins to pull away from the side of the bowl. The dough at this stage should be *very* soft. Flour your hands and pluck off a marble-size piece. If it rolls into a ball but then disintegrates into a sticky glob, it is the right consistency. Too much flour at this point makes it too hard to roll the breadsticks later. Cover the bowl with plastic wrap and with a tightly woven kitchen towel (both coverings are necessary to protect the dough in the refrigerator). Refrigerate for 30 minutes.

7. On a lightly floured work surface, roll the dough into a 9 × 24-inch rectangle. Remove the butter packet from the refrigerator, open it carefully, and position it over the dough rectangle, butter side down, leaving a third of the rectangle uncovered (refer again to the illustrations on page 99). Make sure to leave a ½-inch border of dough at the top, bottom, and one side. Peel off the paper and save it to line the baking sheets later. Fold the uncovered third of dough over the butter. Press the edges at the top and bottom to seal. Fold the dough rectangle in half. You will have three layers of dough and two layers of butter.

8. Roll the dough once again into a 9 × 24-inch rectangle and fold it into thirds as before. Wrap loosely in plastic wrap, leaving enough room for the dough to expand without bursting, and cover with a kitchen towel. Refrigerate for 30 minutes.

9. On a lightly floured board, roll the dough into a 9 × 24-inch rectangle and fold into thirds again.

10. Roll and fold the dough once more (the dough will have been rolled and folded four times in all). Wrap as before and refrigerate for 30 minutes.

11. Divide the dough in half. Roll each piece into a 9 × 12-inch rectangle and cut into 24 half-inch strips. Roll each strip in the remaining cheese and put the strips on parchment-lined baking sheets, 1 inch apart. Cover with a towel and let rise for 45 minutes.

12. About 15 minutes before the end of rising, preheat the oven to 400°F.

13. Carefully twist the ends of the breadsticks in opposite directions. Twist four times. Take care not to deflate the breadsticks; they keep their shape much better if twisted after the rising time.

14. Bake the breadsticks for 15 minutes, or until golden brown. Remove from the baking sheets and cool on a rack.

Roquefort Poppy Seed Breadsticks

1 scant tablespoon or
1 (¼-ounce) package active
dry yeast

1¼ cups warm water (105° to
115°F)

1 tablespoon sugar

1 teaspoon salt

3 ounces Roquefort cheese, at
room temperature, crumbled
(about ⅔ cup)

2 tablespoons poppy seeds

3½ to 4½ cups unbleached
all-purpose flour

2 egg whites, stiffly beaten

**Makes about 144 thin
breadsticks**

Flavored with rich, robust Roquefort cheese, these thin, crispy breadsticks are perfect for snacks or as a party food, or to serve with soups and salads. If you have a hand-cranked pasta machine, use it to make an even thinner variation. These are much more work, but their shape is extremely interesting and the extra crispness makes them tasty.

1. In a large bowl, soften the yeast in the water.

2. Add the sugar, salt, Roquefort, poppy seeds, and 2 cups of the flour to the yeast. Beat vigorously with a dough whisk or a heavy-handled spoon for 2 minutes.

3. Fold the egg whites into the yeast mixture. Gradually add more of the remaining flour, ¼ cup at a time, until the dough forms a mass and begins to pull away from the side of the bowl. Turn the dough out onto a floured work surface.

4. Knead, adding more flour a little at a time as necessary, for 8 to 10 minutes, or until you have a smooth, elastic dough and blisters begin to develop to the surface.

5. Put the dough into an oiled bowl. Turn to coat the entire ball of dough with oil. Cover with a tightly woven kitchen towel and let rise for about 1 hour, until doubled in size.

6. Turn the dough out onto a lightly oiled work surface. Divide the dough into 4 equal pieces. With a rolling pin, roll each piece into a 10 × 12-inch rectangle. Cover with a towel and let rest 5 minutes. Cut into 36 breadsticks, ⅓ inch wide and 10 inches long. Put the breadsticks ½ inch apart on a parchment-lined baking sheet (see Note). Repeat with remaining dough.

7. Cover the breadsticks with towels and let rise for 45 minutes.

8. About 15 minutes before the end of rising, preheat the oven to 325°F.

9. Bake the breadsticks for 9 to 11 minutes, or until lightly toasted. Immediately remove them from the baking sheet and cool on a rack.

VARIATION

To make these breadsticks with a hand-cranked pasta machine, follow the recipe through step 5.

6. Turn the dough out onto a lightly floured work surface and divide it into 12 equal pieces. Sprinkle the pieces with flour. Set the pasta machine at the widest setting. Roll one piece of dough and set aside. Continue until all the dough has been rolled through once. Place the rolled pieces of dough in a row to keep them in the order in which they were rolled. Lightly dust the dough with flour.

7. Turn the pasta machine to the next setting. Roll each piece of dough through the pasta machine in the same order as the first rolling. Lightly dust with flour.

8. Turn the pasta machine to the next setting. Roll each piece of dough through the machine, again in the same order. Lightly dust with flour. Cover with a towel and let rest for 5 minutes.

9. Using the fettuccine cutter, roll each section of dough through the pasta machine. Dust with flour if necessary. Separate the strands of dough, spreading them out on parchment-lined baking sheets about ½ inch apart. Each one will be a thin breadstick. You should have almost 200 breadsticks.

10. Cover the breadsticks with towels and let rise for 45 minutes.

11. About 15 minutes before the end of rising, preheat the oven to 325°F.

12. Bake the breadsticks for 9 to 11 minutes, or until lightly toasted. Immediately remove them from the baking sheet and cool on a rack.

Note: The number of baking sheets you need will depend, of course, on their size. When a pan comes out of the oven, I whisk the paper and breadsticks off the baking sheet and then carefully slip one of the parchment sheets with risen dough onto the baking sheet, to go back into the oven. About halfway through the shaping process, I take a 15-minute break, covering the unshaped dough with a towel, so that I don't have so many breadsticks waiting to get into the oven.

Salzstangen

2 scant tablespoons or
2 (¼-ounce) packages active
dry yeast

½ cup warm water (105° to
115°F)

1½ cups warm milk (105° to
115°F)

2 tablespoons sugar

2 teaspoons salt

3 tablespoons solid vegetable
shortening, melted

5½ to 6½ cups unbleached
all-purpose flour

3 egg whites, very stiffly
beaten

3 tablespoons baking soda

2 quarts water

1 large egg beaten with
1 tablespoon cold water, for
egg wash

Coarse salt or caraway seeds
(optional)

Makes 30

Salzstangen, rolled breadsticks popular in southern Germany, have a dark, bitter, shiny coating on the crust and are usually sprinkled with coarse salt, caraway seeds, or both before baking. In Germany, the breadsticks get their sheen from a wash made with lye; I've substituted baking soda here instead.

1. In a large bowl, soften the yeast in the water.

2. Add the milk, sugar, salt, shortening, and 3 cups of the flour. Beat vigorously with a dough whisk or a heavy-handled spoon for 2 minutes.

3. Stir in the egg whites and beat until no egg white is visible.

4. Gradually add more of the remaining flour, ¼ cup at a time, until the dough forms a mass and begins to pull away from the side of the bowl. Turn the dough out onto a floured work surface.

5. Knead, adding more flour, a little at a time as necessary, for 8 to 10 minutes, or until you have a smooth, elastic dough and blisters begin to develop on the surface.

6. Put the dough into an oiled bowl. Turn to coat the entire ball of dough with oil. Cover with a tightly woven kitchen towel and let rise for about 1 hour, until doubled in size.

7. Turn the dough out onto a lightly oiled work surface and divide it in half. Roll each piece of dough into an 18 × 30-inch rectangle. Cover and let rest for 5 minutes.

8. Cut the dough into 6-inch squares. Starting at one corner, roll each dough square diagonally to the opposite side to form breadsticks the shape of cigars. Place the breadsticks 2 inches apart on parchment-lined baking sheets, loose ends down. Cover with a towel and let rise for 30 minutes.

9. About 15 minutes before the end of rising, preheat the oven to 400°F.

10. Bring 2 quarts of water to boil in a skillet or Dutch oven. Add the baking soda to the boiling water; turn the heat to low. Carefully slip one breadstick into the water and leave it in for just 5 to 10 seconds before removing it with a slotted spoon or skimmer.

As they are poached, put the breadsticks on parchment-lined baking sheets, 3 inches apart.

11. Brush the breadsticks with egg wash, being careful not to let it drip onto the pans. If desired, sprinkle lightly with coarse salt, caraway seeds, or both. Bake for 20 to 25 minutes, or until the breadsticks are light brown (the internal temperature should reach 190°F).

12. Immediately remove from the baking sheets and cool on a rack.

Yeast, like man, luxuriates in warmer temperatures.

Pretzels

2 scant tablespoons or
2 (¼-ounce) packages active
dry yeast

½ cup warm water (105° to
115°F)

2 cups warm milk (105° to
115°F)

¼ cup sugar

½ cup solid vegetable
shortening

6½ to 7½ cups unbleached
all-purpose flour

1 teaspoon baking powder

2 teaspoons salt

2 quarts water

3 tablespoons baking soda

Coarse salt or sesame seeds
(optional)

Makes 24 large pretzels

Making your own jumbo pretzels is a kick—and one that your children will enjoy as much as you do. It is said that pretzels have been made since the Dark Ages, when monks fashioned bread to resemble the crossed arms of praying children and gave the baked bread to pupils who had successfully mastered their lessons. Over the centuries, pretzels, like all breads, underwent various transformations and were adopted and adapted by a number of cultures.

The Germans love to eat big, crusty pretzels with their beer, serving them up in beer halls with plenty of spicy mustard. A small amount of lye in the pretzel wash, called *lauge*, makes German pretzels different from American pretzels, which are dipped in a wash containing baking soda. The pretzels are in the wash for a mere 10 seconds and the measure of lye is so tiny that it does no harm. On the contrary, it gives the pretzels their crispness and sheen. Most pretzel lovers would not dream of eating a salt-free pretzel, but I have found that sesame seeds used instead of salt are very good.

1. In a large bowl, soften the yeast in the warm water.

2. Add the milk, sugar, shortening, and 2 cups of flour. Beat vigorously with a dough whisk or a heavy-handled spoon for 2 minutes. Cover the bowl loosely with plastic wrap and a tightly woven kitchen towel. Let rise for 30 minutes. This sponge will have the consistency of a cake batter; it should be light and full of bubbles.

3. Whisk together the baking powder, salt, and 1 cup of the remaining flour. Add to the sponge and mix well. Beat vigorously for 2 minutes.

4. Gradually add more flour, ¼ cup at a time, until the dough forms a mass and begins to pull away from the side of the bowl. Turn the dough out onto a floured work surface.

5. Knead, adding more flour, a little at a time as necessary, for 8 to 10 minutes, or until you have a smooth, elastic dough and blisters begin to develop on the surface.

6. Put the dough into an oiled bowl. Turn to coat the entire ball of dough with oil. Cover with a towel and let rise for 30 minutes.

7. Turn the dough out onto a lightly oiled work surface and divide it into 24 equal pieces. With your hands, roll each piece into a 24-inch rope (diagram 1). Lay one rope in a U shape (diagram 2). About 2 inches from each end, cross the dough (diagram 3). Cross a second time (diagram 4). Picturing the dough as the face of a clock, bring the ends down and press them into the bottom of the U at 5 and 7 o'clock (diagram 5). Repeat with all the remaining ropes. Cover with a towel and let rest for 20 minutes on the work surface.

8. Meanwhile, preheat the oven to 400°F. Line two or three baking sheets with parchment.

9. Bring 2 quarts of water to boil in a large saucepan or Dutch oven and add the soda. Drop the pretzels, one at a time, into the boiling mixture for 10 seconds and then remove with a slotted spoon or skimmer. Put them on the parchment-lined baking sheets, smooth side up (otherwise, the pretzel could unwrap during baking). Sprinkle with coarse salt or sesame seeds, if desired.

10. Bake for 15 minutes, or until golden. Immediately remove from the baking sheets and cool on a rack.

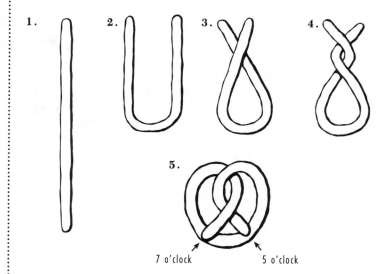

1.   2.   3.   4.

5.

7 o'clock   5 o'clock

4

Whole wheat flour is the most familiar whole grain flour and the one most home bakers think of when they consider healthful breads. It is sold in supermarkets, specialty shops, and health food stores. Because the flour contains the germ and the bran as well as the endosperm of the wheat berry, it does not have the extended shelf life that all-purpose flour does. Buy whole wheat flour as you need it and store it in a tightly lidded canister in a cool cupboard or in the refrigerator or freezer. It keeps for only a few months.

Whole wheat flour has the same gluten-making capabilities as all-purpose flour. But its rising abilities are affected by the presence of the bran and the germ: they weigh the dough down a little, so that the rise may not be as high as with white flour breads. To compensate, let breads made with whole wheat flour alone rise for a little longer than those made with a combination of whole wheat and all-purpose flour. I often add all-purpose flour to lighten the loaves and help the rise.

Whole Wheat Yeast Breads

Once you get used to the flavor of bread made with whole wheat flour only, you might come to prefer its hearty, earthy flavor and not be overly concerned with its height.

I have included recipes for straightforward whole wheat breads as well as whole wheat rolls and buns. Some of the loaves are intricately shaped into attractive, unusual-looking breads that make a splash at a party or as a gift. They are easier than they look—and if you do not have the time to fuss with the shaping, simply form the dough in round or rectangular loaves. They will still taste wonderful.

Whole Wheat Bread

*2 scant tablespoons or
2 (¼-ounce) packages active
dry yeast*

*2½ cups warm water (about
105° to 115°F)*

*¼ cup firmly packed brown
sugar*

2 teaspoons salt

2 tablespoons vegetable oil

2 cups whole wheat flour

*3½ to 4½ cups unbleached
all-purpose flour*

Makes 2 loaves

Just as the Basic White Bread on page 71 is the best introduction to making bread with unbleached all-purpose white flour, this recipe will teach you how to work with whole wheat flour. If you follow the recipe exactly, you will produce a mild-flavored whole wheat bread with a firm texture—bread that is perfect for sandwiches, for toast, and for spreading with homemade strawberry jam.

Once you feel comfortable with the recipe and want to experiment a little, or if you simply like a heartier wheat bread, increase the amount of whole wheat flour and decrease the amount of white flour. Work up to making the bread with whole wheat flour exclusively for an earthy, robust loaf bursting with flavor that seems to hug you from the inside out. But take care not to add too much flour during kneading. Whole wheat flour is heavier than all-purpose flour, and too much of it results in leaden bread. If you use all whole wheat flour in this recipe, increase both rising times by about 15 minutes.

1. In a large bowl, soften the yeast in the water.

2. Add the brown sugar, salt, oil, whole wheat flour, and 2 cups of the all-purpose flour. Beat vigorously with a dough whisk or a heavy-handled spoon for 2 minutes.

3. Gradually add more of the remaining flour, ¼ cup at a time, until the dough forms a mass and begins to pull away from the side of the bowl. Turn the dough out onto a floured work surface.

4. Knead, adding more flour, a little at a time as necessary, for 8 to 10 minutes, or until you have a smooth, elastic dough.

5. Put the dough into an oiled bowl. Turn once to coat the entire ball of dough with oil. Cover with a tightly woven kitchen towel and let rise for about 1 hour, or until doubled in size.

6. Turn the dough out onto a lightly oiled work surface and divide it in half. Form into loaves, following the directions on page 71.

7. Put the loaves, seam side down, into well-greased loaf pans. Cover with a towel and let rise for about 45 minutes.

8. About 15 minutes before the end of rising, preheat the oven to 375°F.

9. Bake the loaves for 25 to 30 minutes, or until they shrink slightly from the sides of the pans and sound hollow when tapped (the internal temperature should reach 190°F). Remove from the pans and cool on a rack.

Make sure to consult the information on flour and other ingredients and on utensils (chapter 1) and the baking class on making yeast breads (chapter 2).

Whole Wheat Garlic Bread

2 scant tablespoons or
2 (¼-ounce) packages active
dry yeast

2½ cups warm water (105° to
115°F)

2 teaspoons sugar

3 teaspoons minced garlic

1 teaspoon salt

4 tablespoons olive oil

3½ to 4½ cups unbleached
all-purpose flour

2 cups whole wheat pastry
flour

Makes 4 sheaves

I like to serve this bread in place of the familiar baguette that most people expect when they hear the term garlic bread. To make this light wheat bread, I combine whole wheat pastry flour with all-purpose flour and then form the dough into four sheaves: loaves that are partially cut on the diagonal before baking so that they resemble wheat sheaves. The sheaves are broken apart at the table into individual pieces. This bread is best served warm and fresh. If allowed to cool completely, the garlic tastes bitter. You can reheat it by setting the loaves on the rack of a 350°F oven for about 10 minutes.

1. In a large bowl, soften the yeast in the water.

2. Add the sugar, 2 teaspoons of the garlic, the salt, 2 tablespoons of the oil, 1 cup of the unbleached flour, and all the pastry flour to the yeast. Beat vigorously with a dough whisk or a heavy-handled spoon for 2 minutes.

3. Gradually add more of the all-purpose flour, ¼ cup at a time, until the dough forms a mass and begins to pull away from the side of the bowl. Turn the dough out onto a floured work surface.

4. Knead, adding more flour, a little at a time as necessary, for 8 to 10 minutes, or until you have a smooth, elastic dough.

5. Put the dough into an oiled bowl. Turn to coat the entire ball of dough with oil. Cover with a tightly woven kitchen towel and let rise for about 1 hour, or until doubled in size.

6. Turn the dough out onto a lightly oiled work surface and divide it into 4 pieces. Roll each piece of dough into a 12-inch rope and put on well-greased baking sheets. Working with one rope at a time and using long-bladed sharp scissors, cut a 45° angle (or V shape) about three-quarters of the way through the dough and about 2 inches from the top (diagram 1). Pull the dough to the right and make a second V (diagram 2). Pull the dough to the left (diagram 3). Continue to cut and pull the dough to opposite sides until you reach the bottom of the loaf. You will make about 10 cuts per loaf. Pinch the bottom, rounded end of the loaf to a point

1.

Cut

2.

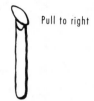

Pull to right

3.

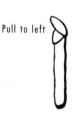

Pull to left

4.

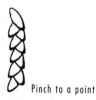

Pinch to a point

5.

(diagram 4). The loaf can also be shaped into a circle after cutting, if desired (diagram 5). Repeat with the remaining three ropes of dough.

7. Cover the dough with a towel and let rise for 45 minutes.

8. About 15 minutes before the end of rising, preheat the oven to 400°F. Put a shallow pan on the lower shelf of the oven.

9. Just before baking, brush the loaves with a little of the remaining olive oil.

10. Put 1 cup of ice cubes in the heated pan on the lower shelf of the oven. Immediately put the loaves in the oven and bake for 10 minutes.

11. Combine the remaining garlic and olive oil. Remove the loaves from the oven and brush this mixture over each loaf. Return the loaves to the oven and bake for 10 to 15 minutes more, or until the loaves are lightly browned (the internal temperature should reach 190°F).

12. Cool the loaves on racks, brushing with any remaining garlic/oil mixture after about 5 minutes. Serve the bread warm.

VARIATION
Shape the dough into 2 round freestanding loaves and place well apart on a well-greased baking sheet. Cover the loaves with a towel and let rise for 45 minutes. Just before baking, score the tops of the loaves ¼ inch deep in two or three places. Bake the loaves 25 to 30 minutes.

Note: I put 2 sheaves on a baking sheet, well apart. If your oven won't fit two sheets side-by-side, shape only 2 of the sheaves at a time. Leave the rest of the dough covered by a towel on the work surface for 15 minutes. That way, the second batch will not over-proof.

Whole Wheat Peggy Tub Bread

1 scant tablespoon or 1 (¼-ounce) package active dry yeast

¼ cup warm water (105° to 115°F)

1½ cups warm milk (105° to 115°F)

¼ cup vegetable oil

2 large eggs

¼ cup sugar

2 teaspoons salt

½ cup toasted wheat germ

2 cups whole wheat flour

3½ to 4½ cups unbleached all-purpose flour, plus additional as needed

1 large egg beaten with 1 tablespoon cold water, for the egg wash

Makes 2 loaves

A peggy tub is an English wash tub used for laundry. According to Elizabeth David's *English Bread and Yeast Cookery*, it was also drafted for other purposes, including salting, brewing, and raising dough. Almost any dough can be used with this technique for letting bread rise. The method is particularly good in hot weather to keep dough from rising too quickly. It works better than letting dough rise in the refrigerator because it allows the dough to rise more uniformly. Breads made by this process are moister than those made in more traditional ways. This is a good method to use when you don't have time to complete the whole recipe at one time.

1. In a large bowl, soften the yeast in the water.

2. Add the milk, oil, eggs, sugar, salt, wheat germ, whole wheat flour, and 2 cups of the all-purpose flour. Beat vigorously with a dough whisk or a heavy-handled spoon for 2 minutes.

3. Gradually add more of the remaining all-purpose flour, ¼ cup at a time, until the dough forms a mass and begins to pull away from the side of the bowl. Turn the dough out onto a floured work surface.

4. Knead, adding more flour, a little at a time as necessary, for 8 to 10 minutes, or until you have a smooth, elastic dough.

5. After kneading the dough, roll it in flour so that it is well coated all over. Sprinkle flour generously on a large, tightly woven kitchen towel and set the dough on the towel. Loosely wrap the towel around the dough, leaving enough room for the dough to rise without forcing the towel open.

6. Fill a large bowl with water. If you want the dough to double in size in about 1 hour, the water should be 80° to 90°F. If you want to prolong the rising for up to 12 hours, the water should be 45° to 55°F. Submerge the wrapped dough in the water with the folded side up, so the dough won't fall out. It will sink to the bottom at first, but will float up as the yeast begins to work. When the dough rises to the surface, it is ready to shape. However, if you wish, it can be left floating in the water for as long as 12 hours.

7. When you are ready to shape the bread, unwrap the dough. If it is tacky, oil your hands. Turn the dough out onto a lightly oiled work surface and divide it in half. Form into loaves following the instructions on page 71.

8. Put the loaves, seam side down, into well-greased loaf pans. Cover with a towel and let rise for about 45 minutes, or until almost doubled in size.

9. About 15 minutes before the end of rising, preheat the oven to 375°F.

10. Just before baking, brush the tops of the loaves with egg wash. (Don't let it drip down into the pans or the bread will stick and not rise to its full potential.)

11. Bake the loaves for 25 to 30 minutes, or until they are golden brown and shrink slightly from the sides of the pans (the internal temperature should reach 190°F). Remove the bread from the pans and cool on a rack.

If you have a small oven or other limitations on your ability to bake on 2 or more baking sheets at the same time, see the Note on page 189.

Whole Wheat Potato Bread

1 scant tablespoon or 1 (¼-ounce) package active dry yeast

¼ cup warm water (105° to 115°F)

½ cup mashed potatoes (instant potatoes are acceptable, but omit the teaspoon of salt called for below)

1 cup warm milk (105° to 115°F)

2 tablespoons brown sugar

1 teaspoon salt

2 tablespoons vegetable oil

1 cup whole wheat flour

1½ to 2½ cups unbleached all-purpose flour

1 large egg beaten with 1 tablespoon cold water, for the egg wash

Makes 1 large wheat-shaped loaf

When this bread is shaped into a loaf resembling a bundle of wheat as described in the recipe, it makes a lovely gift or a centerpiece for a buffet table. But the tasty dough can also be made into a rectangular loaf or 18 dinner rolls.

1. In a large bowl, soften the yeast in the water.

2. Add the potatoes, milk, brown sugar, salt, oil, all the whole wheat flour, and 1 cup of the all-purpose flour. Beat vigorously with a dough whisk or a heavy-handled spoon for 2 minutes.

3. Gradually add more of the all-purpose flour, ¼ cup at a time, until the dough forms a mass and begins to pull away from the side of the bowl. Turn the dough out onto a floured work surface.

4. Knead, adding more flour, a little at a time as necessary, for 8 to 10 minutes, or until you have a smooth, elastic dough.

5. Put the dough into an oiled bowl. Turn to coat the entire ball of dough with oil. Cover with a tightly woven kitchen towel and let rise for about 1 hour, or until doubled in size.

6. Line a 13 × 18-inch baking sheet with parchment paper and set aside.

7. Turn the dough out onto a lightly oiled work surface and divide it in half. Divide both pieces in half again and continue this until there are 32 equal pieces. Knead two of the pieces together into a smooth ball, roll under your palms into a 20-inch rope, and lay it across the baking sheet, about halfway down the 18-inch side, so that it extends an inch on both sides. Roll each remaining piece of dough into a 16-inch rope. Place the ropes lengthwise on the baking sheet on top of the 20-inch rope, bunching them slightly in the middle and spreading them out at each end (diagram 1). You will be stacking many of them on top of others. The loaf should be about 6 inches wide in the middle. Take up the ends of the 20-inch rope and tie them around the bunched ropes (diagram 2). Arrange the bottom ends into a spray. Using sharp, long-bladed scissors, snip a row of V shapes in the top of each rope at an angle (diagram 3) to resemble the top of a sheaf of wheat. Arrange the ropes to

1.

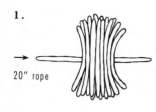

20" rope

2.

3.

4.

look like a bundle of wheat. Bend a few over for a more natural look (diagram 4).

8. Cover the dough with a towel and let rise for about 45 minutes, or until almost doubled in size.

9. About 15 minutes before the end of rising, preheat the oven to 375°F.

10. Just before baking, brush the bread with the egg wash, taking care not to let it drip onto the pan. Bake for 30 to 35 minutes, or until golden (the internal temperature should reach 190°F). Cool on a rack.

VARIATIONS

Standard Loaf: Shape the dough into either 1 round freestanding loaf and place on a well-greased baking sheet, or 1 standard pan loaf (for directions, see page 59) and place in a well-greased loaf pan. Cover the loaf with a towel and let rise for 45 minutes. Just before baking, score the top of the free-standing loaf ¼ inch deep in two or three places. Bake the loaf 25 to 30 minutes.

Rolls: Divide dough into 18 equal pieces and place, evenly spaced, in a well-greased 12-inch round pan (two 8-inch round pans can be used, in which case the rolls will be higher).

Toasty Whole Wheat Bread

1½ cups whole wheat flour

2 scant tablespoons or 2 (¼-ounce) packages active dry yeast

3 cups warm water (105° to 115°F)

2 tablespoons brown sugar

2 tablespoons vegetable oil

¼ cup unprocessed wheat bran

¼ cup wheat germ (raw or toasted), plus additional for sprinkling

¼ cup soy flour

3½ to 4½ cups unbleached all-purpose flour

2 teaspoons salt

1 large egg beaten with 1 tablespoon cold water, for the egg wash

Makes 2 loaves

Toasting the whole wheat flour before you make the dough brings out its earthy flavor so you taste it with every slice. Heating the flour destroys some nutrients, but they are more than made up for in this recipe by the addition of wheat bran, wheat germ, and soy flour. Soy flour conditions the dough without adding flavor so that the bread is pleasantly light.

1. Put the whole wheat flour in a heavy 10-inch skillet over medium-low heat. Stir with a whisk for about 10 minutes until flour is nicely browned and well toasted. Take care the flour does not scorch. Set aside to cool.

2. While the whole wheat flour is cooling, soften the yeast in the water in a large bowl.

3. Add the brown sugar, oil, wheat bran, ¼ cup wheat germ, soy flour, and 2 cups of the all-purpose flour to the yeast. Beat vigorously with a whisk for 2 minutes. The resulting sponge will have the consistency of a cake batter. Cover loosely with plastic wrap and a tightly woven kitchen towel and let rise for 45 minutes. The sponge should be light and full of bubbles.

4. Add the salt and cooled whole wheat flour to the sponge. Beat vigorously with a whisk until well combined.

5. Gradually add the unbleached flour, ¼ cup at a time, until the dough forms a mass and begins to pull away from the side of the bowl. Turn the dough out onto a floured work surface.

6. Knead, adding more flour, a little at a time as necessary, for 8 to 10 minutes, or until you have a smooth, elastic dough.

7. Put the dough into an oiled bowl. Turn to coat the entire ball of dough with oil. Cover with a towel and let rise for about 1 hour, until doubled in size.

8. Turn the dough out onto a lightly oiled work surface and divide it in half. Form into loaves, following the directions on page 71.

9. Fit the loaves, seam side down, into well-greased loaf pans. Cover with a towel and let rise for about 45 minutes, or until almost doubled.

10. About 15 minutes before the end of rising, preheat the oven to 375°F.

11. Just before baking, brush the tops of the loaves with the egg wash, being careful not to let the wash drip onto the pan. Sprinkle lightly with 2 tablespoons wheat germ, if desired.

12. Bake the loaves for 25 to 30 minutes, or until they shrink slightly from the sides of the pan and sound hollow when tapped (the internal temperature should reach 190°F). Immediately remove from the pans and cool on a rack.

Whole Wheat Sunflower Seed Bread

1 cup hulled sunflower seeds

2 scant tablespoons or 2 (¼-ounce) packages active dry yeast

½ cup warm water (105° to 115°F)

2 cups warm milk (105° to 115°F)

2 teaspoons salt

¼ cup solid vegetable shortening

½ cup maple syrup

3 cups whole wheat flour

2½ to 3½ cups unbleached all-purpose flour

Vegetable oil (optional)

Makes 2 loaves

The rich flavor of toasted sunflower seeds is a perfect companion to the nutty, robust flavor of whole wheat. Toasting intensifies the flavor threefold. You can buy toasted sunflower seeds if you do not want to toast them yourself. If the toasted seeds have added salt, decrease the amount of salt in the recipe to 1½ teaspoons.

1. Toast the sunflower seeds by spreading them in a single layer in a dry skillet and setting it over medium-low heat. Cook, stirring occasionally, for about 10 minutes, or until the seeds are lightly toasted. Cool.

2. Meanwhile, in a large bowl, soften the yeast into the warm water.

3. Add the milk, salt, cooled sunflower seeds, shortening, maple syrup, and whole wheat flour. Beat vigorously with a dough whisk or a heavy-handled spoon for 2 minutes.

4. Gradually add some of the all-purpose flour, ¼ cup at a time, until the dough forms a mass and begins to pull away from the side of the bowl. Turn the dough out onto a floured work surface.

5. Knead, adding more flour, a little at a time as necessary, for 8 to 10 minutes, or until you have a smooth, elastic dough.

(continued)

6. Put the dough into an oiled bowl. Turn to coat the entire ball of dough with oil. Cover with a tightly woven kitchen towel and let rise for about 1 hour, until doubled in size.

7. Turn the dough out onto a lightly oiled work surface and divide it in half. Shape into loaves, following the directions on page 71.

8. Fit the loaves, seam side down, into well-greased loaf pans. Cover with a towel and let rise for about 45 minutes, or until almost doubled in size.

9. About 15 minutes before the end of rising, preheat the oven to 375°F.

10. Bake the loaves for 30 to 35 minutes, or until they shrink slightly from the sides of the pan and sound hollow when tapped (the internal temperature should reach 190°F). Immediately remove from the pans to cool on a rack. For a shiny, soft crust, brush the tops of the loaves with oil while they are still warm.

The center of whatever you're baking should be as close to the vertical center of the oven as the racks will allow. This enhances more even baking.

Seeded Whole Wheat Bread

2 scant tablespoons or
2 (¼-ounce) packages active
dry yeast

½ cup warm water (105° to
115° F)

2½ cups warm milk (105° to
115°F)

¼ cup firmly packed brown
sugar

¼ cup vegetable oil

½ cup hulled sunflower seeds

½ cup sesame seeds

½ cup poppy seeds

¼ cup caraway seeds

½ cup flax seeds (see Note,
page 113)

2 teaspoons salt

2 cups whole wheat flour

2½ to 3½ cups unbleached
all-purpose flour

Makes 2 loaves

The large measure of seeds makes this a delicious, full-flavored loaf that is dense, moist, and reminiscent of a popular breakfast bread served throughout Germany. Take care not to add too much flour or the bread will be heavy.

1. In a large bowl, soften the yeast in the water.

2. Add the milk, brown sugar, oil, sunflower seeds, sesame seeds, poppy seeds, caraway seeds, flax seeds, salt, all the whole wheat flour, and 1 cup of the all-purpose flour. Beat vigorously with a dough whisk or a heavy-handled spoon for 2 minutes. Cover the mixture with a tightly woven kitchen towel and let it rest for 10 minutes. This allows the seeds to absorb some of the liquid, which will keep the bread from being too dry.

3. Gradually add more of the all-purpose flour, ¼ cup at a time, until the dough forms a mass and begins to pull away from the side of the bowl. Turn the dough out onto a floured work surface.

4. Knead, adding more flour, a little at a time as necessary, for 8 to 10 minutes, or until you have a smooth elastic dough.

5. Put the dough into an oiled bowl. Turn to coat the entire ball of dough with oil. Cover with a towel and let rise for about 1 hour, until doubled in size.

6. Turn the dough out onto a lightly oiled work surface and divide it in half. Shape into loaves following the instructions on page 71.

7. Fit the loaves, seam side down, into well-greased loaf pans. Cover with a towel and let rise for about 45 minutes, or until almost doubled in size.

8. About 15 minutes before the end of rising, preheat the oven to 375°F.

9. Bake for 25 to 30 minutes, or until the loaves shrink slightly from the sides of the pans and sound hollow when tapped (the internal temperature should reach 190°F). Immediately remove the bread from the pans and cool on a rack.

Grilled Vegetable Wheat Bread

½ cup coarsely chopped onion

½ cup coarsely chopped sweet red bell pepper

2 tablespoons olive oil, plus additional for brushing

½ cup carrots, sliced about ¼ inch thick

½ cup thinly sliced celery, sliced about ¼ inch thick

½ cup broccoli florets (thumbnail size)

½ cup coarsely chopped cauliflower

1 scant tablespoon or 1 (¼-ounce) package active dry yeast

¼ cup warm water (105° to 115°F)

1 cup warm milk (105° to 115°F)

1 tablespoon solid vegetable shortening

1 teaspoon salt

1 teaspoon coarsely cracked pepper

1 tablespoon sugar

1 cup whole wheat flour

2 to 3 cups unbleached all-purpose flour

Makes 6 flat breads

This delicious bread cooks right on the grill rack alongside whatever else you are grilling—and it is done in about 16 minutes. You can also bake it on a baking stone or baking sheet in a hot oven—although on a baking sheet the crust will not be as crunchy. Either way, it is a great bread to serve with simple grilled meats, poultry, and vegetables.

1. Cook the onion and chopped bell pepper in 2 tablespoons of oil over medium heat for about 5 minutes, or until softened but not browned. Set aside to cool.

2. Bring a saucepan of water to a boil. Add the carrots and celery to the boiling water and blanch for about 15 seconds; remove with a slotted spoon and plunge into a large bowl of cold water. Drain and spread on a kitchen towel to dry. Repeat with the broccoli, using the same pan of boiling water, and then with the cauliflower.

3. In a large bowl, soften the yeast in the water.

4. Add the milk, shortening, salt, pepper, sugar, all the whole wheat flour, and 1 cup of the unbleached flour to the yeast. Beat vigorously with a dough whisk or a heavy-handled spoon for 2 minutes.

5. Gradually add more of the all-purpose flour, ¼ cup at a time, until the dough forms a mass and begins to pull away from the side of the bowl. Turn the dough out onto a floured work surface.

6. Cover the dough with the sautéed onion and pepper and the blanched vegetables. Knead the vegetables into the dough, taking care not to mash them. Continue to knead the dough lightly for about 3 minutes, adding only enough flour to make a soft dough that is just a little sticky. Since this is a flat bread, it does not require as much kneading as other bread doughs.

7. Put the dough into an oiled bowl. Turn to coat the entire ball of dough with oil. Cover with a tightly woven kitchen towel and let rise for about 1 hour, or until doubled in size.

8. Turn the dough out onto a lightly oiled work surface and divide it into 6 pieces. Flatten each piece into a disk about ½ inch thick. Put each disk on a separate piece of oiled wax or parchment paper. Cover with a towel and allow to rise for about 45 minutes, or until doubled in size.

9. To bake the bread in the *oven,* put a baking stone or tile on the lower shelf of the oven and preheat the oven to 400°F for 30 minutes. Brush each disk of bread with oil and invert it onto the hot stone. Peel off and discard the paper and quickly brush the top of the bread with oil. Bake for about 15 minutes, or until golden.

10. To bake on the *grill,* position the grill rack about 5 inches from the heat source. Preheat the gas grill or let coals burn until they are completely covered with gray-white ash. Brush each bread disk with oil and carefully turn onto the grill rack. Peel off and discard the paper. Grill for about 8 minutes. Turn the bread over and brush the top with oil. Grill for 8 minutes more, or until golden.

11. Cool the breads on a rack for 10 minutes before eating.

Sesame Whole Wheat Rolls

2 scant tablespoons or
2 (¼-ounce) packages active
dry yeast

½ cup warm water (105° to
115°F)

2 cups lukewarm milk (105°
to 115°F)

¼ cup solid vegetable
shortening

½ cup firmly packed brown
sugar

¼ cup sesame seeds, plus
additional for sprinkling if
desired

¼ cup stone-ground
cornmeal (yellow or white)

2 cups whole wheat flour

3½ to 4½ cups unbleached
all-purpose flour

2 teaspoons salt

1 large egg beaten with
1 tablespoon cold water,
for the egg wash

Makes 32 rolls

Just a touch of sesame seed and cornmeal adds subtle texture and flavor to these soft, light rolls. But if you prefer bolder taste and texture, increase the amount of both. Be sure to decrease the amount of whole wheat flour by the same amount if you increase the cornmeal.

1. In a large bowl, soften the yeast in the water.

2. Add the milk, shortening, brown sugar, sesame seeds, cornmeal, all of the whole wheat flour, and 1 cup of the all-purpose flour. Beat vigorously with a dough whisk or a heavy-handled spoon for 2 minutes. The resulting sponge will have the consistency of cake batter. Cover the sponge with a tightly woven kitchen towel and let rise for 1 hour. It should be light and full of bubbles.

3. Stir the sponge to deflate it. Add the salt and 1 cup of the all-purpose flour and beat vigorously for 1 minute.

4. Gradually add more of the all-purpose flour, ¼ cup at a time, until the dough forms a mass and begins to pull away from the side of the bowl. Turn the dough out onto a floured work surface.

5. Knead, adding more flour, a little at a time as necessary, about 8 to 10 minutes, until you have a smooth, elastic dough.

6. Put the dough into an oiled bowl. Turn to coat the entire ball of dough with oil. Cover with a towel and let rise for about 45 minutes, or until doubled in size.

7. Turn the dough out onto a lightly oiled work surface and divide it in half. Divide both pieces in half again and continue until there are 32 equal pieces. Leave half the pieces covered with a towel on the work surface. Shape each of the first 16 pieces into a 6-inch rope. Coil each end of the rope toward the center until both ends meet and the rolls are shaped like coiled hearts. Arrange the coiled ropes about 2 inches apart on a well-greased baking sheet.

8. Cover the rolls with a towel and let rise for 45 minutes.

9. Shape the other 16 pieces of dough as directed in step 7 and cover to let rise.

10. About 15 minutes before the end of rising of the first batch, preheat the oven to 400°F.

11. Just before baking, brush the tops of the rolls with the egg wash, taking care not to let it drip onto the pan. Sprinkle lightly with sesame seeds. Bake for 12 to 15 minutes, or until golden (the internal temperature should reach 190°F). Repeat with the second batch.

12. Immediately remove the rolls from the baking sheet and cool on a rack or serve warm.

VARIATION

Shape the dough into either 2 round freestanding loaves and place well apart on a well-greased baking sheet, or 2 standard pan loaves (for directions, see page 59) and place in 2 well-greased loaf pans. Cover the loaves with a kitchen towel and let rise for 45 minutes. Just before baking, score the tops of the freestanding loaves ¼ inch deep in two or three places. Bake the loaves 30 to 35 minutes.

Make sure you have at least 1 inch between baking pans inside the oven, and that you have at least 1 inch between the pans and the sides of the oven. Good air circulation is vital to successful bread baking.

Whole Wheat Honey Lemon Rolls

1 scant tablespoon or
1 (¼-ounce) package active
dry yeast

¼ cup warm water (105° to
115°F)

1 cup warm milk (105° to
115°F)

¼ cup honey

¼ cup solid vegetable
shortening

2 tablespoons grated lemon
peel

1 cup whole wheat flour

2½ to 3½ cups unbleached
all-purpose flour

1 large egg beaten with
1 tablespoon cold milk,
for the egg wash

Makes 24 rolls

These rolls are terrific for breakfast with marmalade, but also with such spicy foods as Cajun dishes or Indian curries. The lemon peel makes them slightly sweet, which offsets those piquant flavors. Be sure not to include any of the bitter white pith when grating the lemon. Use only the colored part of the rind.

1. In a large bowl, soften the yeast in the water.

2. Add the milk, honey, shortening, lemon peel, all the whole wheat flour, and 1 cup of the all-purpose flour. Beat vigorously with a dough whisk or a heavy-handled spoon for 2 minutes.

3. Gradually add more of the remaining all-purpose flour, ¼ cup at a time, until the dough forms a mass and begins to pull away from the side of the bowl. Turn the dough out onto a floured work surface.

4. Knead, adding more flour, a little at a time as necessary, for 8 to 10 minutes, or until you have a smooth, elastic dough.

5. Put the dough into an oiled bowl. Turn to coat the entire ball of dough with oil. Cover with a tighly woven kitchen towel and let rise for about 1 hour, or until doubled in size.

6. Turn the dough out onto a lightly oiled work surface and divide it into thirds, then divide each third in half. Divide the pieces in half two more times to make 24 pieces. Leave half the pieces covered with a towel on the work surface. Roll each of the first 12 pieces into an 8-inch rope. Coil the ends in opposite directions to make S-shaped rolls. Arrange the rolls about 2 inches apart on a well-greased baking sheet.

7. Cover with a towel and let rise for about 45 minutes, until almost doubled in size.

8. Meanwhile, after the first batch has risen for 15 minutes, shape the other 12 pieces of dough as directed in step 6. Cover to let rise.

9. About 15 minutes before baking, preheat the oven to 400°F.

10. Just before baking, lightly brush each roll with egg wash, taking care not to let any drop onto the baking sheet. Bake for 18 to 20 minutes, or until golden (the internal temperature should reach 190°F). Repeat with second batch.

11. Remove the rolls from the baking sheet and cool on racks.

VARIATION

Shape the dough into either 2 round freestanding loaves and place well apart on a well-greased baking sheet, or 2 standard pan loaves (for directions, see page 59) and place in 2 well-greased loaf pans. Cover the loaves with a towel and let rise for 45 minutes. Just before baking, score the tops of the freestanding loaves ¼ inch deep in two or three places. Bake the loaves 30 to 35 minutes.

"We take out the germ and nourishment of the wheat and feed it to the pigs and keep the rubbish for ourselves. Who would ever think of trying to fatten a pig on white flour?"—H.S. Joyce, *I Was Born in the Country* (1946).

Whole Wheat Herb Buns

2 scant tablespoons or 2 (¼-ounce) packages active dry yeast

½ cup warm water (105° to 115°F)

2 cups warm milk (105° or 115°F)

¼ cup solid vegetable shortening, cut up

3 tablespoons sugar

2 teaspoons salt

1 teaspoon crushed dried oregano or 1 tablespoon chopped fresh oregano

1 teaspoon crumbled dried sage or 1 tablespoon chopped fresh sage

2 tablespoons chopped dried chives or ¼ cup chopped fresh chives

2 cups whole wheat flour

3½ to 4½ cups unbleached all-purpose flour

Makes 18 buns

I first made these buns in the dead of winter, when all I had was dried herbs. We used them to sandwich a generous amount of smoked turkey, sweet mustard, and lettuce, or to wrap around hamburgers. When summer arrived, I tried them with fresh herbs and they almost tasted like a new recipe. Either way, the soft sandwich buns are absolutely terrific.

1. In a large bowl, soften the yeast in the water.

2. Add the milk, shortening, sugar, salt, oregano, sage, chives, all the whole wheat flour, and 1 cup of the all-purpose flour. Beat vigorously with a whisk for 2 minutes.

3. Gradually add more of the all-purpose flour, ¼ cup at a time, until the dough forms a mass and begins to pull away from the side of the bowl. Turn the dough out onto a floured work surface.

4. Knead, adding more flour, a little at a time as necessary, about 8 to 10 minutes, or until you have a smooth, elastic dough.

5. Put the dough into an oiled bowl. Turn to coat the entire ball of dough with oil. Cover with a tightly woven kitchen towel and let rise for about 1 hour, or until doubled in size.

6. Turn the dough out onto a lightly oiled work surface and divide it into thirds. Divide each piece in half and then into thirds again for a total of 18 pieces.

7. You will need 3 baking sheets to make 18 crusty buns, so shape the pieces in 3 batches, leaving the rest of the dough on the work surface, covered with a towel. Shape each piece into a ball and pat or roll it to flatten into a 3-inch circle. After all the buns in a batch are shaped and flattened, flatten them again to a 3½-inch circle by pressing the centers, not the edges, with your fingers. For soft-sided buns, place the circles of dough on a well-greased baking sheet about ½ inch apart (in this case, they should all fit on 2 baking sheets). For crusty buns, place them on a well-greased baking sheet about 3 inches apart.

8. Cover the buns with a towel and let rise for about 45 minutes, until almost doubled in size.

9. About 15 minutes before the end of rising of the first batch, preheat the oven to 375°F. Bake for 20 to 25 minutes, or until the rolls are golden (the internal temperature should reach 190°F).

10. Remove from the baking sheets and cool on racks.

VARIATION

Shape the dough into either 2 round freestanding loaves and place well apart on a well-greased baking sheet, or 2 standard pan loaves (for directions, see page 59) and place in 2 well-greased loaf pans. Cover the loaves with a towel and let rise for 45 minutes. Just before baking, score the tops of the freestanding loaves ¼ inch deep in two or three places. Bake the loaves 25 to 30 minutes.

5

I have separated these recipes from the preceding ones for whole wheat breads because they include such grains as rye and oats for an array of flavors and textures welcomed by all bread bakers as they move beyond basic loaves. I also include recipes here that call for wheat in different, less familiar guises, such as bran and cracked wheat.

I have a fondness for rye flour. Its robust, distinctive flavor appeals to the sandwich lover in me. Many bread lovers do not realize that pumpernickel bread is simply dark rye bread and bears a resemblance to dark peasant bread. You will find recipes for these and other rye breads on these pages, including one for turtle-shaped loaves perfect for sandwiches and buffet decorations.

These are all hearty, healthful breads. They are full of bold flavors and noticeable textures as different from those of ordinary white bread as thick Scottish porridge is from packaged cream of wheat.

Whole Grain Yeast Breads

Basic Rye Bread

2 scant tablespoons or 2 (¼-ounce) packages active dry yeast

2½ cups warm water (105° to 115°F)

2 tablespoons vegetable oil

¼ cup honey

2 cups rye flour

2 teaspoons salt

2 tablespoons caraway seeds

3½ to 4½ cups unbleached all-purpose flour

Cornmeal, for pan and loaves

Makes 2 round loaves

All home bread bakers need at least one good basic rye bread recipe in their repertoire. Here is my choice. The bread is easy to make and bursts with good rye flavor. Homemade rye bread makes the best sandwiches imaginable, or try it as they eat it in Europe: thinly sliced and spread with butter and thin slices of sweet onion. Freestanding loaves such as these must be flattened before rising; otherwise they will be round as bowling balls when baked rather than slightly rounded.

1. In a large mixing bowl, soften the yeast in the water.

2. Add the oil, honey, rye flour, salt, caraway seeds, and 1 cup of the all-purpose flour. Beat vigorously with a dough whisk or a heavy-handled spoon for 2 minutes.

3. Gradually add more of the remaining flour, ¼ cup at a time, until the dough forms a mass and begins to pull away from the sides of the bowl. Turn the dough out onto a floured work surface.

4. Knead, adding more flour, a little at a time as necessary, for 8 to 10 minutes, or until you have a smooth, elastic dough.

5. Put the dough into an oiled bowl. Turn to coat the entire ball of dough with oil. Cover with a tightly woven kitchen towel and let rise for about 1 hour, or until doubled in size.

6. Sprinkle a large greased baking sheet liberally with cornmeal.

7. Turn the dough out onto a lightly oiled work surface. Divide it in half and gently knead each piece in a circle to form a ball. Take care not to knead roughly and split the smooth outer skin, which will help the bread hold its shape during baking. Roll each ball in cornmeal to coat the entire surface of the loaf. Place the balls well apart on the prepared baking sheet and press each one in the center to flatten slightly.

8. Cover the loaves with a towel and let rise for about 45 minutes, or until almost doubled.

9. About 15 minutes before the end of rising, preheat the oven to 375°F.

10. Just before baking, make 3 slits in the top of each loaf, about ½ inch deep and 1 inch apart. Brush or spray the tops of the loaves with cold water.

11. Bake for 30 to 35 minutes, or until loaves are golden brown and sound hollow when tapped (the internal temperature should reach 190°F). Remove the bread from the baking sheets and cool on a rack.

Old-fashioned Oatmeal Bread

1 cup old-fashioned rolled oats, plus additional as needed

2 cups boiling water

2 scant tablespoons or 2 (1/4-ounce) packages active dry yeast

1/2 cup warm water (105° to 115°F)

1/4 cup vegetable oil

1/2 cup honey

2 teaspoons salt

1 cup whole wheat flour

4 to 5 cups unbleached all-purpose flour

Solid vegetable shortening for greasing pans

1 large egg beaten with 1 tablespoon cold water, for the egg wash

Makes 2 loaves

Not only does soaking the oats before adding them to the dough make the finished bread moist, it increases its shelf life. I also like the large amount of oats in this bread because of the vitamins, minerals, and fiber they supply. This bread is delicious toasted.

1. Add 1 cup rolled oats to the boiling water. Stir, cover, and let sit for about 45 minutes, until cooled to lukewarm.

2. In a large bowl, soften the yeast in the water.

3. Add the oil, honey, salt, all the whole wheat flour, 1 cup of the unbleached flour, and the cooled oat mixture to the yeast. Beat vigorously with a dough whisk or a heavy-handled spoon for 2 minutes.

4. Gradually add more of the remaining flour, 1/4 cup at a time, until the dough forms a mass and begins to pull away from the side of the bowl. Turn the dough out onto a floured work surface.

5. Knead, adding more flour, a little at a time as necessary, for 8 to 10 minutes, or until you have a smooth, elastic dough.

6. Put the dough into an oiled bowl. Turn to coat the entire ball of dough with oil. Cover with a tightly woven kitchen towel and let rise for about 1 hour, until doubled in size.

7. Grease two loaf pans with solid shortening and sprinkle the sides and bottoms of the pans lightly with rolled oats.

8. Turn the dough out onto a lightly oiled work surface and divide it in half. Shape into loaves, following the directions on page 71.

9. Fit the loaves, seam side down, into the prepared loaf pans. Cover with a towel and let rise for 45 minutes.

10. About 15 minutes before the end of the rising time, preheat the oven to 375°F.

11. Just before baking, brush the tops of the loaves with the egg wash, taking care not to let it drip down the sides of the pans. Sprinkle the loaves lightly with additional rolled oats, if desired. Bake for 25 to 30 minutes, or until the loaves shrink slightly from the sides of the pan and sound hollow when tapped (the internal temperature should reach 190°F). Remove the bread from the pans and cool on a rack.

Make sure to consult the information on flour and other ingredients and on utensils (chapter 1) and the baking class on making yeast breads (chapter 2).

Pumpernickel

2 scant tablespoons or
2 (¹/₄-ounce) packages active
dry yeast

2 cups warm water (105° to
115°F)

2 tablespoons molasses

2 teaspoons caraway seeds

2 teaspoons salt

1 cup warm mashed potatoes
(105° to 115°F)

2 cups dark rye or
pumpernickel flour, plus
additional as needed

1 cup unprocessed bran

3¹/₂ to 4¹/₂ cups unbleached
all-purpose or whole wheat
flour

Makes 2 round loaves

The story goes that a German baker named Pumpernickel developed a hearty loaf that used very little wheat flour, which was in
scarce supply during a severe famine sometime around 1450. The
tangy, moist bread, almost black in color and tasting robustly of
rye, remained a favorite with Pumpernickel's customers long after
wheat flour was again available. Today, we still admire the solid,
tasty loaf. I make it with more wheat flour than Herr Pumpernickel
would have thought correct, and to be authentic you may use four
cups of rye flour and only two of wheat flour. Try to plan your
baking schedule so that this bread is eaten the day after baking to
give the crust time to soften and turn chewy.

1. In a large bowl, soften the yeast in the water.

2. Add the molasses, caraway seeds, salt, mashed potatoes,
rye or pumpernickel flour, bran, and 1 cup of the all-purpose or
whole wheat flour. Beat vigorously with a dough whisk or a heavy-
handled spoon for 2 minutes.

3. Gradually add more of the remaining flour, ¹/₄ cup at a
time, until the dough forms a mass and begins to pull away from
the side of the bowl. Turn the dough out onto a floured work
surface.

4. Knead, adding more flour, a little at a time as necessary,
for 8 to 10 minutes, or until you have a smooth elastic dough. You
may not need to use all the flour. It is especially important to add
only as much flour as needed because too much quickly turns this
loaf into a rock-hard hunk of bread. The dough should be elastic
yet still sticky when left to rise.

5. Put the dough into an oiled bowl. Turn to coat the entire
ball of dough with oil. Cover with a tightly woven kitchen towel
and let rise for about 2 hours, or until doubled in size.

6. Turn the dough out onto a lightly oiled work surface and
divide it in half. Shape each piece into a ball. Roll each ball in rye
flour to coat thoroughly. Put each ball on a piece of lightly oiled
parchment paper and flatten the top slightly.

7. Cover the loaves with a towel and let rise for about 1 hour, or until almost doubled in size.

8. About 15 minutes before the end of rising, preheat the oven to 375°F.

9. Just before baking, carefully lift each loaf and hold it under cold running water until the outside is sticky. Place the loaves well apart on a well-greased baking sheet. Use a sharp knife to cut an X about ½ inch deep in the top of each loaf.

10. Bake the loaves for 30 to 35 minutes, or until they are browned and sound hollow when tapped (the internal temperature should reach 190°F). Cool on a rack. The bread is best when eaten the day after baking.

VARIATION

You might also try baking this in a pullman loaf pan. The dough lends itself beautifully to this treatment and the resulting perfectly square slices are a novelty. If you have a pullman pan (see page 41), omit the instructions for rolling the dough in rye flour and for rinsing it under cool water. Add 10 more minutes to the baking time, too.

If you have a small oven or other limitations on your ability to bake on 2 or more baking sheets at the same time, see the Note on page 189.

Honey Cracked Wheat Bread

FOR THE STARTER

1 tablespoon or 1 (¹/₄-ounce) package active dry yeast

2 cups warm water (105° to 115°F)

³/₄ cup cracked wheat (see page 6)

2 cups unbleached all-purpose flour

FOR THE BREAD

1 scant tablespoon or 1 (¹/₄-ounce) package active dry yeast

¹/₂ cup warm water (105° to 115°F)

2 tablespoons vegetable oil

¹/₄ cup honey, plus additional as needed

2 teaspoons salt

1 cup whole wheat flour

1¹/₂ to 2¹/₂ cups unbleached all-purpose flour

Makes 2 loaves

I make this rustic, honey-sweetened bread with a starter not unlike the sourdough starters explained on pages 287–92. This is not sourdough, however, but simply a spongy yeast mixture that gives the finished loaf a marvelous taste and great texture. You can make the starter 12 to 24 hours before beginning the bread, which provides ample leeway in your schedule. For a shiny, sweet crust, I recommend brushing the top of the baked bread with warm honey, which is thin and easy to brush, as opposed to room-temperature honey, which is thick and heavy. I like the bread for sandwiches—but really *love* it toasted!

1. To make the starter, combine all the starter ingredients in a large bowl. Beat vigorously with a dough whisk or a heavy-handled spoon for 2 minutes. Cover with plastic wrap and a tightly woven kitchen towel. Let rise for 12 to 24 hours. Starters are flexible, and this one may rise and collapse during this period, but once more flour is added during mixing and kneading, it will regain its strength.

2. To begin making the bread, soften the yeast in the water.

3. Add the softened yeast, oil, ¹/₄ cup honey, the salt, and the whole wheat flour to the starter. Beat vigorously with a dough whisk or heavy-handled spoon for 2 minutes.

4. Gradually add the all-purpose flour, ¹/₄ cup at a time, until the dough forms a mass and begins to pull away from the side of the bowl. Turn the dough out onto a floured work surface.

5. Knead, adding more flour, a little at a time as necessary, for 8 to 10 minutes, or until you have a smooth, elastic dough.

6. Put the dough into an oiled bowl. Turn to coat the entire ball of dough with oil. Cover with a towel and let rise for about 1 hour, until doubled in size.

7. Turn the dough out onto a lightly oiled work surface and divide it in half. Shape into loaves, following the directions on page 71.

8. Fit the loaves, seam side down, into well-greased loaf pans. Cover with a towel and let rise for 45 minutes.

9. About 15 minutes before the end of rising, preheat the oven to 375°F.

10. Bake the loaves for 30 to 35 minutes, or until they shrink slightly from the sides of the pan and sound hollow when tapped (the internal temperature should reach 190°F). Remove to a rack to cool. For a sweet, shiny crust, brush the tops of the warm loaves with warmed honey.

The center of whatever you're baking should be as close to the vertical center of the oven as the racks will allow. This enhances more even baking.

Full-Grain Bread

2 cups water

¼ cup vegetable oil

½ cup honey

¼ cup bulgur wheat, plus additional as needed

¼ cup cracked wheat (see page 6)

½ cup shredded coconut

¼ cup wheat germ

¼ cup wheat bran

½ cup old-fashioned rolled oats

2 scant tablespoons or 2 (¼-ounce) packages active dry yeast

½ cup warm water (105° to 115°F)

½ cup hulled sunflower seeds

2 large eggs, lightly beaten

2 teaspoons salt

4½ to 5½ cups unbleached all-purpose flour

1 egg white beaten with 1 tablespoon cold water, for the egg wash

Makes 2 loaves

In the town of Poulsbo, Washington, there is an excellent and well-known Scandinavian bakery that turns out some of the tastiest, most wholesome bread you have ever put in your mouth. Although its recipes are top secret, I have adapted this close approximation to the famous Poulsbo Bread. The coconut gives the bread subtle, surprising flavor.

1. Bring the 2 cups of water to a boil in a medium saucepan. Add the oil, honey, the ¼ cup bulgur wheat, cracked wheat, coconut, wheat germ, wheat bran, and rolled oats to the boiling water. Remove from the heat and stir. Cover and let sit for about 45 minutes, or until cooled to about 110°F.

2. In a large bowl, soften the yeast in the water.

3. Add the cooled grain mixture, sunflower seeds, eggs, salt, and 2 cups of the all-purpose flour to the yeast. Beat vigorously with a dough whisk or a heavy-handled spoon for 2 minutes.

4. Gradually add more of the remaining flour, ¼ cup at a time, until the dough forms a mass and begins to pull away from the side of the bowl. Turn the dough out onto a floured work surface.

5. Knead, adding more flour, a little at a time as necessary, for 8 to 10 minutes, or until you have a smooth elastic dough.

6. Put the dough into an oiled bowl. Turn to coat the entire ball of dough with oil. Cover with a tightly woven kitchen towel and let rise for about 1 hour, until doubled in size.

7. Turn the dough out onto a lightly oiled work surface and divide it in half. Using a rolling pin, roll one piece of dough into an 8 × 16-inch rectangle. Using your hands, roll the dough toward you to form an 8-inch cylinder and pinch the ends. With a knife or dough blade, cut the dough in half crosswise so that you have two 4-inch cylinders. Repeat with the remaining piece of dough.

8. Fit the loaves seam-side down into 2 well-greased loaf pans with the cut edges facing the long sides of the pan. This shape is not only attractive; it facilitates breaking the baked bread apart if you want to use half and freeze the rest in smaller loaves. Cover the loaves with a towel and let rise for 45 minutes.

9. About 15 minutes before the end of rising, preheat the oven to 375°F.

10. Just before baking, brush the tops of the loaves with the egg wash, taking care not to let it run down the sides of the pans. Sprinkle with bulgur wheat, if desired. Bake for 25 to 30 minutes, or until the loaves shrink slightly from the sides of the pan and sound hollow when tapped (the internal temperature should reach 190°F).

11. Immediately remove the bread from the pans and cool on a rack.

VARIATION

Shape the dough into either 2 round freestanding loaves and place well apart on a well-greased baking sheet, or 2 standard pan loaves (for directions, see page 59) and place in 2 well-greased loaf pans. Cover the loaves with a towel and let rise for 45 minutes. Just before baking, score the tops of the freestanding loaves ¼ inch deep in two or three places. Bake the loaves 25 to 30 minutes.

Make sure you have at least 1 inch between baking pans inside the oven, and that you have at least 1 inch between the pans and the sides of the oven. Good air circulation is vital to successful bread baking.

Bran Brown Bread

2 scant tablespoons or
2 (¼-ounce) packages active
dry yeast

2 cups warm water (105° to
115°F)

2 teaspoons salt

1½ cups unprocessed bran

2 teaspoons caraway seeds

1 tablespoon instant coffee
powder

¼ cup vegetable oil

¼ cup molasses or honey

¼ cup cider vinegar

1 ounce unsweetened
chocolate, melted

1 cup light rye flour

3½ to 4½ cups unbleached
all-purpose flour

1 teaspoon cornstarch

½ cup cold water

Makes 2 round lattice loaves

This is a variation on peasant bread, made dark and tangy by the addition of chocolate, coffee, molasses, vinegar, and rye flour. Shaping it into lattice loaves makes it especially attractive. If you feel inspired, you might choose to combine this dark dough with a lighter dough, such as the dough for the Basic White Bread (page 71) to make a two-tone lattice, using one dough for the horizontal ropes and the other for the vertical. Try this bread sliced very thin and spread with sweet butter or topped with rare roast beef and hot horseradish.

1. In a large bowl, soften the yeast in the warm water.

2. Add the salt, bran, caraway seeds, instant coffee, oil, molasses, vinegar, chocolate, rye flour, and 1 cup of the all-purpose flour. Beat vigorously with a dough whisk or a heavy-handled spoon for 2 minutes.

3. Gradually add more of the remaining flour, ¼ cup at a time, until the dough forms a mass and begins to pull away from the side of the bowl. Turn the dough out onto a floured work surface.

4. Knead, adding more flour a little at a time as necessary, for 8 to 10 minutes, or until you have a smooth, elastic dough.

5. Put the dough into an oiled bowl. Turn to coat the entire ball of dough with oil. Cover with a tightly woven kitchen towel and let rise for about 1 hour, until doubled in size.

6. Turn the dough out onto a lightly oiled work surface and divide it in half. Divide each piece in half again and continue this until there are 32 equal pieces. Use 16 pieces for each loaf. Cover the pieces for the second loaf with a towel while shaping the first loaf.

7. With your hands, roll each piece of dough into a 12-inch rope. Lay 8 ropes vertically on the work surface, about ½ inch apart (diagram 1). Fold every other rope in half and lay a ninth rope horizontally across the 4 remaining vertical ropes, just above the folded ropes (diagram 2). Keep the ropes ½ inch apart. Straighten the folded ropes back up over the horizontal rope.

1.

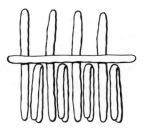

2.

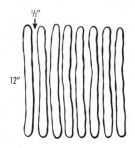

3.

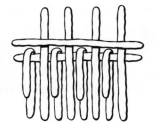

8. Fold the other 4 vertical ropes (not the 4 that were folded before) back over the horizontal rope and lay a second rope horizontally across the vertical ropes, just above the folded ropes (diagram 3). Straighten the folded ropes over the horizontal rope.

9. Repeat until you have used 4 horizontal ropes.

10. Follow the same process with the lower half of the dough until you have used the remaining 4 ropes.

11. Tuck the edges under. Fit the loaf into a well-greased 8-inch round pan.

12. Repeat the process for the second loaf.

13. Cover the loaves with a towel and let rise for 45 minutes.

14. About 15 minutes before the end of rising, preheat the oven to 375°F.

15. Bake the loaves for 25 minutes.

16. While the bread is baking, make the glaze. Combine the cornstarch with the cold water in a small saucepan. Bring the mixture to a boil over medium heat. Reduce the heat to low and cook for 1 minute.

17. When the bread has baked for 25 minutes, brush the loaves with the cornstarch mixture. Return the bread to the oven and cook for 5 to 10 minutes more, or until the loaves shrink slightly from the sides of the pans and sound hollow when tapped (the internal temperature should reach 190°F). Remove from the pans and cool on a rack.

VARIATION

Shape the dough into either 2 round freestanding loaves and place well apart on a well-greased baking sheet, or 2 standard pan loaves (for directions, see page 59) and place in 2 well-greased loaf pans. Cover the loaves with a towel and let rise for 45 minutes. Just before baking, score the tops of the freestanding loaves ¼ inch deep in two or three places. Bake the loaves 30 to 35 minutes.

Dad's Oat Bran Bread

2 cups oat bran

1 tablespoon sugar

1 cup whole wheat flour

4½ to 5½ cups unbleached all-purpose flour

2 scant tablespoons or 2 (¼-ounce) packages active dry yeast

2 teaspoons salt

½ cup corn oil

3 cups hot water (120° to 130°F)

1 large egg beaten with 1 tablespoon cold water, for the egg wash

Makes 3 loaves

Once when my parents were visiting, my father lamented how much he would miss homemade bread when he got home. I gave him a bread baking lesson then and there, and ever since he has been making bread. Like many good bread bakers, he uses recipes as starting points only, letting his creativity and the available ingredients determine the outcome of the loaf. One summer a good supply of oat bran as well as the desire for a bread that would make great tomato sandwiches led him to develop this recipe. Dad used the rapid-mix method (see page 54), which insulates the yeast so the warmer liquid won't harm it.

1. In a large bowl, whisk together the oat bran, sugar, whole wheat flour, 2 cups of the unbleached flour, the yeast, and the salt.

2. Combine the oil and hot water. Add to the dry ingredients and beat vigorously with a dough whisk or a heavy-handled spoon for 2 minutes.

3. Gradually add more of the remaining all-purpose flour, ¼ cup at a time, until the dough forms a mass and begins to pull away from the side of the bowl. Turn the dough out onto a floured work surface.

4. Knead, adding more flour, a little at a time as necessary, for 8 to 10 minutes, or until you have a smooth, elastic dough.

5. Put the dough into an oiled bowl. Turn to coat the entire ball of dough with oil. Cover with a tightly woven kitchen towel and let rise for about 1 hour, or until doubled in size.

6. Turn the dough out onto a lightly oiled work surface and divide into thirds. Form into loaves following the directions on page 71.

7. Fit the loaves, seam side down, into 3 well-greased loaf pans. Cover with a towel and let rise for 45 minutes.

8. About 15 minutes before the end of rising, preheat the oven to 375°F.

9. Just before baking, brush the tops of the loaves with the egg wash, taking care that it doesn't drip down the sides of the pans.

Black Peasant Bread

2 scant tablespoons or
2 (¼-ounce) packages active
dry yeast

2½ cups warm strong black
coffee (105° to 115°F)

¼ cup vegetable oil

¼ cup molasses

2 tablespoons caraway seeds

2 teaspoons salt

½ cup toasted wheat germ

¼ cup cocoa powder

2 cups dark rye or
pumpernickel flour

5 to 6 cups unbleached all-
purpose flour

Cornmeal

Makes 2 loaves

Bake for 25 to 30 minutes, or until the loaves shrink slightly from the sides of the pans and sound hollow when tapped (the internal temperature should reach 190°F). Remove from the pans and cool on a rack.

This is a dark, full-flavored bread that has a slight tang. I call it peasant bread because the combination of coffee, molasses, and cocoa with rye flour helps to re-create the tart, strong-flavored breads baked for centuries by European peasants. The aristocracy took light, white flour milled from the starchy endosperm and left the laborers the remaining coarse mixture of germ and bran. This heavy flour was very different from today's whole wheat flour, and although it no doubt was full of vitamins and fiber, it yielded dense, heavy dark loaves with a noticeably sharp flavor. Peasant wives thriftily used leftover crumbs to add to the flour, which made the baked bread tarter and heavier than ever. Nowadays, we fashion rustic loaves we romantically call peasant breads, savoring their robust flavor; but they most likely bear little resemblance to the heavy, dense originals.

1. In a large bowl, soften the yeast in the coffee.

2. Add the oil, molasses, caraway seeds, salt, wheat germ, cocoa powder, rye or pumpernickel flour, and 1 cup of the unbleached flour to the yeast. Beat vigorously with a dough whisk or a heavy-handled spoon for 2 minutes.

3. Gradually add more of the remaining all-purpose flour, ¼ cup at a time, until the dough forms a mass and begins to pull away from the side of the bowl. Turn the dough out onto a floured work surface.

4. Knead, adding more flour, a little at a time as necessary, for 8 to 10 minutes, or until you have a smooth, elastic dough. You may not need to use all the flour; rye dough is better if it is quite tacky.

(continued)

5. Put the dough into an oiled bowl. Turn to coat the entire ball of dough with oil. Cover with a tightly woven kitchen towel and let rise for about 1 hour, until doubled in size.

6. For a more finely textured bread, leave the dough in the bowl and punch it down. Cover with the towel and let rise again for about 40 minutes, or until doubled in size. (You may omit this step.)

7. Turn the dough out onto a lightly oiled work surface. Divide it in half and gently knead the dough in a circle to form a ball. Take care not to knead roughly and split the smooth outer skin, which holds the bread shape during baking. Roll each ball in flour to coat completely. Place them well apart on a well-greased baking sheet that has been lightly sprinkled with cornmeal. Flatten the top of each loaf slightly to make broad, rounded loaves.

8. Cover the loaves with a towel and let rise for about 45 minutes, or until almost doubled in size.

9. About 15 minutes before the end of rising, preheat the oven to 375°F.

10. Just before baking, make a few slashes in a tic-tac-toe design about ¼ to ½ inch deep in the top of each loaf.

11. Bake the loaves for 30 to 35 minutes, or until they are well browned and sound hollow when tapped (the internal temperature should reach 190°F). Immediately remove the loaves from the baking sheet and cool on a rack.

Broadmoor Baker's Bread

2 scant tablespoons or
2 (¼-ounce) packages active
dry yeast

2½ cups warm water (105° to
115°F)

¼ cup molasses

2 cups whole wheat flour

3½ to 4½ cups unbleached
all-purpose flour

½ cup sesame seeds

½ cup hulled sunflower seeds

½ cup firmly packed brown
sugar

½ cup old-fashioned rolled
oats

¼ cup cracked wheat (see
page 6)

¼ cup poppy seeds

¼ cup hulled pumpkin seeds

¼ cup gluten flour (optional)

2 teaspoons salt

¼ cup soy, safflower, or
canola oil

Makes 2 loaves

When I lived in Seattle, I became fond of the locally produced Broadmoor bread. I discovered that the recipe had been developed by a baking enthusiast who lived in the Broadmoor section of the city. Apparently, he was a renter's broker by day, but during his free time turned to the kitchen and his true love: bread baking. He sold the recipe for the bread to a large commercial bakery, and although the actual formula is not available, I re-created it, relying on my taste buds and the list of ingredients on the package.

1. In a large bowl, soften the yeast in the water.

2. Add the molasses, whole wheat flour, and 1 cup of the unbleached flour. Beat vigorously with a dough whisk or a heavy-handled spoon for 2 minutes. The resulting sponge will have the consistency of cake batter. Cover and let rise for about 1 hour. The sponge should be light and full of bubbles.

3. Stir in the sesame seeds, sunflower seeds, brown sugar, rolled oats, cracked wheat, poppy seeds, pumpkin seeds, gluten flour (if desired—see Note), salt, and oil.

4. Gradually add more of the remaining all-purpose flour, ¼ cup at a time, until the dough forms a mass and begins to pull away from the side of the bowl. Turn the dough out onto a floured work surface.

5. Knead, adding more flour, a little at a time as necessary, for 8 to 10 minutes, or until you have a smooth, elastic dough.

6. Put the dough into an oiled bowl. Turn to coat the entire ball of dough with oil. Cover with a tightly woven kitchen towel and let rise for about 1 hour, or until doubled in size.

7. Turn the dough out onto a lightly oiled work surface and divide it in half. Shape into loaves, following the directions on page 71.

8. Fit the loaves, seam side down, into well-greased loaf pans. With a dough scraper or spatula, make a deep furrow along the whole length of each loaf, pushing through the dough to the bottom. Cover with a towel and let rise for 45 minutes.

(continued)

9. About 15 minutes before the end of rising, preheat the oven to 375°F.

10. Bake for 35 to 40 minutes, or until the bread shrinks slightly from the sides of the pan and the loaves sound hollow when tapped (the internal temperature should reach 190°F). Remove the bread from the pans and cool on a rack.

Note: I include gluten flour in the recipe because it is one of the ingredients listed for the packaged bread. However, I generally avoid using this high-protein flour, feeling that a good hard wheat flour and proper kneading contribute to a lofty rise that needs no boost from the gluten flour.

Raisin Bran Bread

2 scant tablespoons or 2 (¼-ounce) packages active dry yeast

½ cup warm water (105° to 115°F)

2 cups warm milk (105° to 115°F)

2 tablespoons vegetable oil, plus additional as needed

2 teaspoons salt

1 cup unprocessed bran

1 cup whole wheat flour

3½ to 4½ cups unbleached all-purpose flour

1 cup raisins

Makes 2 twisted loaves

This raisin bread has a good, hearty flavor and a pleasingly coarse texture supplied by the unprocessed bran. I suggest buying the bran from a health food store. I like this bread for egg salad and sprout sandwiches—a favorite in our house.

1. In a large bowl, soften the yeast in the water.

2. Add the milk, 2 tablespoons oil, salt, bran, whole wheat flour, and 1 cup of the all-purpose flour. Beat vigorously with a dough whisk or a heavy-handled spoon for 2 minutes.

3. Add the raisins and stir. Gradually add more of the remaining unbleached flour, ¼ cup at a time, until the dough forms a mass and begins to pull away from the side of the bowl. Turn the dough out onto a floured work surface.

4. Knead, adding more flour, a little at a time as necessary, for 8 to 10 minutes, or until you have an elastic dough.

5. Put the dough into an oiled bowl. Turn to coat the entire ball of dough with oil. Cover with a tightly woven kitchen towel and let rise for about 1 hour, or until doubled in size.

6. Turn the dough out onto a lightly oiled work surface and divide it into 4 equal pieces. With your hands, roll each piece into a 12-inch rope. For each loaf, twist 2 ropes together. Be careful not to pull the ropes. Tuck the ends under and put into well-greased loaf pans. Cover with a towel and let rise for 45 minutes.

7. About 15 minutes before the end of rising, preheat the oven to 375°F.

8. Bake for 25 to 30 minutes, or until the bread shrinks slightly from the sides of the pan and sounds hollow when tapped (the internal temperature should reach 190°F). Remove the bread from the pans to cool on a rack. For a soft, shiny crust, brush the tops of the warm loaves lightly with oil.

VARIATION
Shape the dough into either 2 round freestanding loaves and place well apart on a well-greased baking sheet, or 2 standard pan loaves (for directions, see page 59) and place in 2 well-greased loaf pans. Cover the loaves with a towel and let rise for 45 minutes. Just before baking, score the tops of the freestanding loaves ¼ inch deep in two or three places. Bake the loaves 25 to 30 minutes.

In some health food stores you can buy a liquid soy mixture. This used to be called soy milk. When the truth-in-advertising laws went into effect, it could no longer be called milk because it doesn't come from mammary glands. It goes under many names now depending on the manufacturer. This is an ideal liquid to use in yeast breads.

Walnut Rye Bread

2 scant tablespoons or
2 (¹/₄-ounce) packages active
dry yeast

¹/₂ cup warm water (105° to
115°F)

2 cups warm milk (105° to
115°F)

¹/₃ cup honey

2 cups rye flour

¹/₄ cup vegetable oil, plus
additional as needed

2 teaspoons salt

1 tablespoon grated orange
peel

2 teaspoons crushed anise
seeds

1 cup coarsely chopped
walnuts

3¹/₂ to 4¹/₂ cups unbleached
all-purpose flour

Makes 2 round spindle loaves

This is a full-bodied bread that combines the strong, bold flavors of rye and anise with great success. Crush the anise seeds in a mortar with a pestle or by gentle pounding with a hammer on a cutting board. The spindle-shaped loaves are easy to pull apart, but the dough can easily be formed into any shape.

1. In a large bowl, soften the yeast in the water.

2. Add the milk, honey, rye flour, ¹/₄ cup oil, salt, orange peel, anise seeds, walnuts, and 1 cup of the all-purpose flour. Beat vigorously with a dough whisk or a heavy-handled spoon for 2 minutes.

3. Gradually add more of the remaining flour, ¹/₄ cup at a time, until the dough forms a mass and begins to pull away from the side of the bowl. Turn the dough out onto a floured work surface.

4. Knead, adding more flour, a little at a time as necessary, for 8 to 10 minutes, or until you have an elastic dough.

5. Put the dough into an oiled bowl. Turn to coat the entire ball of dough with oil. Cover with a tightly woven kitchen towel and let rise for about 1 hour, or until doubled in size. Meantime, line 2 baking sheets with parchment paper.

6. To shape into spindle loaves, first turn the dough out onto a lightly oiled work surface and divide it in half. Divide each piece in half again and continue this until there are 16 pieces. Shape each piece into a 12-inch rope. Use 8 pieces to form each loaf. Fold each rope into a V shape with the ends about 7 inches apart (diagram 1). Following the diagrams 2, 3, and 4, position the V-shaped ropes on the baking sheet in a circle with the ends (legs) facing outward. Slip the right leg of the last rope under the left leg of the first rope to anchor it (diagram 5).

7. Repeat for the second loaf.

8. Cover the loaves with a towel and let rise for about 45 minutes, until almost doubled in size.

1.

2.

3.

4.

5.

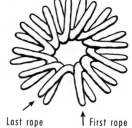

Last rope   ↑ First rope

9. About 15 minutes before the end of rising, preheat the oven to 375°F.

10. Bake for 25 to 30 minutes, or until the loaves are golden brown and sound hollow when tapped (the internal temperature should reach 190°F). Remove the loaves from the baking sheets and cool on racks. For a soft, shiny crust, brush the tops of the warm loaves with oil.

VARIATION

Shape the dough into either 2 round freestanding loaves and place well apart on a well-greased baking sheet, or 2 standard pan loaves (for directions, see page 59) and place in 2 well-greased loaf pans. Cover the loaves with a towel and let rise for 45 minutes. Just before baking, score the tops of the freestanding loaves ¼ inch deep in two or three places. Bake the loaves 25 to 30 minutes.

Apple Oatmeal Bread

2 scant tablespoons or
2 (¼-ounce) packages active
dry yeast

½ cup warm water (105° to
115°F)

2 cups warm milk (105° to
115°F)

2 tablespoons vegetable oil

½ cup firmly packed brown
sugar

2 teaspoons salt

2 cups old-fashioned rolled
oats (not quick-cooking or
instant), plus additional as
needed

1 teaspoon ground cinnamon

4½ to 5½ cups unbleached
all-purpose flour

2 cups chopped tart apples
(peeled or unpeeled)

1 cup coarsely chopped
walnuts

Solid vegetable shortening
for greasing pans

1 large egg beaten with
1 tablespoon cold water, for
the egg wash

Makes 2 loaves

This is a particularly moist, richly textured bread that is good any time of year but seems custom-made for crisp fall days when nothing tastes better than a piece of homemade bread and a mug of hot mulled apple cider. The apples keep the bread moist and the rolled oats give it texture. I leave the apple skins on for extra fiber. Usually I use Granny Smith apples—their tart flavor and firm texture make them perfect for baking—but choose whatever firm, tart apples are in season in your area. Grease the bread pans with vegetable shortening; an oil spray is not effective, since the oats will not adhere to it.

1. In a large bowl, soften the yeast in the water.

2. Add the milk, oil, brown sugar, salt, oats, cinnamon, 2 cups of the flour, the apples, and the walnuts. Beat vigorously with a dough whisk or heavy-handled spoon for 2 minutes.

3. Gradually add more of the remaining flour, ¼ cup at a time, until the dough forms a mass and begins to pull away from the side of the bowl. Turn the dough out onto a floured work surface.

4. Knead, adding more flour, a little at a time as necessary, for 8 to 10 minutes, or until you have an elastic dough.

5. Put the dough into an oiled bowl. Turn to coat the entire ball of dough with oil. Cover with a tightly woven kitchen towel and let rise for about 1 hour, or until doubled in sized.

6. Grease 2 loaf pans with solid vegetable shortening and sprinkle the sides and bottoms with rolled oats.

7. Turn the dough out onto a lightly oiled work surface and divide it in half. Form into loaves (see directions on page 71).

8. Fit the loaves, seam sides down, into the prepared pans. Cover with a towel and let rise for about 45 minutes, or until almost doubled.

9. About 15 minutes before the end of rising, preheat the oven to 375°F.

10. Just before baking, lightly brush the tops of the loaves with the egg wash (taking care that it doesn't drip down into the pans) and sprinkle with additional rolled oats. Bake for 25 to 30 minutes, or until the loaves are golden brown and shrink slightly from the sides of the pan (the internal temperature should reach 190°F). Immediately remove the bread from the pans and cool on a rack.

Millet Bread

2 cups milk

1/4 cup vegetable oil

1 cup millet

2 scant tablespoons or
2 (1/4-ounce) packages active
dry yeast

1/2 cup warm water (105° to
115°F)

2 cups whole wheat flour

2 teaspoons salt

1/4 cup honey

3 1/2 to 4 1/2 cups unbleached
all-purpose flour

Butter or oil (optional)

Makes 2 loaves

I hope you will try this wonderful bread. Millet gives bread subtle flavor and lots of crunch, and this loaf is especially satisfying with a bowl of hot vegetable soup or homemade tomato soup. I always soak millet in liquid before adding it to the other ingredients to prevent the bread from drying out too quickly after baking.

1. Scald the milk in a small saucepan and add the oil and millet. Cover and set aside for about 45 minutes, to cool to about 110°F.

2. In a large bowl, soften the yeast in the water.

3. Add the millet mixture, all of the whole wheat flour, salt, honey, and 1 cup of the all-purpose flour. Beat vigorously with a dough whisk or a heavy-handled spoon for 2 minutes.

4. Gradually add more of the remaining flour, 1/4 cup at a time, until the dough forms a mass and begins to pull away from the side of the bowl. Turn the dough out onto a floured work surface.

5. Knead, adding more flour, a little at a time as necessary, for 8 to 10 minutes, or until you have a smooth, elastic dough.

6. Put the dough into an oiled bowl and turn to coat the entire ball of dough with oil. Cover with a tightly woven kitchen towel and let rise for about 1 hour, or until doubled in size.

7. Turn the dough out onto a lightly oiled work surface and divide it in half. Gently knead one piece of dough in a circle to

(continued)

baking. Flatten the top slightly. Repeat with the remaining piece of dough and put the loaves well apart on a well-greased baking sheet.

8. Cover with a towel and let rise for 45 minutes.

9. About 15 minutes before the end of rising, preheat the oven to 375°F.

10. Just before baking, cut a large X about ½ inch deep in the top of each loaf with a sharp knife.

11. Bake for 30 to 35 minutes, or until the loaves are golden brown and sound hollow when tapped (the internal temperature should reach 190°F). For a soft, shiny crust, rub the top of the loaves with butter or oil. Cool on a rack.

Pretzel Bell Bread

FOR THE SPONGE

1 scant tablespoon or
1 (¼-ounce) package active
dry yeast

1½ cups warm coffee (105° to
115°F)

2 cups rye flour

3 tablespoons caraway seeds

FOR THE BREAD

1 scant tablespoon or
1 (¼-ounce) package active
dry yeast

1 cup warm water (105° to
115°F)

¼ cup molasses (the darker
the better)

2 teaspoons salt

¼ cup vegetable oil, plus
additional as needed

3 squares unsweetened
baking chocolate, melted

1½ cups rye flour

2½ to 3½ cups unbleached
all-purpose flour

Makes 2 round loaves

When my husband, Keith, was at the University of Michigan, the Pretzel Bell was a popular college hangout in Ann Arbor. Everyone who spent time there came to love the dark rye bread served hot from the oven with crocks of fresh sweet butter. I made this loaf for Keith—and we think it is even better than the bread from the Pretzel Bell!

1. To make the sponge, combine the yeast, coffee, rye flour, and caraway seeds in a large bowl. Mix well. The sponge will have the consistency of cake batter. Cover with plastic wrap and let sit for 12 to 24 hours. The sponge should be light and full of bubbles. It may rise at first and then fall again, but it will gain strength when the other ingredients are added.

2. To begin the bread, soften the yeast in the water. Then beat into the sponge.

3. Add the molasses, salt, oil, chocolate, rye flour, and 1 cup of the all-purpose flour. Beat vigorously with a dough whisk or a heavy-handled spoon for 2 minutes.

4. Gradually add more of the remaining all-purpose flour, ¼ cup at a time, until the dough forms a mass and begins to pull away from the side of the bowl. Turn the dough out onto a floured work surface.

5. Knead, adding more flour, a little at a time as necessary, for 8 to 10 minutes, or until you have a smooth, elastic dough.

6. Put the dough into an oiled bowl and turn to coat the entire ball of dough with oil. Cover with a tightly woven kitchen towel and let rise for about 1½ hours, or until doubled in size.

7. Turn the dough out onto a lightly oiled work surface. Divide it in half and shape each piece into a ball. Flatten the tops of the loaves and put them well apart on a well-greased baking sheet. Cover with a towel and let rise for about 1 hour, until almost doubled in size.

8. About 15 minutes before the end of rising, preheat the oven to 375°F.

(continued)

9. Just before baking, cut a tic-tac-toe design about ½ inch deep in the top of each loaf with a sharp knife. Brush or spray the loaves with cold water.

10. Bake for 25 to 30 minutes, or until the loaves sound hollow when tapped (the internal temperature should be 190°F). Remove the bread from the baking sheet and cool on a rack. For a soft, shiny crust, brush the tops of the warm loaves with oil.

Rye Turtles

2 scant tablespoons or
2 (¼-ounce) packages active
dry yeast

2½ cups warm water (105° to
115°F)

1 tablespoon caraway seeds

1 teaspoon salt

2 tablespoons sugar

1 tablespoon vegetable oil

2 cups light rye flour

3½ to 4½ cups unbleached
flour

1 large egg beaten with
1 tablespoon cold water, for
the egg wash

24 whole cloves (optional)

Makes 12 turtles

When we lived in Germany, I frequented a bakery in Cadolzburg that made rye bread turtles similar to these. While the dough can also be shaped into plain rolls or a loaf of bread, the turtles are novel and make a lighthearted presentation for sandwiches.

1. In a large bowl, soften the yeast in the water.

2. Add the caraway seeds, salt, sugar, oil, all of the rye flour, and 1 cup of the unbleached flour. Beat vigorously with a dough whisk or a heavy-handled spoon for 2 minutes.

3. Gradually add more of the remaining all-purpose flour, ¼ cup at a time, until the dough forms a mass and begins to pull away from the side of the bowl. Turn the dough out onto a floured work surface.

4. Knead, adding more flour, a little at a time as necessary, for 8 to 10 minutes, or until you have a smooth, elastic dough.

5. Put the dough into an oiled bowl. Turn to coat the entire ball of dough with oil. Cover with a tightly woven kitchen towel and let rise for about 1 hour, or until doubled in size.

6. Line 2 baking sheets with parchment paper. Turn the dough out onto a lightly oiled work surface, divide into 12 equal pieces, and smooth each piece into a ball. Working with one piece at a time, take two thirds of the dough ball and shape it into an oval for the turtle's body (diagram 1). Place on a prepared baking sheet (arrange so that each sheet will hold 6 turtles spaced 3 inches

1.

2.

3.

4.

5.

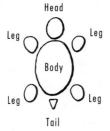

apart) and flatten the top slightly. Picture this oval as a clock face with the narrow ends at 6 and 12 o'clock (diagram 2).

7. Take the remainder of the dough ball and divide it into thirds (diagram 3); set 2 pieces aside. Cut off a sliver of the remaining piece for the tail. Flatten the thicker end of the sliver slightly and place it under the body at 6 o'clock. Shape the remaining bit of dough into an oval for the head and flatten one end slightly. Place the flattened end of the head under the turtle at 12 o'clock.

8. Divide both of the other two sections of dough in half and smooth each piece into a 1-inch-long cylinder for the four legs (diagram 4). Flatten one end of each slightly so it will slide under the body without distorting it. Place the flattened ends of the legs under the body at 2, 4, 8, and 10 o'clock.

9. Repeat the shaping process with the remaining 11 pieces of dough.

10. Cover the turtles with towels and let rise for 45 minutes.

11. About 15 minutes before the end of rising, preheat the oven to 375°F.

12. Just before baking, cut a tic-tac-toe design ¼ inch deep on the back of each turtle with a sharp knife. Stick whole cloves into the heads for eyes if you like (diagram 5) and brush lightly with the egg wash.

13. Bake the turtles for 15 to 20 minutes, or until browned (the internal temperature should reach 190°F). Remove from the baking sheets and cool on a rack.

VARIATION

Shape the dough into either 2 round freestanding loaves and place well apart on a well-greased baking sheet, or 2 standard pan loaves (for directions, see page 59) and place in 2 well-greased loaf pans. Cover the loaves with a towel and let rise for 45 minutes. Just before baking, score the tops of the freestanding loaves ¼ inch deep in two or three places. Bake the loaves 30 to 35 minutes.

Norwegian Rugbrød

2 scant tablespoons or 2 (¼-ounce) packages active dry yeast

½ cup warm water (105° to 115°F)

2 cups warm milk (105° to 115°F)

½ cup honey

¼ cup vegetable oil

2 tablespoons molasses

2 teaspoons salt

1 tablespoon grated orange peel

1 teaspoon crushed fennel seeds

1 teaspoon anise seeds

1 cup dark rye flour

1 cup light rye flour

4 to 5 cups unbleached all-purpose flour

1 egg white beaten with 1 tablespoon cold water, for the egg wash

Makes 2 large loaves

Lightly scented with orange, fennel, and anise, this Norwegian specialty is served at the traditional smorgasbord and is also used for open-faced sandwiches. I suggest using half dark rye flour and half light rye flour, but you may use all of one kind instead. I want to thank Sissel Tangen, who not only helped test many of the recipes in this book but who, being from Norway, was an enormous help to me when I was developing this one.

1. In a large bowl, soften the yeast in the water.

2. Add the milk, honey, oil, molasses, salt, orange peel, fennel seeds, anise seeds, all of the dark and light rye flour, and 1 cup of the unbleached flour. Beat vigorously with a dough whisk or a heavy-handled spoon for 2 minutes.

3. Gradually add more of the remaining all-purpose flour, ¼ cup at a time, until the dough forms a mass and begins to pull away from the side of the bowl. Turn the dough out onto a floured work surface.

4. Knead, adding more flour, a little at a time as necessary, for 8 to 10 minutes, or until you have a smooth, elastic dough.

5. Put the dough into an oiled bowl. Turn to coat the entire ball of dough with oil. Cover with a tightly woven kitchen towel and let rise for about 1 hour, or until doubled in size.

6. To form a twisted loaf, turn the dough out onto a lightly oiled work surface and divide it in half. Shape each piece into a 24-inch rope. Fold the rope in half (diagram 1) and twist twice (diagrams 2 and 3). Put the loaf on a well-greased baking sheet. Repeat with the second rope.

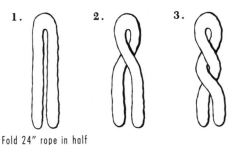

Fold 24″ rope in half

7. Cover the loaves with kitchen towels and let rise for 45 minutes.

8. About 15 minutes before the end of rising, preheat the oven to 375°F.

9. Just before baking, lightly brush each loaf with the egg wash, taking care that it doesn't drip onto the baking sheets. Bake for 30 to 35 minutes, or until the loaves are well browned and sound hollow when tapped (the internal temperature should reach 190°F). Remove from the baking sheets and cool on a rack.

VARIATION

Shape the dough into either 2 round freestanding loaves and place well apart on a well-greased baking sheet, or 2 standard pan loaves (for directions, see page 59) and place in 2 well-greased loaf pans. Cover the loaves with a towel and let rise for 45 minutes. Just before baking, score the tops of the freestanding loaves ¼ inch deep in two or three places. Bake the loaves 30 to 35 minutes.

Fennel seeds were called "meetin' seeds" by the Puritans, who nibbled them at church services to cleanse their breath.

Cracked Wheat Rolls

2 cups milk

2 cups cracked wheat (see page 6)

2 scant tablespoons or 2 (¼-ounce) packages active dry yeast

½ cup warm water (105° to 115°F)

2 tablespoons vegetable oil, plus additional as needed

¼ cup firmly packed brown sugar

½ teaspoon ground ginger

2 teaspoons salt

4 to 5 cups unbleached all-purpose flour

Makes 36 coiled dinner rolls

Soaking cracked wheat in scalded milk softens it enough so that by the time you add it to the bread dough it is the right consistency. It should give the rolls crunch without being so hard that you risk cracking a tooth!

1. Pour the milk into a medium saucepan and heat until scalded (tiny bubbles will appear all around the edge). Add the cracked wheat, stir, and cover. Let the mixture sit until it cools to 105° to 115°F.

2. In a large bowl, soften the yeast in the water.

3. Add the cracked wheat mixture, 2 tablespoons of oil, the brown sugar, ginger, salt, and 2 cups of the flour. Beat vigorously with a dough whisk or a heavy-handled spoon for 2 minutes.

4. Gradually add more of the remaining flour, ¼ cup at a time, until the dough forms a mass and begins to pull away from the side of the bowl. Turn the dough out onto a floured work surface.

5. Knead, adding more flour, a little at a time as necessary, for 8 to 10 minutes, or until you have a smooth, elastic dough.

6. Put the dough into an oiled bowl. Turn to coat the entire ball of dough with oil. Cover with a tightly woven kitchen towel and let rise for about 1 hour, or until doubled in size.

7. Turn the dough out onto a lightly oiled work surface and divide it into thirds, then divide each piece in half. Divide each of these pieces into thirds and then into halves again to make 36 pieces. Shape each piece into a rope about 8 inches long. Wind each rope into a loose coil—if the coil is wound too tightly, the middle will pop up during baking. Flatten the end and tuck it under the coil to keep it from coming uncoiled. Arrange the coils 2 inches apart on well-greased baking sheets (you'll need 3 of them). Cover with a towel and let rise for 45 minutes.

8. About 15 minutes before the end of rising, preheat the oven to 375°F.

9. Bake for 18 to 20 minutes, or until the rolls are browned on top and the internal temperature reaches 190°F. Immediately remove from the baking sheets to cool on racks. For a soft shiny crust, brush the tops of the hot rolls with oil.

VARIATION

Shape the dough into either 2 round freestanding loaves and place well apart on a well-greased baking sheet, or 2 standard pan loaves (for directions, see page 59) and place in 2 well-greased loaf pans. Cover the loaves with a towel and let rise for 45 minutes. Just before baking, score the tops of the freestanding loaves ¼ inch deep in two or three places. Bake the loaves 25 to 30 minutes.

Pecan Oat Rolls

2 scant tablespoons or
2 (¹/4-ounce) packages active
dry yeast

¹/2 cup warm water (105° to
115°F)

2 cups warm milk (105° to
115°F)

¹/4 cup solid vegetable
shortening

2 teaspoons salt

2 tablespoons honey

1¹/2 cups oat flour (see Note)

4 to 5 cups unbleached all-
purpose flour

1 cup coarsely chopped
pecans

Vegetable oil (optional)

Makes 32 rolls

Having grown up in the South, I was raised eating pecans in nearly every baked creation pulled from the oven. I have always loved the flavor and texture they give to breads.

1. In a large mixing bowl, soften the yeast in the water.

2. Add the milk, shortening, salt, honey, all of the oat flour, 2 cups of the all-purpose flour, and the pecans. Beat vigorously with a dough whisk or a heavy-handled spoon for 2 minutes.

3. Gradually add more of the remaining flour, ¹/4 cup at a time, until the dough forms a mass and begins to pull away from the side of the bowl. Turn the dough out onto a floured work surface.

4. Knead, adding more flour, a little at a time as necessary, for 8 to 10 minutes, or until you have an elastic dough and blisters begin to develop on the surface.

5. Put the dough in an oiled bowl. Turn once to coat the entire ball of dough with oil. Cover with a tightly woven kitchen towel and let rise for about 1 hour, or until doubled in size.

6. Turn the dough out onto a lightly oiled work surface and divide it in half. Divide each piece in half again, and continue this until there are 32 equal pieces. Shape each piece into a ball. Put 16 balls just touching each other in a circle on a parchment-lined or well-greased baking sheet (see diagram). Repeat with the remaining balls of dough on a second baking sheet. Alternatively, use one large baking sheet to fit all 32 balls; or shape the dough into either 2 round freestanding loaves or 2 standard pan loaves (for directions, see page 59) and place on a well-greased baking sheet or in well-greased loaf pans.

7. Cover with a towel and let rise for 45 minutes.

8. About 15 minutes before the end of rising, preheat the oven to 375°F.

9. Bake the rolls for 18 to 22 minutes, or until browned; the loaves for 25 to 30 minutes (the internal temperature should reach 190°F). If you put two baking sheets in one oven, switch their position after 10 minutes so that they bake evenly.

10. Immediately remove from the baking sheets to cool on racks. For a soft, shiny crust, brush the tops of the rolls or loaves with oil while they are still warm.

Note: Look for oat flour in health food stores. If unavailable, grind rolled oats in the blender or food processor until they resemble coarse flour. Measure them after grinding.

Only in recent years have oats been used for more than oatmeal or porridge. In the first English dictionary, Dr. Samuel Johnson defined oats as "a grain which is generally given to horses, but in Scotland supports the people." Today, oats appear in most any form of baking, but they are especially flavorful in breads.

Multi-Grain Sandwich Buns

2 scant tablespoons or 2 (¼-ounce) packages active dry yeast

3 cups warm water (105° to 115°F)

½ cup molasses, plus additional as needed

2 teaspoons salt

3 tablespoons vegetable oil

1 cup old-fashioned rolled oats

½ cup cornmeal

½ cup toasted wheat germ

1 cup rye meal or rye flour

2 cups whole wheat flour

2½ to 3½ cups unbleached all-purpose flour

Makes 32 buns

For buns with wonderful texture, use a light hand when adding the flour during kneading. Too much flour results in heavy buns. These are delicious with soups and salads, but I find them best around the holidays when there is plenty of leftover turkey in the house and homemade cranberry relish. What a great sandwich!

1. In a large bowl, soften the yeast in the water.

2. Add the molasses, salt, oil, oats, cornmeal, wheat germ, rye meal, and whole wheat flour. Beat vigorously with a dough whisk or a heavy-handled spoon for 2 minutes.

3. Gradually add some of the unbleached flour, ¼ cup at a time, until the dough forms a mass and begins to pull away from the side of the bowl. Turn the dough out onto a floured work surface.

4. Knead, adding more flour, a little at a time as necessary, for 8 to 10 minutes, or until you have a smooth, elastic dough.

5. Put the dough into an oiled bowl. Turn to coat the entire ball of dough with oil. Cover with a tightly woven kitchen towel and let rise for about 1 hour, or until doubled in size.

6. Turn the dough out onto a lightly oiled work surface and divide it in half. Divide each piece in half again and continue to do this until you have 32 equal pieces. Leave half the pieces covered with a towel on the work surface. Roll each of the first 16 pieces into a ball and flatten the tops. Arrange 2 inches apart on well-greased baking sheets. Cover with a towel and let rise for 45 minutes.

7. Shape the other 16 pieces of dough as instructed above and cover to let rise.

8. About 15 minutes before the end of rising of the first batch, preheat the oven to 375°F.

9. Bake the buns for 20 to 25 minutes, or until they are browned (the internal temperature should reach 190°F). Repeat with second batch. Remove to a rack to cool. For a richer color, brush the buns while still hot with molasses.

VARIATION

Shape the dough into either 2 round freestanding loaves and place well apart on a well-greased baking sheet, or 2 standard pan loaves (for directions, see page 59) and place in 2 well-greased loaf pans. Cover the loaves with a towel and let rise for 45 minutes. Just before baking, score the tops of the freestanding loaves ¼ inch deep in two or three places. Bake the loaves 30 to 35 minutes.

Gruyère Rye Sandwich Buns

2 scant tablespoons or 2 (¼-ounce) packages active dry yeast

2½ cups warm water (105° to 115°F)

2 tablespoons vegetable oil

¼ cup honey

2 teaspoons salt

3½ to 4½ cups unbleached all-purpose flour

2 cups rye flour

8 ounces Gruyère cheese, shredded (about 2 cups)

2 large eggs, separated

Cornmeal (optional)

2 tablespoons olive oil

Makes 20 buns

Keep in mind that all cheese breads, including these buns, taste best if allowed to mellow for at least an hour after baking.

1. In a large bowl, soften the yeast in the water.

2. Add the vegetable oil, honey, salt, 1 cup of the unbleached flour, the 2 cups of rye flour, and 1 cup of the cheese. Beat vigorously with a dough whisk or a heavy-handled spoon for 2 minutes.

3. Beat the egg whites until stiff peaks form. Stir into the dough.

4. Gradually add more of the remaining flour, ¼ cup at a time, until the dough forms a mass and begins to pull away from the side of the bowl. Turn the dough out onto a floured work surface.

5. Knead, adding more flour, a little at a time as necessary, for 8 to 10 minutes, or until the dough is smooth and elastic.

6. Put the dough into an oiled bowl. Turn to coat the entire ball of dough with oil. Cover with a tightly woven kitchen towel and let rise for about 1 hour, or until doubled in size.

7. Turn the dough out onto a lightly oiled work surface, and sprinkle with the remaining 1 cup of cheese. Knead the cheese into the dough slightly—large streaks of cheese should remain visible. Cover with a towel and let rest on the work surface for 5 minutes.

8. For crisp bottom crusts, sprinkle a well-greased baking sheet lightly with cornmeal.

(continued)

9. Divide the dough in half and shape each piece into a 24-inch rope. Form into buns by cutting each rope into 10 equal pieces. Put the buns 2 inches apart on the prepared baking sheets. Flatten the tops so that they are about 2 inches high.

10. Cover the buns with a towel and let rise for 45 minutes.

11. About 15 minutes before the end of rising, preheat the oven to 400°F.

12. Just before baking, beat the egg yolks with the olive oil and brush over the tops and sides of the buns, taking care not to let the mixture drip onto the pans.

13. Bake for 15 to 18 minutes, or until well browned and the internal temperature reaches 190°F. Immediately remove from the baking sheets and cool on a rack.

VARIATION

Shape the dough into either 2 round freestanding loaves and place well apart on a well-greased baking sheet, or 2 standard pan loaves (for directions, see page 59) and place in 2 well-greased loaf pans. Cover the loaves with a towel and let rise for 45 minutes. Just before baking, score the tops of the freestanding loaves ¼ inch deep in two or three places. Bake the loaves 25 to 30 minutes.

Onion Cheese Oat Bran Buns

2 scant tablespoons or
2 (¼-ounce) packages active
dry yeast

2½ cups warm water (105° to
115°F)

1 cup oat bran

2 teaspoons salt

2 tablespoons solid vegetable
shortening

2 tablespoons sugar

10 ounces sharp Cheddar
cheese, shredded (2½ cups)

½ cup finely chopped onion

4½ to 5½ cups unbleached
all-purpose flour

Vegetable oil (optional)

Makes 18 buns

This cheese dough makes terrific hamburger as well as hot dog buns. The cheese is meant to be visible in the dough, not completely mixed into it. The mix of sharp cheese and onion gives the bread just the right bite.

1. In a large bowl, soften the yeast in the water.

2. Add the oat bran, salt, shortening, sugar, 1½ cups of the cheese, the onion, and 2 cups of the flour. Beat vigorously with a dough whisk or a heavy-handled spoon for 2 minutes.

3. Gradually add more of the remaining flour, ¼ cup at a time, until the dough begins to pull away from the side of the bowl. Turn the dough out onto a floured work surface.

4. Knead, adding more flour, a little at a time as necessary, for 8 to 10 minutes, or until you have a smooth, elastic dough and blisters begin to develop on the surface.

5. Put the dough into an oiled bowl. Turn to coat the entire ball of dough with oil. Cover with a tightly woven kitchen towel and let rise for about 1 hour, or until doubled in size.

6. Turn the dough out onto a lightly oiled work surface. Flatten the dough to a 15-inch square with your hands. Sprinkle with the remaining cheese. Roll up the dough and knead a few times, just to marble the cheese throughout the dough. Cover with a towel and let rest on the work surface for 5 minutes.

7. Divide the dough into 18 pieces by cutting it into thirds, dividing each third in half, and dividing each of the resulting 6 pieces into thirds again. For hot dog buns, roll each ball into a cylinder about 4½ inches long and flatten the cylinder until it is about ½ inch thick. For hamburger buns, roll or pat each ball into a flat disk about ½ inch thick. Put the buns on a well-greased baking sheet, about ½ inch apart. Cover with a towel and let rise for 45 minutes.

8. About 15 minutes before the end of rising, preheat the oven to 375°F.

9. Bake the buns for 15 to 20 minutes, or until they are golden brown (the internal temperature should reach 190°F). Immediately

(continued)

remove them from the baking sheet to cool on a rack. For a shiny, soft crust, brush the tops of the buns with oil while still warm.

VARIATION

Shape the dough into either 2 round freestanding loaves and place well apart on a well-greased baking sheet, or 2 standard pan loaves (for directions, see page 59) and place in 2 well-greased loaf pans. Cover the loaves with a towel and let rise for 45 minutes. Just before baking, score the tops of the freestanding loaves ¼ inch deep in two or three places. Bake the loaves 25 to 30 minutes.

6

Filled breads and pizzas are meals in themselves. As you read through these pages, you will see recipes for calzones chock full of cheeses, herbs, Italian sausage, and garlic. You will also find an Italian pane rustica and a German käsebrot—both large, cheese-filled breads that can be a main course or sliced and taken to work or school as a tasty brown-bag sandwich. Along these same lines are the recipes for Reuben bread and pizza bread: yeast breads filled with appetizing ingredients that serve the same purpose as a good sandwich. I also give recipes for feta and lamb-filled buns and for soft Asian buns filled with a gingery mixture of meat and green onions.

Making pizza dough is similar to making any other yeast dough. All you need is time; the rest is easy. But in the interest of time, I explain how to freeze the baked pizza crust for quick meals on the days you do not have time to cook but want something truly wonderful. I have also provided pizza-loving readers with my favorite tomato sauce —and lots of other ideas for delicious novelty pizzas.

Filled Breads and Pizzas

Artichoke and Red Pepper Calzone

4 red bell peppers, seeded and sliced thin (about 2 cups)

4 cloves garlic, chopped fine

1 large onion, sliced thin (about 1 cup)

5 tablespoons olive oil

1 scant tablespoon or 1 (¼-ounce) package active dry yeast

1¼ cups warm water (105° to 115°F)

1 tablespoon sugar

Salt

2½ to 3½ cups unbleached all-purpose flour

1 (6-ounce) jar marinated artichoke hearts, drained and sliced thin (about ¾ cup)

8 ounces mozzarella cheese, shredded (about 2 cups)

4 ounces feta cheese, crumbled (about 1 cup)

1 tablespoon fresh oregano leaves or 1 teaspoon dried

Ground black pepper

Makes 12

Calzone (pronounce the *e*) is a disk of dough folded around a filling and then baked. Some fillings combine meats with vegetables; others have cheeses and herbs. This recipe mixes slowly cooked onions and peppers with artichoke hearts and cheese. I prefer sweet red and yellow peppers, but you could substitute green peppers instead.

1. In a large skillet over medium-low heat, combine the peppers, half the garlic, the onion, and 2 tablespoons of the olive oil. Cook, stirring often, for about 30 minutes, until the onions and peppers are softened. Set aside to cool.

2. In a large bowl, soften the yeast in the water.

3. Add the sugar, 1 teaspoon salt, and 1½ cups of the flour to the yeast. Beat vigorously with a dough whisk or a heavy-handled spoon for 2 minutes.

4. Gradually add more of the remaining flour, ¼ cup at a time, until the dough forms a mass and begins to pull away from the side of the bowl. Turn the dough out onto a floured work surface.

5. Knead, adding more flour, a little at a time as necessary, for 8 to 10 minutes, or until you have a smooth, elastic dough and blisters begin to develop on the surface.

6. Put the dough into an oiled bowl. Turn to coat the entire ball of dough with oil. Cover with a tightly woven kitchen towel and let rise for about 1 hour, until doubled in size.

7. Meantime, in a small saucepan, combine the remaining garlic with the remaining 3 tablespoons olive oil over low heat. Simmer for 20 minutes. (Take care that the garlic does not burn; use a flame tamer if necessary.) Remove from the heat and set aside.

8. When the dough has risen, turn it out onto a lightly oiled work surface and divide it into 12 equal pieces. (You will need 2 baking sheets to make 12 calzones—if your oven is small or if you have only 1 baking sheet, see Note.) Form each piece into a ball. Cover with a towel and let rest for 5 minutes.

(continued)

9. Combine the artichokes, mozzarella, feta, oregano, and cooked pepper mixture. Season with salt and pepper. Divide into 12 equal portions.

10. Using a rolling pin, roll each ball of dough into a 6-inch round. Put a portion of the pepper mixture in the center of each round. Fold the dough over to form a semicircle and press the edges to seal.

11. Line 2 baking sheets with parchment paper, or grease them well. Put 6 calzone on each baking sheet. Cover with a towel and let rest for 25 minutes.

12. About 15 minutes before the end of the resting period, preheat the oven to 400°F. Put a shallow heavy pan on the bottom shelf of the oven.

13. Just before baking, crimp the edges of each calzone with a fork to hold the filling inside. Brush each calzone with the garlic-flavored olive oil and prick the top with a fork to allow steam to escape.

14. Put 1 cup of ice cubes in the heated pan on the bottom shelf of the oven. Immediately put the calzone in the oven and bake for 25 to 30 minutes, or until golden brown. (Testing the calzone with an instant-read thermometer does not work because there is too much filling and not enough dough.)

15. After removing the calzone from the oven, brush once again with the garlic-flavored oil. Immediately transfer from the baking sheets to a rack. Calzone are best served warm, but if you have leftovers, wrap them in plastic and store in the refrigerator for up to three days, or freeze them. Reheat calzone (thawed, if frozen) on a baking sheet set in a 350°F oven for 10 minutes.

VARIATION

Sausage, Spinach, and Cheese Calzone: Remove the skin from 1 pound of spicy Italian sausage and break the meat into chunks. Brown the sausage in a large skillet over medium-low heat. Drain on paper towels. Wipe out the skillet and add 1 large onion, sliced thin (about 1 cup), 2 tablespoons of olive oil, and 2 cloves of finely chopped garlic. Cook slowly over medium-low heat for about 30 minutes, or until the onions are softened and caramelized. Set aside to cool.

Make the dough as in the above recipe. While the dough is rising, make the filling: Remove the stems from 10 ounces (about 4 cups) of rinsed and dried fresh spinach leaves and slice the leaves into ¼-inch strips. Combine the spinach with ½ cup of thinly sliced sun-dried tomatoes, 8 ounces shredded mozzarella cheese (about 2 cups), 4 ounces finely grated Parmesan cheese (about 1 cup), 1 tablespoon fresh oregano leaves (or 1 teaspoon dried), and salt and pepper to taste. Add the cooked sausage and onions and stir well.

Meanwhile, combine 2 cloves of chopped garlic with 3 tablespoons of warm olive oil in a small saucepan and sauté gently for 20 minutes.

Divide the dough into 12 equal portions and continue with the recipe. Just before baking the calzone, brush each with the garlic-flavored oil. After removing them from the oven, brush again with the garlic-flavored oil.

Note: If you have a smaller oven, you may not be able to bake all the calzone—or the full portion in other recipes—in one batch. In that case, here's how to stagger things so that the second batch doesn't overproof and both come out perfect. Shape half the dough. Cover the remaining dough with a towel and let it rest on the the work surface for about two thirds of the cooking time for the first pan. Then shape the second batch, cover, and allow to rise.

Similarly, if you have only 1 baking sheet, it's still possible to make many of the recipes in this book that call for using 2 baking sheets. Follow the same method described above and when you get to shaping the second batch, do so on a sheet of parchment paper. When the first batch is finished, slide the parchment paper onto the baking sheet. (Of course, I heartily recommend that you purchase a second baking sheet!)

Make sure to consult the information on flour and other ingredients and on utensils (chapter 1) and the baking class on making yeast breads (chapter 2).

Greek Lamb and Feta Filled Buns

1 scant tablespoon or
1 (¼-ounce) package active
dry yeast

1¼ cups warm water (105° to
115°F)

1 tablespoon sugar

1 teaspoon salt

1 teaspoon anise seeds,
crushed in a mortar

2½ to 3½ cups unbleached
all-purpose flour

2 cups finely chopped cooked
lamb

1 teaspoon grated lemon peel

1 tablespoon fresh lemon
juice

4 ounces feta cheese,
crumbled (about 1 cup)

¼ cup thinly sliced scallions

1 large egg beaten with
1 tablespoon cold water, for
the egg wash

Sesame seeds (optional)

Makes 12 buns

These are out of this world—great to take along on a picnic, as well as to serve for supper on the patio. I love the flavor of lamb, but the buns are equally good made with beef or chicken. You could also reduce their size and serve them as hors d'oeuvres at a party.

1. In a large bowl, soften the yeast in the water.

2. Add the sugar, salt, anise seeds, and 2 cups of the flour. Beat vigorously with a dough whisk or a heavy-handled spoon for 2 minutes.

3. Gradually add more of the remaining flour, ¼ cup at a time, until the dough forms a mass and begins to pull away from the side of the bowl. Turn the dough out onto a floured work surface.

4. Knead, adding more flour, a little at a time as necessary, for 8 to 10 minutes, or until you have a smooth, elastic dough and blisters begin to develop on the surface.

5. Put the dough into an oiled bowl. Turn to coat the entire ball of dough with oil. Cover with a tightly woven kitchen towel and let rise for about 1 hour, or until doubled.

6. Turn the dough out onto a lightly oiled work surface and divide in thirds. Divide the 3 pieces in half again. Divide in half twice more, until there are 24 equal pieces.

7. Combine the lamb, lemon peel, lemon juice, feta cheese, and scallions. Divide the filling into 12 equal portions.

8. Pat or roll each piece of dough into a 5-inch round. Put a portion of filling in the center of 12 of the rounds. Top each filled round with one of the remaining rounds and press the edges firmly to seal. Arrange the buns 2 inches apart on parchment-lined or well-greased baking sheets.

9. Cover with a towel and let rise for 45 minutes.

10. About 15 minutes before the end of rising, preheat the oven to 400°F.

11. Just before baking, pierce the top of each bun with a fork or knife blade. Using your fingers or the tines of a fork, reseal the edges of the buns to make sure the filling does not come out. Brush the tops of buns with the egg wash. Sprinkle with sesame seeds, if desired.

12. Bake for 20 to 25 minutes, or until lightly browned. (Because of the filling, it is not possible to test these buns with an instant-read thermometer.) Immediately remove from the baking sheets and cool on racks. Serve fresh from the oven. Or you can freeze them, well wrapped in plastic and foil, and then thaw them and refresh for 15 minutes in a preheated 375° oven.

Never oil bread pans. Use butter, shortening, lard, or treated oil spray. The dough absorbs oil, which will most often cause the dough to stick to the pans.

Käsebrot

*1 scant tablespoon or
1 (¹/₄-ounce) package active
dry yeast*

*¹/₄ cup warm water (105° to
115°F)*

4 large eggs

*1 cup warm milk (105° to
115°F)*

2 tablespoons vegetable oil

1 teaspoon salt

2 tablespoons sugar

*3 to 4 cups unbleached all-
purpose flour*

*8 ounces Muenster cheese,
shredded (about 2 cups)*

*8 ounces Emmenthal cheese,
shredded (about 2 cups)*

*8 ounces Parmesan cheese,
grated (about 2 cups)*

¹/₂ cup chopped fresh basil

**Makes 1 large filled loaf;
serves 8 to 12**

This filled bread is a German specialty, bursting with creamy, mild Muenster and Emmenthal cheeses and spiked with a handful of sharp Parmesan. It tastes best served at room temperature and so is wonderful for picnics and tailgate parties. I also like it for supper with a simple green salad.

1. In a large bowl, soften the yeast in the water.

2. Separate 2 of the eggs, reserving the yolks for a glaze during baking. Add the milk, oil, egg whites, salt, sugar, and 2 cups of the flour to the yeast mixture. Beat vigorously with a dough whisk or a heavy-handled spoon for 2 minutes.

3. Gradually add more of the remaining flour, ¹/₄ cup at a time, until the dough forms a mass and begins to pull away from the side of the bowl. Turn the dough out onto a floured work surface.

4. Knead, adding more flour, a little at a time as necessary, for 8 to 10 minutes, or until you have a smooth, elastic dough and blisters begin to develop on the surface.

5. Put the dough into an oiled bowl. Turn to coat the entire ball of dough with oil. Cover with a tightly woven kitchen towel and let rise for about 1 hour, or until doubled in size.

6. Turn the dough out onto a lightly oiled work surface. Do not knead the dough or it will become elastic and difficult to roll. Using a rolling pin, roll the dough into a 20-inch round, so that the center is thicker than the edges. Lift the dough and drape it over the top of a well-greased 9-inch springform pan. Be careful not to puncture the dough. Cover with a towel and let rest for 5 minutes.

7. Carefully ease the dough into the pan. There should be about 2 inches of dough extending over the top edge.

8. Beat the 2 remaining eggs. Mix the cheeses with the beaten eggs and basil and spoon into the center of the dough. Bring the overhanging edges of the dough up and into the center, making 8 evenly spaced pleats. Twist the pleated dough to form a topknot. Cover with a towel and let rise for 30 minutes.

9. While the dough is rising, preheat the oven to 375°F.

10. Bake the käsebrot for 35 mintues. Beat the reserved egg yolks and brush the top of the bread with the beaten yolks. Bake for 15 minutes more, or until golden brown. Remove from the oven and cool in the pan for 15 minutes. Remove the sides and bottom of the springform. Cool the bread on a rack for at least 2 hours before cutting, to allow the cheese to set and mellow. Cut into wedges to serve.

The center of whatever you're baking should be as close to the vertical center of the oven as the racks will allow. This enhances more even baking.

Pane Rustica

¼ cup plus 3 tablespoons olive oil

6 cloves garlic

1 scant tablespoon or 1 (¼-ounce) package active dry yeast

¼ cup warm water (105° to 115°F)

1 cup warm milk (105° to 115°F)

1 teaspoon salt

3½ to 4½ cups unbleached all-purpose flour

2 cups diced mortadella sausage

1 cup shredded provolone cheese

4 cups cleaned and trimmed whole spinach leaves

1 cup ricotta cheese

½ cup coarsely chopped pitted black olives

½ cup coarsely chopped sun-dried tomatoes

1 cup thinly sliced dry salami (a little more than ¼ pound)

3 tablespoons finely chopped fresh basil or 1 tablespoon dried

1 tablespoon finely chopped fresh oregano or 1 teaspoon dried

The Italian pane rustica and the German käsebrot are both large, filled breads baked in springform pans. As a rule, the pane rustica, or country bread, is more dramatic, because it's filled with the colorful, sunny foods that make Italian cooking so marvelous.

1. Heat 3 tablespoons of olive oil in a small saucepan until hot.

2. Make a garlic paste by dropping the garlic cloves through the top of a running blender (a food processor does not work well for this). When the cloves stick to the sides of the blender, scrape them down. With the blender running, slowly add the hot olive oil through the top. You may need to scrape the sides once or twice more. The garlic should be so fine at this point that you can hardly see it. (If you do not have a blender, make the paste in a mortar with a pestle, beginning with finely chopped garlic. Gradually add drops of olive oil to the garlic until all the oil is incorporated.) Set the paste aside.

3. In a large bowl, soften the yeast in the water.

4. Add 2 teaspoons of the garlic paste, the milk, the remaining ¼ cup of olive oil, the salt, and 2 cups of the flour to the yeast. Beat vigorously with a dough whisk or a heavy-handled spoon for 2 minutes.

5. Gradually add more of the remaining flour, ¼ cup at a time, until the dough forms a mass and begins to pull away from the side of the bowl. Turn the dough out onto a floured work surface.

6. Knead, adding more flour, a little at a time as necessary, for 8 to 10 minutes, or until you have a smooth elastic dough and blisters begin to develop on the surface.

7. Put the dough into an oiled bowl. Turn to coat the entire ball of dough with oil. Cover with a tightly woven kitchen towel and let rise for about 1 hour, or until doubled in size.

8. Turn the dough out onto a lightly oiled work surface and divide it in half. Cover one piece of dough with a towel. Using a rolling pin, shape the second piece into a 16-inch round, patting and rolling the outside 5 inches so that it is thinner than the middle of the round. This prevents the top of the loaf from being too doughy.

⅓ teaspoon cracked black pepper

4 ounces mozzarella cheese, shredded (1 cup)

2 ounces Parmesan cheese, grated (½ cup)

1 large egg, beaten

Makes one 9-inch round loaf; serves 8 to 10

1.

2.

Top view

9. Brush the bottom and inside of a 9-inch springform pan with some of the remaining garlic paste. Ease the dough round into the pan, allowing the excess dough to extend over the sides. Take care not to make holes in the dough while doing this or the filling will run out.

10. Spread the mortadella evenly over the bottom of the dough. Spread the provolone evenly over the mortadella. Spread 2 cups of the spinach leaves over the provolone.

11. Combine the ricotta, olives, and sun-dried tomatoes in a small bowl. Spread this mixture over the spinach. Spread the salami over the ricotta and top with the remaining spinach.

12. Combine the basil, oregano, pepper, mozzarella, Parmesan, and beaten egg in a bowl. Spoon this mixture over the spinach layer. Using the back of a spoon, press down to compress the layers. Pleat the edge of the dough over the filling—it will not cover the top completely.

13. Preheat the oven to 400°F.

14. Cut off one third of the remaining ball of dough and set it aside, covered with a kitchen towel. Using a rolling pin, roll the remaining two thirds of dough into a 12-inch round. Lay the dough round over the filling, tucking the excess dough between the edges of the pan and the dough lining.

15. Divide the remaining piece of dough in half. Roll each piece into a 24-inch rope. Twist the ropes together (diagram 1) and lay them around the top edge of the loaf. Brush the loaf liberally with garlic paste. Cut four 1-inch slits in the top to release steam (diagram 2).

16. Bake the pane rustica for 30 minutes, until the top is evenly browned. Put the pan on a baking sheet and remove the outer ring. Bake 5 minutes more, or until the outside turns golden brown. Remove the bottom of the springform and transfer the bread to a rack to cool.

17. Brush the warm pane rustica with the remaining garlic paste. Allow to cool for at least 1 hour before cutting, so that the filling will not run out. Serve at room temperature, cut into wedges.

Reuben Bread

FOR THE BREAD

1 scant tablespoon or 1 (¼-ounce) package active dry yeast

1¼ cups warm water (105° to 115°F)

2 tablespoons solid vegetable shortening

1 cup rye flour

1½ to 2½ cups unbleached all-purpose flour

1 teaspoon salt

2 tablespoons honey

2 teaspoons caraway seeds

FOR THE FILLING

¼ cup Thousand Island dressing

2 tablespoons Dijon mustard

½ pound corned beef, finely chopped (1½ cups)

8 ounces (about 1 cup) packaged sauerkraut, well drained

12 ounces Swiss cheese, shredded (about 3 cups)

Makes 1 large loaf

Reuben sandwiches, those deliciously messy concotions of corned beef, Swiss cheese, Thousand Island dressing, sauerkraut, and rye bread, have long been a favorite of mine. I like to bake the ingredients into a loaf of rye bread for a neater, more compact version of the overloaded sandwiches served in German rathskellers. This makes them feasible for picnics, tailgating, and other events when a sloppy sandwich is definitely *not* welcome. For the filling, use either store-bought Thousand Island dressing or make your own.

1. Begin the bread by softening the yeast in the water in a large bowl.

2. Add the shortening, rye flour, 1 cup of the unbleached flour, the salt, honey, and caraway seeds. Beat vigorously with a dough whisk or heavy-handled spoon for 2 minutes.

3. Gradually add more of the remaining flour, ¼ cup at a time, until the dough forms a mass and begins to pull away from the side of the bowl. Turn the dough out onto a floured work surface.

4. Knead, adding more flour, a little at a time as necessary, for 8 to 10 minutes, or until you have a smooth, elastic dough and blisters begin to develop on the surface.

5. Put the dough into an oiled bowl. Turn to coat the entire ball of dough with oil. Cover with a tightly woven kitchen towel and let rise for about 1 hour, or until doubled in size.

6. Turn the dough out onto a lightly oiled work surface. Pat or roll it into a 10 × 25-inch rectangle.

7. Make the filling by combining the Thousand Island dressing, mustard, corned beef, sauerkraut, and 2 cups of the Swiss cheese in a bowl. Toss to mix thoroughly. Spread the corned beef mixture evenly over the dough, leaving a ½-inch border along the upper 25-inch side. Roll up tightly from the bottom starting with a long side; pinch the seam to seal. Coil the dough cylinder loosely, seam side down, and fit into a well-greased 10-inch round pan (a pizza pan works well for this). Cover with a towel and let rise for about 45 minutes, or until almost doubled in size.

8. About 15 minutes before the end of rising, preheat the oven to 375°F.

9. Just before baking, sprinkle the top of the bread with the remaining 1 cup of Swiss cheese. Bake for 35 to 40 minutes, or until golden brown.

10. Remove to a rack and cool for at least 20 minutes before slicing into wedges.

Make sure you have at least 1 inch between baking pans inside the oven, and that you have at least 1 inch between the pans and the sides of the oven. Good air circulation is vital to successful bread baking.

Asian Steamed Buns

FOR THE DOUGH

*1 scant tablespoon or
1 (¼-ounce) package active
dry yeast*

*1½ cups warm water (105° to
115°F)*

2 tablespoons sugar

*1 tablespoon vegetable
shortening*

*2½ to 3½ cups unbleached
all-purpose flour*

FOR THE FILLING

2 teaspoons sesame oil

*2 cups ground or finely
chopped raw pork, ham, or
beef*

*3 tablespoons chopped
scallions*

½ cup thinly sliced celery

*1 teaspoon peeled and finely
chopped fresh ginger*

2 cloves garlic, chopped fine

2 tablespoons honey

1 tablespoon soy sauce

3 tablespoons cold water

1 tablespoon cornstarch

Makes 12 buns

Steamed buns, a Chinese favorite, can be filled before steaming with a wide choice of ingredients. Usually the filling is spicy. Be sure all the ingredients are chopped to about the same size for even cooking and pleasant eating. The soft buns generally have about three times as much dough as filling and so make a satisfying dim sum dish: the dough tempers the spiciness of the filling so that the buns can be eaten in the morning for Chinese breakfast. If you do not have a bamboo steamer, improvise with a rack set in a large Dutch or French-style oven, or use a vegetable steamer.

1. Begin the dough by softening the yeast in the water in a large bowl.

2. Add the sugar, shortening, and 1½ cups of the flour. Beat vigorously with a dough whisk or a heavy-handled spoon for 2 minutes.

3. Gradually add more of the remaining flour, ¼ cup at a time, until the dough forms a mass and begins to pull away from the side of the bowl. Turn the dough out onto a floured work surface.

4. Knead, adding more flour, a little at a time as necessary, for 8 to 10 minutes, or until you have a smooth, elastic dough and blisters begin to develop on the surface.

5. Put the dough in an oiled bowl. Turn to coat the entire ball of dough with oil. Cover with a tightly woven kitchen towel and let rise for about 1 hour, or until doubled in size.

6. Begin the filling. In a skillet or wok, heat the sesame oil over medium-high heat. Add the meat, scallions, celery, ginger, and garlic and cook, tossing constantly, just until the meat loses its raw color.

7. Combine the honey, soy sauce, and water in a small bowl. Add the cornstarch and whisk until smooth. Pour over the meat mixture and cook, stirring constantly, for about 2 minutes or until the mixture thickens. Remove from the heat and let cool.

8. Cut twelve 3-inch rounds of parchment paper.

9. Turn the dough out onto a lightly oiled work surface and divide it into 12 equal pieces. Shape each piece into a ball. Cover with a towel and let rest on the work surface for 5 minutes.

10. Using a rolling pin, roll each piece into a 4-inch round. Divide the filling into 12 portions and put one portion in the center of each dough round. Picturing the dough round as a clock, bring up the dough at 3, 6, 9, and 12 o'clock. Then gather in the dough at 1:30, 4:30, 7:30, and 10:30. Pinch the dough firmly to seal; if it is not firmly sealed, the filling will come out during steaming. Place each bun, seam side down, on one of the prepared parchment rounds. Cover with a towel and let rest for 10 minutes on the work surface.

11. Put 1 inch of water in the bottom of a large covered pan fitted with a rack or a bamboo steamer. (If you are using a pan with a rack, you may need to raise the rack on a heatproof cup or small bowl.) Bring the water to a boil. Reduce the heat to keep the water at a simmer.

12. Carefully, so as not to burn your fingers, place as many filled buns as will fit (still on their parchment rounds) on the steamer rack and cover. If you are using a metal lid rather than a bamboo steamer, put a thick towel between the pan and the lid to absorb steam so that the liquid does not drip onto the rolls. (If your steamer is not large enough to hold all the rolls at one time, put the remaining rolls in the refrigerator while waiting to steam them. This will keep them from rising any further.) Steam for 15 to 20 minutes—the buns should be a little shiny and slightly springy to the touch.

13. Serve the buns immediately. Refrigerate any leftover buns in an airtight container for up to 3 days and steam for 12 minutes to refresh them. These buns do not freeze well.

Al Larson's Pizza Bread

1 scant tablespoon or
1 (¼-ounce) package active
dry yeast

1¼ cups warm water (105° to
115°F)

½ teaspoon sugar

2½ to 3½ cups unbleached
all-purpose flour

1 teaspoon salt

1 tablespoon olive oil

½ teaspoon garlic salt

¼ teaspoon cayenne pepper

1 tablespoon Italian
seasoning (see Note)

6 ounces provolone cheese,
shredded (about 1½ cups)

8 ounces pepperoni, sliced
thin (2 cups)

2 ounces mozzarella cheese,
shredded (about ½ cup)

Makes one 10-inch loaf

Someone once commented that I must have flour in my veins because I love to bake so much. Al Larson, a student of mine from Washington State, quickly absorbed flour into his veins, too. From the minute the dough began responding to him, he was hooked. This filled loaf, oozing with melted cheese and Italian seasonings, is one of his creations. It is great on a picnic.

1. In a large bowl, soften the yeast in the water. Add the sugar and stir until dissolved. Let sit for 10 minutes.

2. Add 1½ cups of the flour, the salt, and the olive oil. Beat vigorously with a dough whisk or heavy-handled spoon for 2 minutes.

3. Gradually add more of the remaining flour, ¼ cup at a time, until the dough forms a mass and begins to pull away from the side of the bowl. Turn the dough out onto a floured work surface.

4. Knead, adding more flour, a little at a time as necessary, for 8 to 10 minutes, or until you have a smooth, elastic dough and blisters begin to develop on the surface.

5. Put the dough into an oiled bowl. Turn to coat the entire ball of dough with oil. Cover with a tightly woven kitchen towel and let rise for about 1 hour, or until doubled in size.

6. Turn the dough out onto a lightly oiled work surface and use a rolling pin to shape it into a 10 × 25-inch rectangle. Sprinkle the dough evenly with garlic salt, cayenne pepper, Italian seasoning, and half the provolone. Spread the pepperoni and mozzarella in layers on top of the provolone and pat them lightly into place. Using your hands, roll the dough toward you to form a 25-inch cylinder. Roll the cylinder of dough into a coil that fits snugly in a well-greased 10 × 2-inch round pan (a deep-dish pizza pan works well).

7. Cover with a towel and let rise for 15 minutes.

8. While the bread is rising, preheat the oven to 375°F.

9. Bake the bread for 25 minutes. Sprinkle with the remaining provolone and return to the oven for 5 to 10 minutes more, or until the bread is golden brown and the cheese is melted. Immediately remove from the pan to cool on a rack. Allow to cool for at least 20 minutes before cutting into wedges.

Note: Italian seasoning is sold in the spice section of every supermarket—but you can create your own mixture of oregano, thyme, basil, rosemary, savory, and/or sage.

If you have a small oven or other limitations on your ability to bake on 2 or more baking sheets at the same time, see the Note on page 189.

Pizza

2 scant tablespoons or
2 (1/4-ounce) packages active
dry yeast

2 1/2 cups warm water (105° to
115°F)

2 teaspoons salt

1 tablespoon sugar

2 tablespoons olive oil

5 1/2 cups to 6 1/2 cups
unbleached all-purpose flour

Cornmeal (optional)

This recipe makes:
1 (13 × 18-inch)
  **rectangular pizza, about
  1 inch thick**
4 (14-inch) pizzas, about
  1/4 inch thick
2 (14-inch) pizzas, about
  1/2 inch thick
1 (14-inch) pizza, about
  1 inch thick
4 (12-inch) pizzas, about
  3/8 inch thick
3 (12-inch) pizzas, about
  1/2 inch thick
6 (6-inch) pizzas, about
  1/4 inch thick

If you can make yeast bread, you can make pizza crust. Once the crust is baked, it can easily be frozen and kept for as long as six months. Just be sure it is completely cool before freezing. Wrap it first in plastic and then in foil. When you want pizza, take the crust from the freezer, cover it with topping, and place it in a preheated 400°F oven for 10 minutes. No need to thaw the crust. With the following recipe, you can make a number of small pizza crusts or one or two large ones. The rectangular pizza crust is good for deep-dish, or Chicago-style, pizza. Flexibility and imagination are all you need for good pizza!

This pizza crust can also be made in the morning, prebaked (see step 12), and left on a rack covered with a tightly woven kitchen towel until you are ready to top it and finish the baking in the evening. And of course, you do not have to prebake the crust at all. Simply spread the topping on the raw shell and bake the pizza for 20 to 25 minutes at 400°F.

I like to prebake my pizza because I love crisp crust. Using a pizza screen or heated pizza stone makes the crust even crisper than when it is prebaked on a baking sheet or round pizza pan. The choice is yours and whatever you decide, once you and your family sample homemade pizza it will be hard to go back to home delivery from the local pizzeria!

Following this recipe are ways to vary the flavor of the crust so that you can make cornmeal pizza crust, semolina pizza crust, whole wheat pizza crust, and so on. On page 207 is a recipe for my favorite tomato pizza sauce. I have included ideas for other toppings on page 204.

1. In a large bowl, soften the yeast in the water.

2. Add the salt, sugar, oil, and 3 cups of the flour. Beat vigorously with a dough whisk or a heavy-handled spoon for 2 minutes.

3. Gradually add more of the remaining flour, 1/4 cup at a time, until the dough forms a mass and begins to pull away from the side of the bowl. Turn the dough out onto a floured work surface.

4. Knead, adding more flour, a little at a time as necessary, for 8 to 10 minutes, or until you have a smooth, elastic dough and blisters begin to develop on the surface.

5. Put the dough into an oiled bowl. Turn to coat the entire ball of dough with oil. Cover with a tightly woven kitchen towel and let rise for about 1 hour, or until doubled in size.

6. If you wish to use a baking stone for an especially crisp, dry crust, put the stone in the center of the oven while the dough is rising and preheat at 400°F for at least 30 minutes. This heats the stone all the way through. If you are not using a stone, preheat the oven to 400°F about 15 minutes before shaping the dough, as directed in step 10.

7. When the dough has risen, turn it out onto a lightly oiled work surface. Divide it according to the number of pizzas you wish to make and shape into balls.

8. Shape the dough. If you use a rolling pin, you will have a crust of uniform thickness and texture. If you prefer an irregular crust with an uneven texture, pat the dough into shape with the heel of your hand. Or you can shape the dough into a disk 2 to 3 inches smaller than you wish and toss the dough into the air with a spinning motion until the disk reaches the appropriate size. This takes coordination, practice, and a good sense of humor. The finished dough will taste no different.

9. Sprinkle a pizza pan with cornmeal to give added crispness to the crust and help prevent it from sticking. If you are baking directly on a baking stone, liberally sprinkle your work surface with cornmeal so that you can more easily lift the crust with a peel (or piece of cardboard) and slide it onto the stone—the coarseness of the cornmeal makes the dough easy to slide onto and off the peel. If you do not like the gritty texture of cornmeal, eliminate it or use semolina flour. The dough can be put directly into well-greased pans or, if you are using a baking stone, you can shape the dough on parchment paper and put it and the paper onto the stone.

10. Cover the dough with a kitchen towel and let it rest for 25 minutes. About 15 minutes before the end of the resting period, preheat the oven to 400°F.

11. Just before baking, prick the dough in several places with a fork, toothpick, or the point of a knife.

(continued)

PIZZA TOPPING IDEAS

Cheeses

mozzarella
Gouda
Swiss
provolone
Cheddar
goat cheese
Monterey Jack

Meats

browned sausage meat
browned ground beef
salami
pepperoni
thinly sliced and cooked
  Canadian bacon

Vegetables

black or green olives
raw or roasted pepper
  slices
raw or sautéed mushrooms
onions
sun-dried tomatoes

12. Put the crust in the preheated oven and bake for 10 minutes. Check the crust after 5 minutes. If large bubbles have formed, cover your hand with a clean towel and press the air out of the bubbles. The crust should be slightly firm and pale at the end of the 10 minutes. Immediately remove the crust from the pan and cool it on a rack to prevent it from becoming soggy.

13. Top the prebaked crust with the desired sauce and topping. Put the pizza on a screen, back into a pan, or on a preheated baking stone. You may also put it directly on the oven shelf—this gives a crisp crust, but toppings may drip onto the bottom of the oven.

14. Bake the pizza and topping for 10 minutes for regular pizza, 15 to 18 minutes for deep-dish pizza.

VARIATIONS

Cornmeal Crust: Substitute 1 cup of cornmeal (yellow or white) for 1 cup all-purpose flour.

Semolina Crust: Substitute 2 cups semolina flour for 2 cups all-purpose flour.

Whole Wheat Crust: Substitute 2 cups whole wheat flour for 2 cups all-purpose flour.

Rye Crust: Substitute 1½ cups rye flour for 1½ cups all-purpose flour.

Boboli-Style Crust: Add 1 cup shredded mozzarella or grated Parmesan cheese during the kneading process. Boboli should be shaped about ½ inch thick and allowed to rise for 45 minutes rather than resting for 25 minutes. The crust can be prebaked as a pizza crust or baked completely for 15 to 18 minutes. It is perfect for Cold Vegetable Pizza (see page 206).

PIZZA VARIATIONS

Mexican Pizza: Spread 2 cups of taco sauce or salsa over a 14-inch prebaked cornmeal pizza crust. Top with 1 cup of shredded Cheddar, 1 cup of shredded Monterey Jack, 2 cups of chopped fresh tomatoes, ½ cup of sliced green olives, ½ cup of sliced black olives, and ½ cup of drained chopped canned green chilies. Bake for 10 minutes at 400°F, or for 20 minutes if the pizza crust is not prebaked. Spread the warm pizza with 1 cup of sour cream and top with slices of avocado.

Greek Pizza: Spread 1½ cups Best-Ever Pizza Sauce (page 207) over a 14-inch prebaked semolina pizza crust. Sprinkle with 2 cups of shredded mozzarella, 2 cups of sautéed chopped onions, 2 cups of sautéed chopped green peppers, ½ cup of halved pitted Greek olives, and 1 cup of crumbled feta cheese. Bake for 10 minutes at 400°F or for 20 minutes if the pizza crust is not prebaked.

Blue Cheese and Walnut Pizza: Spread the contents of an 8-ounce package of softened cream cheese over a 14-inch prebaked pizza crust. Sprinkle 1 cup of crumbled blue cheese and ¾ cup of coarsely chopped walnuts over the cream cheese. Bake for 10 minutes at 400°F or for 20 minutes if the pizza crust is not prebaked.

Pesto, Pear, and Brie Pizza: Spread ½ cup of homemade or good-quality store-bought pesto over a 14-inch pizza crust. Lay thin slices of pear over the crust with the wider parts closest to the edges of the pizza. Top evenly with about 1 cup of diced ripe Brie. Bake for 10 minutes at 400°F or for 20 minutes if the pizza crust is not prebaked.

Fresh Tomato and Basil Pizza: Sprinkle the crust with 2 cups shredded cheese (provolone is my favorite, but any cheese is good) or spread with a soft cheese (chèvre, Brie, etc.). Alternately lay thinly sliced fresh tomatoes with fresh basil leaves over the cheese, overlapping each slightly. Brush liberally with olive oil. Bake 10 minutes at 400°F or for 20 minutes if the pizza crust is not prebaked.

Goat Cheese and Sun-dried Tomato Pizza: Sprinkle the crust with 2 cups shredded mozzarella cheese, ½ cup thinly sliced sun-dried tomatoes, and 1½ cups diced chèvre, Montrachet, or Bucheron (goat cheese). Bake 10 minutes at 400°F or for 20 minutes if the pizza crust is not prebaked. (Once I forgot the mozzarella: the pizza was entirely different, yet extremely good.)

Cold Vegetable Pizza

1 (12-inch) baked pizza crust (see page 202)

3 ounces cream cheese, softened

$^1/_4$ cup plain yogurt or mayonnaise

1 tablespoon grainy mustard

$^1/_4$ teaspoon garlic powder

Salt and pepper to taste

$^1/_4$ cup fresh dillweed

$^1/_2$ cup broccoli florets, broken into small pieces

1 cup shredded or finely chopped carrots

$^1/_2$ cup pitted black olive halves

$^1/_4$ cup thinly sliced sun-dried tomatoes

4 ounces Cheddar cheese, shredded (about 1 cup)

Makes one 12-inch pizza

My son Mark was introduced to the joys of cold pizza the summer he worked in the kitchen at Camp Orkila on the San Juan Islands in Washington State. Once you learn how to make pizza crust, keep an extra one or two in the freezer to use for this versatile light supper, particularly when the weather is hot and no one feels like spending much time in the kitchen. I usually blanch the vegetables to improve their color before chilling them to crisp them. However, you could substitute another herb and yellow summer squash or zucchini, tomatoes, radishes, or bell peppers.

1. Preheat the oven to 400°F.

2. Bake the crust for 5 minutes to refresh it and make it crisp. Transfer the crust from the oven to a rack to prevent it from steaming and becoming soggy.

3. In a small bowl, combine the cream cheese, yogurt, mustard, garlic powder, salt, and pepper. Mix until smooth. Spread evenly over the warm pizza crust.

4. Sprinkle the dill, broccoli, carrots, olives, tomatoes, and Cheddar over the cream cheese. Serve at room temperature.

Best-Ever Pizza Sauce

¼ cup olive oil

1 cup finely chopped onion

6 cloves garlic, finely chopped

3 (1-pound) cans tomatoes (about 8 cups), chopped and undrained

3 tablespoons chopped fresh oregano or 1 tablespoon crushed dried leaves

½ teaspoon sugar

½ teaspoon salt

½ teaspoon cracked pepper

1 (6-ounce) can tomato paste

Maskes about 8 cups

Basic tomato and cheese pizza remains a favorite with my family, and I usually keep a portion of this sauce frozen along with several baked pizza crusts. Spoon premeasured portions of sauce into a zip-style freezer bag; when it's time to eat, defrost it in the bag (5 minutes in the microwave). Spread the sauce on the frozen, pre-baked pizza crust, top it with cheese and anything else you desire, pop into a 400°F oven, and 10 minutes later it's pizza!

1. Put the olive oil in a large, heavy pan over medium heat. Add the onions and garlic and cook for about 5 minutes, or until the onions are transparent.

2. Add the tomatoes, basil, oregano, sugar, salt, pepper, and tomato paste. Stir to combine and bring to a boil. Reduce heat to low and simmer uncovered for 1 hour, stirring occasionally.

3. Remove the sauce from the heat and cool before using.

7

The yeast breads in this chapter are perfect for all those times when you want something sweet and a candy bar or piece of cake simply won't do. For me, sweet yeast breads always outrank more ordinary confections. They combine the warm, soul-satisfying tastes and textures of bread with flavors we all cherish: cinnamon, orange, nuts, butter, fruit, honey . . . and on and on.

I begin this chapter with Gooey Cinnamon Rolls, follow these with more breakfast treats, and then offer a selection of brunch breads, coffee breads, and tea breads. All can be mixed and matched. Do not hesitate to serve a tea bread for breakfast, Buttery Brunch Twists for tea, or Orange Macadamia Swirl Loaf with morning coffee.

I end the chapter with a collection of holiday breads. The holidays are a special time for baking. As we work in the kitchen, with the lovely aroma of holiday breads wafting from the oven, we often are overcome with feelings of well-being. Nothing is more gratifying during these winter celebrations than baking something from the heart for our friends and loved ones.

Sweet Yeast Breads

(continued)

Gooey Cinnamon Rolls

FOR THE DOUGH

1 scant tablespoon or 1 (¼-ounce) package active dry yeast

¼ cup warm water (105° to 115°F)

1 cup warm milk (105° to 115°F)

3 tablespoons solid vegetable shortening

2 large eggs, at room temperature

¼ teaspoon ground ginger

1 teaspoon salt

3½ to 4½ cups unbleached all-purpose flour

FOR THE SYRUP

2 tablespoons unsalted butter

¾ cup firmly packed brown sugar

½ cup light corn syrup

FOR THE FILLING

4 tablespoons (½ stick) unsalted butter, melted

1 tablespoon cinnamon

¾ cup firmly packed brown sugar

(continued)

These luscious cinnamon rolls are hard to resist. The ginger in the recipe lightens the dough—it adds no flavor. The rolls are baked in syrup and the pan inverted after baking, so that the syrup drips down the sides of the rolls.

1. Begin the dough by softening the yeast in the water in a large bowl.

2. Add the milk, shortening, eggs, ginger, salt, and 2 cups of the flour. Beat vigorously with a dough whisk or a heavy-handled spoon for 2 minutes.

3. Gradually add more of the remaining flour, ¼ cup at a time, until the dough forms a mass and begins to pull away from the side of the bowl. Turn the dough out onto a floured work surface.

4. Knead, adding more flour, a little at a time as necessary, for 8 to 10 minutes, or until you have a smooth, elastic dough and blisters begin to develop on the surface.

5. Put the dough into an oiled bowl. Turn to coat the entire ball of dough with oil. Cover with a tightly woven kitchen towel and let rise for about 1 hour, or until doubled in size.

6. Make the syrup by melting the 2 tablespoons of butter in a small saucepan. Add the brown sugar and corn syrup and stir to combine. Bring the mixture to a boil over medium heat. Immediately remove from the heat and divide evenly into 2 well-greased 9 × 2-inch round pans. Set aside to cool.

7. Turn the dough out onto a lightly oiled work surface. Using a rolling pin, shape it into an 18 × 24-inch rectangle.

8. Prepare the filling by brushing the 4 tablespoons of melted butter over the entire surface of the dough, leaving a ½-inch border along the upper long side to make it easier to seal after rolling. Sprinkle the dough evenly with the cinnamon and brown sugar and, if desired, with the raisins and nuts.

9. Using your hands and starting at the filled edge, roll the dough to form a 24-inch cylinder. Pinch all along the edge to seal. Cut the cylinder into 16 equal pieces (see Note).

(continued)

1 cup raisins (optional)

1 cup chopped nuts (optional)

Makes 16 large rolls

Apple Fritters

1 scant tablespoon or 1 (¼-ounce) package active dry yeast

¼ cup warm water (105° to 115°F)

¾ cup warm milk (105° to 115°F)

3 tablespoons granulated sugar

1½ teaspoons ground cinnamon

½ teaspoon salt

10. Arrange 8 rolls in each pan on top of the cooled syrup, cut side up. Cover with a towel and let rise for about 50 minutes, until almost doubled.

11. About 15 minutes before the end of rising, preheat the oven to 350°F.

12. Bake the rolls for 25 to 30 minutes, or until they are pale gold (the internal temperature should reach 190°F). Let them cool in the pans for 3 minutes and then invert onto plates. Leave the pans on top of the rolls for another 2 minutes before removing to give the syrup opportunity to drip down the sides.

Note: I find the best way to cut rolled breads so that they keep their shape is with a 14-inch length of plain, unwaxed dental floss. Wrap the floss around the index finger of each hand and pull taut. Lightly score the top of the cylinder with the floss so that you know where to cut. Slip the floss under the roll at the scoring, bring up the ends, cross them, and pull them straight out to the sides.

When we lived in Seattle, a Saturday morning trip to the Pike Place Market was a weekly highlight. I always made a point of stopping by the Three Girls Bakery, where the owner, Zelda, banters with regular and walk-in customers alike. I would relish the opportunity to have a quick breakfast of hot coffee and deep-fried apple fritters—made with marvelous Washington State apples—while catching up on the local gossip. I have re-created the fritter recipe here. The fritters are best made with the freshest tart apples you can buy. Granny Smiths are always a good choice.

1. In a large bowl, soften the yeast in the water.

2. Add the milk, granulated sugar, cinnamon, salt, and 2 cups of the flour. Beat vigorously with a dough whisk or a heavy-handled spoon for 2 minutes.

3. Add the apples and mix well.

3½ to 4½ cups unbleached all-purpose flour

2 cups finely chopped tart apples, such as Granny Smith

Peanut oil, for deep frying

2 cups confectioners' sugar

4 to 6 tablespoons milk

Makes about 48 fritters

4. Gradually add more of the remaining flour, ¼ cup at a time, until the dough begins to pull away from the side of the bowl. The dough will form a ball in the center of the bowl when the flour is added but, as you continue to stir, it will spread out again and stick to the bowl, rather like a very thick batter.

5. Cover the dough with a tightly woven kitchen towel and let it rise for about 1 hour, or until doubled in size.

6. About 10 minutes before the end of rising, pour the oil into a deep, heavy 10- or 12-inch pan to a depth of 2 inches. Place over medium heat and heat until it is hot but not smoking (375°F on a deep-frying thermometer).

7. Without deflating the dough, drop it by tablespoons into the hot oil, making only a few fritters at a time. Cook for 3 minutes, until golden brown on one side; turn and cook for 2 more minutes. Remove the fritters with a slotted spoon as they are cooked and drain on paper towels.

8. In a shallow bowl, combine the confectioners' sugar with enough milk to make a thick, runny icing about the consistency of honey. Dip the fritters in the icing and turn them to glaze both sides. Drain on a wire rack set over parchment or wax paper to catch the icing drips.

Note: You may choose to drizzle pure maple syrup over the fritters instead of icing them, or simply pop the warm fritters in a bag full of confectioners' sugar and shake gently to coat.

The center of whatever you're baking should be as close to the vertical center of the oven as the racks will allow. This enhances more even baking.

Jam Coils

2 scant tablespoons or
2 (¼-ounce) packages active
dry yeast

½ cup warm water (105° to
115°F)

1 cup warm milk (105° to
115°F)

½ cup solid vegetable
shortening

2 large eggs, at room
temperature

2 teaspoons salt

½ teaspoon ground ginger

½ cup granulated sugar

5 to 6 cups unbleached all-
purpose flour

½ cup jam or preserves, such
as raspberry, strawberry,
blueberry, or peach

1 cup confectioners' sugar

4 to 6 tablespoons heavy
cream

Makes 24 rolls

Using different flavors of jams and preserves makes a tasty assortment of coiled breakfast rolls. I do not recommend jelly, since it
melts and toughens in the oven. For more variety, substitute a cup
of whole wheat flour for a cup of all-purpose—the bread will taste
a little nutty. As with the cinnamon rolls on page 211, I include
ginger in the recipe to lighten and condition the dough—it adds
no flavor.

1. In a large bowl, soften the yeast in the water.

2. Add the milk, shortening, eggs, salt, ginger, granulated
sugar, and 3 cups of the flour. Beat vigorously with a dough whisk
or a heavy-handled spoon for 2 minutes.

3. Gradually add more of the remaining flour, ¼ cup at a
time, until the dough forms a mass and begins to pull away from
the side of the bowl. Turn the dough out onto a floured work
surface.

4. Knead, adding more flour, a little at a time as necessary,
for 8 to 10 minutes, or until you have a smooth, elastic dough and
blisters begin to develop on the surface.

5. Put the dough into an oiled bowl. Turn to coat the entire
ball of dough with oil. Cover with a tightly woven kitchen towel
and let rise for about 1 hour, or until doubled in size.

6. Turn the dough out onto a lightly oiled work surface and
divide it into thirds, then divide each third in half. Divide the
pieces in half two more times to make 24 equal pieces. Using your
hands, roll each piece into a 20-inch rope. Flatten the ends of the
rope by pushing down on each end. On a parchment-lined or well-
greased baking sheet, coil each rope very loosely, beginning at one
flattened end. As you coil the rope, leave a little space so that it
does not touch itself—if the dough is coiled too tightly, the center
will fill in and there will be no space for the jam. Tuck the other
flattened end under the coil to prevent it from coming loose. Cover
the coils with a towel and let rise for about 50 minutes, or until
doubled in size.

7. About 15 minutes before the end of rising, preheat the
oven to 375°F.

8. Just before baking, make a deep indentation in the center of each coil with your thumb or finger. Press all the way down to the bottom and make a hole about ¼ inch deep and 1 inch in diameter. Fill each indentation with 1 teaspoon of jam. If the hole is not large enough, when the dough rises it will squeeze the jam out.

9. Bake the coils for 15 to 18 minutes, or until they are lightly browned (the internal temperature should reach 190°F). Immediately remove from the baking sheets and cool on a rack for 20 minutes.

10. Combine the confectioners' sugar with sufficient heavy cream to make it the consistency of honey. Drizzle the icing over the tops of the coils.

If you have a small oven or other limitations on your ability to bake on 2 or more baking sheets at the same time, see the Note on page 189.

Danish Pastries

FOR THE PASTRIES

1 pound (4 sticks) unsalted butter, at room temperature

4½ to 5½ cups unbleached all-purpose flour

2 scant tablespoons or 2 (¼-ounce) packages active dry yeast

1½ cups warm water (105° to 115°F)

½ cup granulated sugar

1 teaspoon salt

½ teaspoon ground cardamom

1 teaspoon vanilla extract

2 large eggs plus 2 egg yolks, at room temperature

Fillings (see page 221)

1 egg, well beaten

FOR THE GLAZE

2 cups confectioners' sugar

1 teaspoon vanilla extract

About 4 tablespoons heavy cream or fresh orange juice

Makes approximately 48 pastries

Danish pastries are a cross between a buttery, flaky croissant and a sweet bread. When making these pastries, be sure to use unsalted butter, keep the dough chilled, and work in a cool environment. It is also important to let the dough rise in a cool place. Otherwise, the butter melts, leaving the pastries heavy and greasy. I have provided recipes for fillings on page 221. Use the ones that most appeal to you for the pastry shapes that call for them. In Denmark, these pastries are called Viennese pastries, because they were developed by Austrian bakers who were imported to Denmark some time in the last century to replace striking local pastry chefs.

These pastries freeze very well.

1. Cut a piece of parchment paper 36 inches long and 15 inches wide. Put the paper on the work surface with the long edge facing you and make creases 3½ inches from the top and bottom edges. Crease the paper 10 inches from the left and right sides.

2. Combine the butter with ½ cup of the flour. Spread this mixture into the 8 × 16-inch rectangle in the center of the creased parchment paper (follow diagrams 1–3 on page 99). Fold in the sides of the paper at the creases, and then fold in the top and bottom creases. Flip the packet over on the work surface. Using a rolling pin, carefully roll the butter inside the packet to an even thickness. Hold the packet up to the light to check for thick or thin places.

3. Lay the butter packet flat on a refrigerator shelf to chill while working with the dough.

4. In a large bowl, soften the yeast in the water.

5. Add 2 cups flour, the granulated sugar, salt, cardamom, vanilla extract, 2 eggs, and the egg yolks to the yeast. Beat vigorously with a dough whisk or a heavy-handled spoon for 2 minutes.

6. Add more of the remaining flour, ¼ cup at a time, until the dough begins to pull away from the side of the bowl. At this stage, the dough should be very soft. Flour your hands and break off a marble-size piece of dough. If it rolls into a ball before disintegrating, it is the right consistency. Adding too much flour at this point makes it hard to roll the pastries later. Cover the bowl lightly with plastic wrap and a tightly woven kitchen towel. Refrigerate for 30 minutes.

7. On a well-floured work surface, using a floured rolling pin, roll the dough into a 9 × 24-inch rectangle. Remove the butter packet from the refrigerator and lay it over two thirds of the dough, leaving one third uncovered (again, follow diagrams 4–6 on page 99). Fold over the unbuttered third and then the buttered third so that you have 3 layers of dough alternating with 2 layers of butter. Give the dough a quarter turn so that the longer edge is facing you.

8. Take a rolling pin and press it firmly on one of the short edges of the dough (diagram 7, page 100). Make sure the board is covered with flour or the dough will tear and the butter will break through. (If this happens, pat the butter with flour and continue.) Lift the rolling pin and press down about 2 inches from the first pressing. Be sure to press the dough, not roll it. Continue pressing at 2-inch intervals across the dough (diagram 8, page 100).

9. Lift the dough carefully to make sure there is still a good coating of flour underneath. Using the rolling pin, press it across the dough as before but in the opposite direction. The dough now has trenches in two directions (diagram 9, page 100). This waffling technique distributes the butter evenly without breaking the dough packet.

10. Roll the waffled dough into a 10 × 18-inch rectangle, then fold the dough into thirds. Cover with plastic wrap and a tightly woven kitchen towel and refrigerate for 20 minutes.

11. Waffle, roll, fold, and chill the dough two more times, as described above, making sure the work surface is well floured. Cover with plastic wrap and a towel and refrigerate for 30 minutes or overnight. (Both coverings are necessary to protect the dough from forming a crust in the refrigerator.)

12. Turn the dough out onto a lightly oiled work surface. Shape it into one of the following shapes. Then proceed to step 17.

(continued)

13. For *coils* (diagrams 1–5): Roll the dough into a 12-inch square and cut it into twenty-four 12-inch strips. Following the diagrams, coil the dough into the desired shape. When you coil the dough, make sure the cut side is up so that the layers of dough are facing you.

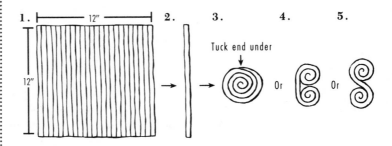

14. For *twists* (diagrams 6–10): Roll the dough into a 12 × 24-inch rectangle. Cut the dough into twenty-four 12-inch strips. Holding one end of a strip firmly, twist the other end of the dough 8 times. Twist the remaining strips in the same way.

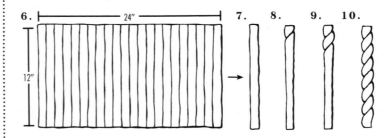

15. For *envelopes, pillows, triangles, foldovers, cockscombs,* and *pinwheels:* Roll the dough into a 9 × 24-inch rectangle. Cut the dough into twenty-four 3-inch squares (diagram 11). Following diagrams 12–32, fill with the filling of your choice and form the dough into desired shapes. Use about 1 tablespoon of filling for each pastry. Brush the edges of the dough with the beaten egg and press together to seal.

(continued)

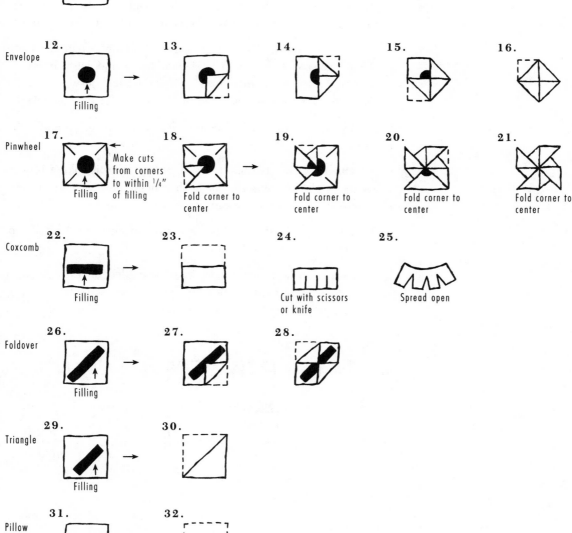

11. 3″
3″

Envelope 12. Filling → 13. 14. 15. 16.

Pinwheel 17. Filling — Make cuts from corners to within ¼″ of filling 18. Fold corner to center → 19. Fold corner to center 20. Fold corner to center 21. Fold corner to center

Coxcomb 22. Filling → 23. 24. Cut with scissors or knife 25. Spread open

Foldover 26. Filling → 27. 28.

Triangle 29. Filling → 30.

Pillow 31. Filling → 32.

16. For *bear claws* (diagrams 33–37): Roll the dough into an 18 × 16-inch rectangle. Cut the dough into twenty-four 2 × 6-inch rectangles. Following the diagrams, fill with the filling of your choice and shape the claws, putting about 1 tablespoon of filling at the fold line. Brush the edges of the dough with the beaten egg and press together to seal and then cut according to the diagram.

17. Arrange the pastries 3 inches apart on parchment-lined baking sheets. Cover with a kitchen towel and let rise for 30 minutes at room temperature—this should not be warmer than 75°F or the butter will melt and the pastries will fall when baked.

18. About 15 minutes before the end of rising, preheat the oven to 375°F.

19. Bake the pastries for 20 minutes, or until golden brown. Because of the amount of fat in the dough, an instant-read thermometer is not a good test for doneness.

20. Immediately remove the pastries from the baking sheets and cool on a rack for 20 minutes.

21. To make the glaze, combine the confectioners' sugar with the vanilla extract and enough heavy cream or orange juice to give it the consistency of honey. Drizzle the glaze over the pastries.

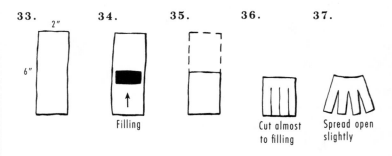

33.   34.   35.   36.   37.

Filling   Cut almost   Spread open
to filling   slightly

Danish Pastry Fillings

ALMOND PASTE FILLING

1 cup blanched whole
almonds, ground very fine

¾ cup confectioners' sugar

1 large egg white

1 teaspoon almond extract

1 teaspoon grated lemon peel

Pinch of salt

PRUNE FILLING

8 ounces (about 2 cups)
prunes, finely chopped

½ teaspoon grated lemon
peel

1 teaspoon grated orange
peel

¼ teaspoon grated nutmeg

3 tablespoons unsalted
butter, melted

½ cup finely chopped walnuts

2 teaspoons granulated sugar

CHEESE FILLING

8 ounces cream cheese, at
room temperature

½ cup creamed cottage
cheese

1 large egg yolk

½ cup confectioners' sugar

1 tablespoon grated lemon
peel

**Each recipe makes enough to
fill about 24 pastries**

Combine all the ingredients in a bowl and work to a stiff paste. Alternatively, combine the ingredients in a food processor and process just until combined to make a stiff paste. Store in the refrigerator. This filling freezes well.

Put all the ingredients in a bowl and stir to combine. Alternatively, combine the ingredients in a food processor and process just until combined. Store in the refrigerator. This filling freezes well.

Put all the ingredients in a bowl and stir to combine. For best results, make this filling by hand—it becomes too runny if made in a food processor. Store in the refrigerator for up to 1 week. The filling does not freeze well.

Savarin

FOR THE DOUGH

*1 scant tablespoon or
1 (¼-ounce) package active
dry yeast*

*¼ cup warm water (105° to
115°F)*

*1½ cups unbleached all-
purpose flour*

3 tablespoons sugar

½ teaspoon salt

*3 large eggs, at room
temperature*

*8 tablespoons (1 stick)
unsalted butter, at room
temperature*

FOR THE SYRUP

1 cup boiling water

¾ cup sugar

2 tablespoons lemon juice

*¼ cup Kirsch or other
cherry-flavored liqueur*

FOR THE ASSEMBLY

¼ cup red currant jelly

2 pints strawberries

*Whipped heavy cream,
crème fraîche, or fresh
yogurt*

Makes 1 large loaf

The savarin is a rich dessert or brunch bread made by the batter method and soaked in syrup. It is baked in a large ring mold called a savarin, named after the famous French food writer Brillat-Savarin. Unlike ordinary tube and Bundt pans, the savarin's tube is about five inches in diameter so that the hole in the center of the baked bread is generous enough to fill with fresh fruit. Strawberries are conventional, but peaches, nectarines, blueberries, and raspberries are tasty, too.

1. Begin the dough by softening the yeast in the warm water in a large bowl.

2. Add the flour, sugar, salt, and eggs. Beat vigorously with a dough whisk or heavy-handled spoon for 2 minutes.

3. Cut the butter into 8 pieces. Add to the yeast mixture, 1 piece at a time, beating well after each addition.

4. When the butter is thoroughly incorporated, cover the bowl with plastic wrap and a tightly woven kitchen towel, and refrigerate for at least 2 and up to 24 hours. (Both coverings are necessary to protect the dough in the refrigerator. If the dough rises at room temperature, the butter absorbs flour and the finished bread is heavy.)

5. Stir the dough and scrape it into a well-greased 6-cup savarin mold. Cover with a towel and let rise for 1½ hours at room temperature (no cooler than 65°F and no warmer than 80°F). Time the rising rather than watching the dough; because of the eggs and butter, this dough does not rise like regular yeast dough.

6. About 15 minutes before the end of rising, preheat the oven to 375°F.

7. Bake the savarin for 25 to 30 minutes, or until it is well browned and shrinks slightly from the mold (the internal temperature should reach 190°F). Watch the bread carefully toward the end of the baking time—it browns quickly. If it becomes too brown before it is done, cover loosely with foil, shiny side up.

8. Immediately remove the bread from the mold to cool on a rack for 10 minutes while you make the syrup. Reserve the mold; you will be using it again.

9. Combine the boiling water, sugar, and lemon juice in a heavy saucepan and stir until the sugar dissolves. Bring the mixture to a rolling boil over medium-high heat. Lower the heat and cook slowly for 8 minutes. Remove from the heat and add the Kirsch.

10. Put ½ cup of syrup in the savarin mold. Return the savarin to the mold. Spoon the remaining syrup over the savarin until it is completely absorbed. Let sit for 20 minutes.

11. Remove the savarin from the mold. Heat the jelly until melted and brush it on all sides of the savarin. Serve with fresh strawberries and dollops of cream, crème fraîche, or yogurt.

Make sure you have at least 1 inch between baking pans inside the oven, and that you have at least 1 inch between the pans and the sides of the oven. Good air circulation is vital to successful bread baking.

Buttery Brunch Twists

*1 scant tablespoon or
1 (¼-ounce) package active
dry yeast*

*½ cup warm water (105° to
115°F)*

*4½ to 5½ cups unbleached
all-purpose flour*

1 teaspoon salt

*6 large eggs, at room
temperature*

*8 tablespoons (1 stick)
unsalted butter, at room
temperature*

*½ cup very finely chopped
pecans*

*½ cup firmly packed brown
sugar*

*2 teaspoons ground
cinnamon*

¾ cup red currant jelly

1 cup confectioners' sugar

About 2 tablespoons milk

Makes 24 twists

These ultra-rich twists are perfect to serve for brunch or any time you want to splurge—how about afternoon tea in front of the fire? I have made them with currant jelly, but you can use others to vary the recipe. Orange marmalade gives them a pleasantly tart flavor. For a whimsical presentation, stand them on end in a basket or flowerpot.

1. In a large bowl, soften the yeast in the water.

2. Add 2 cups of the flour, the salt, eggs, and butter. Beat vigorously with a dough whisk or heavy-handled spoon for 2 minutes.

3. Gradually add more of the remaining flour, ¼ cup at a time, until the dough begins to pull away from the side of the bowl into a firm ball.

4. Cover the bowl lightly with plastic wrap and a tightly woven kitchen towel. Refrigerate for at least 2 and up to 24 hours. (Both coverings are necessary to protect the dough from forming a crust in the refrigerator.)

5. In a small bowl, combine the pecans, brown sugar, and cinnamon. Set aside.

6. Remove the dough from the refrigerator and turn out onto a lightly oiled work surface. Using a rolling pin, roll the dough into a 12 × 24-inch rectangle. Spread the pecan mixture over two thirds of the dough, leaving a ½-inch border around the edges. Fold the uncovered third of dough over one third of the filling. Press lightly to seal the edges and compress the filling. Fold the dough in half so that you have 3 layers of dough and 2 layers of filling.

7. Cover the dough with a towel and let rest on the work surface for 10 minutes.

8. Roll the dough again into a 12 × 24-inch rectangle. Let it rest for 5 minutes to allow the gluten to relax. Starting with a short side, cut the dough into twenty-four 1-inch strips. Twist each strip 4 times and place about 2 inches apart on a parchment-lined baking sheet. When all the strips are twisted, cover with a towel and let rise for about 45 minutes, or until almost doubled.

9. About 15 minutes before the end of rising, preheat the oven to 400°F.

10. Bake the twists for 15 minutes, or until golden brown. Remove from the baking sheets to a rack.

11. Heat the currant jelly in a small saucepan over medium heat until melted. Lightly brush over the tops of the twists.

12. Combine the confectioners' sugar with enough milk to make a mixture the consistency of honey. Drizzle lightly over the tops of the twists.

Sweet Orange Rye Bread

2 scant tablespoons or
2 (¼-ounce) packages active
dry yeast

1½ cups warm water (105° to
115°F)

1 (14-ounce) can sweetened
condensed milk

1 teaspoon orange extract

2 teaspoons salt

½ teaspoon ground cloves

1 tablespoon grated orange
peel

1 cup raisins

1½ cup rye flour

3½ to 4½ cups unbleached
all-purpose flour

Makes 1 large 8-strand braid

Although there are not a lot of recipes for sweet rye breads, those that exist are spectacular. An eight-strand braid may sound intimidating, but it truly is one of the easiest braids of all to make—and it looks so impressive! Any leftover sweet rye bread makes outstanding French toast.

1. In a large bowl, soften the yeast in the water.

2. Measure ¼ cup of the condensed milk and set it aside.

3. Add the remaining condensed milk to the yeast, along with the orange extract, salt, cloves, orange peel, raisins, rye flour, and 1 cup of the all-purpose flour. Beat vigorously with a dough whisk or a heavy-handled spoon for 2 minutes.

4. Gradually add more of the remaining flour, ¼ cup at a time, until the dough forms a mass and begins to pull away from the side of the bowl. Turn the dough out onto a floured work surface.

5. Knead, adding more flour, a little at a time as necessary, for 8 to 10 minutes, or until you have an elastic dough.

6. Put the dough into an oiled bowl. Turn to coat the entire ball of dough with oil. Cover with a tightly woven kitchen towel and let rise for about 2 hours, or until doubled in size.

7. Turn the dough out onto a lightly oiled work surface and divide it into 8 equal pieces. Using your hands, roll each piece into a rope about 20 inches long. Lay 4 strands at an angle on the left and four on the right, leaving the center free (diagram 1). Pinch all 8 strands together firmly at the top (diagram 2). Take the outside right strand across 3 strands and place it so that it becomes the fifth strand from the left (diagram 3). Take the outside left strand across 4 strands and place it so it becomes the fourth strand from the right (diagram 4). Continue taking the outside strands from alternating sides and bringing them to the center in this fashion until the ends become too short to cross (diagram 5). You will have to keep moving the strands outward to make room for the center strands. Pinch the strands together at the bottom of the braid and turn them under. Lift the braid onto a parchment-lined or well-

1.

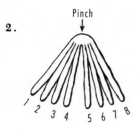

20"

1 2 3 4   1 2 3 4

2.

Pinch

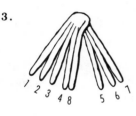

1 2 3 4   5 6 7 8

3.

1 2 3 4 8   5 6 7

4.

2 3 4 8   1 5 6 7

5.

greased baking sheet. Tuck about an inch of the top of the braid under to neaten it.

8. Cover the braid with a towel and let rise about 1 hour. Let this dough rise by timing it rather by waiting until it is almost doubled in size. It will not rise much now, but will rise more in the oven.

9. About 15 minutes before the end of rising, preheat the oven to 375°F.

10. Bake the bread for 20 minutes. Remove it from the oven and brush lightly with a little of the reserved condensed milk.

11. Return the braid to the oven and continue to bake for 10 minutes more, or until it is golden brown and sounds hollow when tapped (the internal temperature should reach 190°F). Remove from the baking sheet to cool on a rack.

12. Drizzle the top of the braid while still warm with the remaining condensed milk

VARIATION

Shape the dough into 2 round freestanding loaves and place well apart on a well-greased baking sheet. Cover the loaves with a towel and let rise for 45 minutes. Just before baking, score the tops of the loaves ¼ inch deep in two or three places. Bake the loaves 30 to 35 minutes.

Whole Wheat Orange-Date Lattice Bread

FOR THE DOUGH

1 scant tablespoon or
1 (¼-ounce) package active
dry yeast

¼ cup warm water (105° to
115°F)

¾ cup warm milk (105° to
115°F)

¼ cup solid vegetable
shortening

½ cup granulated sugar

1 large egg, beaten, at room
temperature

1 tablespoon orange peel

1 teaspoon salt

2½ to 3½ cups unbleached
all-purpose flour

1 cup whole wheat flour

FOR THE FILLING

1 cup finely chopped pitted
dates

1 cup fresh orange juice

1 teaspoon grated orange
peel

1 tablespoon unsalted butter

This sweet yeast bread looks gorgeous on a buffet table and tastes wonderful, too. I like the dates for their bold sweetness, but plump prunes also work well. For even more variety, add a half cup of finely chopped nuts to the filling. Whatever your choice, be sure the filling is sufficiently cool when it is spread over the dough.

1. Begin the dough by softening the yeast in the water in a large bowl.

2. Add the milk, shortening, sugar, egg, orange peel, salt, 1 cup of the unbleached flour, and all of the whole wheat flour to the yeast. Beat vigorously with a dough whisk or a heavy-handled spoon for 2 minutes.

3. Gradually add more of the remaining all-purpose flour, ¼ cup at a time, until the dough forms a mass and begins to pull away from the side of the bowl. Turn the dough out onto a floured work surface.

4. Knead, adding more flour, a little at a time as necessary, for 8 to 10 minutes, or until you have a smooth, elastic dough.

5. Put the dough into an oiled bowl. Turn to coat the entire ball of dough with oil. Cover with a tightly woven kitchen towel and let rise for about 1 hour, until doubled in size.

6. To make the filling, in a heavy saucepan combine the dates, orange juice, orange peel, and butter. Bring to a boil over medium heat. Reduce the heat to low and simmer for 10 minutes, or until mixture is thick. Set aside to cool to room temperature.

7. Turn the dough out directly onto a parchment-lined baking sheet. Roll or pat it into a 9 × 14-inch rectangle.

8. On both 14-inch sides, cut the dough to make 3-inch attached strips about 1 inch apart. Spread the cooled filling down the center of the dough between the cuts (diagram 1).

9. Starting at the top and alternating from side to side, fold the strips over the filling toward the center (diagram 2). When you reach the bottom of the loaf, tuck the ends under (diagram 3). The

FOR THE GLAZE

1½ cups confectioners' sugar

3 to 5 tablespoons fresh orange juice

Makes 1 large lattice loaf

strips of dough will cover the filling. Cover the dough with a towel and let rise for about 45 minutes, or until almost doubled.

10. About 15 minutes before the end of rising, preheat the oven to 375°F.

11. Bake the bread for 30 to 35 minutes, or until the loaf is golden brown (the internal temperature should reach 190°F). Immediately remove from the pan and cool on a rack for 20 minutes.

12. For the glaze, combine the confectioners' sugar with enough orange juice to make a mixture the consistency of honey. Drizzle lightly over the top of the bread.

1.

2.

3.

Swiss Fruit Bread

½ cup brandy

½ cup each coarsely chopped dried apples, dried cherries, dried pears, dried apricots, raisins, and figs (or a combination of your favorite dried fruits to equal 3 cups)

1 scant tablespoon or 1 (¼-ounce) package active dry yeast

¼ cup warm water (105° to 115°F)

1 cup warm milk (105° to 115°F)

4 tablespoons (½ stick) unsalted butter, at room temperature, cut up

¼ cup honey

1 teaspoon salt

1 teaspoon ground cinnamon

½ teaspoon grated nutmeg

¼ teaspoon ground ginger

2 large eggs, beaten

3½ to 4½ cups unbleached all-purpose flour, plus 2 tablespoons for the dried fruit

1 cup blanched almonds

Confectioners' sugar

Makes 1 loaf

Give yourself plenty of time for this fruit-filled loaf. Not only does the fruit need a full 24 hours to macerate in the brandy, but the bread tastes best when permitted to mellow for 2 days before you slice into it. The bread is dark with spices and generously studded with fruit. Slice it thin and spread it with cream cheese. It is divine all year along.

1. The day before baking the bread, combine the brandy with the fruits in a glass bowl. Stir occasionally for maximum absorption.

2. On baking day, soften the yeast in the water in a large bowl.

3. Add the milk, butter, honey, salt, cinnamon, nutmeg, ginger, eggs, and 2 cups of the flour to the yeast. Beat vigorously with a dough whisk or a heavy-handled spoon for 2 minutes.

4. Gradually add more of the remaining flour, ¼ cup at a time, until the dough forms a mass and begins to pull away from the side of the bowl. Turn the dough out onto a floured work surface.

5. Knead, adding more flour, a little at a time as necessary, for 8 to 10 minutes, or until you have a smooth, elastic dough and blisters begin to develop on the surface.

6. Put the dough into an oiled bowl. Turn to coat the entire ball of dough with oil. Cover with a tightly woven kitchen towel and let rise for about 1 hour, or until doubled in size.

7. Toast the almonds in a 375°F oven, for 10 minutes or until lightly browned. Allow them to cool. Drain the dried fruit mixture and toss the fruit with the 2 tablespoons of flour.

8. Lightly oil your hands and the work surface. Turn the dough out onto the work surface and knead in the fruit and almonds—the mixture will be sticky but do not add extra flour. Knead only until the fruit and nuts are incorporated. Shape the dough into a ball and cover with a towel. Let the dough rest on the work surface for 5 minutes.

9. Punch a large hole in the center of the ball with your finger. Stretch the hole until it is large enough to fit over the center post of a well-greased 12-cup tube or Bundt pan. Cover with a towel and let rise for about 1 hour, or until almost doubled in size.

10. About 15 minutes before the end of rising, preheat the oven to 375°F.

11. Bake for 40 to 45 minutes, or until the internal temperature reaches 190°F. Immediately transfer from the pan to a rack. Allow the loaf to cool completely before serving. This bread is best baked at least 2 days in advance. Wrap the cooled loaf in plastic and store at room temperature to allow the flavors to mellow.

12. Just before serving, sprinkle the bread liberally with confectioners' sugar.

You can eliminate salt completely from a recipe with a few adjustments. Cut the amount of yeast in half, knead the dough about half the usual time, shape it, and put it in the pan, allowing only one rising time. Watch it carefully—if the dough is allowed to rise more than double, it may fall during baking. Salt-free bread doesn't have a lot of flavor, so don't eliminate salt unless you've been told to do without it completely. The amount of salt per serving is minimal.

Six-Strand Lemon Almond Braid

*2 scant tablespoons or
2 (¹⁄₄-ounce) packages active
dry yeast*

*¹⁄₂ cup warm water (105° to
115°F)*

*1 cup warm milk (105° to
115°F)*

*¹⁄₂ cup firmly packed brown
sugar*

2 teaspoons salt

*¹⁄₂ cup solid vegetable
shortening*

*3 large eggs, at room
temperature*

1 large egg, separated

2 teaspoons vanilla extract

*2 tablespoons grated lemon
peel*

*1 (7-ounce) package almond
paste, crumbled*

*5¹⁄₂ to 6¹⁄₂ cups unbleached
all-purpose flour*

*Pärlsocker (see page 30) or
coarsely broken sugar cubes
(optional)*

**Makes 1 large braid; serves 10
to 12**

For many, a six-strand braided loaf is the most challenging of all shaped breads. This almond-flavored bread, gently infused with lemon, is a wonderful one for braiding. But if you are not feeling adventurous, try the bread anyhow. It's less visually exciting but just as delicious shaped into ordinary loaves.

1. In a large bowl, soften the yeast in the water.

2. Stir in the milk, brown sugar, salt, shortening, the 3 whole eggs, egg yolk, vanilla, lemon peel, almond paste, and 3 cups of the flour. Beat vigorously with a dough whisk or a heavy-handled spoon for 2 minutes.

3. Gradually add more of the remaining flour, ¹⁄₄ cup at a time, until the dough forms a mass and begins to pull away from the side of the bowl. Turn out onto a floured work surface.

4. Knead, adding more flour, a little at a time as necessary, for 8 to 10 minutes, or until you have a smooth, elastic dough and blisters begin to develop on the surface.

5. Put the dough into an oiled bowl. Turn to coat the entire ball of dough with oil. Cover with a tightly woven kitchen towel and let rise for about 1 hour, or until doubled in size.

6. Turn the dough out onto a lightly oiled work surface and divide it into 6 equal pieces. Using your hands, roll each piece into a 20-inch rope. Lay the ropes vertically on the work surface, side by side, and pinch them together at the top (diagram 1). Braiding the ropes is much easier than you might think, and there is a pattern and rhythm to it that you will quickly learn:

(a) Take the far right rope and lay it horizontally over the other 5 ropes (diagram 2). Take the far left rope and lay it horizontally over the remaining 4 ropes; then spread the 4 ropes apart, 2 to the right and 2 to the left, to leave more room in the center (diagram 3). You will do this each time you are left with 4 vertical ropes.

(b) Take the top horizontal rope from the left and lay it between the separated vertical ropes (diagram 4). Handle the ropes of dough gently, taking care not to pull them.

(c) Take the right vertical rope and lay it horizontally over the 4 vertical ropes (diagram 5); then spread the 4 vertical ropes apart,

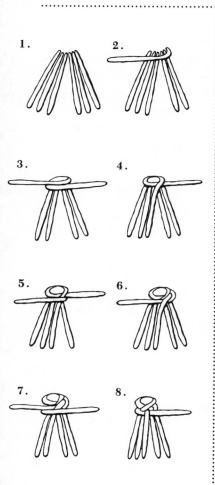

1.

2.

3.

4.

5.

6.

7.

8.

9.

10.

as described above. Take the top horizontal rope from the right and lay it between the separated vertical ropes (diagram 6).

(*d*) Take the left vertical rope and lay it horizontally over the 4 vertical ropes (diagram 7).

(*e*) Take the top horizontal rope from the left and lay it between the separated vertical ropes (diagram 8).

(*f*) Take the right vertical rope and lay it horizontally over the 4 vertical ropes (diagram 9).

Repeat the braiding process from step *c* until you are about 2 inches from the bottom ends of the ropes. Bring all the ends to the center, press them together, and tuck underneath the braid. For a neater braid, tuck underneath about 1 inch from the top (diagram 10). Put the braid on a parchment-lined or well-greased baking sheet. Cover with a towel and let rise for about 45 minutes, or until almost doubled in size.

7. About 15 minutes before the end of rising, preheat the oven to 375°F.

8. Just before baking, beat the egg white until frothy. Brush lightly over the top and sides of the braid, taking care not to let it drip onto the pan. Sprinkle with pärlsocker or crushed sugar.

9. Bake for 40 to 45 minutes, or until the braid is golden brown and sounds hollow when tapped (the internal temperature of the bread should reach 190°F). Remove from the baking sheet and cool on a rack.

VARIATION

Shape the dough into either 2 round freestanding loaves and place well apart on a well-greased baking sheet, or 2 standard pan loaves (for directions, see page 59) and place in 2 well-greased loaf pans. Cover the loaves with a towel and let rise for 45 minutes. Just before baking, score the tops of the freestanding loaves ¼ inch deep in two or three places. Bake the loaves 30 to 35 minutes.

Cherry Almond Honeyed Fantans

1 scant tablespoon or
1 (¼-ounce) package active
dry yeast

½ cup warm water (105° to
115°F)

1½ cups warm milk (105° to
115°F)

1 teaspoon almond extract

2 tablespoons unsalted
butter, at room temperature

1 teaspoon salt

¼ cup granulated sugar

3 tablespoons soy flour

2 cups whole wheat flour

2½ to 3½ cups unbleached
all-purpose flour

1 cup finely chopped dried
cherries

1 cup finely chopped
almonds

½ cup firmly packed brown
sugar

½ cup warm honey

Makes 24 fantans

Fantans are attractively shaped rolls baked in muffin tins and, in this case, filled with a mixture of dried cherries, brown sugar, and almonds. Once you try them, I am sure dried cherries will become a favorite of yours just as they are of mine—they are tart and sweet, and deliciously chewy. If you cannot find them, substitute raisins or another dried fruit, or mail order the cherries from *The King Arthur Flour Baker's Catalogue* (see page 411) or another reputable source.

1. In a large bowl, soften the yeast in the water.

2. Add the milk, almond extract, butter, salt, granulated sugar, all of the soy flour and whole wheat flour, and 1 cup of the all-purpose flour. Beat vigorously with a dough whisk or a heavy-handled spoon for 2 minutes.

3. Gradually add more of the remaining unbleached flour, ¼ cup at a time, until the dough forms a mass and begins to pull away from the side of the bowl. Turn the dough out onto a floured work surface.

4. Knead, adding more flour, a little at a time as necessary, for 8 to 10 minutes, or until you have a smooth, elastic dough. For extra-light fantans, add the minimum amount of flour and keep the dough very tacky.

5. Put the dough into an oiled bowl. Turn to coat the entire ball of dough with oil. Cover with a tightly woven kitchen towel and let rise for about 1 hour, or until doubled in size.

6. Combine the cherries, almonds, and brown sugar. Set this filling aside.

7. Turn the dough out onto a lightly oiled work surface. Using a rolling pin, roll into an 18 × 12-inch rectangle. Sprinkle the filling over two thirds of the dough, leaving a ½-inch border around the edges. Fold the uncovered third of dough over the center third and press the top and bottom edges to seal. Fold the double thickness of dough over the remaining third so that you have a 6 × 12-inch rectangle with 3 layers of dough and 2 layers of filling.

8. Give the dough a quarter turn. Using a rolling pin, carefully roll the dough again into an 18 × 12-inch rectangle, taking care that it does not break open so that the filling bursts through. Fold the dough into thirds. Cover with a towel and let rest on the work surface for 10 minutes.

9. Using a knife, cut the dough into three 12-inch strips. Cut each strip into 8 equal pieces. Put the pieces, cut side up, into lightly oiled muffin pans.

10. Cover with a towel and let rise for about 45 minutes, or until almost doubled.

11. About 15 minutes before the end of rising, preheat the oven to 375°F.

12. Bake the fantans for 15 to 20 minutes, or until they are golden (the internal temperature should reach 190°F). Let cool for 5 minutes in the pans.

13. Remove the fantans from the pans and and dip them in the warm honey. Cool on a rack.

English Cheese Ring

FOR THE DOUGH

2 scant tablespoons or
2 (¼-ounce) packages active
dry yeast

½ cup warm water (105° to
115°F)

8 tablespoons (1 stick)
unsalted butter, at room
temperature

1 cup sour cream, at room
temperature

2 large eggs, at room
temperature

½ cup granulated sugar

1 teaspoon salt

5 to 6 cups unbleached all-
purpose flour

FOR THE FILLING

8 ounces cream cheese, at
room temperature

½ cup granulated sugar

2 large eggs, at room
temperature

1 teaspoon vanilla extract

FOR THE GLAZE

1 cup orange marmalade

Confectioners' sugar
(optional)

Makes 1 large ring

This large, sweet cheese-filled bread traditionally is served at tea-time, but it is good anytime. I have served it for brunch, for dessert, and with midmorning coffee. I urge you to add the flour very slowly during kneading, because the sour cream in the dough absorbs the flour quite differently from other liquids. If you add too much flour, the dough will toughen, and for this bread in particular the dough should be delicate. Simply changing the type of jam spread over the outside of the bread allows you to change its nature. I like a good orange marmalade, but you might prefer currant, black-berry, raspberry, or apricot.

1. Begin the dough by softening the yeast in the water in a large bowl.

2. Add the butter, sour cream, eggs, granulated sugar, salt, and 2 cups of the flour. Beat vigorously with a dough whisk or a heavy-handled spoon for 2 minutes.

3. Gradually add more of the remaining flour, ¼ cup at a time, until the dough forms a mass and begins to pull away from the side of the bowl. Turn the dough out onto a floured work surface.

4. Knead, adding more flour, a little at a time as necessary, for 8 to 10 minutes, or until you have a smooth, elastic dough and blisters begin to develop on the surface.

5. Put the dough into an oiled bowl. Turn to coat the entire ball of dough with oil. Cover with a tightly woven kitchen towel and let rise for about 1 hour, or until doubled in size.

6. Make the filling by beating the cream cheese with the sugar, eggs, and vanilla until light and fluffy. Set aside.

7. Turn the dough out onto a lightly oiled work surface and, using a rolling pin, roll into an 18-inch circle. Drape the circle over a well-greased 10-inch tube or Bundt pan. Ease the dough partway into the pan, leaving about ½ inch extending over the top edge. Try not to make a hole in the dough—if you do, pinch it together. (If the dough is properly kneaded, it will be elastic and strong and should not tear.) It is not necessary to press the dough all the way to the bottom of the pan, since the weight of the filling will do that.

8. Spoon the filling evenly into the dough-lined pan. Bring the outer edges of the dough up over the filling, pleating it to fit. Cut a cross in the dough covering the center post of the pan. Fold each triangle formed back over the pleated dough. Cover with a towel and let rise for 45 minutes. Because of the filling, you will not be able to tell how much the dough has risen.

9. About 15 minutes before the end of rising, preheat the oven to 375°F.

10. Bake the cheese ring for 35 to 40 minutes, or until golden. Because of the filling, you cannot use an instant-read thermometer.

11. Remove from the oven and cool in the pan for 10 minutes to allow the filling to set. Turn the bread out onto a rack and cool for 30 minutes.

12. For the glaze, heat the marmalade in a small saucepan over low heat until melted. Spoon over the cooled ring and let sit for 10 minutes. Just before serving, sprinkle with confectioners' sugar, if desired.

Orange Cheesecake Purses

FOR THE DOUGH

*1 scant tablespoon or
1 (¹/₄-ounce) package active
dry yeast*

*¹/₄ cup warm water (105° to
115°F)*

2 tablespoons vegetable oil

*1 cup warm milk (105° to
115°F)*

3 tablespoons honey

*2 large eggs, at room
temperature*

*2 egg yolks, at room
temperature*

¹/₄ teaspoon vanilla extract

1 teaspoon salt

1 teaspoon ground mace

*4¹/₂ to 5¹/₂ cups unbleached
all-purpose flour*

FOR THE FILLING

*1 pound cream cheese, at
room temperature*

1 cup confectioners' sugar

¹/₄ teaspoon almond extract

1 large egg, beaten

*2 tablespoons finely chopped
candied ginger*

*2 teaspoons grated orange
peel*

Orange-flavored sweetened cream cheese is a tasty filling for these little bundles of dough, named after the savory appetizer called beggar's purses because of their shape: they resemble pieces of gathered cloth secured with a rope. Try this filling, too, with the Holiday Lattice Loaf on page 276.

1. Begin the dough by softening the yeast in the water in a large bowl.

2. Add the oil, milk, honey, eggs, egg yolks, vanilla, salt, mace, and 2 cups of the flour. Beat vigorously with a dough whisk or a heavy-handled spoon for 2 minutes.

3. Gradually add more of the remaining flour, ¹/₄ cup at a time, until the dough forms a mass and begins to pull away from the side of the bowl. Turn the dough out onto a floured work surface.

4. Knead, adding more flour, a little at a time as necessary, for 8 to 10 minutes, or until you have a smooth, elastic dough and blisters begin to develop on the surface.

5. Put the dough into an oiled bowl. Turn to coat the entire ball of dough with oil. Cover with a tightly woven kitchen towel and let rise for about 1 hour, or until doubled in size.

6. Make the filling. Combine the cream cheese, confectioners' sugar, almond extract, beaten egg, candied ginger, and orange peel in a bowl. Mix thoroughly. Cover and refrigerate until ready to use.

7. Turn the dough out onto a lightly oiled work surface and divide it into thirds, then divide each third in half. Divide the pieces in half two more times to make 24 equal pieces. Set aside 6 pieces of dough and cover with a towel. Using a rolling pin, roll the remaining 18 pieces into 6-inch rounds. Put 2 scant tablespoons of filling in the center of each round. Pleat the edges of the dough and pinch together firmly just above the filling. Flare the top of each purse slightly.

8. Divide the reserved 6 pieces of dough into thirds so that you have 18 pieces. Using your hands, roll each piece into a 9-inch

2 egg whites beaten with 2 tablespoons cold water, for the egg wash

Makes 18 purses

rope. Pinch the dough purses again, just above the filling. Loosely tie a rope around the pinched top of each purse.

9. Arrange the purses 2 inches apart on parchment-lined baking sheets. Cover with a towel and let rest for 20 minutes in the refrigerator. If the purses rise too quickly or for too long, they will split open during baking.

10. While the dough is resting, preheat the oven to 375°F.

11. Just before baking, brush each purse thoroughly but lightly with egg wash, making sure no excess wash runs down the sides of the purses and puddles on the baking sheet. A feather pastry brush works well.

12. Bake the purses for 20 minutes, or until golden brown. Because of the filling, an instant-read thermometer does not work as a test for doneness. Immediately remove the purses from the baking sheets and cool on a rack.

Make sure to consult the information on flour and other ingredients and on utensils (chapter 1) and the baking class on making yeast breads (chapter 2).

Spiced Hazelnut Twist

FOR THE DOUGH

2 scant tablespoons or
2 (¼-ounce) packages active
dry yeast

½ cup warm water (105° to
115°F)

1 cup warm milk (105° to
115°F)

4 tablespoons (½ stick)
unsalted butter, at room
temperature

¼ cup granulated sugar

2 teaspoons salt

2 large eggs, at room
temperature

2 egg yolks, at room
temperature (use whites in
filling)

2 teaspoons grated lemon
peel

3½ to 4½ cups unbleached
all-purpose flour

½ teaspoon ground
cardamom

½ teaspoon ground ginger

½ teaspoon grated nutmeg

You can change the character of this loaf by substituting another nut. I use the food processor to grind the nuts; but take care not to overgrind or they turn into paste.

1. Begin the dough by softening the yeast in the water in a large bowl.

2. Add the milk, butter, granulated sugar, salt, eggs, egg yolks, and the lemon peel and stir until mixed.

3. Whisk 3 cups of the flour with the cardamom, ginger, and nutmeg to combine. Add to the yeast mixture and beat vigorously with a dough whisk or a heavy-handled spoon for 2 minutes.

4. Gradually add more of the remaining flour, ¼ cup at time, until the dough forms a mass and begins to pull away from the side of the bowl. Turn the dough out onto a floured work surface.

5. Knead, adding more flour, a little at a time as necessary, for 8 to 10 minutes, or until you have a smooth, elastic dough and blisters begin to develop on the surface.

6. Put the dough into an oiled bowl. Turn to coat the entire ball of dough with oil. Cover with a tightly woven kitchen towel and let rise for about 1 hour, or until doubled in size.

7. Make the filling. Combine the hazelnuts, brown sugar, cinnamon, and rum in a bowl. In a separate bowl, using an electric mixer, beat the egg whites until stiff peaks form. Gently fold the egg whites into the filling. Set the filling aside.

8. Turn the dough out onto a lightly oiled work surface. Divide it in half and, using a rolling pin, shape each piece into a 16 × 18-inch rectangle.

9. Spread half the hazelnut mixture on each rectangle (diagram 1), leaving a ½-inch border along one of the long edges. Starting at the other long edge, roll up the filled dough to form an 18-inch cylinder (diagram 2). Pinch all along the edge to seal (diagram 3). Put each cylinder on a separate parchment-lined baking sheet.

10. Cut 1 cylinder in half lengthwise and turn the cut sides up (diagram 4). Loosely twist the 2 halves together, turning, if necessary, so that the cut side stays up—it tends to twist under.

FOR THE FILLING

2 cups ground hazelnuts or filberts (8 ounces shelled nuts)

½ cup firmly packed brown sugar

2 teaspoons ground cinnamon

3 tablespoons rum (the darker the color, the stronger the flavor)

2 egg whites

FOR THE GLAZE

¼ cup warm honey

Makes 2 loaves

Pinch the ends to seal (diagram 5). Repeat with the second dough cylinder.

11. Cover the twists with a towel and let rise for about 45 minutes, until almost doubled.

12. About 15 minutes before the end of rising, preheat the oven to 375°F.

13. Bake the twists for 30 to 35 minutes, or until lightly browned (the internal temperature should reach 190°F). Remove from the baking sheets to a rack.

14. Brush the hot loaves with honey. Let sit for at least 20 minutes before cutting.

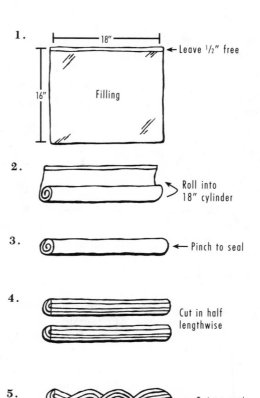

Orange Macadamia Swirl Loaf

FOR THE DOUGH

*1 scant tablespoon or
1 (¼-ounce) package active
dry yeast*

*¼ cup warm water (105° to
115°F)*

*1 cup warm orange juice
(105° to 115°F)*

½ cup granulated sugar

*¼ cup solid vegetable
shortening*

1 teaspoon vanilla extract

*2 large eggs, at room
temperature*

1 teaspoon salt

¼ teaspoon ground ginger

*4½ to 5½ cups unbleached
all-purpose flour*

*2 tablespoons unsalted
butter, melted*

FOR THE FILLING

*½ cup firmly packed brown
sugar*

*2 tablespoons grated orange
peel*

*1 cup finely chopped
macadamia nuts*

The rich, buttery flavor of macadamia nuts combines especially well with the sweet, bright flavor of oranges in this breakfast loaf. If you can find only salted macadamia nuts, spread them on a terrycloth kitchen towel and rub as much salt from them as you can. For intense macadamia flavor, toast the whole nuts for about 15 minutes or until golden in a 375°F oven. You can substitute walnuts, almonds, or another nut for the macadamias, but the flavor will be different.

1. Begin the dough by softening the yeast in the water in a large bowl.

2. Add the orange juice, granulated sugar, shortening, vanilla, eggs, salt, ginger, and 2 cups of the flour. Beat vigorously with a dough whisk or a heavy-handled spoon for 2 minutes.

3. Gradually add more of the remaining flour, ¼ cup at a time, until the dough forms a mass and begins to pull away from the side of the bowl. Turn the dough out onto a floured work surface.

4. Knead, adding more flour, a little at a time as necessary, for 8 to 10 minutes, or until you have a smooth, elastic dough and blisters begin to develop on the surface.

5. Put the dough into an oiled bowl. Turn to coat the entire ball of dough with oil. Cover with a tightly woven kitchen towel and let rise for about 1 hour, or until doubled in size.

6. Turn the dough out onto a lightly oiled work surface. Using a rolling pin, shape the dough into a 24 × 18-inch rectangle. Brush lightly with the melted butter, leaving a ½-inch border along one long edge.

7. To make the filling, combine the brown sugar, orange peel, and macadamia nuts. Spread the mixture evenly over the buttered dough (diagram 1). Using your hands, roll the dough toward the unbuttered edge to form a 24-inch cylinder (diagram 2) and pinch all along the edge to seal. Carefully lift the cylinder onto a parchment-lined or well-greased baking sheet, seam side down. Bring the ends together, without pinching them, to form a circle (diagram 3).

FOR THE GLAZE

1 cup confectioners' sugar

3 to 4 tablespoons fresh orange juice

Makes 1 loaf

8. Starting about 1 inch to the right of the join, cut the dough at 1-inch intervals all around the circle with long-bladed scissors. Cut from the outside to within ½ inch of the center, making sure you cut through both the top and bottom layers of dough (diagram 4). You should have 23 cuts and 24 rolls.

9. To create the swirl, begin with the second roll from the join. The first roll will act as anchor to keep the end in place until you've worked your way around. It will be the last roll twisted into shape. Lift roll 2 and twist it so it lies on its side where the coiled center shows. Do the same with roll 3. Take roll 4 and twist it in the opposite direction from rolls 2 and 3 and lay it on its side in the center of the wreath (diagram 5).

10. Continue around the wreath, twisting two rolls in one direction and the third in the opposite direction to the center (diagram 6). Once you have shaped all the rolls, you will have 16 rolls twisted around the outside edge of the wreath and 8 twisted in the opposite direction in the center (diagram 7).

(continued)

1.
24"
Leave ½" free
18"
Melted butter and filling

2.
Roll into 24" cylinder

TOP VIEWS

3.
Join
Butt ends together

4.
Join

5.
4
3
2

6.

7.

11. Hold the parchment paper in place with one hand. With the other hand, gently push around the outside of the circle to press the rolls together and give the loaf a better shape.

12. Cover the loaf with a towel and let rise for about 45 minutes, until almost doubled.

13. About 15 minutes before the end of rising, preheat the oven to 375°F.

14. Bake the loaf for 25 to 30 minutes, or until golden (the internal temperature should reach 190°F). Remove from the baking sheet and cool on a rack for 20 minutes before glazing.

15. To make the glaze, combine the confectioners' sugar with enough orange juice to give the mixture the consistency of honey. Drizzle the glaze over the warm loaf.

Note: For a quick, easy filling, use a food processor. Process the orange peel and brown sugar together, and when the rind is finely chopped, add the macadamia nuts and process until they are well ground. Be sure not to include any of the bitter white pith with the colored part of the peel.

Pain d'Épice

2 scant tablespoons or
2 (¼-ounce) packages active dry yeast

½ cup warm water (105° to 115°F)

1½ cups warm milk (105° to 115°F)

½ cup honey

2 teaspoons salt

2 teaspoons anise seeds

This is another recipe (besides the Sweet Orange Rye Bread on page 226) for a sweet bread made in part with rye flour. The spiced loaf is produced in nearly every region of France, differing slightly from town to town and village to village according to the grind of flour, the measure of spices, and the hand of the baker. It is traditionally sweetened with honey, and it may be leavened with yeast, baking soda, carbonate of ammonia, or potash. In France, Pain d'Épice is treasured for its keeping qualities, and many bakers prefer to wrap the bread tightly and store it for 2 to 3 days before eating it. If the bread lasts long enough to turn stale, cut it into ½-inch slices and dry them out in a 300°F oven for about 30 minutes. Dip the slices into a hearty sweet wine as you would Italian biscotti.

1. In a large bowl, soften the yeast in the water.

1 teaspoon ground cinnamon

½ teaspoon ground ginger

½ teaspoon ground mace

¼ teaspoon ground cloves

1 cup finely ground almonds

2 cups rye flour

3½ to 4½ cups unbleached all-purpose flour

Softened butter (optional)

Makes 2 loaves

2. Add the milk, honey, salt, anise seeds, cinnamon, ginger, mace, cloves, almonds, all of the rye flour, and 2 cups of the all-purpose flour. Beat vigorously with a dough whisk or a heavy-handled spoon for 2 minutes.

3. Gradually add more of the remaining unbleached flour, ¼ cup at a time, until the dough begins to pull away from the side of the bowl. Turn the dough out onto a floured work surface.

4. Knead, adding more flour, a little at a time as necessary, for 8 to 10 minutes, or until you have a smooth, elastic dough. Take special care not to add too much flour in this recipe—rye dough should be fairly tacky at the end of the kneading process; otherwise, the bread will be heavy.

5. Put the dough in an oiled bowl. Turn to coat the entire ball of dough with oil. Cover with a tightly woven kitchen towel and let rise for about 1 hour, or until doubled in size.

6. Turn the dough out onto a lightly oiled work surface and divide it in half. Shape into loaves following the directions on page 71.

7. Fit the loaves, seam sides down, into well-greased loaf pans. Cover with a towel and let rise for about 45 minutes, or until almost doubled in size.

8. About 15 minutes before the end of rising, preheat the oven to 375°F.

9. Bake for 30 to 35 minutes, or until the loaves have shrunk slightly from the sides of the pan and sound hollow when tapped (the internal temperature should reach 190°F). Immediately remove the bread from the pans to cool on a rack.

10. For a soft, shiny crust, rub the tops of the loaves with softened butter.

Peanut Butter and Jelly Loaf

1 scant tablespoon or 1 (¼-ounce) package active dry yeast

¼ cup warm water (105° to 115°F)

1 cup warm milk (105° to 115°F)

¾ cup smooth peanut butter

2 large eggs, lightly beaten

¼ cup granulated sugar

1 teaspoon salt

1 cup coarsely chopped peanuts

2½ to 3½ cups unbleached all-purpose flour

½ cup jelly or jam

½ cup confectioners' sugar

About 2 tablespoons milk

Makes 1 large loaf

Who doesn't like the flavor combination of peanut butter and jelly? It appeals to children of all ages, and it is combined here in a sweet loaf perfect for breakfast, lunch, dessert, or an afterschool snack. If you prefer, use chunky peanut butter in the dough, but the glaze is best made with smooth peanut butter.

1. In a large bowl, soften the yeast in the water.

2. Add the milk, ½ cup of the peanut butter, the eggs, granulated sugar, salt, peanuts, and 1 cup of the flour. Beat vigorously with a dough whisk or a heavy-handled spoon for 2 minutes. Reserve the remaining peanut butter for the glaze.

3. Gradually add more of the remaining flour, ¼ cup at a time, until the dough forms a mass and begins to pull away from the side of the bowl. Turn the dough out onto a floured work surface.

4. Knead, adding more flour, a little at a time as necessary, for 8 to 10 minutes, or until you have a smooth, elastic dough and blisters begin to develop on the surface.

5. Put the dough into an oiled bowl. Turn to coat the entire ball of dough with oil. Cover with a tightly woven kitchen towel and let rise for about 1 hour, or until doubled in size.

6. Turn the dough out onto a piece of lightly oiled parchment paper, cut to fit a large baking sheet. Using a rolling pin, roll the dough into a 14-inch circle. Put a 3-inch-diameter glass tumbler or can in the center of the circle (diagram 1). Using a dough blade or knife, and visualizing the dough as a clock, cut from the tumbler to the edge of the circle at 12, 3, 6, and 9 o'clock (diagram 2). The outer ring of dough is now cut into fourths. Cutting from the edge of the dough to the tumbler, cut each quarter into 6 equal strips (diagram 3), so that you have 24 strips in all. Remove the tumbler.

7. Twist 2 strips of dough together. Twist the adjacent 2 strips together (diagram 4) and continue around the circle until you have 12 twists. Coil one of the twists into the center of the dough (where the tumbler was), making sure the ends are tucked under so that they will not come undone during rising and baking (diagram 5). Coil each of the remaining 11 twists in the same direction around

1.

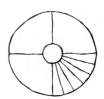

14" circle

2.

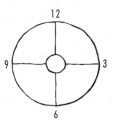

3.

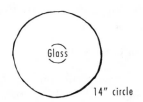

4.

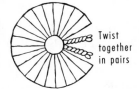

Twist together in pairs

5.

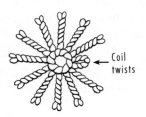

← Coil twists

6.

the center coil (diagram 6). Carefully slide the parchment paper with the shaped dough onto a baking sheet. Cover with a towel and let rise for about 45 minutes, or until almost doubled in size.

8. About 15 minutes before the end of rising, preheat the oven to 375°F.

9. Bake the bread for 30 to 35 minutes, or until lightly browned (the internal temperature should reach 190°F). Remove from the baking sheet and transfer to a rack.

10. While the bread is still hot, drop ½ teaspoon jelly or jam into the center of each coil. Allow to cool for 20 minutes.

11. In a measuring cup, combine confectioners' sugar and the remaining ¼ cup of peanut butter with enough milk to make a thick, runny icing about the consistency of honey. Drizzle from the spout of the cup in a zigzag pattern over the top of the bread.

Mexican Wedding Bread

1 scant tablespoon or
1 (¼-ounce) package active
dry yeast

¼ cup warm water (105° to
115°F)

1 cup warm milk (105° to
115°F)

½ cup granulated sugar

2 large eggs, beaten

2 teaspoons vanilla extract

4½ to 5½ cups unbleached
all-purpose flour

1 teaspoon salt

1 cup finely ground pecans

1 cup confectioners' sugar

3 tablespoons water

Makes 18 individual breads

Traditionally, this bread is served at weddings in southern Mexico to signify the joining of two people into one couple.

1. In a large bowl, soften the yeast in the water.

2. Add the milk, granulated sugar, eggs, vanilla, and 2 cups of the flour. Beat vigorously with a dough whisk or heavy-handled spoon for 2 minutes. The sponge will have the consistency of cake batter. Cover the bowl with plastic wrap and a tightly woven kitchen towel and let rise for 45 minutes, or until the sponge is light and full of bubbles. (Both coverings are necessary to protect the dough.)

3. Add the salt, pecans, and 1 cup of the remaining flour to the sponge and beat for 1 minute.

4. Gradually add more of the remaining flour, ¼ cup at a time, beating until the dough forms a mass and begins to pull away from the side of the bowl. Turn the dough out onto a floured work surface.

5. Knead, adding more flour, a little at a time as necessary, for 8 to 10 minutes, or until you have a smooth, elastic dough and blisters begin to develop on the surface.

6. Put the dough into an oiled bowl. Turn to coat the entire ball of dough with oil. Cover with a towel and let rise for about 45 minutes, or until doubled in size.

7. Turn the dough out onto a lightly oiled work surface. Divide it into thirds and then divide each piece in half. Divide each piece into thirds and then in half again to make 36 equal pieces. Using your hands, roll each piece into a 8-inch rope. Pinch the ends of one rope together to form a circle (diagram 1). Take another rope, slip it through the first circle (diagram 2), and pinch the ends together (diagram 3). Put the two interlinked circles on a

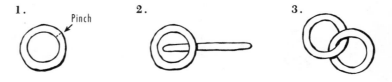

1.   Pinch   2.   3.

parchment-lined or well-greased baking sheet. Repeat with the remaining ropes of dough to make 18 individual links, spacing them 2 inches apart on two separate sheets (see Note, page 189). Cover with a towel and let rise for about 45 minutes, until almost doubled in size.

8. About 15 minutes before the end of rising, preheat the oven to 375°F.

9. Bake for 15 to 20 minutes, or until golden brown. The rolls are too thin to be tested for doneness with an instant-read thermometer.

10. While the rolls are baking, combine the confectioners' sugar with the water in a shallow bowl.

11. As soon as the rolls are done, remove them from the baking sheets and dip the tops into the bowl of icing. Put them on a rack for about 30 minutes to allow the icing to set.

Sculpted breads can be traced back 4,000 years, to when Egyptian bakers baked bread into flower and bird shapes to use as offerings to the gods.

Pan de los Muertos

MEXICAN BREAD OF THE DEAD

1 tablespoon anise seeds

¼ cup boiling water

2 scant tablespoons or 2 (¼-ounce) packages active dry yeast

½ cup warm water (105° to 115°F)

½ cup granulated sugar

8 tablespoons (1 stick) unsalted butter, melted

6 large eggs, lightly beaten

1 tablespoon orange blossom water

1 tablespoon grated orange peel

2 teaspoons salt

5½ to 6½ cups unbleached all-purpose flour

2 cups confectioners' sugar

¼ cup milk

1 tablespoon unsalted butter, at room temperature

1 teaspoon vanilla extract

Makes 6 small loaves

This rich, spicy bread flavored with anise and orange may sound dismal but actually is a celebration loaf baked to commemorate the departed members of one's family on All Souls' Day, November 2. Mexican bakers fashion the bread into any number of shapes—a doll, cross, flower, or plain loaf—and may write the name of the deceased on the top with sugar icing or beans. The orange blossom water called for here is sold at specialty stores and also through *The King Arthur Flour Bakers's Catalogue* (see page 411).

1. Combine the anise seeds and the boiling water in a heatproof measuring cup or bowl. Cover and steep for about 15 minutes, until cool.

2. In a large bowl, soften the yeast in the water.

3. Add the anise water, granulated sugar, melted butter, eggs, orange blossom water, orange peel, salt, and 3 cups of the flour to the yeast mixture. Beat vigorously with a dough whisk or a heavy-handled spoon for 2 minutes.

4. Gradually add more of the remaining flour, ¼ cup at a time, until the dough forms a mass and begins to pull away from the side of the bowl. Turn the dough out onto a floured work surface.

5. Knead, adding more flour, a little at a time as necessary, for 8 to 10 minutes, or until you have a smooth, elastic dough and blisters begin to develop on the surface.

6. Put the dough into an oiled bowl. Turn to coat the entire ball of dough with oil. Cover with a tightly woven kitchen towel and let rise for about 1 hour, or until doubled in size.

7. Turn the dough out onto a lightly oiled work surface and divide it into 6 pieces. Line 2 baking sheets with parchment, or grease them well. Shape the pieces of dough into any of the shapes illustrated and arrange them on the prepared baking sheets. Alternately, shape the dough into 2 round loaves. Cover with a towel and let rise for 45 minutes.

8. About 15 minutes before the end of rising, preheat the oven to 375°F.

9. Bake the breads for 25 to 30 minutes, or until they are well browned and the internal temperature reaches 190°F. If baking 2 large loaves, bake 30 to 35 minutes. Remove bread from the baking sheets and cool on a rack for 15 minutes.

10. Make a glaze by combining the confectioners' sugar with the milk, butter, and vanilla. Whisk well so that the glaze is thin enough to apply with a pastry brush. Brush the glaze thinly over the bread.

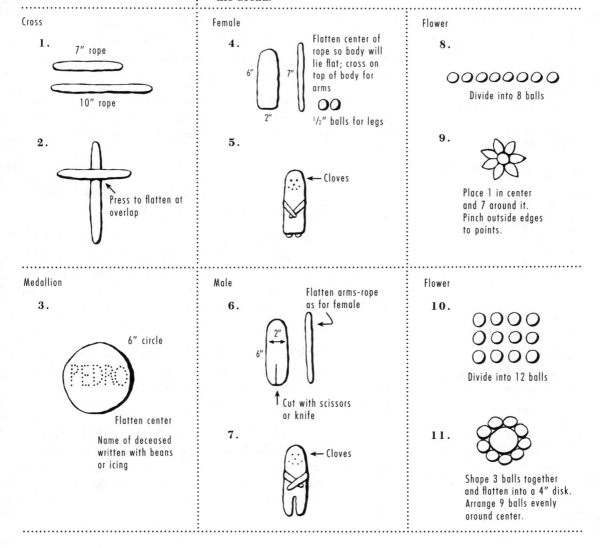

Cross

1. 7" rope / 10" rope

2. Press to flatten at overlap

Medallion

3. 6" circle / PEDRO / Flatten center / Name of deceased written with beans or icing

Female

4. 6" / 7" / Flatten center of rope so body will lie flat; cross on top of body for arms / 2" / ½" balls for legs

5. Cloves

Male

6. 2" / 6" / Flatten arms-rope as for female / Cut with scissors or knife

7. Cloves

Flower

8. Divide into 8 balls

9. Place 1 in center and 7 around it. Pinch outside edges to points.

Flower

10. Divide into 12 balls

11. Shape 3 balls together and flatten into a 4" disk. Arrange 9 balls evenly around center.

Norwegian Princess Bread

FOR THE DOUGH

1 scant tablespoon or 1 (¼-ounce) package active dry yeast

¼ cup warm water (105° to 115°F)

½ teaspoon salt

¼ cup granulated sugar

½ teaspoon ground cardamom

2 teaspoons grated lemon peel

3½ to 4½ cups unbleached all-purpose flour

8 tablespoons (1 stick) unsalted butter, well chilled

1 cup warm milk (105° to 115°F)

FOR THE CUSTARD

2 tablespoons granulated sugar

2 tablespoons unbleached all-purpose flour

1 cup milk

2 egg yolks

1 teaspoon vanilla extract

These sweet, light cinnamon-kissed rolls are nestled on a bed of custard that is a complete surprise. I got this recipe from my good friend Sissel Tangen, who has shared so many of her native Norwegian recipes with me. I use a springform pan for the bread, but you may use any similarly sized pan if you first line the bottom with parchment paper to make removing the bread easy.

1. Begin the dough by softening the yeast in the water in a small bowl or cup.

2. In a large bowl, whisk together the salt, sugar, cardamom, lemon peel, and 3 cups of the flour. Cut the cold butter into 8 pieces. Using a pastry blender or 2 knives, cut the butter into the flour mixture until it resembles grains of rice.

3. Add the milk and softened yeast to the flour mixture and stir to combine. Add just enough of the remaining flour to make a ball of dough that will retain its shape without sagging. This dough is not kneaded.

4. Put the dough into an oiled bowl. Turn to coat the entire ball of dough with oil. Cover with a tightly woven kitchen towel and let rise for about 1½ hours, or until doubled.

5. Prepare the custard. In a small heavy saucepan, whisk together the sugar and flour. Add the milk and egg yolks and whisk to combine. Cook over medium-low heat, stirring often, for about 5 minutes, or until the sauce thickens enough to coat the back of a spoon. Remove from the heat, add the vanilla, and set aside to cool.

6. Meanwhile, turn the dough out onto a lightly oiled work surface. Cut off one third of the dough with a knife or dough divider. Cover the remaining two thirds with a kitchen towel while working with the first piece.

7. Using a rolling pin, roll the dough into a 10-inch circle. Line a well-greased 9-inch springform pan with the rolled dough, allowing ½ inch to come up the sides of the pan. Using your fingertips, press this dough to flatten it until it extends about 1 inch up the sides of the pan. Cover the pan with a towel and set aside.

FOR THE FILLING

2 tablespoons unsalted butter, melted

1 teaspoon ground cinnamon

2 tablespoons granulated sugar

FOR THE GLAZE

1 cup confectioners' sugar

1 teaspoon rum extract

2 to 4 tablespoons heavy cream

Makes 12 large rolls

8. Using a rolling pin, roll the remaining dough into an 18-inch square. Spread the dough with melted butter, leaving a ½-inch border along one edge. Combine the cinnamon and granulated sugar and sprinkle over the butter. Using your hands, roll the dough toward the ½-inch unfilled border to form an 18-inch cylinder. Pinch all along the loose edge to seal.

9. Cut the cylinder into 12 equal pieces (see the technique described in Note, page 212).

10. Spread the prepared cooled custard over the dough in the bottom of the springform pan. Arrange the rolls, cut side up, on top of the custard. Cover with a towel and let rise for about 45 minutes, or until almost doubled in size.

11. About 15 minutes before the end of rising, preheat the oven to 375°F.

12. Bake for 30 to 35 minutes, or until the rolls are brown (the internal temperature should reach 190°F). Immediately remove the bread from pan and cool on a rack for 20 minutes before glazing.

13. For the glaze, combine the confectioners' sugar with the rum and enough heavy cream to make a spreadable mixture. Spread the glaze over the top of the bread. Princess bread is best served warm.

Babas au Rhum

FOR THE DOUGH

1 scant tablespoon or
1 (¼ ounce) package active
dry yeast

1 teaspoon sugar

¼ cup warm water (105° to
115°F)

2 cups unbleached all-
purpose flour

4 large eggs, lightly beaten,
at room temperature

1 tablespoon honey

1 teaspoon salt

8 tablespoons (1 stick)
unsalted butter, at room
temperature

¾ cup golden raisins

FOR THE SYRUP AND GLAZE

1½ cups sugar

2 cups boiling water

¼ cup plus 1 tablespoon dark
rum

1 cup strained apricot
preserves

Makes 12

When Polish king Stanislas Leszcynski was exiled to Lorraine, he found the customary *kouglof* too dry for his liking and dipped his bread in rum. So enchanted was he with his creation that he named it after his favorite hero from *A Thousand and One Nights,* the clever Ali Baba. Later, his pastry chef refined the sweet bread by using brioche dough. The result is a light, airy yeast cake that is coated with a sticky, fruity crust. Babas au Rhum are best served soon after baking, slightly warm or at room temperature, but you may make them in advance and then reheat them in a 400°F oven for about 5 minutes. They taste heavenly topped with whipped cream or plain yogurt.

Baba molds, sold in kitchenware shops, are about 3 inches deep, tapering upward from a narrow 2-inch base to a 3-inch mouth. You can improvise with popover pans, brioche molds, custard cups, or muffin tins. If you use glass custard cups, reduce the oven temperature to 350°F.

1. Begin the dough by stirring the yeast and 1 teaspoon sugar into the warm water in a large bowl. Let sit for 10 minutes, until it has doubled and is very bubbly.

2. Add the flour, eggs, honey, and salt to the yeast mixture. Beat vigorously with a dough whisk or heavy-handled spoon for 2 minutes.

3. Cut the butter into 16 pieces. Press each piece into the dough, distributing evenly. Cover the bowl with a tightly woven kitchen towel and let rise for 1 hour at room temperature.

4. Fold the raisins into the dough, and stir until the butter is thoroughly incorporated.

5. Fill well-greased baba cups halfway with dough. Cover with a towel and let rise 20 minutes. Uncover and let rise for 20 minutes more.

6. While the dough is rising, preheat the oven to 375°F.

7. Bake the babas for about 15 minutes or until lightly golden on top (the internal temperature should reach 190°F). Remove from the cups to cool on a rack.

8. Prepare the syrup. In a medium saucepan, combine the 1½ cups sugar and boiling water and stir until the sugar dissolves. Bring the mixture to a rolling boil, reduce the heat and simmer for 2 minutes. Remove from the heat and stir in ¼ cup rum.

9. Submerge the babas, one at a time, in the hot syrup for about 5 seconds. The outside should absorb some of the syrup, but should not get soggy. Put the babas on the rack and let them stand for 30 minutes.

10. Reheat the syrup until very hot. Dip the babas in the syrup mixture for another 5 seconds and return to the rack.

11. Heat the apricot preserves over low heat until melted. Add the remaining 1 tablespoon rum. Brush the glaze over the babas to cover them completely. Serve warm or at room temperature.

Bread is low in calories; it's what you put *on* bread that can be devastating. Certainly, butter or margarine enhances bread, but unadorned bread or bread dipped in soup is wonderful.

Colomba di Pasqua

2 scant tablespoons or
2 (¼-ounce) packages active
dry yeast

½ cup warm water (105° to
115°F)

8 tablespoons (1 stick)
unsalted butter, at room
temperature

8 ounces almond paste

½ cup sugar, plus additional
as needed

4 large eggs, at room
temperature

2 tablespoons grated lemon
peel

1 tablespoon vanilla extract

1 teaspoon salt

½ cup warm milk (105° to
115°F)

4½ to 5½ cups unbleached
all-purpose flour

1 cup thinly sliced almonds

Makes 1 large loaf

This almond-decorated Easter loaf shaped like a dove has its origins in both Portugal and Italy. Many versions of the bread have a bit of almond paste spread on the wings and tail. Since these sections seemed to be the first devoured in my family, I decided to make the bread with the almond paste baked into the dough so that the desired flavor was present throughout the loaf. Do not be concerned if the dough does not rise as much as you expect—the almond paste weighs it down.

1. In a small cup or bowl, soften the yeast in the water.

2. In a large bowl, beat the butter, almond paste, and sugar together until light and fluffy. Separate one of the eggs and set aside.

3. Add the softened yeast, lemon peel, vanilla, salt, 3 of the eggs, the egg yolk, milk, and 3 cups of the flour to the butter mixture. Beat vigorously with a dough whisk or heavy-handled spoon for 2 minutes.

4. Gradually add more of the remaining flour, ¼ cup at a time, until the dough forms a mass and begins to pull away from the side of the bowl. Turn the dough out onto a floured work surface.

5. Knead, adding more flour, a little at a time as necessary, for 8 to 10 minutes, or until you have a smooth, elastic dough.

6. Put the dough into an oiled bowl. Turn to coat the entire ball of dough with oil. Cover with a tightly woven kitchen towel and let rise for about 1½ hours. Because of the almond paste, the dough will not double in size.

7. Turn the dough out onto a lightly oiled work surface. Divide it in half and smooth each half into a ball. Cover with a towel and let rest for 5 minutes.

8. Shape one ball of dough into a half oval 12 inches long and 4 inches wide at the center (diagram 1). Put it in the center of a parchment-lined baking sheet. This will be the wings of the bird. Flatten the center slightly.

9. Shape the other ball of dough into an 8 × 16 × 16-inch triangle with rounded rather than pointed angles (diagram 2).

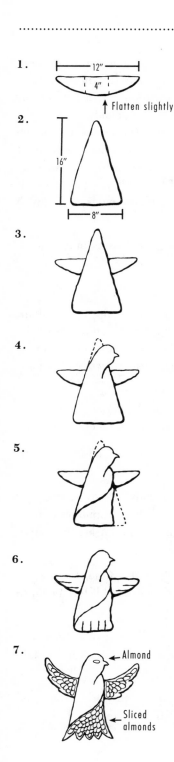

1.

12"

4"

↑ Flatten slightly

2.

16"

8"

3.

4.

5.

6.

7.

← Almond

Sliced
almonds

Center the triangle over the half circle (diagram 3). Fold the top point of the triangle over to make the head and pinch its tip to form a beak (diagram 4). Twist the base of the triangle in the opposite direction to form the tail (diagram 5). Cut 2-inch slits along the bottom edge of the tail and the ends of the wings. Fan them out like feathers (diagram 6). Cover with a towel and let rise for 45 minutes. The dough will not rise as high as other yeast doughs, but it will rise a little and then rise more in the oven.

10. About 15 minutes before the end of rising, preheat the oven to 375°F.

11. Beat the egg white until frothy. Lightly brush the dove with the beaten egg white and spread the almonds, overlapping slightly, on the tail and wings to simulate feathers, reserving a small piece of almond to make the dove's eye (diagram 7). Carefully brush the almonds with the remaining egg white and sprinkle the dove with granulated sugar, if desired.

12. Bake for 20 minutes. Cover the bread loosely with aluminum foil, shiny side up. Continue to bake for 10 to 15 more minutes, or until golden brown and hollow sounding when tapped (the internal temperature should reach 190°F).

13. Remove the dove from the baking sheet and cool on a rack.

Betsy's Stollen

FOR THE DOUGH

1 cup raisins

1 cup mixed candied fruits (see page 281)

¼ cup orange juice or rum

2 scant tablespoons or 2 (¼-ounce) packages active dry yeast

¼ cup warm water (105° to 115°F)

1 cup warm milk (105° to 115°F)

8 tablespoons (1 stick) unsalted butter, softened

4½ to 5½ cups unbleached all-purpose flour

½ cup granulated sugar

½ teaspoon ground mace

2 tablespoons grated lemon peel

2 large eggs, lightly beaten

2 teaspoons salt

1 cup chopped almonds

2 tablespoons unsalted butter, melted

FOR THE FILLING

2 tablespoons granulated sugar

1 tablespoon cinnamon

I have always had a special fondness for stollen, the fruited nut bread from Germany that is so much a part of the Christmas holidays. Therefore, it was with great excitement that I tasted my first "authentic" German stollen when my husband, Keith, and I moved to Germany with the army. Much to my dismay, the stollen was dry and cakey—not at all like the ones I had made at home. I worked on perfecting my private idea of stollen and have come up with a wonderfully moist bread that I top with a sugary glaze. If you prefer, brush the stollen with melted butter and then dust with confectioners' sugar.

1. Begin the dough by combining the raisins and candied fruits with the orange juice or rum. Set aside.

2. In a large bowl, soften the yeast in the water.

3. Add the milk, 8 tablespoons butter, 2 cups of the flour, ½ cup granulated sugar, the mace, lemon peel, and eggs to the yeast. Beat vigorously with a dough whisk or heavy-handled spoon for 2 minutes. The sponge will have the consistency of cake batter.

4. Cover the bowl with plastic wrap and a tightly woven kitchen towel. Let rise for 30 minutes, or until the sponge is light and full of bubbles. (Both coverings are necessary to protect the sponge.)

5. Stir the sponge to deflate it. Add the salt, raisin-fruit mixture, and almonds and mix well.

6. Gradually add more of the remaining flour, ¼ cup at a time, until the dough forms a mass and begins to pull away from the side of the bowl. Turn the dough out onto a lightly floured work surface.

7. Knead, adding more flour, a little at a time, for 8 to 10 minutes, or until you have an elastic dough and blisters begin to develop on the surface.

8. Put the dough into an oiled bowl and turn to coat the entire ball of dough with oil. Cover with a towel and let rise for about 45 minutes, or until doubled in size.

9. Turn the dough out onto a lightly oiled work surface and divide it in half. Shape each half into a 9 × 13-inch oval. Brush 1

FOR THE ICING

1 cup confectioners' sugar

About 6 tablespoons heavy cream

Red and green candied cherries (optional)

Makes 2 stollens

tablespoon of melted butter on each oval. Stir together the 2 tablespoons of granulated sugar and the cinnamon. Sprinkle the cinnamon sugar lengthwise over half of each oval, dividing it equally between them. Fold each oval in half lengthwise. Carefully lift the stollens onto a parchment-lined baking sheet. Press the folded side of each loaf slightly to help the stollen keep its shape during rising and baking.

10. Cover with a towel and let rise for 45 minutes.

11. About 15 minutes before the end of rising, preheat the oven to 375°F.

12. Bake for 25 to 30 minutes, or until golden brown (the internal temperature of the stollen should reach 190°F). Remove from the baking sheet to cool on a rack. Let sit for 30 minutes before icing.

13. For the icing, combine the confectioners' sugar with enough heavy cream to make it the consistency of honey. Drizzle the icing over the tops of the stollen.

14. If desired, cut the red cherries into sixths and put them on top of the stollen in the shape of flower petals. Cut the green cherries into fourths to make stems and leaves.

Stale bread makes excellent croutons, bread crumbs, or French toast.

Gingerbread Men

2 scant tablespoons or
2 (¼-ounce) packages active
dry yeast

½ cup warm water (105° to
115°F)

2 cups whole wheat flour

2 teaspoons salt

½ cup sugar

1 teaspoon powdered
mustard

1 teaspoon ground cinnamon

1 teaspoon ground ginger

½ teaspoon ground cloves

2 cups warm milk (105° to
115°F)

½ cup dark or light molasses

¼ cup solid vegetable
shortening

5 to 6 cups unbleached all-
purpose flour

1 large egg beaten with 1
tablespoon cold milk, for the
egg wash

Raisins, for decoration

Makes 16

True to the old tale of the gingerbread man, these little guys are well worth the chase, whether it's down the road or into the kitchen. The inclusion of mustard may sound odd, but it enhances the other flavors. You can shape this spicy yeast dough into any sort of loaf, but I like the fanciful gingerbread men best.

1. In a large bowl, soften the yeast in the water.

2. Whisk the whole wheat flour, salt, sugar, mustard, cinnamon, ginger, and cloves together to distribute the spices evenly through the flour. Add the mixture to the yeast with the milk, molasses, shortening, and 1 cup of the all-purpose flour. Beat vigorously with a dough whisk or a heavy-handled spoon for 2 minutes.

3. Gradually add more of the remaining flour, ¼ cup at a time, until the dough forms a mass and begins to pull away from the side of the bowl. Turn the dough out onto a floured work surface.

4. Knead, adding more flour, a little at a time as necessary, for 8 to 10 minutes, or until you have a smooth, elastic dough and blisters begin to develop on the surface.

5. Put the dough into an oiled bowl. Turn to coat the entire ball of dough with oil. Cover with a tightly woven kitchen towel and let rise for about 1 hour, or until doubled in size.

6. Turn the dough out onto a lightly oiled work surface and divide it in half. (You'll be using 2 baking sheets—if you have a small oven or only 1 baking sheet, see Note, page 189.) Divide each piece in half again and continue until there are 16 equal pieces. Working with one piece at a time, pinch off a piece of dough about the size of a golf ball. Shape it into a smooth ball and set aside. Shape the remainder of the piece of dough into a smooth ball and gently roll this into a 4-inch cylinder; this will be the body (diagram 1). Put the smaller ball at the top for a head. Using scissors, cut the dough to make arms and legs (diagram 2). Put the dough on a parchment-lined baking sheet and spread it out to make a gingerbread man (diagram 3). Cover with a towel. Shape the remaining pieces of dough into gingerbread men in the same way, spacing them 2 inches apart on the baking sheets. Let rise, covered, for 45 minutes.

7. About 15 minutes before the end of rising, preheat the oven to 375°F.

8. Just before baking, lightly brush each man with the egg wash. Decorate with raisins for eyes, nose, mouth, and buttons. Using a toothpick, press the raisins firmly into the dough or they will come off when the dough rises during baking (diagram 4).

9. Bake the gingerbread men for 25 to 30 minutes, or until they are well browned (the internal temperature should reach 190°F). Remove from the baking sheets and cool on a rack.

1.

2.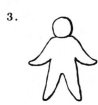

3.

4.

Orange Wreath with Orange Butter

FOR THE DOUGH

½ cup granulated sugar

½ cup boiling water

½ cup fresh orange juice

3 tablespoons grated orange peel

1 scant tablespoon or 1 (¼-ounce) package active dry yeast

½ cup warm water (105° to 115°F)

1 cup warm orange juice (105° to 115°F)

¼ cup solid vegetable shortening

2 large eggs, at room temperature

1 teaspoon salt

4½ to 5½ cups unbleached all-purpose flour

FOR THE ORANGE BUTTER

½ pound (2 sticks) unsalted butter, at room temperature

1 tablespoon reserved sugared orange peel

This lightly sweetened bread shaped into a wreath is big and showy —just right for a holiday party. The orange butter, while not absolutely necessary, adds bittersweet flavor and an attractive touch when served in a bowl in the center of the wreath.

1. Combine the granulated sugar with the boiling water, ½ cup orange juice, and the orange peel in a heavy saucepan over medium heat. Stir until the sugar dissolves and bring the mixture to a rolling boil. Reduce the heat and simmer, uncovered, for about 30 minutes, or until the mixture is reduced by half and thickened. Strain, reserving the orange syrup and the sugared orange peel separately. Allow to cool.

2. In a large bowl, soften the yeast in the water.

3. Add 2 tablespoons of the sugared orange peel, the warm orange juice, shortening, eggs, salt, and 2 cups of the flour to the yeast. Beat vigorously for 2 minutes.

4. Gradually add more of the remaining flour, ¼ cup at a time, until the dough forms a mass and begins to pull away from the side of the bowl. Turn the dough out onto a floured work surface.

5. Knead, adding more flour, a little at a time as necessary, for 8 to 10 minutes, or until you have a smooth elastic dough and blisters begin to develop on the surface.

6. Put the dough into an oiled bowl. Turn to coat the entire ball of dough with oil. Cover with a tightly woven kitchen towel and let rise for about 1 hour, or until doubled in size.

7. Turn the dough out onto a lightly oiled work surface. Cut or break off one fourth of the dough; set aside and cover with a towel. Divide the remaining dough in half and with your hands roll each piece into a 30-inch rope. Loosely twist the two ropes together (diagram 1) and join the ends to form a circle. The top rope should connect with the bottom rope from the opposite side (diagram 2). Put the circle on a well-greased or parchment-lined baking sheet and cover with a towel.

8. Divide the reserved dough into quarters. Roll each piece into a pencil-thin rope about 28 inches long (diagram 3). Loosely twist 2 of the ropes together. Repeat with the remaining 2 ropes.

1 cup confectioners' sugar

¼ cup reserved orange syrup (or an orange-flavored liqueur such as Grand Marnier, or fresh orange juice)

Makes 1 large wreath

1.

2.

3.

4.

Loosely wrap a small twist around the large twist, gently lifting portions of large wreath so that it is encircled—lay the small twist in the creases (diagram 4) and tuck the end underneath. Continue with the second small twist so that the wreath is wrapped all the way around.

9. Butter the outside of a 5-inch ovenproof bowl and put it in the center of the wreath. Gently push the wreath so that the bowl fits snugly in the middle. Cover with a towel and let rise for 30 minutes. Take care not to let the dough rise for too long or the larger twist will break the smaller ones.

10. About 15 minutes before the end of rising, preheat the oven to 375°F.

11. Bake the wreath for 25 to 30 minutes, or until it is golden brown (the internal temperature should reach 190°F). Remove from the baking sheet to cool on a rack. Remove the bowl from the center of the wreath.

12. To make the orange butter, cut the butter up roughly into tablespoon-size pieces. Combine all the ingredients for the orange butter and beat until light and fluffy. Brush some of the butter over the warm wreath. Let cool for 5 minutes and brush again. Put the remaining orange butter in the same bowl used to form the wreath. Just before serving, return it to its niche in the center of the wreath, this time setting the bread on a buffet table.

Cherry Almond Wreath

2 scant tablespoons or
2 (¼-ounce) packages active
dry yeast

½ cup warm water (105° to
115°F)

1½ cups warm milk (105° to
115°F)

8 ounces almond paste,
crumbled

8 tablespoons (1 stick)
unsalted butter, at room
temperature

2 teaspoons salt

3 large eggs, lightly beaten

2 teaspoons grated lemon
peel

5½ to 6½ cups unbleached
all-purpose flour

2 cups coarsely chopped red
candied cherries

2 cups coarsely chopped
green candied cherries

2 cups finely chopped
almonds

1 large egg beaten with
1 tablespoon cold water, for
the egg wash

Pärlsocker (see page 30) or
coarsely broken sugar cubes
(optional)

Makes 2 wreaths

I add almond paste to the dough for this fruit-filled holiday wreath to make it as tasty as it is unusual. The resulting bread makes a magnificent gift from your kitchen and your heart, one that is sure to be appreciated by everyone. If you prefer, substitute dried apricots or dried cherries for the candied fruit. It is good either way.

1. In a large bowl, soften the yeast in the water.

2. Add the milk, almond paste, butter, salt, eggs, lemon peel, and 3 cups of the flour. Beat vigorously with a dough whisk or a heavy-handled spoon for 2 minutes.

3. Gradually add more of the remaining flour, ¼ cup at a time, until the dough forms a mass and begins to pull away from the side of the bowl. Turn the dough out onto a floured work surface.

4. Knead, adding more flour, a little at a time as necessary, until you have a smooth, elastic dough and blisters begin to develop on the surface.

5. Put the dough into an oiled bowl and turn once to coat the entire ball of dough with oil. Cover with a tightly woven kitchen towel and let rise for about 1 hour, or until doubled in size. Line 2 baking sheets with parchment.

6. Turn the dough out onto a lightly oiled work surface. Using a rolling pin, roll into a 22 × 16-inch rectangle. Let rest for 5 minutes. Cut into four 22-inch strips.

7. Combine the red and green cherries with the almonds. Sprinkle this mixture evenly down the center of each dough strip and, using your hands, roll into a 22-inch cylinder. Loosely twist two of the cylinders together (diagram 1). Lift the dough twist carefully onto a prepared baking sheet and bend to form a circle. Join the end of the bottom left strip to the end of the top right strip (diagram 2) and lay the end of the bottom right strip on top of the join. Stretch the top left strip slightly so that it covers the end of the bottom right strip (diagram 3) and tuck it under the wreath (diagram 4).

8. Repeat with the remaining 2 cylinders of dough. Cover the wreaths with a towel and let rise for about 45 minutes, or until almost doubled in size.

9. About 15 minutes before end of rising, preheat the oven to 375°F.

10. Just before baking, lightly brush each wreath with egg wash. Sprinkle with parlsöcker or coarse sugar, if desired.

11. Bake the wreaths for 25 to 30 minutes, or until they are golden brown (the internal temperature should reach 190°F). Remove from the baking sheets and cool on a rack.

1.

2.

3.

4.

Hazelnut Holiday Tree

FOR THE DOUGH

*2 scant tablespoons or
2 (¹/₄-ounce) packages active
dry yeast*

*¹/₂ cup warm water (105° to
115°F)*

*1¹/₂ cups warm milk (105° to
115°F)*

¹/₂ cup honey

*4 tablespoons (¹/₂ stick)
unsalted butter, at room
temperature*

2 large eggs, lightly beaten

2 teaspoons salt

*5¹/₂ to 6¹/₂ cups unbleached
all-purpose flour*

FOR THE FILLING

1¹/₂ cups hazelnut or filberts

*8 tablespoons (1 stick)
unsalted butter, at room
temperature*

1¹/₂ cups confectioners' sugar

1 tablespoon vanilla extract

¹/₂ teaspoon grated nutmeg

FOR THE ICING

2 cups confectioners' sugar

*3 ounces cream cheese, at
room temperature*

2 to 4 tablespoons milk

Makes 2 trees

Hazelnuts are combined here with butter and sugar and a whisper of nutmeg for a sweet, full-bodied filling that makes this holiday loaf, shaped like a tree, a special breakfast or brunch treat as well as a welcome gift.

1. Begin the dough by softening the yeast in the water in a large bowl.

2. Add the milk, honey, 4 tablespoons butter, eggs, salt, and 2 cups of the flour. Beat vigorously with a dough whisk or a heavy-handled spoon for 2 minutes.

3. Gradually add more of the remaining flour, ¹/₄ cup at a time, until the dough forms a mass and begins to pull away from the side of the bowl. Turn the dough out onto a floured work surface.

4. Knead, adding more flour, a little at a time as necessary, for 8 to 10 minutes, or until you have a smooth, elastic dough and blisters begin to develop on the surface.

5. Put the dough into an oiled bowl. Turn to coat the entire ball of dough with oil. Cover with a tightly woven kitchen towel and let rise for about 1 hour, or until doubled in size.

6. Meanwhile, preheat the oven to 350°F. Line the baking sheets with parchment.

7. Prepare the filling. Put the nuts on an ungreased baking sheet and bake for 20 minutes, or until they are golden brown under the skin. Remove from the oven and place the nuts in a rough-textured towel (such as terrycloth). Rub the nuts in the towel to remove as much of the skin as possible. Finely chop the skinned nuts—this is easily done in a food processor or blender.

8. Turn off the oven but keep the door closed to hold in the heat.

9. Beat the 8 tablespoons butter with the 1¹/₂ cups confectioners' sugar, vanilla, and nutmeg until fluffy. Fold in the nuts. Set the filling aside.

10. Turn the dough out onto a lightly oiled work surface. Divide it in half and roll each piece into a 10 × 12-inch rectangle.

1.

2.

3.

4.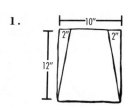

5.

6.

7.

11. Position one dough rectangle in front of you so that the shorter edges are at the top and bottom. Using the point of a knife, mark the dough 2 inches from the top left and right corners. Trim the dough from the marks to the bottom left and right corners to make a trapezoid (diagram 1). Reserve the dough trimmings in their original triangular shape.

12. Spread half the filling evenly over the dough, leaving a ½-inch border all around. Bring the sides of the dough to the center and pinch together firmly to seal (diagram 2). Fold up the bottom edge of the dough and pinch to seal (diagram 3). Turn the filled dough seam side down and place on a prepared baking sheet.

13. Using scissors, make angled 2-inch cuts about 1 inch apart down each long side of the dough so that it resembles a spruce tree (diagram 4).

14. Put the reserved dough trimmings together to form a rectangle as shown in diagram 5. Loosely twist the rectangle (diagram 6). Bend the twist into a U shape (diagram 7). Put the loose ends under the bottom of the dough tree to form the trunk.

15. Shape and fill the remaining piece of dough in the same way. Cover the filled dough trees with a towel and let rise for about 45 minutes, or until almost doubled in size.

16. About 15 minutes before the end of rising, preheat the oven to 375°F.

17. Bake the loaves for 30 to 35 minutes, or until they are golden brown (the internal temperature should reach 190°F).

18. Remove to a rack and let cool for 20 minutes before icing.

19. For the icing, beat the 2 cups confectioners' sugar with the cream cheese until smooth. Add enough milk to make a spreadable icing. Spread the icing on top of the filled dough trees.

Pan Dulce

2 scant tablespoons or
2 (¼-ounce) packages active
dry yeast

½ cup warm water (105° to
115°F)

1¾ cups warm milk (105° to
115°F)

8 tablespoons (1 stick)
unsalted butter, at room
temperature

¾ cup sugar

1 teaspoon salt

2 large eggs, lightly beaten

5½ to 6½ cups unbleached
all-purpose flour

1 teaspoon fennel seeds

1 cup golden raisins

½ cup currants

½ cup candied lemon peel
(see page 280)

½ cup candied orange peel
(see page 280)

1 cup finely chopped
almonds

1 egg yolk beaten with
2 tablespoons water, for the
egg wash

Makes 2 loaves

Serve this Mexican fruit and spice bread instead of fruitcake for a change during the winter holidays. Try it toasted, too, spread with butter or cream cheese.

1. In a large bowl, soften the yeast in the water.

2. Add the milk, butter, sugar, salt, eggs, 2 cups of the flour, the fennel seeds, raisins, currants, lemon peel, orange peel, and almonds. Beat vigorously with a dough whisk or a heavy-handled spoon for 2 minutes.

3. Gradually add more of the remaining flour, ¼ cup at a time, until the dough forms a mass and begins to pull away from the side of the bowl. Turn the dough out onto a floured work surface.

4. Knead, adding more flour, a little at a time as necessary, for 8 to 10 minutes, or until you have a smooth, elastic dough.

5. Put the dough into an oiled bowl. Turn to coat the entire ball of dough with oil. Cover with a tightly woven kitchen towel and let rise for about 1½ hours, or until doubled in size.

6. Turn the dough out onto a lightly oiled work surface and divide it in half. Shape each piece into a ball and place well apart on a parchment-lined baking sheet. Flatten each ball slightly. Cover with a towel and let rise for about 1 hour, or until almost doubled in size.

7. About 15 minutes before the end of rising, preheat the oven to 375°F.

8. Just before baking, make three cuts in the top of each loaf to form a triangle. Brush the egg wash lightly over the top and sides of each loaf.

9. Bake for 40 to 45 minutes, or until the loaves are well browned and sound hollow when tapped (the internal temperature should reach 190°F). Watch carefully during the last 10 minutes of baking. If the bread starts to become too brown, cover the top loosely with a piece of foil, shiny side up.

10. Remove from the baking sheet and cool on a rack.

Panettone

1 scant tablespoon or
1 (¼-ounce) package active
dry yeast

¼ cup warm water (105° to
115°F)

1½ cups warm milk (105° to
115°F)

½ cup sugar

1 teaspoon salt

4½ to 5½ cups unbleached
all-purpose flour

2 teaspoons crushed anise
seeds

¾ cup golden raisins

½ cup pine nuts

½ cup shelled pistachio nuts

½ cup finely chopped
candied lemon peel

½ cup finely chopped
candied citron

2 tablespoons grated orange
peel

4 tablespoons (½ stick)
unsalted butter, at room
temperature

Makes 1 loaf

Chock full of candied citrus rind, raisins, pistachios, and pine nuts, gently spiced with anise, this is one of my all-time favorite Christmas breads. When baked in a traditional panettone pan, it is gloriously domed, designed to represent the domed church steeples of Italy. I have seen recipes recommending coffee cans, brown paper bags, and soufflé dishes fitted with paper collars as viable substitutes for hard-to-find panettone pans. I find none of these particularly satisfactory and so have developed a recipe using a Bundt or kugelhopf pan.

1. In a large bowl, soften the yeast in the water.

2. Add the milk, sugar, salt, 2 cups of the flour, the anise seeds, raisins, pine nuts, pistachio nuts, lemon peel, citron, orange peel, and the butter. Beat vigorously with a dough whisk or heavy-handled spoon for 2 minutes.

3. Gradually add more of the remaining flour, ¼ cup a time, until the dough forms a mass and begins to pull away from the side of the bowl. Turn the dough out onto a floured work surface.

4. Knead, adding more flour, a little at a time as necessary, for 8 to 10 minutes, or until you have an elastic dough and blisters begin to develop on the surface.

5. Put the dough into an oiled bowl. Turn to coat the entire ball of dough with oil. Cover with a tightly woven kitchen towel and let rise for about 1½ hours, or until doubled in size.

6. Turn the dough out onto a lightly oiled work surface and shape it into a ball. Punch a large hole in the center of the ball with your finger. Stretch the hole to about 3 inches in diameter. Fit the dough into a large, well-greased tube pan with the center post protruding through the hole. Cover with a towel and let rise for about 1 hour, or until almost doubled in size.

7. About 15 minutes before the end of rising, preheat the oven to 375°F.

8. Bake the bread for 45 to 50 minutes, or until it is well browned and hollow sounding when tapped (the internal temperature should reach 190°F). Remove from the pan and cool on a rack.

Scottish Black Bun

1 scant tablespoon or
1 (¼-ounce) package active
dry yeast

¼ cup warm water (105° to
115°F)

1 cup warm milk (105° to
115°F)

2 large eggs, at room
temperature

2 tablespoons unsalted
butter, at room temperature

¼ cup sugar

1 teaspoon salt

¼ teaspoon ground pepper

1 teaspoon ground cinnamon

1 teaspoon ground ginger

4 to 5 cups unbleached
all-purpose flour

2 cups currants

1 cup dark raisins

2 tablespoons finely chopped
candied or crystallized
ginger

½ cup finely chopped
candied orange peel
(see page 280)

½ cup finely chopped
candied lemon peel
(see page 280)

2 cups finely chopped
walnuts, pecans, cashews,
almonds, or other nuts

½ cup honey

Scottish black bun is a loaf of moist bread served during the Christmas holidays and especially at New Year's Eve. To form the bread, a portion of the dough is mixed with fruits and nuts and the fruited dough is then wrapped in the rest of the dough. During rising and baking, the bread should be weighted to compress both doughs so that the finished loaf is uniform and dense in texture. Although Scottish bun traditionally is made into one loaf, you can make smaller loaves by baking the bread in 5 × 3½-inch loaf pans. These small versions make lovely gifts.

1. In a large bowl, soften the yeast in the water.

2. Add the milk, eggs, butter, sugar, salt, pepper, cinnamon, ground ginger, and 2 cups of the flour. Beat vigorously with a dough whisk or heavy-handled spoon for 2 minutes.

3. Gradually add more of the remaining flour, ¼ cup at a time, until the dough forms a mass and begins to pull away from the side of the bowl. Turn the dough onto a floured work surface.

4. Knead, adding more flour, a little at a time as necessary, for 8 to 10 minutes, or until you have an elastic dough and blisters begin to develop on the surface.

5. Put the dough into an oiled bowl. Turn to coat the entire ball of dough with oil. Cover with a tightly woven kitchen towel and let rise for about 1 hour, or until doubled in size.

6. In a large bowl, combine the currants, raisins, candied ginger, candied orange and lemon peel, nuts, and honey. Add the brandy if desired. Stir until well mixed.

7. Turn the dough out onto a lightly oiled work surface. Cut or break off a third of the dough, set it aside, and cover with a towel.

8. Coat your hands with a thin film of cooking oil. Combine the two thirds of dough with the fruit and nut mixture by squeezing the fruit into the dough with your fingers. Use a plastic dough scraper or spatula on the work surface to help with this sticky and messy procedure, and keep your hands and the work surface lightly oiled. Do not add more flour. Alternatively, use a heavy-duty mixer to combine the fruit with the dough.

¼ cup brandy (optional)

1 egg beaten with 1 tablespoon cold water, for the egg wash

Makes 1 large loaf

9. Shape the fruited dough into a ball. Cover with a towel and set aside.

10. Take the reserved dough and break off one third of it. Set the small piece aside and cover with a towel.

11. On a lightly oiled work surface, roll the larger portion of the reserved dough into a 15-inch round. Carefully ease the rolled dough into a well-greased 9-inch springform pan, with the excess dough extending over the sides of the pan.

12. Put the fruited dough ball into the dough-lined pan. The heavier, fruited dough may pull the plain dough (lining the pan) into the pan. If so, stretch the plain dough up so that you are able to encase the fruited dough. Pleat the plain dough evenly over the top of the fruited dough.

13. On a lightly oiled work surface, roll the remaining third of dough into a 9-inch round. Center it on the top of the pleated dough in the springform pan, making sure it reaches the edges of the pan. Cover with a towel and let rest for 30 minutes.

14. About 15 minutes before the end of the rest period, preheat the oven to 375°F.

15. Just before baking, prick holes through the top layer of dough into the fruited dough, about 1 inch deep, using a skewer or toothpick. Weight the dough with something flat, such as a cake pan that has been greased on the under surface or an ovenproof plate; then place a heavier object (such as a small brick, thick kitchen tile, or heavy ovenproof measuring cup) on top of that. This compresses the dough and controls the rising so the finished loaf is uniform and dense in texture. Bake for 1½ hours (smaller loaves should bake only 1 hour).

16. Remove the weight from the top of the loaf; unclasp and remove the outside ring from the springform pan and place the loaf upside down on a parchment-lined baking sheet. Brush the top and sides of the loaf with the egg wash, taking care not to let it spill onto the baking sheet.

17. Return the bread to the oven and bake for 5 to 10 minutes more, or until the loaves are golden brown (the internal tempera-

(continued)

Striezel

2 scant tablespoons or
2 (¼-ounce) packages active
dry yeast

½ cup warm water (105° to
115°F)

1 cup warm milk (105° to
115°F)

½ cup sugar

1 teaspoon salt

8 tablespoons (1 stick)
unsalted butter, at room
temperature

2 large eggs

2 large egg yolks

2 teaspoons vanilla extract

5½ to 6½ cups unbleached
all-purpose flour

1½ cups mixed candied fruit
(see page 281)

2 egg whites beaten with
1 tablespoon cold water,
for the egg wash

Pärlsocker (see page 30) or
coarsely broken sugar cubes

**Makes 1 large double
braided loaf**

ture should reach 190°F). Another test is to stick a pick into the center of the loaf. If it comes out clean with no dough sticking to it, it is done. The bread is best if left to mellow for at least 6 hours before serving.

In the United States, European holiday traditions are passed down from generation to generation not only as treasured ties to the past but because they taste so good. This light and buttery Austrian bread, seductively flavored with candied fruit, is fashioned into a large double braid for a pretty presentation or elegant gift.

1. In a large bowl, soften the yeast in the water.

2. Add the milk, sugar, salt, butter, eggs, yolks, vanilla, and 3 cups of the flour. Beat vigorously with a dough whisk or a heavy-handled spoon for 2 minutes. Add the candied fruit and stir to combine.

3. Gradually add more of the remaining flour, ¼ cup at a time, until the dough forms a mass and begins to pull away from the side of the bowl. Turn the dough out onto a floured work surface.

4. Knead, adding more flour, a little at a time as necessary, for 8 to 10 minutes, or until you have an elastic dough and blisters begin to develop on the surface.

5. Put the dough into an oiled bowl. Turn to coat the entire ball of dough with oil. Cover with a tightly woven kitchen towel and let rise for about 1 hour, or until doubled in size.

6. Turn the dough out onto a lightly oiled work surface and divide it into quarters. Set one piece of the dough aside and cover with a towel. Roll the three remaining pieces of dough into 20-inch ropes. Lay the ropes side by side on a parchment-lined or well-greased baking sheet.

7. Braid the dough, beginning in the center for a more balanced braid. Bring the right rope over the center rope and then the left rope over the center, the right over the center, the left over the center, continuing until the ropes are too short to braid. Pinch the ends together and tuck them under.

8. To braid the other end of the loaf, turn it so the braided portion is at the top and the ropes are at the bottom. Bring the center rope over the right rope and then the center rope over the left, the center over the right, the center over the left, and continue until the ends are too short to braid. Pinch the ends together and tuck them under.

9. With the side of your hand, make an indentation down the center of the braid. This helps keep the top braid in place.

10. Divide the remaining piece of dough into thirds. Roll each piece into a 22-inch rope. Braid as described above, but do not tuck the ends under when they become too short to braid. Lay the small braid down the center of the large braid in the indentation. Fold the ends of the small braid under the ends of the large braid.

11. Cover the braids with a towel and let rise for about 45 minutes, until almost doubled in size.

12. About 15 minutes before the end of rising, preheat the oven to 375°F.

13. Just before baking, lightly brush the top of the braids with the egg wash, taking care not to let it drip down onto the pan. Sprinkle with pärlsocker, if desired.

14. Bake for 35 to 40 minutes, or until golden brown and the loaf sounds hollow when tapped (the internal temperature of the braid should reach 190°F). Remove from the baking sheet and cool on a rack.

Christopsomo

½ cup finely chopped figs

¼ cup sweet red wine

2 scant tablespoons or
2 (¼-ounce) packages active
dry yeast

½ cup warm water (105° to
115°F)

1 cup warm milk (105° to
115°F)

½ pound (2 sticks) unsalted
butter, at room temperature

4 large eggs, beaten

½ cup honey

1 tablespoon crushed anise
seeds

1 tablespoon grated orange
peel

2 teaspoons salt

5½ to 6½ cups unbleached
all-purpose flour

1 egg white, beaten

8 candied cherry halves or
8 walnut halves

Makes 2 loaves

This Greek Christmas bread is decorated with the likeness of an early form of the Christian cross. It is a rich, round loaf scented with wine-soaked figs, anise, and orange. I think you will find it marvelous thinly sliced and spread with sweet butter. It is also delicious when toasted.

1. Combine the figs and wine in a glass bowl. Cover and let stand at room temperature for 2 hours.

2. In a large bowl, soften the yeast in the water.

3. Add the milk, butter, eggs, honey, anise seeds, orange peel, salt, 2 cups of the flour, and the fig mixture to the yeast. Beat vigorously with a dough whisk or a heavy-handled spoon for 2 minutes.

4. Gradually add more of the remaining flour, ¼ cup at a time, until the dough forms a mass and begins to pull away from the side of the bowl. Turn the dough out onto a floured work surface.

5. Knead, adding more flour, a little at a time as necessary, for 8 to 10 minutes, or until you have an elastic dough and blisters begin to develop on the surface.

6. Put the dough into an oiled bowl. Turn to coat the entire ball of dough with oil. Cover with a tightly woven kitchen towel and let rise for about 1 hour, or until doubled in size.

7. Turn the dough out onto a lightly oiled work surface and divide it in half. Pinch off 1 golf ball–size piece of dough from each half. Divide these small balls in half and then use your hands to roll each half into a 12-inch rope (you will have 4 ropes). Shape the remaining pieces of dough into 2 smooth balls and put them far apart on a parchment-lined 13 × 18-inch baking sheet. Flatten each ball of dough into an 8-inch round, about 2 inches thick. Lay 2 ropes across the center of each round to form a cross (diagram 1). Make a 3-inch cut into the end of each rope and curl the ends back to form circles (diagram 2).

8. Cover the loaves with a towel and let rise for about 45 minutes, or until almost doubled in size.

9. About 15 minutes before the end of rising, preheat the oven to 375°F.

10. Just before baking, lightly brush each loaf with the beaten egg white. Put a cherry or walnut in the center of each circle.

11. Bake for 35 to 40 minutes, or until the loaves are golden brown and sound hollow when tapped (the internal temperature should reach 190°F). Cool on a rack.

1.

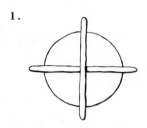

2.

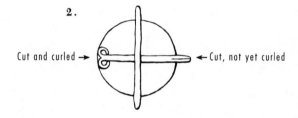

Cut and curled →   ← Cut, not yet curled

Holiday Lattice Loaf

FOR THE BREAD

1 scant tablespoon or
1 (1/4-ounce) package active
dry yeast

1/4 cup warm water (105° to
115°F)

3/4 cup warm milk (105° to
115°F)

1/4 cup solid vegetable
shortening

1/4 cup honey

2 large eggs, lightly beaten

1 teaspoon vanilla extract

1 teaspoon salt

4 cups unbleached all-
purpose flour

FOR THE FILLING

1 cup mixed candied fruit
(see page 281)

1 cup finely chopped nuts

FOR THE GLAZE

1 cup confectioners' sugar

4 to 6 tablespoons fresh
orange juice

Makes 1 loaf

I developed this lattice-shaped loaf for the holidays and filled it with the expected and much loved candied fruit and nuts, but you could also fill it with a mixture of apples, cinnamon, sugar, nuts, and raisins for a completely different character. Or reduce the honey by half, omit the vanilla extract, and fill the bread with a mixture of spinach, walnuts, sun-dried tomatoes, and cream cheese. How wonderful that would be at a holiday open house!

1. Begin the dough by softening the yeast in the water in a large bowl.

2. Add the milk, shortening, honey, eggs, vanilla, salt, and 2 cups of the flour. Beat vigorously with a dough whisk or heavy-handled spoon for 2 minutes.

3. Gradually add more of the remaining flour, 1/4 cup at a time, until the dough forms a mass and begins to pull away from the side of the bowl. Turn the dough out onto a floured work surface.

4. Knead, adding more flour, a little at a time as necessary, for 8 to 10 minutes, or until you have a smooth, elastic dough and blisters begin to develop on the surface.

5. Put the dough into an oiled bowl. Turn to coat the entire ball of dough with oil. Cover with a tightly woven kitchen towel and let rise for about 1 hour, or until doubled in size.

6. Turn the dough out directly onto a parchment-lined baking sheet. Roll or pat it into a 9 × 14-inch rectangle.

7. Along both 14-inch sides, snip the dough with kitchen scissors to make a row of 3-inch attached strips, each about 1 inch wide (diagram 1).

8. For the filling, combine the candied fruit and nuts. Spread the filling down the center of the dough in the 3-inch strip between the cuts.

9. Starting at the top and alternating from side to side, fold the strips over the filling toward the center (diagram 2). Stop when you reach the middle of the loaf (diagram 3). Turn the pan around and repeat from the other end. The strips will cover the filling. Twist together the excess dough in the center and shape into loops

1.

2.

3.

4.

to resemble a bow (diagram 4). Cover the loaf with a towel and let rise for about 45 minutes, or until almost doubled in size.

10. About 15 minutes before the end of rising, preheat the oven to 375°F.

11. Bake the loaf for 30 to 35 minutes, or until it is golden brown (the internal temperature should reach 190°F). Transfer to a rack and allow to cool for 15 minutes before glazing.

12. For the glaze, combine the confectioners' sugar with enough orange juice to give it the consistency of honey. Drizzle over the top of the warm loaf.

Fruited Pull-Apart Bread

1 scant tablespoon or
1 (¼-ounce) package active
dry yeast

¼ cup warm water (105° to
115°F)

½ cup warm milk (105° to
115°F)

4 tablespoons (½ stick)
unsalted butter, at room
temperature

1 cup whole wheat flour

1 to 2 cups unbleached all-
purpose flour

¼ cup granulated sugar

¼ teaspoon ground mace

1 tablespoon grated lemon
peel

1 large egg, lightly beaten

1 teaspoon salt

½ cup finely chopped
almonds

1 cup finely diced mixed
candied or dried fruits

4 tablespoons (½ stick)
butter, melted

1 cup granulated sugar
mixed with 2 teaspoons
ground cinnamon

Confectioners' sugar
(optional)

Makes 1 large loaf

I use whole wheat flour for this festive, fun bread baked in a tube or Bundt pan, although you may choose to use all white flour. After the loaf is inverted onto a serving plate, guests separate the slices with a fork, pulling off as many as they like. This bread is made with mixed candied fruit or any mixture of dried fruit. Choose the fruits depending on the season and your preferences.

1. In a large bowl, soften the yeast in the water.

2. Add the milk, butter, all of the whole wheat flour, ½ cup of the all-purpose flour, the sugar, mace, lemon peel, egg, salt, almonds, and diced fruit. Beat vigorously with a dough whisk or heavy-handled spoon for 2 minutes.

3. Gradually beat in more of the remaining flour, ¼ cup at a time, until the dough forms a mass and begins to pull away from the side of the bowl. Turn the dough out onto a floured work surface.

4. Knead, adding more flour, a little at a time as necessary, until you have an elastic dough.

5. Put the dough into an oiled bowl. Turn to coat the entire ball of dough with oil. Cover with a tightly woven kitchen towel and let rise for about 1 hour, or until doubled in size.

6. Turn the dough out onto a lightly oiled work surface and divide it in half. Using a rolling pin roll each piece into a 24 × 9-inch rectangle and let it rest for 5 minutes. Cut each rectangle into twenty-four 3-inch squares. Dip each square into melted butter and then into the sugar-cinnamon mixture. Position each square in a well-greased tube or Bundt pan so that each one is standing on end.

7. Cover with a towel and let rise for about 45 minutes, or until almost doubled in size.

8. About 15 minutes before the end of rising, preheat the oven to 375°F.

9. Bake for 35 to 40 minutes, or until the loaf has shrunk slightly from the side of the pan and sounds hollow when tapped (the internal temperature should reach 190°F). Immediately turn out of the pan and cool on a wire rack. Dust with confectioners' sugar, if desired.

Bread is extremely personal. Three people can follow the same recipe and the end results would produce three entirely different masterpieces. The way each person measures, or doesn't measure, the method of mixing ingredients, the length of time bread is kneaded, the types of pans, the weather, and the oven, are among the many variables. Each bread is entirely you and no one else can completely duplicate it.

Candied Fruit Peel

*4 large grapefruit (or 6 large
navel oranges or 10
tangerines or 12 large
lemons)*

2½ cups plus 1 cup sugar

*2 tablespoons light corn
syrup*

1½ cups water

**Makes about 4 cups
(1½ pounds)**

Since some of my recipes call for candied fruit peel, I am providing you with a method for making it. Candied peel is sold in many areas of the country during the holidays but is generally hard to find at other times of the year. Homemade candied peel keeps well and has much more flavor than store-bought. Rough-skinned citrus fruits have thicker peel and more white pith than smoother-skinned varieties, which are better for juice. If there is too much white pith, trim the peel with a sharp knife so that the peel is about a quarter-inch thick.

1. To remove any waxy preservative, wash the fruit with a dishcloth or towel and mild detergent. Rinse thoroughly.

2. Remove the peel from the fruit. There are gadgets available in cookware stores that remove only the peel. If you do not have one, cut the fruit into fourths and separate the peel from the pulp and trim excess white pith so that the peel is about ¼ inch thick. Cut the peel into ¼-inch dice.

3. Put the peel into a heavy saucepan and cover with water. Bring to a boil over medium-high heat. Reduce the heat, simmer for 5 minutes, and strain through a sieve.

4. Return the peel to the saucepan and repeat step 3. Strain the peel.

5. Combine 2½ cups of the sugar with the corn syrup in the saucepan. Add 1½ cups of water and bring the mixture to a boil over medium-high heat, stirring constantly until the sugar dissolves. After the sugar dissolves, there is no need to stir.

6. Add the peel to the sugar mixture and return to a boil. Reduce the heat and simmer uncovered for 45 minutes.

7. Strain the mixture through a sieve. (If desired, reserve the syrup to sweeten drinks—it is especially good in iced tea, lemonade, or mixed drinks calling for simple syrup where you might want a sharp citrus flavor.)

8. Pour the remaining 1 cup of sugar into a plastic bag. Add the peel and shake the bag until the peel is completely coated with sugar. Separate the pieces of peel if they stick together.

9. Line a large baking sheet with parchment or wax paper. Spread the peel out on the paper to cool and air dry for 6 hours, or until it is completely dry. Store in an airtight container for up to 2 weeks or in the freezer for up to 4 months.

Candied Fruit

½ cup peeled and diced fresh ginger (in ¼-inch pieces)

1 cup washed and pitted sour cherries

½ cup lemons, washed, cut into ¼-inch slices and then into ½-inch wedges

1 cup oranges, washed, cut into ¼-inch slices and then into ½-inch wedges

2 cups fresh cranberries, washed

2 cups peeled and cored fresh pineapple, cut into ¼-inch dice

4 cups plus 2 cups sugar

¼ cup light corn syrup

Makes about 6 cups (2¼ pounds)

Using your own candied fruit mixture for holiday baking adds a tremendous amount of intense fruit flavor without the strong sugary taste of commercially prepared fruit. Because the color isn't as bright in homemade mixtures, I add cranberries for both color and flavor. Cranberries may split open during cooking but still look lovely. I also add fresh ginger to perk up the flavor. Limes can be used with lemons or in place of them, but their green color fades during cooking. Citron can also be added, but I have trouble finding it in local American markets.

1. Put the ginger in a saucepan, cover with water, place over medium-high heat, and bring to a boil. Once the water reaches a full boil, cook the ginger for 15 minutes. Drain and discard the water. Set aside.

2. Put the cherries, lemons, oranges, and cranberries in a saucepan, cover with water, place over medium-high heat, and bring to a full boil. Once the water reaches a full boil, cook the fruit for 10 minutes. Drain and discard the water. Set aside.

3. Put the pineapple in a large heavy pan with 4 cups of water. Place over medium-high heat and bring to a full boil. Once the water reaches a full boil, cook for 10 minutes. Remove the fruit from the water with a slotted spoon or skimmer. Set aside.

4. Add 4 cups of sugar, the corn syrup, and the ginger to the pineapple water. Place over medium-high heat and bring the mixture to a full boil. Boil for 10 minutes.

5. Add the cherries, lemons, oranges, cranberries, and pineapple. Return to a full boil and cook for 15 minutes. Stir the mixture often but gently.

(continued)

6. Remove the fruit from the boiling mixture and drain. I use pizza screens (see page 43), since the fruit tends to fall through the average baker's rack. The fruit can be placed in a colander and shaken to remove the excess syrup. (If desired, reserve the syrup to sweeten drinks or use as a base for a holiday punch.)

7. Preheat the oven to 200°F.

8. Spread the fruit out on parchment-lined or well-greased baking sheets. If the fruit is sticky and clumps together, separate it with 2 forks. Place it in the oven for 2 hours to dry it slightly.

9. Put the remaining 2 cups of sugar into a large plastic or paper bag. Add the fruit and shake the bag to completely coat the fruit with sugar.

10. Spread the fruit out on parchment or wax paper and allow to cool and air dry for about 6 hours. When it is completely dry, store in an airtight container for up to 2 weeks or in the freezer for up to 4 months.

PART
TWO

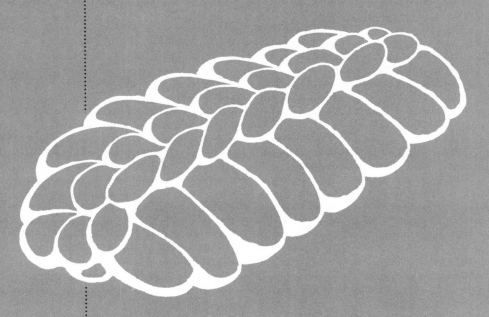

8

Until relatively recently, using a sourdough starter was the only way to make leavened bread. The middle of the nineteenth century witnessed the arrival of packaged yeast and, as a result, the departure of a centuries-old tradition. Since ancient times, bakers had been using starters to leaven bread. Although no one knows for certain, it was mostly likely the Egyptians who discovered (no doubt accidentally) that a fermented slurry of flour and water caused magical things to happen to an ordinary loaf of bread: the bread rose, developed a sturdy texture, and tasted better than the flat, unleavened hearth breads that were the staples of early man.

Our own West was tamed by men and women who subsisted on hunted game and bread made from starters carefully toted across the prairies and mountains. More important than pigs, cattle, or sheep, starters were part of brides' dowries and were jealously guarded by pioneer wives as their caravans trundled across the country. These women

Baking Class:
Making Breads with Sourdough Starters and Other Natural Yeast Leaveners

kneaded the starter into a firm ball, nestled it in the flour barrel, and softened it with water when they needed to bake bread. They always saved a piece of the starter, burying it again deep in the flour barrel. The starter meant life, and as prospectors rushed to California and then to the Yukon and Alaska, they, too, carried a supply of starter for biscuits and other sustaining breads.

Because starters taste strongest near the ocean, breads baked in San Francisco and other coastal towns took on a distinctive, pungent flavor, earning the name "sourdough" and becoming identified with the Gold Rush, the high life in San Francisco, and the drearier life in small mining towns stretching into Alaska. Perhaps the starters' greatest use, other than for baking, was as the base for "hooch." The liquid that naturally forms on the top of the starter is alcoholic—and not surprisingly was treasured by prospectors and other Western adventurers. Hooch most likely kept many a lonely man good company on cold nights.

The Return of Sourdough

Bread baking during the past ninety years has been dominated by packaged yeast. Many home bakers do not have the time to use a starter, fewer understand how to keep one active, and many feel starters are unpredictable. Luckily, a number of dedicated and stubborn bakers have kept the art of sourdough baking alive, sharing their starters with friends and neighbors and personalizing them with various types of flour, liquids, and sweeteners. A friend gave me some starter that he claimed was descended from a batch carried across the country by his great grandmother in a covered wagon more than one hundred years ago.

Although it does not have to be a hundred years old, a good starter matures with time, getting better whenever it is used. Bakers call starters mothers, and just like the human counterpart, each one has its own personality. As already mentioned, starters are more pungent when kept near sea water, which explains why a starter carried home to Minneapolis, for instance, from San Francisco will never produce a loaf with the sour flavor of the California bread. But it will make an excellent loaf.

Today, sourdough refers more to the method of preparation than to the flavor of the bread. Numerous home and professional bakers are turning out marvelous sourdough breads, happily reviving the art of using starters to leaven loaves.

THE FLOUR

Ingredients for a Sourdough Starter

I use unbleached all-purpose flour for starters, but I also have recipes for starters using cornmeal, or mashed potatoes, or yogurt, along with one that relies only on whole wheat flour. These yield loaves with varying flavors. The cornmeal-based starter is the strongest flavored; the potato-based starter is the mildest. They are meant to intrigue you once you have mastered the basics of sourdough baking. Begin with the Yeast Sourdough Starter on page 298, and when you feel comfortable baking with it, try the others.

Try to avoid bleached all-purpose flour and bread flour. I feel that bleaches, bromates, and other additives interfere with the flavor of the bread. Bleach shortens gluten strands, which are so necessary to a good, sturdy loaf.

THE LIQUID

Water is my liquid of choice, although some bakers make starters with milk. Milk-fed starters sometimes spoil, but I have never had trouble with water-fed ones. Pure well water or bottled spring water is the best for a good starter. Read the label carefully to be sure no salt has been added to the bottled water; salt retards the yeast development. If you use tap water, it is usually a good idea to let it sit for 24 hours to give any chemicals the chance to evaporate.

THE YEAST

Old-fashioned starters were made of flour and water only. The mixture was left to stand for several days so it would attract wild yeast spores occurring naturally in the air and from the wheat itself. The starter fermented and swelled. Once it had started, most bakers kept the batch alive for years, replenishing it every time they baked. I make starters in a similar way, although for the basic Yeast Sourdough Starter (page 298) I rely on a teaspoon of active dry yeast to stimulate the mixture.

Wild yeasts are in the air around us all the time. Different ones work with liquids, grains, or fruits to develop yogurt, cheese, beer and wine, and of course sourdough starters. Like its commercial cousin, wild yeast does not fare well when it comes into contact with high temperatures; it prefers gentle warmth. Although commercial yeast reverts to its wild state a few days after a starter is made, it is entirely possible to make starters without ever using packaged yeast. For instructions for doing so, see opposite.

Making a Sourdough Starter

WITH COMMERCIAL YEAST

To make starter using commercial yeast, begin by softening the yeast in warm water in a ceramic or glass bowl and then adding flour to the mixture. Stir it well (but do not fret over lumps—they disappear as the mixture ferments) and cover it loosely with plastic wrap. Lay the wrap over the top of the bowl so that air can circulate. I usually prick holes in the plastic with a toothpick for circulation. Without the plastic, the starter will dry out. If the plastic is too tightly stretched over the container, no natural yeast spores will get through and the starter will not ferment.

Leave the starter at room temperature (65° to 80°F) for 3 days. During that time it will rise and fall at least once. When it is ready, it will look runny and bubbly and smell slightly sour. It is now ready to use.

Transfer the starter to a pottery or glass storage container with a ceramic or plastic lid. I use a 4-cup clear glass bowl, which gives the starter plenty of room to expand. It is also easy to clean. Even though starter kept in a sufficiently large container never touches the lid, metal lids corrode. I also discourage the use of plastic containers, because starters erode some types of plastic.

WITH NATURAL WILD YEAST

To make a natural wild yeast starter, combine 1 cup of warm water (about 100°F) with 1½ cups of flour. If possible, use freshly ground flour. If not, use unbleached all-purpose or whole wheat flour. Stir the mixture until combined and put it in a glass or ceramic container capable of holding 4 times the volume of the mixture. Cover with a tightly woven kitchen towel and place in a draft-free area that is between 75° and 80°F. Stir the starter twice a day for 5 days. When the starter develops a pungent aroma and is full of bubbles, it is ready to use. Care for it as you would any starter.

F or recipes calling for sourdough starter, remove ½ cup of starter from the container—or however much the recipe calls for. Mix it as instructed in the recipe to make a sponge. In my recipes, I suggest letting the sponge mellow for 12 to 36 hours. I prefer a relatively short time, since I use sourdough starters mostly as leaveners. For the tart flavor often associated with sourdough, a longer time is better. Depending on the warmth of your kitchen, the sponge may rise and fall after only a few hours. It will also become bubbly and light. Do not be alarmed if it collapses after rising; it will regain its strength when combined with flour and water again.

When the sponge is ripe, combine it with the other ingredients called for in the recipe. Most sourdough bread doughs are treated similarly to other yeast doughs (see pages 51–68 for more information). They are kneaded, left to rise, shaped, left to rise again, and then baked. The difference is that sourdough breads need about 2 hours or longer for the first rising and about 1½ hours for the second. They also require about 5 minutes more baking time. The

Using a Sourdough Starter

recipes that follow include sourdough quick breads, muffins, and biscuits. These, too, are begun with a sponge and require a lengthy mellowing period—but their flavor is well worth the wait.

FEEDING THE STARTER

Every time you remove starter from the container, you must feed what is left with more flour and water. Most home bakers keep about a cup of starter on hand, taking about half of that every time they bake a loaf. To replenish this amount, add ½ cup of warm water and ¾ cup of unbleached all-purpose flour to it. Stir the mixture, cover the bowl with a loose layer of plastic wrap, as described above, and let it sit at room temperature for 24 hours—time for the starter to rise and then fall.

After 24 hours, cover with a plastic lid or double thickness of plastic wrap held in place with a strong rubber band and refrigerate it. However, if you plan to bake with the starter within 4 days, keep it at room temperature.

Some bakers go for years without cleaning their sourdough crocks, feeding and replenishing their starter as needed in the same encrusted container. However, I feel that it's important to clean the sourdough crock every time I feed the starter. I scrub it clean and rinse it well with hot water, on the theory that unwanted bacteria that can kill the starter may build up in the container.

If you do not use the starter for 12 to 14 days, divide it in half and replenish one half as described with flour and water. Either discard the other half of the starter or feed it and give it to a friend. Sharing sourdough starter with a fellow baker is a friendly way to keep the art of sourdough baking thriving.

I find it helpful to date the container every time I replenish it so that I am reminded to feed the starter even if I do not use it. This constant and regular feeding keeps the starter alive and also strengthens it. Every time it is fed, it becomes more full bodied and will flavor bread differently. These differences are subtle—although over months and years a starter changes dramatically, getting better with age if well cared for.

FREEZING THE STARTER

There may be times when you cannot feed the starter regularly. While it is preferable to keep it refrigerated and fed, you may freeze a starter for as long as 6 months without loss of potency.

To freeze it, put half a cupful in a sturdy airtight container. I find freezer-weight zip-style plastic bags ideal, as they are sufficiently heavy and it is easy to remove excess air from them. This is important because ice crystals form on starters stored in containers that are not airtight.

When you are ready to activate the starter, thaw it in the refrigerator and then transfer it to a glass or ceramic bowl. Add ¼ cup of unbleached all-purpose flour and ¼ cup of warm water to the ½ cup of thawed starter; stir and cover it with a loose layer of plastic wrap. Let the starter stand at room temperature for 48 hours and then add the same amounts of flour and water again. After another 2 days, the starter will be bubbly and active. Maintain it as explained above, feeding it every 12 to 14 days and keeping it refrigerated in a pottery or glass container.

B aking with starters presents its own set of questions and problems. If you follow the recipes carefully and are diligent about caring for the starter, you should have great success. Nevertheless, you may have difficulties, especially at first.

Common Difficulties with Sourdough Starters

THE LOAF DOES NOT RISE HIGH ENOUGH

If you feel the bread is not as high in volume as it should be, you may choose to add a little active dry yeast to the recipe to give the starter a boost. Purists may argue with me on this point, but I feel that because baking is so personal, what really matters is that you are happy with the final product. And there are times when a little yeast can make your day!

To add yeast, soften a scant tablespoon of active dry yeast (one ¼-ounce package) in the water called for in the recipe *after* the sponge has mellowed for 12 to 36 hours. Mix this into the sponge and proceed with the recipe. With the added yeast, the dough will rise in 1 hour the first time and in 45 minutes the second time.

If the recipe does not call for water, substitute ¼ cup of water for whatever liquid it does call for. Soften the yeast in the water and proceed with the recipe.

BAKING AT A HIGH ALTITUDE

Sourdough breads baked at 2,000 feet or above are wonderfully flavorful. They rise faster and higher and the starter expands more than at sea level. Keep a close watch on the dough so that it does not rise too much. It will not require the full 2 hours that breads at lower altitudes need.

ADDING SUGAR TO THE STARTER

If you like the sweetness provided by a little sugar, by all means add some to the starter. I suggest 1 tablespoon for every cup of starter you make. Add the same amount of sugar every time you replenish the starter to keep the flavor sweet. If you decide you do not like the sweetness, stop adding sugar when you feed the starter, and after one or two feedings you will never know it was there in the first place.

SUBSTITUTING STARTER FOR YEAST IN OTHER RECIPES

Once you have mastered baking yeast bread by feel, you can use a sourdough starter to leaven any yeast bread. Begin the recipe by making a sponge with ½ cup of starter, ⅓ cup of warm water, and ½ cup of unbleached all-purpose flour. Stir in the mixture and then cover it loosely with plastic and let it mellow for 12 to 36 hours. Use the sponge in place of the yeast and in place of ½ cup of liquid called for in the recipe.

ORANGE- OR PINK-LOOKING HOOCH

The liquid that naturally forms on top of the starter is called hooch, and when the starter is healthy and well fed, the hooch looks gray. Orange- or pink-looking hooch indicates a ruined starter. Discard it and begin again.

SEPARATED STARTER OR STARTER THAT IS MORE THAN A THIRD HOOCH

Weak-looking, watery, or separated starter may be strengthened by adding an extra ½ cup of flour when you feed it.

FORGETTING TO FEED THE STARTER

If you neglect to feed the starter you may be able to salvage it as long as the hooch is not pink or orange colored. Discard all but 2 tablespoons of starter. Put the 2 tablespoons in a clean glass or ceramic bowl and add ¼ cup warm (90°F) water and ¼ cup un-bleached all-purpose flour. Stir, cover loosely with plastic wrap, and let the starter stand for 24 hours. Add another ¼ cup each of flour and water after 24 hours and again after 48 hours. The starter should be bubbly and light by then. If not, discard it and start again.

Other Natural Yeast Leaveners

I have included recipes in Chapter 11 for breads made with two other starters: levain and desem. Both resemble sourdough starters, but the technique for each is different and both produce breads that are different, too, from traditional sourdough breads.

LEVAIN

A starter perfected by French bakers, levain (pronounced luh-VANE) relies solely on naturally occurring yeast spores to leaven a wonderfully open-textured loaf. Usually shaped as a baguette or round loaf, levain loaves are best eaten the same day they are baked, since the crisp crusts turn soggy after a few hours. Even slightly soggy levain bread makes outstanding sandwiches, French toast, and croutons.

While the initial mother takes 9 days to make, levain starter may be kept alive from loaf to loaf. Once made, levain stores well in the refrigerator and forms the basis for such delicious, simple bread that you will be pleased you invested the time.

Levain starter is made with unbleached all-purpose flour and water. The *bread* is made with cold water, flour, salt, and the starter. I have supplied a recipe for levain starter on page 343 and levain bread on page 344.

DESEM

Desem (pronounced DAY-zum) produces a bold, sweet-tasting bread with discernible wheat flavor. The robust bread made this way is wonderful for toasting, sandwiches, and snacks. The starter, which is of Flemish origin, is best made with freshly ground wheat flour, but I've tried it with store-bought whole wheat flour, bleached all-purpose flour, and unbleached all-purpose—all easier to purchase than freshly ground wheat flour. The results were disappointing: breads made with the bleached-flour desem tasted like chemicals, and those made with unbleached all-purpose and whole wheat flours were not nearly as flavorful as those made from freshly ground wheat flour. If you can locate a mill that grinds wheat into flour, use its flour for desem. Barring that, buy whole wheat flour from a health food store or order it from a reliable catalogue, such as *The King Arthur Flour Baker's Catalogue* (see page 411). Most important, find flour that is additive-free. I also recommend using well water or bottled spring water without added sodium. If you use tap water, let it sit for 24 hours to give any chemicals time to evaporate.

Desem bread is made from a desem sponge, which itself is made from desem starter. The starter needs 8 days to ripen, the sponge another 24 hours.

During the process, the starter is buried deep in a container of flour and left to ripen. Nearly every day, it is removed from the flour, its hard, dry, crusty outer layer peeled off, and the soft inside mixed with more water and flour. By the eighth day, the starter is ready to use as the base for the desem sponge. It can also be refrigerated at this point and kept for a month. I suggest using 2 cups for the first desem sponge. Refrigerate the remaining ¾ cup to use later to make subsequent sponges. You can also substitute desem starter for sourdough starter by increasing the liquid by ½ cup.

9

All the breads in this section require a starter, and I have provided recipes for four good ones. The next step is to make a sponge using the starter as the base. This yields a full-flavored, evenly textured, and pleasantly light bread. Although many yeast breads in the earlier chapters are made without sponges, I strongly urge you to try breads that use them. Sourdough sponges need to mellow for 12 to 36 hours, and the longer they sit the better their flavor. But there is nothing difficult or tricky about using one. On the contrary, they make bread baking foolproof: you *see* the bubbling and swelling taking place and know that your bread will rise to lofty heights.

I suggest you begin with the Yeast Sourdough Starter on page 298. When you have made several breads with it, make another starter. All provide slightly different flavor, and all are satisfying to use. Sometimes it is just fun to try something new.

In this chapter are recipes for classic sourdough breads, rolls, apple-filled bread, and cinnamon

Sourdough Starters and Sourdough Breads

bread. I also have a recipe for a rye sourdough bread (the bauernbrot) and a rustic ten-grain bread. Try them all and then experiment on your own. There may be a recipe for yeast bread earlier in the book that you especially like. Try it using sourdough starter rather than yeast.

Although sweet breads made with sourdough may seem like a contradiction, they are far from it. When the sponge is allowed to ripen for only 12 hours, it leavens the bread without imparting any tart flavor. Second, a sponge allowed to ripen for up to 36 hours produces a bread that is delightfully tasty. None of these breads is very sweet, since too much sugar or honey would mask the flavor of the sourdough and upset the balance of flavors and textures. I like cinnamon, orange, and dried fruits in sourdough breads. Their slight tang blends well with the naturally occurring tartness in the dough.

Before you begin, please read the baking class on using sourdough starters beginning on page 285. This explains exactly what sourdough is, how to maintain the starter, and how to bake with it. I know you will soon love this old-fashioned method for making absolutely delicious breads as much as I do.

Yeast Sourdough Starter

1 teaspoon active dry yeast

¾ cup lukewarm water (90° to 100°F)

1½ cups unbleached all-purpose or whole wheat flour

Makes about 1 cup

This is the basic starter, recommended to all beginning sourdough bakers and to experienced bakers who want to make a new starter. I begin with a little commercial active dry yeast, but once the starter is going there is no reason to add more yeast. The pungent, extremely active starter makes wonderful bread.

1. In a 2-quart glass or pottery bowl, soften the yeast in the water. Set aside for 5 minutes.

2. Add the flour to the softened yeast and stir to combine. Any lumps will disappear during fermentation. Cover loosely with plastic wrap; leave a small opening along one edge or pierce the wrap with a toothpick 5 or 6 times. Let stand at room temperature (65° to 80°F) for 3 days.

3. The starter will get runny as it begins to work. After 3 days, it will have risen and fallen, will be bubbly, and will have a slightly sour aroma. The more you use and maintain a starter, the more pungent it becomes.

4. Use the starter in any recipe calling for sourdough starter. Use ½ cup of starter to make the sponge for the recipe and the remaining ½ cup to maintain the mother. Store, covered, in the refrigerator. For more information, read the baking class beginning on page 285.

Make sure to consult the information on flour and other ingredients and on utensils (chapter 1) and the last baking class on making breads with sourdough starters and other natural yeast leaveners (chapter 8).

Cornmeal Sourdough Starter

¾ cup lukewarm water (90° to 100°F)

1 cup unbleached all-purpose flour

2 tablespoons yellow or white cornmeal

1 teaspoon sugar

Makes about 1 cup

Cornmeal produces the most pungent starter, which after a while develops a strong smell. This is natural. The flavor of the cornmeal cannot be detected and you can use the starter with any recipe for sourdough bread. It gives the bread good sourdough taste. This starter relies on airborne wild yeast spores. For more on wild yeast, see page 289.

1. In a 2-quart glass or pottery bowl, combine the water, flour, cornmeal, and sugar. Stir to combine. Any lumps will disappear during fermentation. Cover loosely with plastic wrap; leave a small opening along one edge or pierce the wrap with a toothpick 5 or 6 times. Let stand at room temperature (65° to 80°F) for 3 days. Stir once each day.

2. After 3 days, the mixture should have risen and fallen and will be bubbly and have a pungent sour aroma. The more you use and maintain a starter, the more pungent it becomes.

3. Use the starter in any recipe calling for sourdough starter. Use ½ cup of starter to make the sponge for the recipe and the remaining ½ cup to maintain the mother. For more information, read the baking class beginning on page 285.

4. To maintain the starter add ½ cup warm water, ½ cup unbleached all-purpose flour, 2 tablespoons cornmeal, and 1 teaspoon sugar to the reserved ½ cup of starter. Stir the mixture, cover loosely with plastic wrap, and let stand for 24 hours at room temperature. Then cover tightly and store in the refrigerator.

Potato Sourdough Starter

¼ cup unseasoned, freshly mashed potatoes

¾ cup water (preferably potato water)

1 tablespoon sugar

1 cup unbleached all-purpose flour

Makes about 1 cup

Starters made with mashed potatoes (no seasonings!) do not rise as much as other starters. This does not affect how high the bread rises, however. This starter captures airborne wild yeasts, and the result is a starter with a milder aroma than others. The resulting taste and texture are similar to those of yeast breads.

1. In a 2-quart glass or pottery bowl, combine the potatoes, water, sugar, and flour. Stir to combine. Any lumps will disappear during fermentation. Cover loosely with plastic wrap; leave a small opening along one edge or pierce the wrap with a toothpick 5 or 6 times. Let stand at room temperature (65° to 80°F) for 3 days. Stir once each day.

2. After 3 days, the mixture should be bubbly and will have risen slightly and then fallen.

3. Use the starter in any recipe calling for sourdough starter. Use ½ cup of starter to make the sponge for the recipe and the remaining ½ cup to maintain the mother. Store in the refrigerator. For more information, read the baking class beginning on page 285. This starter benefits from the addition of 2 teaspoons of sugar with each feeding.

Yogurt Sourdough Starter

¾ *cup plain yogurt*

½ *cup water*

1½ *cups unbleached all-purpose or whole wheat flour*

Makes about 1 cup

Y ou can use regular low-fat or nonfat yogurt for this starter, which works beautifully in any recipe for sourdough bread in the book. The advantage to using yogurt is that there is an existing active culture that encourages fermentation and ensures success.

1. In a 2-quart glass or pottery bowl, combine the yogurt, water, and flour. Cover loosely with plastic wrap; leave a small opening along one edge or pierce the wrap with a toothpick 5 or 6 times. Let stand at room temperature (65° to 80°F) for 3 days. Stir once a day.

2. After 3 days, the starter should be bubbly and have a slightly pungent aroma. If there is any liquid on the top, stir it back into the mixture.

3. Use the starter in any recipe calling for sourdough starter. Use ½ cup of starter to make the sponge for the recipe and the remaining ½ cup to maintain the mother. Store in the refrigerator. For more information, read the baking class beginning on page 285.

If you have a small oven or other limitations on your ability to bake on 2 or more baking sheets at the same time, see the Note on page 189.

Crusty Sourdough Bread

FOR THE SPONGE

½ cup sourdough starter (pages 298–301)

1 cup warm water (105° to 115°F)

1½ cups unbleached all-purpose flour

FOR THE DOUGH

1½ cups warm water (105° to 115°F)

2 teaspoons salt

5 to 6 cups unbleached all-purpose flour

Makes 2 loaves

This bread is crusty because the loaves are brushed with cold water before being baked in a steam-filled oven, all of which encourages a crisp crust. If you prefer a softer crust, eliminate these steps and, while the finished loaves are still warm, brush the tops with softened butter or oil.

1. At least 12 hours in advance, combine the starter, water, and flour in a large glass or pottery bowl. The sponge will have the consistency of a cake batter. Cover with plastic wrap and let ripen at room temperature for at least 12 hours but no longer than 36 hours.

2. When ready to make the bread, add the 1½ cups water, the salt, and 3 cups of the flour to the sponge. Beat vigorously with a dough whisk or heavy-handled spoon for 2 minutes.

3. Gradually add more of the remaining flour, ¼ cup at a time, until the dough begins to pull away from the side of the bowl. Turn the dough out onto a floured work surface.

4. Knead for 8 to 10 minutes, adding more flour, a little at a time as necessary, until you have a smooth, elastic dough and blisters begin to develop on the surface.

5. Put the dough into an oiled bowl. Turn to coat the entire ball of dough with oil. Cover with a tightly woven kitchen towel and let rise at room temperature for about 2 hours.

6. Turn the dough out onto a lightly oiled work surface and divide it in half. Shape each piece into a ball, cover with a towel, and let rest for 15 minutes.

7. Shape each piece of dough into a ball again. Flatten the centers slightly and place them well apart on a well-greased baking sheet. Cover with a towel and let rise for about 1½ hours, or until almost doubled in size.

8. About 15 minutes before the end of rising, preheat the oven to 400°F. Put a shallow pan on the bottom shelf of the oven.

9. Brush the loaves with cold water.

10. Put 1 cup of ice cubes in the hot pan on the bottom shelf of the oven. Immediately put the bread on the shelf above and bake for 25 to 30 minutes, or until the loaves are lightly browned and sound hollow when tapped (the internal temperature should reach 190 to 200°F).

11. Remove from the baking sheet and cool on a wire rack.

VARIATION

Crusty Sourdough Rolls: Divide the dough in half. Divide each piece in half and continue this until you have 32 equal pieces. Shape the dough into 4-inch cylinders and put them on well-greased baking sheets, 2 inches apart. Cover with a towel. Let rise for about 1½ hours, or until almost doubled in size. Bake as for loaves above, brushing with water and using steam for 15 to 20 minutes, until rolls are lightly browned and sound hollow when tapped (the internal temperature should reach 190 to 200°F). Remove from the baking sheets and cool on a wire rack.

The center of whatever you're baking should be as close to the vertical center of the oven as the racks will allow. This enhances more even baking.

Sourdough Cornmeal Cheese Rings

FOR THE SPONGE

½ cup sourdough starter (pages 298–301)

1¼ cups unbleached all-purpose flour

1 cup warm water (105° to 115°F)

1 cup yellow or white stone-ground cornmeal

FOR THE RINGS

2 teaspoons salt

1 cup warm water (105° to 115°F)

¼ cup sugar

3½ to 4½ cups unbleached all-purpose flour

8 ounces sharp Cheddar cheese, shredded (2 cups)

Cornmeal (optional)

Makes 36 rolls

The cornmeal gives a pleasant coarseness to these cheese rings—and the sourdough starter supplies its own special flavor. Use any sourdough starter for the rolls. Serve these cheese rings, which taste best when allowed to mellow for several hours, at a buffet piled on a spindle so that your guests can simply lift them off, one at a time. A pretty wooden upright paper towel holder works well.

1. At least 12 hours in advance, combine the starter with the flour, water, and the cornmeal in a large glass or pottery bowl. The sponge will have the consistency of cake batter. Cover with plastic wrap and let ripen for at least 12 hours but no longer then 36 hours.

2. When ready to make the rings, add the salt, 1 cup of warm water, sugar, 2 cups of the flour, and the cheese to the sponge. Beat vigorously with a dough whisk or heavy-handled spoon for 2 minutes.

3. Gradually add more of the remaining flour, ¼ cup at a time, until the dough forms a mass and begins to pull away from the side of the bowl. Turn the dough out onto a floured work surface.

4. Knead, adding more flour, a little at a time as necessary, for 8 to 10 minutes, or until you have a smooth, elastic dough and blisters begin to develop on the surface.

5. Put the dough into an oiled bowl. Turn to coat the entire ball of dough with oil. Cover with a tightly woven kitchen towel and let rise at room temperature for about 2 hours.

6. Turn the dough out onto a lightly oiled work surface, cover with a towel, and let rest for 15 minutes.

7. Divide the dough in half. Divide each piece in half again and then into thirds. Divide each piece into thirds, so that there are 36 equal pieces. With your hands, roll each piece into an 8-inch rope. Join the ends together, pinching them to seal, and roll them in cornmeal. Put the rings 2 inches apart on well-greased baking sheets. Cover with plastic wrap and a towel (the cornmeal should prevent the wrap from sticking to the dough). Let rise for about 1½ hours, or until almost doubled in size.

8. About 15 minutes before the end of rising, preheat the oven to 400°F.

9. Bake the rolls for 20 to 25 minutes, or until they are pale gold and sound hollow when tapped (the internal temperature should reach 190°F). Remove from the pans and cool on a wire rack.

VARIATION

Shape the dough into either 2 round freestanding loaves and place well apart on a well-greased baking sheet, or 2 standard pan loaves (for directions, see page 59) and place in 2 well-greased loaf pans. Cover the loaves with a towel and let rise for 1½ hours. Just before baking, score the tops of the freestanding loaves ¼ inch deep in two or three places. Bake the loaves 30 to 35 minutes.

Make sure you have at least 1 inch between baking pans inside the oven, and that you have at least 1 inch between the pans and the sides of the oven. Good air circulation is vital to successful bread baking.

Sourdough Oat Bran Cloverleaf Rolls

FOR THE SPONGE

*½ cup sourdough starter
(pages 298–301)*

*1½ cups unbleached
all-purpose flour*

*1 cup warm water (105° to
115°F)*

FOR THE ROLLS

*1½ cups warm milk (105° to
115°F)*

2 tablespoons vegetable oil

*2 tablespoons barley malt or
honey*

2 teaspoons salt

*2 cups oat bran, plus
additional as needed*

*3½ to 4½ cups unbleached
all-purpose flour*

*1 large egg beaten with
1 tablespoon cold water,
for the egg wash*

Makes 36 rolls

Cloverleaf rolls are so attractive that the time it takes to shape them is well worth it. My family fondly refers to these rolls as "Grandma rolls" because I make dozens of them when my mother-in-law visits. I roll and shape them as we happily sit and chat in the kitchen—and the time just flies! The same dough also makes a good sandwich loaf or ordinary round rolls. If you don't need 36 rolls, freeze some of them, or divide the dough in two and bake half into a loaf, half into 18 rolls.

1. At least 12 hours in advance, combine the starter, flour, and water in a large glass or pottery bowl. The sponge will have the consistency of cake batter. Cover with plastic wrap and let ripen for at least 12 hours but no longer than 36 hours.

2. When ready to make the rolls, add the milk, oil, barley malt, salt, the 2 cups of oat bran, and 2 cups of the flour to the sponge. Beat vigorously with a dough whisk or heavy-handled spoon for 2 minutes.

3. Gradually add more of the remaining flour, ¼ cup at a time, until the dough forms a mass and begins to pull away from the side of the bowl. Turn the dough out onto a floured work surface.

4. Knead, adding more flour, a little at a time as necessary, for 8 to 10 minutes, or until you have a smooth, elastic dough.

5. Put the dough into an oiled bowl. Turn to coat the entire ball of dough with oil. Cover with a tightly woven kitchen towel and let rise at room temperature for about 2 hours.

6. Divide the dough into thirds and divide each piece in half. Repeat, dividing into thirds, next halves, and then thirds until there are 108 equal pieces. Shape each piece into a ball. Put 3 balls together on a work surface to form a triangle. The balls should touch one another. Pinch the balls together from the bottom (diagram 1). Pick them up, turn them over, taking care not to separate the balls, and, using the thumb and index finger of your other hand, squeeze the three balls together gently from the top (diagram 2).

1.

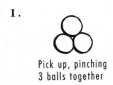

Pick up, pinching
3 balls together

2.

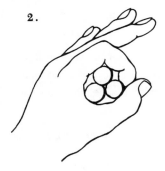

Do this only enough so that they will fit into a muffin pan. Put the joined balls into a well-greased muffin pan. They will spread and fill the cups as they rise. Repeat with the remaining balls of dough until you have 36 rolls. Cover with a towel and let rise for about 1½ hours, or until almost doubled in size.

7. About 15 minutes before the end of rising, preheat the oven to 400°F.

8. Just before baking, lightly brush the tops of the rolls with the egg wash, taking care not to let it drip onto the pans, and sprinkle with oat bran, if desired.

9. Bake the rolls for 20 to 25 minutes, or until they are golden brown (the internal temperature should reach 190°F).

10. Immediately remove the rolls from the pans and cool on a rack.

VARIATIONS

Sourdough Oat Bran Rolls: You may also make plain rolls by dividing the dough into 36 pieces, shaping them into balls, and putting them in well-greased muffin pans to rise. Cover with towel and let rise for about 1½ hours, or until almost doubled in size. Continue with steps 7–10, above.

Sourdough Oat Bran Bread: Shape the dough into either 2 round freestanding loaves and place well apart on a well-greased baking sheet, or 2 standard pan loaves (for directions, see page 59) and place in 2 well-greased loaf pans. Cover the loaves with a towel and let rise for 1½ hours. Just before baking, score the tops of the freestanding loaves ¼ inch deep in two or three places. Bake the loaves 30 to 35 minutes.

Sourdough Sun-Dried Tomato and Romano Focaccia

FOR THE SPONGE

½ cup sourdough starter (pages 298–301)

1 cup unbleached all-purpose flour

½ cup warm water (105° to 115°F)

FOR THE FOCACCIA

½ cup thinly sliced or coarsely chopped oil-packed sun-dried tomatoes (see Note)

½ cup finely chopped onion

¾ cup warm water (105° to 115°F)

1 teaspoon salt

2½ to 3½ cups unbleached all-purpose flour

Cornmeal or semolina for sprinkling pan

4 ounces Romano cheese, shredded (about 1 cup)

Makes 1 flat loaf

Focaccia is an Italian flat bread that can be baked plain, with olive oil and salt as a topping, or flavored with any number of tasty ingredients. The thin, crisp version can be broken apart at the table or—in its thick, breadlike incarnation—cut into generous wedges. It often serves as a major part of a light meal. This delightfully savory version is at its best served warm from the oven. Be warned that you should figure on 4 to 5 hours additional preparation time *after* the sponge has ripened. Plan your meal accordingly.

1. At least 12 hours in advance, mix together the starter, flour, and water in a large glass or pottery bowl. The sponge should have the consistency of cake batter. Cover with plastic wrap and let ripen for at least 12 hours but no longer than 36 hours.

2. When ready to make the bread, drain the tomatoes, reserving the oil.

3. Add the onion, water, salt, tomatoes, and 2 cups of the flour to the sponge. Beat vigorously with a dough whisk or heavy-handled spoon for 2 minutes.

4. Gradually add more of the remaining flour, ¼ cup at a time, until the dough forms a mass and begins to pull away from the side of the bowl. Turn the dough out onto a floured work surface.

5. Knead, adding more flour, a little at a time as necessary, for 8 to 10 minutes, or until the dough is elastic and blisters begin to develop on the surface.

6. Put the dough into an oiled bowl. Turn to coat the entire ball of dough with oil. Cover with a tightly woven kitchen towel and let rise at room temperature for about 2 hours.

7. Turn the dough out onto a lightly oiled work surface, cover with a towel, and let it rest for 15 minutes.

8. Grease a 10 × 2-inch round pan (a deep-dish pizza pan works well), and sprinkle it with cornmeal.

9. Put the dough in the prepared pan and with the heel of your hand press it into a 10-inch circle.

10. Cover the dough with a towel and let rise for 1 hour.

11. Sprinkle the cheese evenly over the dough. Press your fingers into the dough about 1 inch apart and right to the bottom of the pan, to dimple the entire surface. Drizzle with the reserved oil from the tomatoes, allowing it to collect in the indentations.

12. Cover the dough lightly with plastic wrap and a towel. Let rise for 45 minutes more.

13. About 15 minutes before the end of rising, preheat the oven to 400°F. Put a shallow pan on the bottom shelf of the oven.

14. Just before baking, mist or spray water over the top of the focaccia.

15. Put 1 cup of ice cubes in the hot pan on the bottom shelf of the oven. Immediately put the focaccia in the oven and bake for 25 to 30 minutes, or until the crust is golden brown (the internal temperature should reach 190°F).

15. Remove the focaccia from the pan and cool on a rack for 15 minutes before serving.

Note: If you can find only dry-packed tomatoes, mix ½ cup of chopped sun-dried tomatoes with 3 tablespoons of olive oil and heat gently for about 8 minutes. Let the tomatoes and oil cool before adding them to the sponge.

Sourdough Cinnamon Apple Bread

FOR THE SPONGE

½ cup sourdough starter (pages 298–301)

1½ cups unbleached all-purpose flour

1 cup warm water (105° to 115°F)

FOR THE BREAD

½ cup warm milk (105° to 115°F)

1 cup applesauce

2 tablespoons vegetable oil

2 tablespoons sugar

2 teaspoons salt

2 cups old-fashioned rolled oats, plus additional as needed

3½ to 4½ cups unbleached all-purpose flour

2 tablespoons cinnamon

1 large egg beaten with 1 tablespoon cold water, for the egg wash

Makes 2 loaves

The applesauce makes this a moist and tasty bread, perfect for toasting. The cinnamon swirling through the bread makes it look as though you had combined two different doughs for the loaf.

1. At least 12 hours in advance, combine the starter, flour, and water in a large glass or pottery bowl and mix thoroughly. The resulting sponge will have the consistency of cake batter. Cover with plastic wrap and let ripen for at least 12 hours but no longer than 36 hours.

2. When ready to make the bread, add the milk, applesauce, oil, sugar, salt, 2 cups of oats, and 2 cups of the flour to the sponge. Beat vigorously with a dough whisk or heavy-handled spoon for 2 minutes.

3. Gradually add more of the remaining flour, ¼ cup at a time, until the dough forms a mass and begins to pull away from the side of the bowl. Turn the dough out onto a floured work surface.

4. Knead, adding more flour, a little at a time as necessary, for 8 to 10 minutes, or until you have a smooth, elastic dough.

5. Put the dough into an oiled bowl. Turn to coat the entire ball of dough with oil. Cover with a tightly woven kitchen towel and let rise at room temperature for about 2 hours.

6. Turn the dough out onto a lightly oiled work surface and divide into thirds. Put two thirds of the dough aside, covered with a towel.

7. Sprinkle the cinnamon on the work surface and knead it into the remaining third of the dough until the dough is a light brown color. Divide the dough in half and put it under the towel with the other two pieces. Let it rest for 15 minutes.

8. Using a rolling pin, roll one of the plain sections of dough into an 8 × 18-inch rectangle. Roll one of the pieces of cinnamon dough into an 8 × 18-inch rectangle and lay it on top of the first rectangle. With the rolling pin, roll the 2 dough rectangles together to seal. If air pockets develop, pierce them with a toothpick.

9. Using your hands, roll the short sides of the dough toward each other until they meet in the center. Put the dough in a well-greased loaf pan, rolled sides up. Repeat with the remaining dough.

10. Cover the loaves with a towel and let rise for about 1½ hours, or until almost doubled in size.

11. About 15 minutes before the end of rising, preheat the oven to 375°F.

12. Just before baking, brush the tops of the loaves with the egg wash, taking care not to let it drip onto the pans. Sprinkle lightly with additional oats, if desired.

13. Bake the loaves for 35 to 40 minutes, or until they shrink slightly from the sides of the pan and sound hollow when tapped (the internal temperature should reach 190°F). Remove from the pans and cool on a rack.

Sourdough Onion Braid

FOR THE SPONGE

½ cup sourdough starter (pages 298–301)

1½ cups whole wheat flour

1 cup warm water (105° to 115°F)

FOR THE BREAD

2 tablespoons vegetable oil, plus additional as needed

1 cup finely chopped onions

2 cloves garlic, finely chopped

1½ cups warm milk (105° to 115°F)

1 tablespoon caraway seeds

2 teaspoons salt

2 tablespoons sugar

1½ cups whole wheat flour

3½ to 4½ cups unbleached all-purpose flour

Makes 2 braids

Onions, garlic, and caraway all are considered friends of yeast. Their presence causes a chemical reaction with both active dry yeast and the naturally occurring yeast in sourdough starters that significantly lightens the bread. This bread is pleasantly light and moist and makes wonderful toast.

1. At least 12 hours in advance, combine the starter, flour, and water in a large glass or pottery bowl and mix well. The resulting sponge will have the consistency of cake batter. Cover with plastic wrap and let ripen for at least 12 hours but no longer than 36 hours.

2. When ready to make the bread, heat the 2 tablespoons of oil in a heavy skillet over medium-low heat and add the onions and garlic. Cook, stirring often, for about 15 minutes, until the onions are transparent. Remove from the heat and cool to room temperature.

3. Add the cooled onion mixture to the sponge along with the milk, caraway seeds, salt, sugar, all of the whole wheat flour, and 1 cup of the all-purpose flour. Beat vigorously with a dough whisk or heavy-handled spoon for 2 minutes.

4. Gradually add more of the remaining flour, ¼ cup at a time, until the dough forms a mass and begins to pull away from the side of the bowl. Turn the dough out onto a floured work surface.

5. Knead, adding more flour, a little at a time, for 8 to 10 minutes, or until you have a smooth, elastic dough.

6. Put the dough into an oiled bowl. Turn to coat the entire ball of dough with oil. Cover with a tightly woven kitchen towel and let rise at room temperature for about 2 hours.

7. Turn the dough out onto a lightly oiled work surface and divide it into 8 pieces. Cover with a towel and let rest for 15 minutes. Meanwhile, grease 2 baking sheets or line them with parchment.

8. With your hands, shape each piece of dough into an 18-inch rope. Use 4 ropes for each loaf. Pinch 4 ropes together at

1.

2.

3.

4.

5.

6.

one end (diagram 1). Take the rope on the far left and lay it over 2 ropes (diagram 2). Lay the second rope from the left over the second rope from the right, then move the 2 center ropes over to the right so that there is 1 rope on the left and 3 close to one another on the right (diagram 3). Take the rope on the far right and lay it over 2 ropes (diagram 4). Take the second rope from the right and lay it over the second rope from the left (diagram 5). Move the 2 center ropes over to the left. Continue braiding in this manner until the ropes are too short to work with. Gather the ends together in the center and pinch them firmly. Fold about 1 inch under the loaf for a more finished end. Pinch the other end of the loaf firmly and fold under about 1 inch (diagram 6).

9. Braid the remaining 4 ropes in the same way. Carefully transfer the loaves to the prepared baking sheets. (If you prefer, the loaves could be braided directly on the parchment paper.) Cover with a towel and let rise for about 1½ hours, or until almost doubled in size.

10. About 15 minutes before the end of rising, preheat the oven to 375°F.

11. Bake the loaves for 30 to 35 minutes, or until they are golden brown and sound hollow when tapped (the internal temperature should reach 190°F). Immediately remove from the pans and cool on a rack.

12. For a soft, shiny crust, lightly brush the warm braids with oil.

VARIATION

Shape the dough into either 2 round freestanding loaves and place well apart on a well-greased baking sheet, or 2 standard pan loaves (for directions, see page 59) and place in 2 well-greased loaf pans. Cover the loaves with a towel and let rise for 1½ hours. Just before baking, score the tops of the freestanding loaves ¼ inch deep in two or three places. Bake the loaves 30 to 35 minutes.

Sourdough Cracked Wheat Cottage Loaf

FOR THE SPONGE

1/2 cup sourdough starter (pages 298–301)

1 1/4 cups unbleached all-purpose flour

1 cup warm water (105° to 115°F)

1 cup cracked wheat (see page 6)

FOR THE BREAD

1 1/2 cups warm milk (105° to 115°F)

2 tablespoons solid vegetable shortening

2 teaspoons salt

2 tablespoons sugar

4 to 5 cups unbleached all-purpose flour

Vegetable oil

Makes 2 large loaves

Cracked wheat is added to the sponge in this recipe, so that the wheat absorbs a good portion of the liquid and becomes soft. This gives the baked bread a nice texture, with no hard bits of cracked wheat in the crumb. For a more robust wheat flavor, use bulgur instead of cracked wheat, or toast the cracked wheat before adding it to the sponge (be sure to let it cool completely first).

1. At least 12 hours in advance, combine the starter, flour, water, and cracked wheat in a large glass or pottery bowl and stir well. The resulting sponge will have the consistency of cake batter. Cover with plastic wrap and let ripen for at least 12 but no longer than 36 hours.

2. When ready to make the bread, add the milk, shortening, salt, sugar, and 2 cups of the flour to the sponge. Beat vigorously with a dough whisk or heavy-handled spoon for 2 minutes.

3. Gradually add more of the remaining flour, 1/4 cup at a time, until the dough forms a mass and begins to pull away from the side of the bowl. Turn the dough out onto a floured work surface.

4. Knead, adding more flour, a little at a time as necessary, for 8 to 10 minutes, or until the dough is smooth and elastic.

5. Put the dough into an oiled bowl. Turn to coat the entire ball of dough with oil. Cover with a tightly woven kitchen towel and let rise at room temperature for about 2 hours.

6. Turn the dough out onto a lightly oiled work surface and divide in half. Break off one third of each piece of dough. Shape all 4 pieces of dough into balls, 2 large and 2 small. Cover with a towel and let rest on the work surface for 10 minutes.

7. Put the 2 larger balls of dough about 4 inches apart on a well-greased baking sheet. Flatten the balls into 8-inch rounds about 2 inches high. Flatten the 2 smaller balls of dough directly on the work surface into 5-inch rounds about 2 inches high. Center the small rounds of dough on top of the large rounds. Using your finger or the handle of a wooden spoon, press through both rounds right down to the baking sheet. Brush the dough with oil.

8. Cover the dough lightly with plastic wrap and a towel and let rise for about 1½ hours, or until almost doubled in size.

9. About 15 minutes before the end of rising, preheat the oven to 400°F.

10. Just before baking, brush the loaves once again with oil. Bake for 40 to 45 minutes, or until the loaves are golden brown and sound hollow when tapped (the internal temperature should reach 190°F). Remove from the baking sheet and cool on a rack.

There are no preservatives in homemade bread. The more fat in the bread, the longer it keeps, which is why French breads don't last long. Slice your bread, freeze it, then you can bring it out a slice at a time. This is better than trying to keep it fresh in humid climates where bread molds quickly. Bread stored in the refrigerator goes stale quickly.

Sourdough Wheat Germ Honey Bear Bread

FOR THE SPONGE

½ cup sourdough starter (pages 298–301)

1½ cups unbleached all-purpose flour

1 cup warm water (about 105° to 115°F)

FOR THE BREAD

1½ cups warm milk (105° to 115°F)

½ cup honey

2 teaspoons salt

2 cups toasted wheat germ, plus additional as needed

4 to 5 cups unbleached all-purpose flour

1 large egg beaten with 1 tablespoon cold water, for the egg wash

Makes 1 bear-shaped loaf; serves 8 to 10

This recipe combines the tang of sourdough with wheat germ and honey for a flavorful balance of sweet and sour. It's fun to shape the dough into a bear and then glaze it and sprinkle it with wheat germ to represent the bear's fur—but you can also make it into conventional loaves or rolls.

1. At least 12 hours in advance, combine the starter, flour, and water in a large glass or pottery bowl and mix well. The sponge will have the consistency of cake batter. Cover with plastic wrap and let ripen for at least 12 but no longer than 36 hours.

2. When ready to make the bread, add the milk, honey, salt, the 2 cups of wheat germ, and 2 cups of the flour to the sponge. Beat vigorously with a dough whisk or heavy-handled spoon for 2 minutes.

3. Gradually add more of the remaining flour, ¼ cup at a time, until the dough forms a mass and begins to pull away from the side of the bowl. Turn the dough out onto a floured work surface.

4. Knead, adding more flour, a little at a time as necessary, for 8 to 10 minutes, or until you have a smooth, elastic dough.

5. Put the dough into an oiled bowl. Turn to coat the entire ball of dough with oil. Cover with a tightly woven kitchen towel and let rise at room temperature for about 2 hours.

6. Turn the dough out onto a lightly oiled work surface and divide in half. Shape one piece of dough into a ball and put it on a parchment-lined or well-greased baking sheet. Flatten the ball slightly in the center—this is the bear's body.

7. Remove one third of the remaining piece of dough. Shape it into a ball and put it at the top of the body to form the bear's head.

8. Round the remaining dough into a ball and divide it into thirds. Set aside one third of the dough and cover it with a towel. Divide the remaining two pieces of dough in half and shape them into 4-inch cylinders. Flatten the ends of the cylinders and put them under the body of the bear to represent the 4 limbs.

9. Divide the remaining piece of dough into thirds and shape each piece into a ball. Flatten each ball to about ½ inch thickness. Put 1 piece on the head portion for the nose. Put the other 2 pieces under the head for the ears (see diagram).

10. Cover the bear with a towel and let rise for about 1½ hours, or until almost doubled in size.

11. About 15 minutes before the end of rising, preheat the oven to 375°F.

12. Just before baking, brush the bear lightly with egg wash, taking care not to let the egg drip onto the baking sheet, and, if desired, sprinkle with wheat germ. Bake for 40 to 45 minutes, or until golden brown and hollow sounding when tapped (the internal temperature should reach 190°F). Immediately remove from the baking sheet and cool on a rack.

VARIATION

Shape the dough into either 2 round freestanding loaves and place well apart on a well-greased baking sheet, or 2 standard pan loaves (for directions, see page 59) and place in 2 well-greased loaf pans. Cover the loaves with a towel and let rise for 1½ hours. Just before baking, score the tops of the freestanding loaves ¼ inch deep in two or three places. Bake the loaves 30 to 35 minutes.

Sourdough Wild Rice Oat Bread

FOR THE SPONGE

*½ cup sourdough starter
(pages 298–301)*

*½ cup old-fashioned rolled
oats*

1 cup whole wheat flour

*1 cup warm water (105° to
115°F)*

FOR THE BREAD

1 cup hulled sunflower seeds

*1½ cups warm milk (105° to
115°F)*

2 tablespoons vegetable oil

¼ cup honey

1 cup cooked wild rice

2 teaspoons salt

½ cup rye flour

*3½ to 4½ cups unbleached
all-purpose flour*

*1 egg beaten with
1 tablespoon cold milk,
for the egg wash*

*Old-fashioned rolled oats
(optional)*

Makes 2 loaves

The combination of cooked wild rice, with its marvelously nutty flavor, and sourdough results in a hearty bread that is especially good for sandwiches. The flavor intensifies when the bread is toasted.

1. At least 12 hours in advance, combine the starter with the rolled oats, whole wheat flour, and water in a large glass or pottery bowl and mix well. The sponge will have the consistency of cake batter. Cover with plastic wrap and let ripen for at least 12 but no longer than 36 hours.

2. When ready to make the bread, toast the sunflower seeds in a skillet over low heat for about 5 minutes, stirring until they are lightly browned. Allow to cool. Combine the milk, oil, honey, sunflower seeds, wild rice, salt, rye flour, and 1 cup of the all-purpose flour with the sponge. Beat vigorously with a dough whisk or heavy-handled spoon for 2 minutes.

3. Gradually add more of the remaining flour, ¼ cup at a time, until the dough forms a mass and begins to pull away from the side of the bowl. Turn the dough out onto a floured work surface.

4. Knead, adding more flour, a little at a time as necessary, for 8 to 10 minutes, or until you have a smooth, elastic dough.

5. Put the dough into an oiled bowl. Turn to coat the entire ball of dough with oil. Cover with a tightly woven kitchen towel and let rise at room temperature for about 2 hours.

6. Turn the dough out onto a lightly oiled work surface and divide it in half. Shape each piece into a ball, cover with a towel, and let rest for 15 minutes.

7. Shape each piece of dough into a ball again. Flatten the centers slightly and place them well apart on a well-greased baking sheet. Cover with a towel and let rise for about 1½ hours, or until almost doubled in size.

8. About 15 minutes before the end of rising, preheat the oven to 375°F.

9. Just before baking, cut three ¼-inch-deep slits 1 inch apart in the tops of the loaves. Lightly brush the tops of the loaves with the egg wash, taking care not to let it drip onto the baking sheet. Sprinkle oats on the tops, if desired.

10. Bake the loaves for 35 to 40 minutes, or until they are golden brown and sound hollow when tapped (the internal temperature should reach 190°F). Remove from the baking sheet and cool on a rack.

To reheat frozen bread, thaw it in its original wrapping, then wrap it in foil with the shiny side out. Put in a preheated 350°F oven for 10 minutes. Open the foil and heat 5 minutes longer. Using the foil with the shiny side out reflects the heat rays so the bread heats through to the middle without browning.

Sourdough German-Style Bauernbrot

FOR THE SPONGE

½ cup sourdough starter (pages 298–301)

1 cup dark rye flour

1 cup warm water (105° to 115°F)

FOR THE BREAD

2 cups dark rye flour

1 cup warm water (105° to 115°F.)

2 teaspoons salt

2 teaspoons sugar

3 tablespoons caraway seeds

2½ to 3½ cups unbleached all-purpose flour

Cornmeal (optional)

Makes 2 round loaves

A true German Bauernbrot, or farmer's bread, is made with 100 percent rye flour. When I lived in Germany I obtained several recipes from German bakers for the bread and the sourdough starter called *sauerteig*. Every time I tried one of the German recipes, the bread was as heavy as a brick and did not taste as wonderful as I remembered. Obviously something was lost in the translation! This version is my own devising and I think it captures the character and flavor of the real thing.

1. At least 12 hours in advance, combine the starter, rye flour, and water in a large glass or pottery bowl and mix well. The sponge will have the consistency of cake batter. Cover with plastic wrap and let ripen for at least 12 but no longer than 36 hours.

2. When ready to make the bread, add the rye flour, water, salt, sugar, caraway seeds, and 1 cup of the all-purpose flour to the sponge. Beat vigorously with a dough whisk or heavy-handled spoon for 2 minutes.

3. Gradually add more of the remaining flour, ¼ cup at a time, until the dough forms a mass and begins to pull away from the side of the bowl. Turn the dough out onto a floured work surface.

4. Knead, adding more flour, a little at a time as necessary, for 8 to 10 minutes, or until you have a smooth, elastic dough.

5. Put the dough into an oiled bowl. Turn to coat the entire ball of dough with oil. Cover with a tightly woven kitchen towel and let rise at room temperature for about 2 hours.

6. For a crunchy bottom crust, sprinkle a baking sheet generously with cornmeal.

7. Turn the dough out onto a lightly oiled work surface and divide in half. Shape each piece into a ball. Flatten the tops slightly and place them well apart on the prepared baking sheet. Cover with plastic wrap and towel. Let the loaves rise for about 1½ hours, or until almost doubled in size.

8. About 15 minutes before the end of rising, preheat the oven to 400°F. Put a shallow pan on the lower shelf of the oven.

9. Just before baking, cut 3 slits about ½ inch deep and 1 inch apart on top of each loaf.

10. Place 1 cup of ice cubes in the hot pan on the lower shelf of the oven. Immediately put the bread into the oven and bake for 40 to 45 minutes, or until the bread sounds hollow when tapped (the internal temperature should reach 190°F). Remove from the baking sheet and cool on a rack. This bread is much better if allowed to cool completely before cutting or eating. It takes at least 2 hours for the flavors to develop.

Sourdough Cinnamon Rolls

FOR THE SPONGE

½ cup sourdough starter (pages 298–301)

1½ cups unbleached all-purpose flour

1 cup warm milk (105° to 115°F)

FOR THE ROLLS

2 teaspoons salt

1 cup warm milk (105° to 115°F)

½ cup granulated sugar

2 large eggs, beaten, at room temperature

5 to 6 cups unbleached all-purpose flour, or 2 cups whole wheat flour combined with 3½ to 4½ cups unbleached all-purpose flour

FOR THE FILLING

4 tablespoons (½ stick) unsalted butter, melted

2 cups firmly packed brown sugar

1 tablespoon cinnamon

1 cup raisins (optional)

1 cup chopped nuts (optional)

This is a winning combination of full-bodied sourdough and sweet cinnamony filling. For nuttier, fuller flavor, try these rolls with whole wheat flour, as suggested in the recipe.

1. At least 12 hours in advance, mix together the starter, flour, and milk in a large glass or pottery bowl. The resulting sponge will have the consistency of cake batter. Cover with plastic wrap and let ripen for at least 12 but no longer than 36 hours.

2. When ready to make the rolls, add the salt, milk, granulated sugar, eggs, and 3 cups of the flour to the sponge. Beat vigorously with a dough whisk or heavy-handled spoon for 2 minutes.

3. Gradually add more of the remaining flour, ¼ cup at a time, until the dough forms a mass and begins to pull away from the side of the bowl. Turn the dough out onto a floured work surface.

4. Knead, adding more flour, a little at a time as necessary, for 8 to 10 minutes, or until the dough is smooth and elastic (and, if you are using only all-purpose flour, until blisters begin to develop on the surface).

5. Put the dough into an oiled bowl. Turn to coat the entire ball of dough with oil. Cover with a tightly woven kitchen towel and let rise at room temperature for about 2 hours.

6. Turn the dough out onto a lightly oiled work surface. Let it rest while you line a 13 × 18-inch baking sheet with parchment. (If you do not have a baking sheet this large, grease two 9 × 13-inch baking pans or ovenproof glass baking dishes.)

7. Divide the dough in half. Using a rolling pin, roll each piece into an 18 × 24-inch rectangle. Brush with melted butter, leaving a ½-inch border along one long edge without butter or filling, for sealing. Sprinkle the dough evenly with the brown sugar and cinnamon. Sprinkle with raisins and nuts, if desired. With your hands, roll the dough, starting with a long end, into a 24-inch cylinder. Pinch the seam to seal.

8. Cut each cylinder into 12 equal pieces (see the technique described on page 212). Arrange the rolls, cut side up, ½ inch apart

FOR THE ICING

2 cups confectioners' sugar

6 to 8 tablespoons heavy cream

Makes 24 large rolls

on the prepared baking sheet. Cover with plastic wrap and a towel and let rise for about 1½ hours, or until almost doubled in size.

9. About 15 minutes before the end of rising, preheat the oven to 375°F. (If using glass dishes, preheat to 350°F.)

10. Bake the rolls for 25 to 30 minutes, or until they are golden brown (the internal temperature should reach 190°F). Immediately remove from the baking sheet and cool on a rack for 15 minutes.

11. For the icing, combine the confectioners' sugar with enough heavy cream to give the mixture the consistency of honey. Drizzle over the tops of the warm rolls.

Biscuits are a quick bread, usually with a high fat content to make them tender. They are best eaten fresh from the oven. In the British Isles biscuits are what Americans refer to as cookies. Rolls are small breads that are most often served with a meal. When they are larger they are referred to as buns. They usually have at least twice as much volume as a roll. Buns can be eaten as an accompaniment to a meal, but we are most familiar with them used to wrap sandwiches or burgers.

Sourdough Cherry Heart

FOR THE SPONGE

½ cup sourdough starter (pages 298–301)

1 cup unbleached all-purpose flour

½ cup warm water (105° to 115°F)

2 tablespoons granulated sugar

FOR THE BREAD

½ cup warm milk (105° to 115°F)

1 large egg, at room temperature

1 teaspoon vanilla extract

2 tablespoons granulated sugar

1 teaspoon salt

½ teaspoon grated nutmeg

2½ to 3½ cups unbleached all-purpose flour

FOR THE FILLING

1½ cups (16-ounce jar) maraschino cherries, finely chopped, juice reserved

1 cup finely chopped walnuts

Make this heart-shaped wreath for Valentine's Day, or any other time you feel the need to say "I love you." You can also form the dough into a round wreath for Christmas and use a combination of red and green cherries for decoration.

1. At least 12 hours in advance, combine the starter, flour, water, and granulated sugar in a large glass or pottery bowl and mix well. The sponge will have the consistency of cake batter. Cover with plastic wrap and let ripen for at least 12 but no longer than 36 hours.

2. When ready to make the bread, add the milk, egg, vanilla, granulated sugar, salt, nutmeg, and 1 cup of the flour to the sponge. Beat vigorously with a dough whisk or heavy-handled spoon for 2 minutes.

3. Gradually add more of the remaining flour, ¼ cup at a time, until the dough forms a mass and begins to pull away from the side of the bowl. Turn the dough out onto a floured work surface.

4. Knead, adding more flour, a little at a time as necessary, for 8 to 10 minutes, or until you have a smooth, elastic dough and blisters begin to form on the surface.

5. Put the dough into an oiled bowl. Turn to coat the entire ball of dough with oil. Cover with a tightly woven kitchen towel and let rise at room temperature for about 2 hours.

6. To make the filling, toss the cherries and nuts together. Set aside.

7. Turn the dough out onto a lightly oiled work surface. Using a rolling pin, roll it into a 12 × 24-inch rectangle. Spread the filling evenly over the rectangle, leaving a ½-inch border along one long edge (diagram 1). Using your hands, roll the dough, starting with a long end, into a 24-inch cylinder. Pinch the seam to seal (diagram 2).

8. Lay the dough, seam side down, in a heart shape or a circle on a parchment-lined or well-greased baking sheet. If forming a circle, join the ends of the cylinder. They needn't form a perfectly smooth joint. If forming a heart, use the blunt edge of a knife blade to crease the dough at the inside bottom of the heart without

FOR THE ICING

1 cup confectioners' sugar

2 to 4 tablespoons reserved cherry juice or milk

Makes 1 heart-shaped wreath

cutting through the dough. Pinch the outside bottom edge to form a rounded point (diagram 3).

9. Using long-bladed scissors, make cuts about 1½ inches apart around the outside edge of the dough, cutting nearly through the dough. Turn each cut piece slightly so that a little of the cherry filling is showing (diagram 4). Cover the dough with a towel and let rise for about 1½ hours, or until almost doubled in size.

10. About 15 minutes before the end of rising, preheat the oven to 375°F.

11. Bake the bread for 30 to 35 minutes, or until it is golden brown (the internal temperature should reach 190°F). Remove from the baking sheet and cool on a rack for 20 minutes.

12. For the icing, combine the confectioners' sugar with enough cherry juice or milk to give the mixture the consistency of honey. Drizzle over the warm bread.

VARIATION

Chopped dates, prunes, or any mixture of moist dried fruits makes a delicious filling. If you use dried fruits such as apricots or apples, moisten them with water until they are sticky and pasty.

1.

Filling — 20" — ½" — 14"

2.

3.

4.

Sourdough Semolina Apricot Ring

FOR THE SPONGE

½ cup sourdough starter (pages 298–301)

1 cup semolina flour

1 cup warm milk (105° to 115°F)

FOR THE BREAD

½ cup warm water (105° to 115°F)

1 teaspoon salt

½ teaspoon ground ginger

½ cup granulated sugar

3 to 4 cups unbleached all-purpose flour

FOR THE FILLING

2 cups finely chopped dried apricots (about 8 ounces)

½ cup fresh orange juice

½ cup firmly packed brown sugar

2 tablespoons unsalted butter, at room temperature

1 teaspoon almond extract

1 large egg beaten with 1 tablespoon cold water, for the egg wash

Pärlsocker or coarsely broken sugar cubes (see page 30)

Makes 1 loaf

Semolina is a grain that develops excellent flavor in a sourdough bread, particularly when combined with dried fruits, such as the apricots used in this bread (dried cherries are another good choice). Pärlsocker, or pearl sugar, is a very white Scandinavian sugar about the consistency of sesame seeds. It keeps its color and texture when baked, yet melts instantly in your mouth. It is available at Scandinavian specialty stores or from *The King Arthur Flour Baker's Catalogue* (see page 411). Do not confuse pärlsocker with krystal sugar, which is hard.

1. At least 12 hours in advance, combine the starter, semolina flour, and milk in a large glass or pottery bowl and mix well. The sponge will have the consistency of cake batter. Cover with plastic wrap and let ripen for at least 12 but no longer than 36 hours. If your semolina is coarsely ground, the sponge may look curdled. This is natural.

2. When you are ready to make the bread, add the water, salt, ginger, granulated sugar, and 2 cups of the flour to the sponge. Beat vigorously with a dough whisk or heavy-handled spoon for 2 minutes.

3. Gradually add more of the remaining flour, ¼ cup at a time, until the dough forms a mass and begins to pull away from the side of the bowl. Turn the dough out onto a floured work surface.

4. Knead, adding more flour, a little at a time as necessary, for 8 to 10 minutes, or until you have a smooth, elastic dough.

5. Put the dough into an oiled bowl. Turn to coat the entire ball of dough with oil. Cover with a tightly woven kitchen towel and let rise at room temperature for about 2 hours.

6. To begin the filling, combine the apricots, orange juice, and brown sugar in a medium-size saucepan. Cook over medium-low heat for about 15 minutes, stirring often, until the mixture thickens. Remove from the heat and stir in the butter and almond extract. Let the mixture cool.

7. Cut a sheet of parchment paper to fit your baking sheet. Put the paper on the work surface, turn the dough out onto the paper, and roll it into a 16-inch square. The dough will overlap the

1.

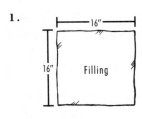

2.

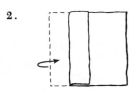

3.

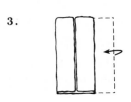

4.

Open seam →

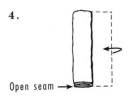

5.

parchment, but will fit later when folded. Spread the filling evenly over the entire surface of the dough (diagram 1). Fold 4 inches of dough from the left side toward the center (diagram 2). Fold 4 inches of dough from the right side toward the center (diagram 3). Then fold the dough in half so that you have a 4 × 16-inch rectangle (diagram 4).

8. Carefully slide the parchment paper on to a baking sheet. Using long-bladed scissors, make cuts in the dough about 1 inch apart along the open-seamed side to within ½ inch of the other edge (diagram 5). Twist the dough so that the cut side faces upward. (The dough can also be formed into a circle after cutting, and the cut sides turned up to form a flower shape.)

9. Cover the dough with a towel and let rise for about 1½ hours, or until almost doubled in size.

10. About 15 minutes before the end of rising, preheat the oven to 375°F.

11. Just before baking, lightly brush the bread with the egg wash and sprinkle liberally with pärlsocker.

12. Bake for 30 to 35 minutes, or until golden brown (the internal temperature should reach 190°F). Immediately remove from the baking sheet and cool on a rack.

Sourdough Pumpkin Swirl Bread

FOR THE SPONGE

½ cup sourdough starter
(pages 298–301)

1 cup unbleached all-purpose
flour

½ cup warm water (105° to
115°F)

½ cup granulated sugar

FOR THE DOUGH

½ cup warm milk (105° to
115°F)

1 teaspoon salt

1 teaspoon ground cinnamon

½ teaspoon ground ginger

2½ to 3½ cups unbleached
all-purpose flour

FOR THE FILLING

1 cup unsweetened canned
pureed pumpkin

1 teaspoon ground cinnamon

1 cup finely chopped pecans

½ cup brown sugar, firmly
packed

For this bread, the filling is kneaded into a portion of the dough, which gives the bread interesting color and also prevents the filling from oozing out during the baking. Cinnamon is incorporated into all the dough for heightened flavor and attractive color.

1. At least 12 hours in advance, combine the starter, flour, water, and granulated sugar in a large glass or pottery bowl and mix well. The sponge will have the consistency of cake batter. Cover with plastic wrap and let ripen for at least 12 hours and no longer than 36 hours.

2. When ready to make the dough, add the milk, salt, cinnamon, ginger, and 1 cup of the flour to the sponge. Beat vigorously with a dough whisk or heavy-handled spoon for 2 minutes.

3. Gradually add more of the remaining flour, ¼ cup at a time, until the dough forms a mass and begins to pull away from the side of the bowl. Turn the dough out onto a floured work surface.

4. Knead, adding more flour, a little at a time as necessary, for 8 to 10 minutes, or until the dough is smooth and elastic and blisters begin to develop on the surface.

5. Break off one third of the dough and set aside for the filling. Form the remaining dough into a ball and put it into an oiled bowl. Turn to coat the entire ball of dough with oil. Cover with a tightly woven kitchen towel and let rise at room temperature for about 2 hours.

6. For the filling, add the pumpkin, cinnamon, pecans, and brown sugar to the smaller piece of dough. Using your hands, a food processor, or a pastry blender, mix the ingredients with the dough until well combined. This is a messy step. Cover the bowl with plastic wrap and set aside.

7. When the plain dough has risen, turn it out onto a lightly oiled work surface. Using a rolling pin, roll it into an 11 × 20-inch rectangle. Spread the pumpkin mixture evenly over the rectangle (diagram 1). Roll one of the shorter edges to the center (diagram 2). Roll the dough from the other short edge to the center (diagram 3). Carefully lift the dough and put it on a parchment-lined or a well-greased baking sheet.

FOR THE ICING

3 ounces cream cheese, at room temperature

2 cups confectioners' sugar

2 to 4 tablespoons milk

Makes 1 loaf

8. Using long-bladed scissors, make cuts along one side of the dough to the center, about 1 inch apart, cutting almost all the way to the center. Repeat on the other side. Turn the cut pieces on their sides with the cut side facing up. The cut pieces can be turned in the same direction or turned in alternating directions.

9. Cover the dough with a towel and let rise for about 1½ hours, or until almost doubled in size.

10. About 15 minutes before the end of rising, preheat the oven to 375°F.

11. Bake the bread for 25 to 40 minutes, or until golden brown (the internal temperature should reach 190°F). Remove from the baking sheet and let sit for 20 minutes on a rack.

12. For the icing, combine the cream cheese and confectioners' sugar with enough milk to make a spreadable icing. Spread over the top of the warm bread.

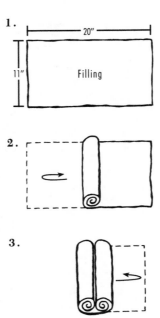

Sourdough Date Nut Orange Twist

FOR THE SPONGE

½ cup sourdough starter (pages 298–301)

1 cup unbleached all-purpose flour

½ cup warm water (105° to 115°F)

FOR THE BREAD

¼ cup granulated sugar

¾ cup warm milk (105° to 115°F)

1 teaspoon vanilla extract

1 tablespoon grated orange peel

2 tablespoons solid vegetable shortening

1 teaspoon salt

2 to 3 cups unbleached all-purpose flour

FOR THE FILLING

2½ cups pitted dates (about 1 pound)

1 cup walnuts

¼ cup brown sugar, firmly packed

If you prefer breads that are not very sweet, omit the brown sugar from the filling—the dates provide nice sweetness on their own. However, the sugar seems to highlight the flavor of the dates and the orange, too. Try it both ways. Either way it's a winner.

1. At least 12 hours in advance, combine the starter, flour, and water in a large glass or pottery bowl and mix well. The sponge will have the consistency of cake batter. Cover with plastic wrap and let ripen for at least 12 but no longer than 36 hours.

2. When ready to make the bread, add the sugar, milk, vanilla, orange peel, shortening, salt, and 1 cup of the flour to the sponge. Beat vigorously with a dough whisk or heavy-handled spoon for 2 minutes.

3. Gradually add more of the remaining flour, ¼ cup at a time, until the dough forms a mass and begins to pull away from the side of the bowl. Turn the dough out onto a floured work surface.

4. Knead, adding more flour, a little at a time as necessary, for 8 to 10 minutes, or until you have a smooth, elastic dough and blisters begin to develop on the surface.

5. Put the dough into an oiled bowl and turn once to coat with oil. Cover with a tightly woven kitchen towel and let rise at room temperature for about 2 hours.

6. Turn the dough out onto a lightly oiled surface and roll it into a 14-inch square. Cover with a towel and let rest while preparing the filling.

7. To make the filling, combine the dates, walnuts, and brown sugar in a food processor and process until very finely chopped—the walnuts should be almost ground. The mixture can also be chopped by hand.

8. Spread the filling evenly over the dough, leaving a ½-inch border along the top edge. Using your hands, roll the dough into a 14-inch cylinder. Pinch all along the edge to seal. Put the dough seam side down on a parchment-lined or well-greased baking sheet.

9. Using a knife, cut the cylinder lengthwise right through to the pan (diagram 1), leaving 2 inches uncut at each end. Carefully

FOR THE TOPPING

¼ cup orange marmalade

Confectioners' sugar (optional)

Makes 1 large twist

turn the cut sides so that they are facing up. Lift the center of one side and cross it over the other. Pull the bottom side out from under the top one (diagram 2). For a prettier shape, tuck 1 inch of each end under.

10. Cover the dough with a towel and let rise for about 1½ hours, or until almost doubled in size.

11. About 15 minutes before the end of rising, preheat the oven to 375°F.

12. Bake the twist for 25 to 30 minutes, or until golden brown (the internal temperature should reach 190°F). Check carefully during the last 10 minutes of baking, since the dates tend to scorch and turn dark. If this starts to happen, lay a piece of foil loosely over the top of the loaf, shiny side up.

13. Remove from the oven and transfer to a rack.

14. For the topping, heat the marmalade over low heat until melted. Brush over the top and sides of the warm bread. Just before serving, sprinkle with confectioners' sugar, if desired.

1.

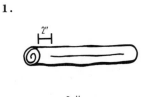

2.

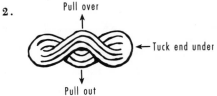

Sourdough Ten-Grain Bread

FOR THE SPONGE

½ cup sourdough starter (pages 298–301)

1¼ cups unbleached all-purpose flour

1 cup 10-grain cereal

1 cup warm water (105° to 115°F)

FOR THE BREAD

1 cup warm milk (105° to 115°F)

2 teaspoons salt

½ cup honey

4½ to 5½ cups unbleached all-purpose flour

Vegetable oil (optional)

Makes 2 loaves

Try this hearty, full-bodied bread with stew or chili. Health food stores carry 10-grain cereal, as well as 7-grain cereal, which can be used in equal measure. You will also find a mail-order source for the cereal in *The King Arthur Flour Baker's Catalogue* on page 411.

1. At least 12 hours in advance, combine the starter, the all-purpose flour, 10-grain cereal, and water in a large glass or pottery bowl and mix well. The sponge will have the consistency of cake batter. Cover with plastic wrap and let ripen for at least 12 but no longer than 36 hours.

2. When ready to make the bread, add the milk, salt, honey, and 3 cups of the flour to the sponge. Beat vigorously with a dough whisk or heavy-handled spoon for 2 minutes.

3. Gradually add more of the remaining flour, ¼ cup at a time, until the dough forms a mass and begins to pull away from the side of the bowl. Turn the dough out onto a floured work surface.

4. Knead, adding more flour, a little at a time as necessary, for 8 to 10 minutes, or until the dough is smooth and elastic.

5. Put the dough into an oiled bowl. Turn once to coat the entire ball of dough with oil. Cover with a tightly woven kitchen towel and let rise at room temperature for about 2 hours.

6. Turn the dough out onto a lightly oiled work surface and divide in half. Shape into loaves, following the directions on page 71.

7. Fit the loaves, seam sides down, into well-greased loaf pans. Cover with plastic wrap and a towel and let rise for about 1½ hours, or until almost doubled in size.

8. About 15 minutes before the end of rising, preheat the oven to 375°F.

9. Bake the bread for 35 to 40 minutes, or until well browned and hollow sounding when tapped (the internal temperature should reach 190°F). Immediately remove from the pans to cool on a rack.

10. For a soft, shiny crust, brush the tops of the warm loaves with oil.

10

Quick breads made with sourdough are not as fast to prepare as other quick breads, but they are faster than many other sourdough breads. All require a starter and most require that you make a sponge that must mellow for 12 to 36 hours before baking. From this point on, the ingredients are mixed and baked right away. The wait can be welcome, since it gives you time to plan ahead. And the time has purpose: the biscuits, muffins, and breads are truly delicious and quite different from more familiar quick breads as they have the unmistakable but never overwhelming tang of sourdough.

As with all the recipes in this section, use any of the four sourdough starters on pages 298–301. Each one works well for the biscuits, muffins, and breads that follow. Please read the baking class beginning on page 285 for more on working with sourdough and starters before attempting any of these breads.

Sourdough Quick Breads

Sourdough Pioneer Biscuits

FOR THE SPONGE

½ cup sourdough starter (pages 298–301)

1 cup unbleached all-purpose flour

1 cup warm water or milk (105° to 115°F)

FOR THE BISCUITS

1½ cups whole wheat flour

2 tablespoons sugar

2 teaspoons baking powder

½ teaspoon salt

½ cup solid vegetable shortening, bacon fat, or lard

Makes about 12 biscuits

Sourdough biscuits were a staple of pioneer families. They are usually made with bacon fat, but in some cases they were made with bear fat! Today, we rely on vegetable shortening. I make them with whole wheat flour to represent the coarse flour no doubt used by settlers. The biscuits are rustic and full flavored, quite unlike the tender white biscuits from the Old South. Try these with butter and honey. Delicious!

1. At least 12 hours before baking, combine the starter, flour, and water in a large glass or pottery bowl and mix well. The sponge will have the consistency of cake batter. Cover with plastic wrap and let ripen for at least 12 but no longer than 36 hours.

2. When ready to make the biscuits, preheat the oven to 450°F.

3. In a medium bowl, whisk together the whole wheat flour, sugar, baking powder, and salt. Using 2 knives or a pastry blender, cut the shortening into the dry ingredients until the mixture forms rice-size pieces. Add the sourdough sponge and toss lightly to combine. Do not overmix, or the biscuits will be tough and will not rise properly.

4. Turn the dough out onto a floured work surface. Pat the dough into a 10-inch square, fold in half and then into quarters. Pat the dough into a square again and fold into quarters twice more.

5. Flatten the dough to a thickness of about 1 inch. Cut into 2-inch squares (or cut with a 2-inch biscuit cutter). Put the biscuits, almost touching, in an ungreased heavy 10-inch skillet with an ovenproof handle or on an ungreased baking sheet. Bake for 15 to 20 minutes, or until lightly browned. Remove from the pan and serve immediately.

Make sure to consult the information on flour and other ingredients and on utensils (chapter 1) and the last baking class on making breads with sourdough starters and other natural yeast leaveners (chapter 8).

Sourdough Muffins

2¾ cups unbleached all-purpose flour

1 teaspoon baking soda

1 teaspoon salt

¼ cup sugar

½ cup sourdough starter (pages 298–301)

1½ cups warm milk (105° to 115°F)

2 large eggs, beaten

¼ cup melted shortening, melted butter, or vegetable oil

Makes 12 muffins

Although no sponge is required for sourdough muffins, you must mix the batter 12 hours before baking the muffins. In effect, the entire batter is a sponge. Mix these the night before if you want muffins for breakfast (great for weekend entertaining), or mix up a batch in the morning and bake them for dinner. The variations that follow the basic recipe turn this single recipe into eleven smashing ones.

1. In a large bowl, whisk together the flour, baking soda, salt, and sugar until well combined.

2. Combine the starter, milk, eggs, and shortening.

3. Add the starter mixture to the dry ingredients all at once. Stir just enough to moisten the dry ingredients. The batter will be slightly lumpy. Cover with plastic wrap and let sit for about 12 hours.

4. When ready to bake the muffins, preheat the oven to 400°F. Butter 12 standard-size muffin cups or line them with paper liners.

5. If the batter has separated, stir just to combine. Spoon the batter into the prepared muffin cups so that they are two-thirds full. For extra-large muffins, fill the cups to the top.

6. Bake for 20 minutes, or until lightly browned (the internal temperature should reach 190°F). Immediately remove from the pan and serve warm.

VARIATIONS

Date and Lemon Muffins: Toss 1½ cups chopped pitted dates and 1 tablespoon grated lemon peel with the dry ingredients.

Orange Muffins: Toss 1½ cups drained, coarsely chopped canned mandarin oranges and 1 tablespoon grated orange peel with the dry ingredients.

Almond Pear Muffins: Toss 2 cups coarsely chopped peeled and cored pears and 1 cup slivered almonds with the dry ingredients. Add 1 teaspoon almond extract to the liquid ingredients.

Spiced Muffins: Add 1 teaspoon ground cinnamon, ½ teaspoon ground ginger, and a pinch of ground cloves to the dry ingredients.

Apple Spice Muffins: Substitute brown sugar for the granulated sugar. Add 2 cups chopped tart apples (peel if you like, but I like the fiber and leave them) and 1 teaspoon ground cinnamon to the dry ingredients.

Herbed Muffins: Add 2 tablespoons minced fresh or 2 teaspoons crumbled dried herbs to the dry ingredients. Use your favorite herb or a combination.

Cheddar Cheese Muffins: Decrease the sugar to 2 tablespoons and add 2 cups shredded Cheddar cheese to the dry ingredients.

Chili and Corn Muffins: Decrease the sugar to 2 tablespoons and add ½ cup drained and chopped canned green chilies and 1 cup canned, frozen, or fresh corn to the dry ingredients.

Artichoke and Parmesan Muffins: Decrease the sugar to 2 tablespoons and add 1 cup chopped marinated artichoke hearts and 1 cup grated Parmesan cheese to the dry ingredients.

Greek Muffins: Decrease the sugar to 2 tablespoons and add 1 cup crumbled feta cheese, ½ cup chopped pitted Greek olives, and ¼ cup chopped sun-dried tomatoes to the dry ingredients.

Make sure you have at least 1 inch between baking pans inside the oven, and that you have at least 1 inch between the pans and the sides of the oven. Good air circulation is vital to successful bread baking.

Sourdough Blueberry Bran Muffins

FOR THE SPONGE

½ cup sourdough starter (pages 298–301)

1 cup warm milk (105° to 115°F)

1¼ cups unbleached all-purpose flour

FOR THE MUFFINS

¼ cup vegetable oil

¼ cup honey

1 egg, beaten

¾ cup whole wheat flour

1½ cups unprocessed bran

2 teaspoons baking powder

½ teaspoon salt

2 teaspoons ground cinnamon

1 cup fresh or frozen blueberries

FOR THE TOPPING

2 teaspoons grated lemon peel

2 tablespoons sugar

Makes 18 muffins

These muffins are out of this world! Because I like them on the tart side, I usually let the starter sit for longer than the minimum 12 hours. Remember that the longer the sponge mellows, the stronger its flavor. If you like milder muffins, bake them after only 12 hours.

1. At least 12 hours before baking, combine the starter, milk, and flour in a large glass or pottery bowl and mix well. The sponge will have the consistency of cake batter. Cover with plastic wrap and let ripen for at least 12 but no longer than 36 hours.

2. When ready to make the muffins, preheat the oven to 425°F. Butter 18 standard-size muffin cups or line them with paper liners.

3. Add the oil, honey, and egg to the starter. Stir to combine.

4. In a large bowl, whisk together the whole wheat flour, bran, baking powder, salt, and cinnamon until well combined. Add the blueberries and toss gently.

5. Add the sponge to the dry ingredients all at once. Stir just until the dry ingredients are moistened, taking care not to overmix. The mixture will be lumpy. Spoon the batter into the prepared cups so that they are two-thirds full.

6. For the topping, combine the lemon peel and the sugar. Sprinkle the mixture on top of the muffins.

7. Bake the muffins for 20 minutes, or until lightly browned and a toothpick inserted in the center of a muffin comes out clean.

Sourdough Banana Nut Bread

FOR THE SPONGE

½ cup sourdough starter (pages 298–301)

1¼ cups unbleached all-purpose flour

1 cup warm water (105° to 115°F)

FOR THE BREAD

2 large eggs, beaten

1½ cups mashed ripe bananas (about 3 bananas)

¾ cup melted vegetable shortening

1¼ cups unbleached all-purpose flour

1½ cups sugar

1½ teaspoons baking soda

1½ teaspoons salt

1½ cups coarsely chopped walnuts

Makes two 8½ × 4½-inch loaves, four 5 × 3½-inch loaves, or six 15-ounce cans

This is a very straightforward banana nut bread, the sort that makes a nice gift or that you take to the parents' meeting at school. But there is a difference: this one is sourdough. Try it spread with cream cheese or butter and served with soup and salad, or slice it and eat it plain with a cup of coffee or tea. Banana bread freezes well—keep some on hand for drop-in company. For the use of cans, see page 391.

1. At least 12 hours before baking, combine the starter, flour, and water in a large glass or pottery bowl and mix well. The sponge will have the consistency of cake batter. Cover with plastic wrap and let ripen for at least 12 but no longer than 36 hours.

2. When ready to make the bread, preheat the oven to 350°F. Grease two 8½ × 4½-inch pans, four 5 × 3½ inch pans, or six 15-ounce cans. Sprinkle the sides and bottoms of the pans with flour.

3. Add the eggs, bananas, and shortening to the starter and mix well.

4. In a large bowl, whisk together the flour, sugar, soda, and salt until well combined. Add the walnuts and toss to mix.

5. Add the sponge to the dry ingredients all at once and stir just until mixed, taking care not to overmix. The mixture will be lumpy. Spoon the batter into the prepared pans.

6. Bake the 8½ inch loaves for about 1 to 1¼ hours; 5-inch loaves for 35 to 40 minutes; 15-ounce cans for 25 to 30 minutes. When done, the loaves will shrink slightly from the sides of the pans and feel springy to the touch (the internal temperature should reach 190°F). Cool in the pans for 10 minutes before turning out onto a rack to cool completely.

The center of whatever you're baking should be as close to the vertical center of the oven as the racks will allow. This enhances more even baking.

Sourdough Currant Nut Bread

FOR THE SPONGE

½ cup sourdough starter (pages 298–301)

1½ cups unbleached all-purpose flour

1¼ cups warm water (105° to 115°F)

FOR THE BREAD

¾ cup milk

2 large eggs, beaten

¾ cup honey

2¼ cups unbleached all-purpose flour

2¼ teaspoons baking soda

1½ teaspoons salt

¾ cup coarsely chopped walnuts, pecans, or almonds

1 cup currants

Makes two 8½ × 4½-inch loaves, four 5 × 3½-inch loaves, or six 15-ounce cans

This basic fruit and nut bread is good with any dried fruit (raisins, apricots, apples) and any kind of nut. It freezes well.

For the use of cans, see page 391.

1. At least 12 hours before baking, combine the starter, flour, and warm water in a large glass or pottery bowl and mix well. The sponge will have the consistency of cake batter. Cover with plastic wrap and let ripen for at least 12 but no longer than 36 hours.

2. When ready to make the bread, preheat the oven to 350°F. Butter and flour two 8½ × 4½-inch pans; four 5 × 3½-inch pans; or six 15-ounce cans.

3. Combine the starter, milk, eggs, and honey and stir to mix thoroughly.

4. In a large bowl, whisk together the flour, baking soda, and salt until well combined. Stir in the nuts and currants.

5. Add the sponge to the flour mixture all at once, stirring just until mixed. The batter will be lumpy. Pour into the prepared pans. If using cans, fill them halfway.

6. Bake the 8½-inch loaves for 1 hour; the 5-inch loaves for 30 minutes; the 15-ounce cans for 25 minutes. When fully baked, the bread will shrink slightly from the sides of the pan and feel springy to the touch (the internal temperature should reach 190°F). Cool in the pans for 10 minutes before turning out onto a rack to cool completely.

11

In this chapter are recipes for levain and desem—two natural yeast starters that raise breads very much as sourdough starters do—and the breads that require them. These starters do not share the tart flavor of sourdough, but they do produce lovely, full-flavored breads. Levain breads are light, while desem breads are hearty. In both cases, the starters take a while to make, and once made are perpetuated from their sponges. Read more about levain and desem starter on pages 293–94.

The starters in this chapter are made from the wild airborne yeast, as are the cornmeal and potato starters on pages 299–300. Experiment with levain as a natural starter for other bread recipes, but when you use it for the French bread on page 344, keep it pure by replenishing it with water, white flour, and salt.

Other Natural Yeast Starters and Breads

Levain Starter

2½ cups unbleached all-purpose flour

2½ cups lukewarm water (about 100°F)

Makes about 3 cups

This starter requires 9 days to make. It needs daily tending, but no single step is difficult. The resulting starter makes an open-textured bread with a crisp crust, the kind of bread you associate with French bread *from* France. There is no way to make successful levain in a quantity less than 3 cups. Either use all 3 to make 3 recipes of levain French bread or discard 2 cups, since you need only 1 for the recipe. Levain does not freeze well. Once the bread dough is made, you will separate a cup's worth to use as the levain for subsequent loaves of bread.

1. Combine ½ cup of the flour with ½ cup of the water in a 2-quart glass or pottery bowl. Stir to mix and cover the bowl with plastic wrap. Pierce the plastic with a toothpick or knife point in five or six places. The purpose is to allow a little air to come in but not so much as to make the dough dry out. Cover the plastic wrap with a tightly woven kitchen towel. Let the mixture sit at room temperature (65° to 80°F) for 24 hours.

2. The next day, add ¼ cup of the remaining flour and ¼ cup lukewarm water to the mixture. Stir to combine. Cover with plastic wrap and let sit at room temperature for 24 hours.

3. Continue adding ¼ cup flour and ¼ cup water each day until all the flour and water is used (a total of 9 days, including the first day). At this time, the mixture should be light and full of bubbles. It will have a wholesome, fresh wheat taste without the tartness usually associated with sourdoughs. Only 1 cup is needed to make 1 bread recipe.

Make sure to consult the information on flour and other ingredients and on utensils (chapter 1) and the last baking class on making breads with sourdough starters and other natural yeast leaveners (chapter 8).

French Bread with Levain

1 cup Levain Starter (page 343)

3 cups cold water (about 70°F)

2 teaspoons salt

6½ to 7½ cups unbleached all-purpose flour

Cornmeal (optional)

Makes 4 baguettes

These baguettes of bread are as close to real French bread as you can get on this side of the Atlantic. Try making them at least once. It is a long process but a very satisfying one.

1. In a large bowl, combine the levain with the cold water, salt, and 4 cups of the flour. Beat vigorously with a dough whisk or heavy-handled spoon for 2 minutes.

2. Gradually add more of the remaining flour, ¼ cup at a time, until the dough forms a mass and begins to pull away from the side of the bowl. Turn the dough out onto a floured work surface.

3. Knead, adding more flour, a little at a time as necessary, for 8 to 10 minutes, or until you have a smooth, elastic dough and blisters begin to develop on the surface.

4. Break off 1 cup of the dough and put it in a glass or pottery container with a nonmetallic lid. This is the levain for another recipe of French bread. The container should be large enough to hold the levain when it doubles in size. Put the container in the refrigerator or a cool (55°F) place.

5. Put the remaining dough into an oiled bowl and turn to coat the entire ball of dough with oil. Cover loosely with plastic wrap and a tightly woven kitchen towel and let rise for about 12 hours.

6. Turn the dough out onto a lightly oiled work surface and divide it into quarters. Using the side of your hand, pound each piece of dough into a 6 × 12-inch oval. Roll each oval into a 12-inch cylinder. Cover with a towel and let rest on the work surface for 15 minutes.

7. If you wish, lightly sprinkle 2 parchment-lined or well-greased baking sheets with finely ground cornmeal or semolina to give the bottom of the loaves extra crispness. (See Note, page 189.)

8. Using the side of your hand, pound each piece of dough into a 6 × 14-inch oval. Starting at a long side, roll each oval tightly to form a 14-inch cylinder and pinch along the edge to seal. Put your finger crosswise on the cylinder, about ½ inch from the end, and pull it toward the middle of the loaf, about another ½ inch.

Pinch the end of the loaf to taper. Repeat with the other end of the loaf. Put 2 loaves seam side down on each baking sheet, spacing them well apart. Cover lightly with plastic wrap and a towel and let rise for 12 hours in the refrigerator or a cool room.

9. About 15 minutes before the end of rising, preheat the oven to 400°F. Put a shallow pan on the lower shelf of the oven.

10. Just before baking, cut several diagonal slashes in the tops of the loaves with a sharp serrated blade, about ½ inch deep and 2 inches apart. Brush the loaves with cold water. Let sit for 5 minutes and brush again with cold water.

11. Put 1 cup of ice cubes in the hot pan on the lower shelf of the oven. Quickly put the loaves on the shelf above and close the oven door to preserve the steam.

12. Bake the bread for 20 to 25 minutes, or until the loaves are pale gold and sound hollow when tapped (the internal temperature should reach 200°F). Immediately remove from the baking sheet and cool on a rack.

Make sure you have at least 1 inch between baking pans inside the oven, and that you have at least 1 inch between the pans and the sides of the oven. Good air circulation is vital to successful bread baking.

Desem Starter

Water

6½ to 7½ cups whole wheat flour (preferably organically grown and/or freshly milled)

Flour for burying starter

Makes about 2¾ cups

This starter is used to make a desem sponge. As with all starters, the more you use this one, the more active it becomes and the more flavorful the bread. Date the container holding the starter after each use, to remind yourself to use it soon again. This starter is not fed, as is a sourdough starter. Instead, some of the sponge is saved every time you make it and *this* is the starter for the *next* sponge. (Note it must then be ripened for at least 12 hours.)

1. Pour 1 cup of room-temperature water (70° to 80°F) into a large glass or ceramic bowl. Add about 2 cups of whole wheat flour to make a firm, kneadable mass.

2. Knead the dough for 10 minutes, adding more flour only if necessary. The dough should be firm enough to remain in a rounded ball when allowed to sit on the work surface for 2 full minutes.

3. Bury the ball of dough in a very large container filled with flour. There should be at least 5 inches of flour surrounding the dough on all sides. Cover the container with plastic wrap or a lid. Let the dough sit for 48 hours in a cool place no warmer than 70°F. I suggest a cellar, the floor of a cool closet, or even an ice chest with a few pieces of ice in it. If the environment is too warm, the dough will not ripen.

4. After 2 days, remove the ball of dough and peel off the hard outer layer with a sharp knife and discard, leaving the soft center. You will have about ¾ cup of dough.

5. Put the soft dough in a bowl and add ¼ cup room-temperature water. Squeeze the dough and water through your fingers until the water is absorbed by the gooey dough. Add about ¾ cup of flour and knead the dough for about 5 minutes. When the baseball-size piece of dough can hold its shape for 2 minutes, bury it again in the flour. Let the dough sit for 24 hours.

6. Repeat this procedure daily, 3 more times (the fourth, fifth, and sixth days).

7. On the seventh day, repeat the process, adding ½ cup of water to the dough and squeezing it until absorbed. Next, add about 1 cup of flour and knead the dough for about 10 minutes, adding more flour only as needed to keep the dough soft and springy. Put the slack dough in a clean bowl, cover it with plastic wrap, and leave it in a cool place for 24 hours. At the end of this time, the dough will be slacker than when it was placed in the bowl.

8. On the eighth day, add ½ cup of water to the dough, squeeze the dough, and add about ¾ cup of flour. After kneading for about 10 minutes, you will have approximately 2¾ cups of dough. It is now ready for making the sponge.

9. Remove ¾ cup of the dough, put it in a 1-quart freezer-weight zip-style plastic bag or an airtight glass container, and store in the refrigerator. This is the starter that is used each time to make a sponge. It may be refrigerated for up to 1 month.

10. After removing the starter for storage, you will have about 2 cups left. This is the sponge. Put the dough in a large bowl and cover with plastic wrap. Put the bowl in a cool place (about 65°F.) to ripen for 12 to 24 hours. The sponge triples in size as it ripens. Once ripened, it is ready to use.

RIPENING A STORED DESEM STARTER

¾ cup desem starter (from step 9, above)

1½ cups room-temperature water (60° to 70°F)

3½ to 4½ cups unbleached all-purpose flour

Makes 2 cups ripened starter

1. Put the starter in a bowl, add the water, and squeeze the starter through your fingers in the water until dissolved.

2. Stir in the flour a little at a time until the dough is stiff enough to knead. Turn dough out onto a floured surface.

3. Knead for 10 minutes, adding more flour as needed, until you have a very firm ball of dough that stays rounded when left on the work surface for 1 minute. If the dough flattens on top, add more flour.

4. Remove ¾ cup (8 ounces) of the dough to your starter container. Cover, let it sit in a cool place for 12 hours, then return it to the refrigerator. This is the starter, to be used for another recipe.

5. Put the remaining dough in a large bowl. This is the sponge. Cover the bowl with plastic wrap and let the sponge ripen in a cool place (about 65°F) for 12 to 24 hours. The sponge will almost triple in size. Once ripened, it is ready to use. Use in any recipe calling for 2 cups of ripened desem sponge.

Basic Desem Bread

2 cups (approximately) ripened desem sponge (pages 346–47)

1½ cups warm water (105° to 115°F)

2 teaspoons salt

3½ to 4½ cups whole wheat or unbleached all-purpose flour

Makes 2 round loaves

This is an extremely flavorful loaf that can be made with whole wheat or unbleached all-purpose flour. The whole wheat makes it heavier and tasting more of the grain. The desem starter on page 346 is made with whole wheat flour and so, for a lighter loaf, you may prefer to use unbleached all-purpose flour for the bread. Or try the bread with half whole wheat and half unbleached all-purpose flour.

1. Mix together the sponge and water in a large bowl until well combined.

2. Add the salt and 2 cups of the flour to the sponge. Beat vigorously with a dough whisk or heavy-handled spoon for 2 minutes.

3. Gradually add more of the remaining flour, ¼ cup at a time, until the dough forms a mass and begins to pull away from the side of the bowl. Turn the dough out onto a floured work surface.

4. Knead, adding more flour, a little at a time as necessary, for 8 to 10 minutes, or until you have a smooth, elastic dough. Try to add as little flour as possible or the bread will be very heavy.

5. Put the dough into an oiled bowl. Turn to coat the entire ball of dough with oil. Cover with a tightly woven kitchen towel and let rise at room temperature for about 2 hours, or until doubled in size.

6. Turn the dough out onto a lightly oiled work surface. Divide it in half and shape each piece into a ball. Let rest, covered, on the work surface for 15 minutes.

7. Knead each piece of dough into a ball again. Roll in flour until well coated. Flatten the tops slightly and put the loaves well apart on a well-greased baking sheet. Shaping the bread twice gives an added lift to the final loaf.

8. Cover the loaves with a towel and let rise for 1 hour.

9. About 15 minutes before the end of rising, preheat the oven to 400°F.

10. Just before baking, cut slits across the top of each loaf, about 1 inch apart and ½ inch deep, starting about an inch from the edge and cutting from end to end.

11. Bake the loaves for 35 to 40 minutes, or until they are lightly browned and sound hollow when tapped (the internal temperature should reach 190°F). Immediately remove from the baking sheet and cool on a rack.

The center of whatever you're baking should be as close to the vertical center of the oven as the racks will allow. This enhances more even baking.

Desem Semolina Sunflower Bread

1 cup sunflower seeds, plus additional seeds for sprinkling

2 cups (approximately) ripened desem sponge (pages 346–47)

2 cups warm water (105° to 115°F)

¼ cup honey

2 teaspoons salt

½ cup unseasoned mashed potatoes

1 cup semolina flour

3½ to 4½ cups unbleached all-purpose flour

1 egg white beaten with 1 tablespoon cold water, for the egg wash

Makes 2 loaves

For maximum effect, the sunflower seeds are toasted in this recipe. The semolina, which always works well with breads raised by natural starters, adds a nutlike flavor to the loaves.

1. Toast the sunflower seeds in a skillet over low heat for about 5 minutes, stirring until they are lightly browned. Set aside until cool.

2. In a large bowl, combine the sponge, water, honey, salt, potatoes, 1 cup toasted sunflower seeds, semolina flour, and 2 cups of the all-purpose flour. Beat vigorously with a dough whisk or heavy-handled spoon for 2 minutes.

3. Gradually add more of the remaining unbleached flour, ¼ cup at a time, until the dough forms a mass and begins to pull away from the side of the bowl. Turn the dough out onto a floured work surface.

4. Knead, adding more flour, a little at a time as necessary, for 8 to 10 minutes, or until you have a smooth, elastic dough.

5. Put the dough into an oiled bowl. Turn to coat the entire ball of dough with oil. Cover with a tightly woven kitchen towel and let rise for about 2 hours, or until doubled in size.

6. Meanwhile, grease 2 loaf pans with solid vegetable shortening or butter. Sprinkle the sides and bottom of the pans with sunflower seeds.

7. Turn the dough out onto a lightly oiled work surface and divide it in half. Form into loaves, following the directions on page 71.

8. Fit the loaves, seam sides down, into the prepared pans. Cover with a towel and let rise for 1 hour.

9. About 15 minutes before the end of rising, preheat the oven to 400°F.

10. Just before baking, brush the tops of the loaves with the egg wash, taking care not to let it drip into the pans. Sprinkle with additional sunflower seeds.

Desem Whole Wheat Rye Bread

2 cups (approximately) ripened desem sponge (pages 346–47)

2 cups warm water (105° to 115°F)

3 tablespoons honey

2 teaspoons salt

1 tablespoon caraway seeds

2 cups dark rye flour (see Note)

3½ to 4½ cups unbleached all-purpose flour

Makes 2 round loaves

11. Bake the loaves for 35 to 40 minutes, or until they are lightly browned and sound hollow when tapped (the internal temperature should reach 190°). Remove from the pans and cool on a rack.

This hearty whole grain bread is similar to dark peasant bread; it should be robust without being heavy. If the loaves are heavy, take care to add less flour next time.

1. In a large bowl, mix together the sponge and water until well combined.

2. Add the honey, salt, caraway seeds, rye flour, and 1 cup of the unbleached flour to the sponge. Beat vigorously with a dough whisk or heavy-handled spoon for 2 minutes.

3. Gradually add more of the remaining all-purpose flour, ¼ cup at a time, until the dough forms a mass and begins to pull away from the side of the bowl. Turn the dough out onto a floured work surface.

4. Knead, adding more flour, a little at a time as necessary, about 8 to 10 minutes, or until you have a smooth, elastic dough.

5. Put the dough into an oiled bowl. Turn to coat the entire ball of dough with oil. Cover with a tightly woven kitchen towel and let rise for about 2 hours, until doubled in size.

6. Turn the dough out onto a lightly oiled work surface and divide it in half. Shape each piece into a ball and let rest on the work surface, covered with a towel, for 15 minutes.

7. Knead each piece of dough into a ball again. Flatten the tops slightly and place well apart on a well-greased baking sheet. (Shaping the bread twice gives an added lift to the final loaf.) Cover with a towel and let rise for 1 hour.

8. About 15 minutes before the end of rising, preheat the oven to 400°F. Put a shallow pan on the lower shelf of the oven.

(continued)

9. Just before baking, cut a large X, about ½ inch deep, on top of each loaf. Brush the loaves with cold water, let sit for 5 minutes, and brush with cold water again.

10. Put 1 cup of ice cubes in the hot pan on the lower shelf in the oven. Quickly put the loaves on the shelf above and close the oven door to hold in the steam.

11. Bake the loaves for 30 to 35 minutes, or until they are brown and sound hollow when tapped (the internal temperature should reach 190°F). Remove from the baking sheet and cool on a rack.

Note: Dark rye flour is essential for the correct color and flavor in this bread, but if you cannot find it, use 1½ cups regular rye flour and add 2 tablespoons of unprocessed wheat bran and 1 tablespoon of wheat germ in its place. The bread will taste as though it was made with dark rye flour.

If you have a small oven or other limitations on your ability to bake on 2 or more baking sheets at the same time, see the Note on page 189.

PART
THREE

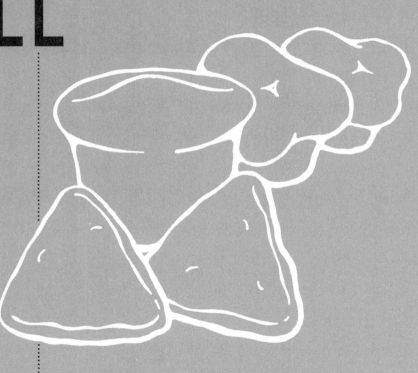

12

Quick breads are breads leavened with baking powder or baking soda instead of yeast. They are mixed and baked in swift succession, and many of them are eaten hot from the oven. They require little or no kneading, rising, or careful shaping. Muffins, biscuits, scones, popovers, and most cornbreads are quick breads. The category also includes all those pleasingly crumbly or wickedly dense creations such as Banana Date Nut Bread, Irish Soda Bread, and Vi's Brown Bread. Quick breads can accompany simple suppers of soup and salad; they can be served spread with sweet butter, cream cheese, or chutney for afternoon tea or as cocktail fare topped with exotic tidbits—and frequently show up on the breakfast table, too.

For consistent results, quick breads require accurate measuring of ingredients—especially dry ingredients such as flour, sugar, and cornstarch. Use measuring cups designed for dry ingredients. These cups generally are made of metal or plastic and have no space above the measuring line so that the flour (or whatever) can be leveled with the sweep of a kitchen knife or other flat utensil. Measuring cups designed for liquids have ample space above the measuring line and usually have a spout to facilitate pouring. For more on measuring cups, turn to page 37.

Also, reread "A Word about Technique," in chapter 2, page 52.

Baking Class:
Making Quick Breads

Leaveners and Flour

Quick breads are leavened with chemical leaveners, such as baking powder and baking soda. As explained on pages 18–19, these produce a balanced alkaline/acid reaction that creates carbon dioxide and thus raises the bread. Most recipes call for double-acting baking powder, which is a carefully blended mixture of baking soda, cornstarch, cream of tartar, and sodium aluminum sulfate or primary calcium phosphate. When combined with liquids, the baking powder releases carbon dioxide bubbles which cause the batter to swell. Most of the leavening action takes place when the moistened batter is exposed to the heat of the oven. Baking soda, an alkaline, reacts with acidic ingredients in the recipe such as yogurt, lemon juice, buttermilk, or molasses, and so may sometimes be the sole leavener in a recipe, depending on the ingredients.

Because gluten formation is the last thing you want for quick breads, they often are made with soft wheat flour such as cake, pastry, or self-rising flour. Soft wheat flour has little gluten-forming potential (for more on flour, review pages 2–6). However, unbleached all-purpose flour produces excellent breads and I generally prefer it, unless you can procure *unbleached* pastry flour.

As the name implies, self-rising flour contains leaveners. You can make your own self-rising flour by combining 1½ teaspoons of double-acting baking powder with ½ teaspoon of salt for every cup of all-purpose flour. Combine the ingredients in a bowl and whisk them thoroughly. Keep the self-rising flour in an airtight canister stored in a cool, dry place. It will remain potent for 1 month or more, but if exposed to air for too long will quickly lose its leavening abilities.

Muffins and Quick Loaves

Muffins and quick bread loaves are made from identical batters. It is the muffin pan that makes the muffin and allows it to form the characteristic domed crown. If the same batter is spooned into a loaf pan, it becomes a quick bread. Both muffins and quick loaves may be savory or sweet, and both take well to chunky ingredients such as chopped apples, nuts, or blueberries and to moist ones such as squash or mashed bananas.

To make the batter, first combine the dry ingredients, whisking them well to blend. Sifting the dry ingredients only layers them on top of one another—whisking is more efficient. Next, mix the liquid ingredients together, and finally combine the two, stirring just until the dry ingredients are moistened. I suggest using a Danish dough whisk (described on page 46) for quick breads and muffins. Its configuration makes it difficult to overmix the batter (overmixing can result in air tunnels in the baked bread and tough crumb). Once the wet and dry ingredients are combined you have no choice but to continue with the recipe through baking. Unlike with yeast breads, there are no methods for stalling the procedure in these recipes. However, you can mix the dry ingredients well before it is time to bake and the wet ingredients shortly before. Keep them separate and mix only when you are ready to bake the bread or muffins.

Some quick bread and muffin recipes (although none of mine) call for creaming the fat and the sugar as you do for a cake. This yields a cakelike muffin that I find neither as appetizing nor as easy as a more traditional muffin.

Once the batter is mixed, spoon it into greased muffin tins or well-greased loaf pans. Quick breads can be baked in nearly any size pan, including cans. The smaller the pan, the less chance there is the baked bread will crack on top. I find it handy to line the loaf pan with a strip of parchment paper that covers the bottom of the pan and overlaps the ends by an inch or two. When the bread is baked, simply run a knife along the long sides, between the bread and the pan, and then lift the loaf out by the parchment paper handles.

For muffins, fill the cups only two-thirds full, leaving ample room for the batter to rise and form the domed crown. If you do not use every muffin cup, fill the empty ones with water. This prevents the muffin tins from warping in the heat of the oven and also contributes to even baking. Remember that muffins do not take as long to bake as larger loaves, so watch them carefully.

With the exception of cornbread and biscuits, quick breads do not like high heat. Bake quick breads in a 350° to 375°F oven.

Just as muffins bake more quickly than loaves, they also cool faster. Let them cool in the muffin pans for about 2 minutes before you turn them out to cool on wire racks.

Let loaves cool for about 10 minutes in the pans. Always let quick breads cool completely before serving. If not, they will crumble when broken apart or sliced.

Scones and Biscuits

Scones and biscuits are quick breads, too. A scone (rhymes with "gone") is a rich Scottish quick bread that resembles a biscuit but is a bit heavier and heartier. Biscuits, originally from England, were perfected in the American South, where soft white flour and careful cooking practices helped to create a tender classic.

Biscuits are meant to be served piping hot and must be made shortly before the meal. They do not take long to bake and often are put in the oven as the final preparations for the rest of the meal are being completed. Scones are more forgiving; they should be freshly baked but may be served warm or even at room temperature.

The dough for scones and biscuits begins with the dry ingredients mixed together in a large bowl. Next, the fat is cut into the flour mixture, as it is for pie crust. Use either a pastry cutter or two knives to mix the fat with the flour, working it until the fat is about the size of rice grains or tiny peas. Next, sprinkle liquid gently over the top of the flour and toss lightly with a fork or Danish dough whisk. Stir and toss the dough, adding liquid as necessary, just until the mixture holds together when you pinch a small amount together. Overmixing results in tough scones and biscuits that will not rise high.

To knead, turn the dough onto a lightly floured work surface and knead it *4 or 5 times* until it forms a smooth ball. Do not knead it any longer or gluten will develop and the baked scones and biscuits will be tough and chewy.

Pat or roll the dough until it is about ½ inch thick and then fold it into thirds and pat or roll it out again to the thickness called for in the recipe. The patting and rolling conditions the dough so that the scones and biscuits rise higher than they otherwise would.

For scones, shape the dough into 6- or 7-inch circles each about ½ inch thick. Lay the circles on an ungreased baking sheet and, using a knife or dough scraper, cut the circles into 6 unseparated wedges. During baking they will join together but they will be easy to break apart afterward. Serve the scones immediately or let them cool on a wire rack.

Shape biscuits by patting or rolling the dough out on the work surface to a thickness of ½ inch to 1 inch. Use a knife, a biscuit cutter, or a glass to cut out squares or circles 2 to 3 inches in diameter. Cut straight down with the knife or cutter. Do not saw the dough with the knife or twist the cutter—either motion seals the sides of the biscuits so that they do not rise as high as they should. If you prefer soft-sided biscuits, set them on a baking sheet so that the sides touch. For crisp-sided biscuits, set them about 2 inches apart. Serve biscuits right away. They should be piping hot so that butter melts on contact.

Some scones and biscuits are dropped by the spoonful onto baking sheets or into hot skillets and, not surprisingly, are called drop scones and drop biscuits. These are easier to make than the other kind, but their texture is not as light and flaky.

Other Quick Breads

Cornbread is a term encompassing all baked goods made with cornmeal. I include four recipes for quick cornbreads, including one for hush puppies, a Southern tradition, and one for spoon bread, another tradition that is a cross between a bread and a soufflé. For the loaf I call Company Cornbread, I mix cornmeal with wheat flour to ensure a good rise. The cornmeal, with its sweet crunch, supplies the unmistakable flavor. Because I am a Southerner by birth, I prefer the white cornmeal most often used in the South. I now live in New England, where yellow cornmeal is commonly used. Both taste wonderful, and I recommend that regardless of the color, you seek out stone-ground cornmeal for the best flavor. As I mentioned earlier, cornbread should be baked in a hot oven. Two of my recipes are baked in 450°F ovens; the spoon bread is baked at 400° and the hush puppies are deep fried in oil heated to 375°.

Popovers are quick breads that perhaps deserve their nomenclature more than any other. These light, airy puffs, leavened only by eggs, are crisp on the outside and hollow inside. Once baked, they must be eaten quickly. Like cornbread, popovers need a hot oven where they inflate as they fill with air. They are best baked in a special popover pan, although you can substitute a muffin tin, custard cups, or ovenproof ramekins. If you heat the pan before spooning in the batter, the popovers will have a crisper crust than if you spoon the batter into cool pans. The choice is yours. Do not open the oven door once the popovers are baking or they will deflate. When they are done, turn them out onto a rack and pierce each one with a sharp knife to allow steam to escape. This will keep them from becoming soggy. Serve them at once.

13

I have described biscuits, scones, cornbread and popovers in the preceding chapter. Please read it carefully before attempting any of the following recipes. But once you have read it, try all of them. Hot biscuits and crumbly scones give character to the simplest meal or tea tray; rich-tasting cornbread and airy popovers turn a cold meal of salads and sliced meat into a small feast. Serve any of these with your favorite homemade jams and jellies or, depending on the menu, with spicy pickles and chutneys.

Biscuits and Scones, Cornbreads and Popovers

Southern-Style Biscuits

3 cups unbleached all-purpose flour

2 teaspoons cream of tartar

1½ teaspoons baking soda

1 teaspoon salt

12 tablespoons (¾ cup) lard or solid vegetable shortening

1¼ cups buttermilk

Makes about 12 large biscuits

I learned to make these biscuits from my grandmother, Mamone, who baked them so often she could make the dough with her eyes closed. She always used cream of tartar and baking soda rather than store-bought baking powder, and I have continued the tradition in this recipe. The biscuits are light and tender, just as old-fashioned Southern biscuits should be. For true Southern-style biscuits, use a pan with sides and arrange the biscuits so close together that they almost touch. This makes them soft. For crusty biscuits, arrange them on an ungreased baking sheet about 2 inches apart.

I always make plenty of biscuits when I bake. Any leftovers can be split open, spread lightly with butter, and then toasted under the broiler. Mamone used to mash butter and cane syrup together as a topping for hot biscuits. You can substitute light molasses for the cane syrup. One bite and I am back home in Georgia.

1. Preheat the oven to 450°F.

2. In a large bowl, whisk together the flour, cream of tartar, baking soda, and salt until well combined. Using a pastry blender or 2 knives, cut the lard or shortening into the dry ingredients until it forms rice-size pieces. Add the buttermilk and toss gently with a fork or dough whisk to combine.

3. Turn the dough out onto a floured board and knead lightly 4 or 5 times, just until the mixture holds together.

4. Roll or pat the dough out to a ½-inch thickness. Fold the dough in half and roll or pat to ½-inch thickness again. Cut out biscuits with a 3-inch cutter. Press the cutter straight down without twisting or the biscuits will not rise properly.

5. Put the biscuits, barely touching, into an ungreased 12-inch round pan with sides, such as a deep-dish pizza pan. Bake for 13 to 15 minutes, or until golden. Serve at once.

VARIATIONS

Oat Biscuits: Process 1 cup of rolled oats in a blender or food processor until finely ground. Substitute for 1 cup of flour.

Whole Wheat Biscuits: Substitute 1 cup of whole wheat flour (preferably whole wheat pastry flour) for 1 cup of all-purpose flour.

Sesame or Poppy Biscuits: Cover a work surface with sesame or poppy seeds before the final rolling of the dough so that the seeds become embedded in it. Put the biscuits in the pan seeded side up.

Cheese Biscuits: Reduce the lard or shortening to ½ cup and add 1 cup of shredded cheese (Cheddar, Swiss, Edam, or Gouda) after the fat is cut in.

Sweet Biscuits: These are great for strawberry shortcake. Mix ¼ cup granulated sugar with the dry ingredients.

Cream Biscuits

3 cups unbleached all-purpose flour

1½ teaspoons salt

1½ tablespoons baking powder

3 teaspoons sugar

1½ cups heavy cream

Makes 12 large biscuits

Cream biscuits are made with heavy cream rather than solid shortening and taste nearly as good as the Southern-Style Biscuits. Many people prefer making these because the ingredients are simply mixed together—there is no fat to cut into the flour.

1. Preheat the oven to 450°F.

2. In a large bowl, whisk together the flour, salt, baking powder, and sugar until well combined. Add the heavy cream to the flour mixture and stir just until combined.

3. Turn out the dough onto a floured work surface and knead lightly 4 or 5 times. Roll or pat the dough to a ½-inch thickness and cut into rounds with a 3-inch cutter. Press the cutter straight down without twisting or the biscuits will not rise properly.

4. Arrange the biscuits, barely touching, in an ungreased 12-inch round pan with sides. Bake for 13 to 15 minutes, or until golden. Serve at once.

Light and Flaky Whole Wheat Biscuits

2 cups unbleached all-purpose flour

1 cup whole wheat pastry flour

2 teaspoons cream of tartar

1½ teaspoons baking soda

2 tablespoons sugar

1 teaspoon salt

¾ cup (1½ sticks) butter or solid vegetable shortening

1 large egg, beaten

1½ cups buttermilk

Makes about 12 biscuits

Similar to Southern-Style Biscuits (page 362), these taste nuttier because of the whole wheat flour. Like all biscuits, these are quick and easy to prepare and appropriate to serve with any meal. Keep the dough nice and moist so that the biscuits will be light—if the whole wheat flour seems to absorb too much liquid, add 1 more tablespoon of buttermilk.

1. Preheat the oven to 450°F.

2. In a large bowl, whisk together the all-purpose flour, whole wheat pastry flour, cream of tartar, baking soda, sugar, and salt until well combined.

3. Using a pastry blender or 2 knives, cut the butter into the dry ingredients until it forms rice-size pieces.

4. Combine the egg with the buttermilk. Add to the flour mixture and stir just until combined.

5. Turn the dough out onto a floured board and knead 4 to 5 times. Roll or pat dough to ½-inch thickness. Cut into rounds with a 3-inch cutter. Press the cutter straight down without twisting or the biscuits will not rise properly.

6. Arrange the biscuits, barely touching, in an ungreased 12-inch round pan with sides. Bake for 13 to 15 minutes, or until golden. Serve at once.

Make sure to consult the information on flour and other ingredients and on utensils (chapter 1) and the last baking class on making quick breads (chapter 12).

Benne Biscuits

½ cup sesame seeds

2 cups unbleached all-purpose flour

2 teaspoons baking powder

½ teaspoon salt

½ cup solid vegetable shortening

¾ cup cold milk

Makes about 24 biscuits

Benne seeds are sesame seeds, deriving their name from the African term for the seed. They have long been popular in Southern cooking, no doubt because slaves brought the seeds with them. For robust sesame flavor, toast the seeds and let them cool completely before adding them to the biscuit dough. The benne seed dough is traditionally rolled thinner than the dough for other biscuits and the biscuits are cut a little smaller, too.

1. Toast the sesame seeds in a dry heavy skillet over moderate heat, stirring, for 4 or 5 minutes, or until golden. Remove from skillet at once to cool.

2. Preheat the oven to 450°F.

3. In a large bowl, whisk together the flour, baking powder, salt, and sesame seeds until well combined.

4. Using a pastry blender or 2 knives, cut the shortening into the dry ingredients until the mixture forms rice-size pieces. Add the milk to the flour mixture and stir just until the dry ingredients are moistened. Take care not to overmix.

5. Turn the dough out onto a floured work surface. Knead lightly 4 or 5 times.

6. Roll or pat the dough to ¼-inch thickness. Cut out biscuits with a 2-inch cutter. Press the cutter straight down without twisting or the biscuits will not rise properly.

7. Arrange the biscuits just barely touching on an ungreased baking sheet. Bake for 10 minutes or until golden. Serve at once.

The center of whatever you're baking should be as close to the vertical center of the oven as the racks will allow. This enhances more even baking.

Beaten Biscuits

5 cups unbleached
all-purpose flour

2 teaspoons salt

2 tablespoons sugar

2 teaspoons baking powder

½ pound (1 cup) lard or solid
vegetable shortening

2 cups cold milk,
approximately

Makes about 48 biscuits

Beaten biscuits are as much a part of the Old South as ham and red-eye gravy. They are not hard to make, but to do so by hand takes time and energy. (Wealthy families whose kitchen staff cooked for them, thought nothing of the 45 minutes of beating the dough required.) This long beating time strengthens the gluten and hence gives the biscuits their pleasant, dry texture and long shelf life. Some kitchens were equipped with a special apparatus that resembled an old washing machine wringer through which the dough was flattened. I tried flattening the dough with my pasta machine, but found the task too fussy. I kept experimenting, however, and discovered that both the food processor and heavy-duty electric mixer produce doughs that are as good as hand-beaten ones. In this recipe I explain how to make the biscuits by hand and in the machines. The high proportion of fat makes this version tender, unlike the traditional chewy, hardtacklike biscuits that kept forever. In the old days, lard was used exclusively, but nowadays vegetable shortening works just fine. Try making them with your children—kids seem to enjoy pounding the dough.

Beaten biscuits are smaller than other biscuits, last longer, and should always be pried apart with a fork, not cut with a knife. You might, if you are an antique shop browser, find a 6-pronged fork designed specifically for opening beaten biscuits.

TO MAKE THE BISCUIT DOUGH BY HAND: In a large bowl, whisk together the flour, salt, sugar, and baking powder until well combined.

With a pastry blender, two knives, or your fingers, work the lard into the dough to distribute it evenly. Add 1½ cups of the milk and stir to mix. Continue adding milk, 2 tablespoons at a time, until all the flour is moistened and the dough forms a ball when the mixture is stirred.

Turn the dough out onto a floured board and knead for 5 minutes. Cover with a tightly woven kitchen towel and let rest for 5 minutes. Using the side of a rolling pin, beat the dough into a 10 × 15-inch rectangle. Fold the dough into thirds to form a 10 × 5-inch rectangle. Give it a quarter turn and beat it into a 10 × 15-inch rectangle again. Continue beating and folding the dough for about 45 minutes, until it is full of tiny blisters. Shape and bake as directed below.

TO MAKE THE BISCUIT DOUGH IN A FOOD PROCESSOR: Combine all the ingredients but the milk in a food processor fitted with the plastic dough blade. Pulse until the lard is evenly distributed throughout the mixture. With the machine running, gradually add milk until the dough forms a ball on top of the blade. Continue to process the dough for 4 minutes. Shape and bake as directed below.

TO MAKE THE BISCUIT DOUGH IN A HEAVY-DUTY MIXER: Combine all the ingredients but the milk in a heavy-duty mixer fitted with the paddle attachment. With the mixer on low speed, gradually add milk until the dough pulls away from the side of the bowl and forms a ball in the center. Remove the paddle and replace it with the dough hook. With the mixer on medium speed, knead the dough for 15 minutes, keeping the dough as soft as possible. Shape and bake as directed.

TO SHAPE AND BAKE THE BISCUITS:

1. Preheat the oven to 350°F.

2. Roll the dough out on a lightly floured surface so that it is ¼ inch thick.

3. Using a 2-inch biscuit cutter, cut the dough into rounds and put them, barely touching, on an ungreased baking sheet. (Do not attempt to reshape the scraps, which is difficult—traditionally, they were fed to horses, pigs or the dog as a treat.) Pierce the center of each biscuit with a fork, going all the way through. This helps keep the biscuit flat.

4. Bake the biscuits for 30 minutes, until very lightly browned on the bottom, cream colored on top, and dry all through. (If the biscuits are not dry, they will get moldy.) Serve at once or let the biscuits cool on wire racks.

Cream Cheese and Chive Biscuits

3 cups unbleached
all-purpose flour

2 teaspoons cream of tartar

1½ teaspoons baking soda

1 teaspoon salt

½ cup chopped fresh chives

1 (8-ounce) package cream
cheese, softened

1¼ cups buttermilk

**Makes 12 large or 30 small
biscuits**

These biscuits are a rich, flavorful accompaniment to a meal. The cream cheese makes them especially tender and the chives add a subtle but unmistakable oniony flavor. The next time you give a cocktail party, consider making these in the smaller size, and fill the tiny baked and split biscuits with thin slices of ham, turkey, or roast beef.

1. Preheat the oven to 450°F.

2. In a large bowl, whisk together the flour, cream of tartar, baking soda, salt, and chives, until well combined.

3. Using a pastry blender or 2 knives, cut the cream cheese into the dry ingredients until it forms pea-size pieces. Add the buttermilk to the flour mixture and stir just until combined.

4. Turn the dough out onto a floured work surface and knead lightly 4 or 5 times. Roll or pat to ½-inch thickness. Cut into 12 rounds with a 3-inch cutter (for 30 tiny biscuits, use a 1½-inch cutter). Press the cutter straight down without twisting or the biscuits will not rise properly.

5. Put the biscuits, barely touching each other, in an ungreased 12-inch round pan. Bake either size biscuit for 13 to 15 minutes or until golden. Serve at once.

Basic Scones

3 cups unbleached all-purpose flour

4 teaspoons baking powder

1½ teaspoons salt

½ teaspoon baking soda

½ cup lard or 8 tablespoons (1 stick) unsalted butter, chilled

1 cup buttermilk, or as needed

Makes 12 scones

There are many good variations for scones, both in Great Britain and in America. The variations for Southern-Style Biscuits (page 362) work well with this recipe.

1. Preheat the oven to 400°F.

2. In a large bowl, whisk together the flour, baking powder, salt, and soda until well combined. Using a pastry blender or 2 knives, cut the lard into the flour mixture until it forms rice-size pieces.

3. Add 1 cup buttermilk to the dry ingredients all at once. Toss lightly with a fork or Danish dough whisk just until the mixture begins to hold together. If the mixture doesn't hold together, add more buttermilk, 1 tablespoon at a time, until it does.

4. Gather the dough into a ball and knead 4 or 5 times. Divide the dough in half. Put the halves well apart on an ungreased baking sheet and pat into rounds, about 6 inches in diameter. Cut each round into 6 equal wedges, using a sharp knife or dough scraper. Cut all the way through, but do not separate the wedges.

5. Bake the scones for 15 to 20 minutes, or until lightly brown. Serve at once or let the scones cool on wire racks.

Make sure you have at least 1 inch between baking pans inside the oven, and that you have at least 1 inch between the pans and the sides of the oven. Good air circulation is vital to successful bread baking.

Whole Wheat Lemon Raisin Scones

1 cup whole wheat pastry flour

2 cups unbleached all-purpose flour

¼ cup firmly packed brown sugar

1 tablespoon baking powder

½ teaspoon baking soda

½ teaspoon salt

1 tablespoon grated lemon peel

1½ sticks (12 tablespoons) unsalted butter, chilled

1 cup golden raisins

1½ cups buttermilk

Makes 12 scones

I use whole wheat pastry flour in these scones to give them a full, nutty flavor that blends nicely with the lemon. If you cannot find golden raisins (also called sultanas), substitute dark raisins.

1. Preheat the oven to 400°F.

2. In a large bowl, whisk together the pastry flour, all-purpose flour, brown sugar, baking powder, soda, salt, and lemon peel until well combined.

3. Using a pastry blender or 2 knives, cut the butter into the flour mixture until it forms rice-size pieces. Add the raisins and toss to mix. Add the buttermilk to the dry ingredients and toss lightly with a fork or dough whisk, just until mixture begins to hold together.

4. Gather the dough into a ball and knead 4 or 5 times. Divide the dough in half and shape each piece into a ball. Place the balls well apart on an ungreased baking sheet and pat into 6-inch circles. Cut each circle into 6 equal wedges, using a sharp knife or dough scraper. Cut all the way through but do not separate the wedges.

5. Bake the scones for 15 to 20 minutes, until golden brown. Serve at once or let the scones cool on wire racks.

Martha's Cornbread

2 cups white cornmeal,
preferably stone-ground

1 teaspoon salt

1 tablespoon double-acting
baking powder

1 large egg, lightly beaten

1¼ cups milk

2 tablespoons fat (bacon
drippings or vegetable oil)

**Makes one 7-inch-round
bread; serves 6 to 8**

This is my sister Martha's recipe for the best Southern-style cornbread I have ever tasted. No wheat flour is used in authentic Southern cornbread, which is supposed to be coarsely textured and taste very much like corn. Martha uses self-rising white cornmeal, and if you can find it, go ahead and use it. (Leave out the salt and baking powder in the recipe, because they are incorporated into the self-rising cornmeal.) Baking the cornbread in a cast-iron skillet or heavy pan that can tolerate the high oven temperature gives the bread a good crust.

1. Preheat the oven to 450°F.

2. Grease a 7-inch cast iron skillet or heavy-duty pan. Put the skillet in the hot oven for about 5 minutes to heat the pan.

3. Combine all the ingredients for the cornbread and mix well. Pour the mixture into the heated pan.

4. Bake for 15 to 20 minutes, or until the bread is golden brown and springy to the touch. Immediately turn out of the pan. Serve the cornbread hot from the oven.

Note: My grandmother mashed equal amounts of cane syrup and butter as a topping for cornbread (and for biscuits). If you want to try this and cannot find cane syrup, use light molasses instead.

The South and North vie for the best cornbreads. Traditionally, Southerners favor white cornmeal while Northerners favor yellow. Southern cornbread has no wheat flour or sweetener. An expression from the Old South states "If there's sweetener in the cornbread, a damn Yankee's been in the kitchen!"

Company Cornbread

1 to 2 tablespoons fat (bacon drippings, butter, solid vegetable shortening, or vegetable oil)

1½ cups white or yellow cornmeal, preferably stone-ground

½ cup unbleached all-purpose or whole wheat flour

1 teaspoon baking soda

2 teaspoons baking powder

½ teaspoon salt

2 tablespoons sugar (optional)

2 large eggs, beaten

2½ cups buttermilk

Makes one 10-inch round bread

As a Southerner, I usually make this with white cornmeal, although yellow cornmeal tastes good, too. My mother tested this recipe for me and admitted that it was similar to hers, but, she said, "No self-respecting Southerner puts sugar in cornbread." She claimed she tried to add the sugar, but it "just wouldn't go in the bowl!" Also try the variation following the recipe—adding the cheese, tomatoes, and peppers turns this into a very different bread.

1. Preheat the oven to 450°F.

2. Put the fat in a 10-inch cast iron skillet. Put the skillet in the hot oven to melt the fat and heat the pan.

3. In a large bowl, whisk together the cornmeal, flour, baking soda, baking powder, salt, and sugar until well combined.

4. Whisk together the eggs and buttermilk. Add the liquid ingredients to the dry ingredients all at once. Stir just until combined.

5. Pour the batter into the hot skillet. Bake for 25 minutes, or until golden brown and springy to the touch. Immediately turn the cornbread out of the pan. Serve hot.

VARIATION

Cheese and Pepper Cornbread: After all the ingredients are combined, add 1 cup shredded sharp Cheddar cheese, ½ cup chopped sun-dried tomatoes, and 1 cup chopped green, red, or yellow bell peppers—or a combination of all three colors to equal 1 cup—to the batter. Stir to mix. Pour the mixture into the skillet and bake as directed.

Southerners split leftover cornbread, spread it with butter, and toast it. Northerners crumble their leftover cornbread into a bowl, sprinkle it with sugar, and pour milk over it as though it was a cereal.

Hush Puppies

Vegetable oil for frying

1½ cups white or yellow cornmeal, preferably stone-ground

1 teaspoon baking powder

½ teaspoon baking soda

½ teaspoon salt

¾ cup buttermilk

1 large egg, beaten

½ cup finely chopped onion

Makes about 30

These fried cornmeal cakes are fun to make, as much because you have the opportunity to tell the story of their origin as because the little morsels taste so good.

Hush puppies were named by Southern fishermen who tossed pieces of quickly fried cornbread batter to the hungry, whining dogs who accompanied them on their treks to fishing camps. As the men tossed the scraps of cornbread to the hounds, they called out, "Hush, puppies!" The dogs' bread was crude and probably fairly tasteless, having been made from the leftover cornmeal used to bread the fish. Southern cooks have added leaveners and other ingredients such as chopped onion, but the spirit of the bread remains: it is simple and easy and tastes good served with fish. For authenticity, fry the hush puppies in the same oil you use to fry fish, but if you are not frying fish, use vegetable oil with a high smoking point, such as soy or corn oil. Dip a spoon or a small ice cream scoop in oil before scooping up the batter. This way, the batter slips right off the scoop into the hot oil.

1. Pour oil into a large deep pan to a depth of 3 inches and heat to 375°F.

2. While the oil is heating, whisk together the cornmeal, baking powder, baking soda, and salt in a large bowl until well combined.

3. Add the buttermilk, egg, and onion and stir just until the mixture holds together.

4. Drop 1 heaping tablespoon of batter at a time into the hot oil. Do not crowd the pan. Fry for about 1½ minutes on each side, or until golden brown. Remove from the oil with a long-handled slotted spoon and drain on paper towels. Let the oil regain its temperature and continue frying the hush puppies until all are cooked. Serve at once.

Southern Spoon Bread

1 cup white cornmeal, preferably stone-ground

1 teaspoon baking powder

1 teaspoon salt

2 tablespoons melted bacon fat or vegetable oil

3 large eggs, separated

3 cups milk

Serves 6

Spoon bread is a Southern bread that is similar to a soufflé but not quite as light or fragile. The bread is brought to the table directly from the oven and spooned onto plates. Usually it is served with meat and gravy, and the gravy is poured over the spoon bread as well as the meat. For instance, this would be good with ham and red eye gravy, roast chicken and gravy, or roast pork and gravy. You can also drizzle it with melted butter mixed with cane syrup or light molasses. The variation for Cheese Spoon Bread is full flavored enough to stand on its own as a meal, served with a green salad.

1. Preheat the oven to 400°F.

2. Liberally grease a 1½-quart soufflé dish or tall ovenproof casserole.

3. In a large bowl, whisk together the cornmeal, baking powder, and salt until well combined.

4. Combine the bacon fat with the egg yolks and milk. Whisk until well combined. Add the liquid ingredients to the dry ingredients and stir just until blended.

5. Beat the egg whites until stiff peaks form—almost to the dry stage. If they are not stiff enough, the cornmeal will sink to the bottom.

6. Stir ½ cup of the cornmeal mixture into the egg whites to lighten the batter. Gently fold the egg whites into the remaining batter, taking care not to deflate the whites. Pour the mixture into the prepared dish.

7. Bake for 45 minutes, or until the spoon bread is lightly browned and a knife inserted into the center comes out clean. Serve hot.

VARIATION

Cheese Spoon Bread: Combine 2 cups shredded cheese (such as Monterey Jack, Cheddar, Swiss, or any pepper cheese) with the dry ingredients in step 3.

Popovers

3 large eggs, well beaten

1 cup milk

1 tablespoon vegetable oil or melted butter

1 cup unbleached all-purpose flour

½ teaspoon salt

Makes 11 popovers

Classic popovers are a rich quick bread leavened only by eggs. Once in the oven, they expand to double their size, filling with hot air that leaves them crisp on the outside and hollow on the inside. Heating the pan before baking the popovers gives them a crisp crust. If you prefer a softer crust, do not heat the pan. Whichever you choose, do not open the oven during baking or the popovers will fall. I serve popovers with butter and jam; they are also great cut open while still hot and filled with turkey or chicken salad.

1. Preheat the oven to 375°F. Butter a popover pan and put it in the preheated oven for 5 minutes, until very hot. Alternatively, butter and heat muffin pans, custard cups, ramekins, or any oven-proof cup.

2. In a medium bowl, whisk together the eggs, milk, oil, flour, and salt until smooth.

3. Spoon the batter into the hot pan, filling each cup between half and two-thirds full.

4. Put in the oven immediately and bake for 35 to 40 minutes. Do not open the oven during cooking or the popovers will fall.

5. Remove the popovers from the pan to a rack. Pierce each popover with the point of a knife or a fork to allow the steam to escape. Serve while still warm.

VARIATIONS

Cheese Popovers: Just before pouring the batter into the hot pan, stir in ¾ cup shredded cheese (such as Cheddar, Swiss, Gruyère, Parmesan, or Romano).

Herb Popovers: Add 1 tablespoon of fresh herbs or 1 teaspoon dried herbs just before pouring the batter into the hot pan.

Garlic Popovers: Just before pouring the batter into the hot pan, add 2 finely chopped cloves of garlic.

Orange Popovers: Add 1 teaspoon grated orange rind and 2 tablespoons granulated sugar to the batter.

Lemon Popovers: Add 1 teaspoon grated lemon peel and 2 tablespoons granulated sugar to the batter.

Sweet Popovers: Add 3 tablespoons granulated sugar to the batter.

14

The idea of beginning the day with a glass of fresh juice, a freshly baked muffin, and a cup of freshly brewed coffee or tea is delightful. On these pages, I have recipes for muffins, which I then follow with an assortment of quick loaves. With very few exceptions, the muffin recipes can be baked in loaf pans, and the bread recipes can be baked in muffin cups. I would not suggest, however, trying to bake Irish Soda Bread or the Tortone into muffins.

Once you master mixing muffin and quick loaf batters, you will be able to do so in a twinkling, and fresh breads can become part of your daily routine. Take care not to overmix the batter; it is supposed to be slightly lumpy. Unlike yeast breads, these must be baked soon after mixing—no resting, rising, or shaping is required. The leaveners, which usually are double-acting baking powder and baking soda, go to work as soon as they are mixed with liquid and continue to work in the oven.

Muffins and quick loaves are good ways to incor-

Muffins and Quick Loaves

porate fresh and dried fruit and moist vegetables such as carrots and squash into baked products. The batters welcome chunky ingredients, which taste delicious nestled in the firm yet moist crumb of a perfectly baked bread. As with all bread baking, I urge you to use these recipes as starting points. Once you are comfortable, experiment on your own, incorporating your own favorite flavors and ingredients into the breads.

In a few of the loaf recipes I suggest baking the bread in cans. This is fun and produces perfectly round slices. Your children will love the idea, too. Make sure the cans are completely clean. Fill them about two thirds of the way so that in the oven the bread does not expand over the lip, and be sure to set the cans upright on the oven shelf. Quick breads baked in cans need about the same time in the oven as those baked in loaf pans, but I suggest checking them after 20 minutes or so—when a skewer or toothpick is inserted in the center of the loaf, no crumbs or batter should cling to it (the internal temperature should be 190°F on an instant thermometer).

Betsy's Basic Muffins

3 cups unbleached all-purpose flour

1½ tablespoons baking powder

1½ teaspoons salt

½ cup sugar

2 large eggs, beaten

1½ cups milk

½ cup melted shortening, butter or vegetable oil

Makes about 12 large muffins

This is my favorite recipe for a plain muffin, one that tastes good just as it is but which also may be dressed up in many guises. A number of ideas for sweet and savory muffins follow, all beginning with this basic recipe. Try a few of my variations and then experiment on your own, keeping in mind that if an ingredient is dry, add it to the other dry ingredients; if it is wet, add it to the liquid ingredients.

1. Preheat the oven to 400°F. Grease 12 standard (7-tablespoon) muffin cups or line them with paper liners.

2. In a large bowl, whisk together the flour, baking powder, salt, and sugar until well combined.

3. Combine the eggs, milk, and shortening. Add the liquid ingredients to the dry ingredients all at once and stir just until combined. Take care not to overmix—the mixture should be slightly lumpy.

4. Spoon the batter into the prepared muffin cups so that they are two-thirds full. If you want extra-large muffins, fill the cups to the top. (For even baking, fill any empty cups with water.)

5. Bake for 20 to 25 minutes, or until lightly browned (the internal temperature of the muffins should reach 190°F). Immediately remove the muffins from the pans and serve warm, or cool on a rack.

VARIATIONS

Date and Lemon Muffins: Toss 1½ cups chopped pitted dates and 1 tablespoon grated lemon peel with the dry ingredients.

Fig Muffins: Toss 1½ cups chopped figs with the dry ingredients.

Orange Muffins: Toss 1½ cups drained, coarsely chopped canned mandarin oranges and 1 tablespoon grated orange peel with the dry ingredients. Substitute orange juice for the milk.

Almond Pear Muffins: Toss 2 cups coarsely chopped peeled and cored pears and 1 cup slivered almonds with the dry ingredients. Add 1 teaspoon almond extract to the liquid ingredients.

(continued)

Apple Cinnamon Muffins: Substitute brown sugar for the granulated sugar. Add 2 cups chopped tart apples (peel if you like, but I like the fiber and leave them) and 1 teaspoon cinnamon to the dry ingredients.

Mixed Nut Muffins: Add ½ cup each coarsely chopped hazelnuts, pecans, walnuts, Brazil nuts, and almonds to the dry ingredients.

Spiced Muffins: Add 1 teaspoon ground cinnamon, ½ teaspoon ground ginger, and a pinch of cloves to the dry ingredients.

Chocolate Chip Muffins: Toss 1½ cups chocolate chips (preferably minichips) with the dry ingredients.

Gorp Muffins: Add ½ cup each unsweetened shredded coconut, peanuts, sunflower seeds, plain M&M's candy, and raisins to the dry ingredients.

Hot and Spicy Muffins: Add 2 cups cinnamon "red hots" candy to the dry ingredients.

Herbed Muffins: Add 2 tablespoons minced fresh or 2 teaspoons crumbled dried herbs to the dry ingredients. Use your favorite herb or a combination.

Cheddar Cheese Muffins: Decrease the sugar to 2 tablespoons and add 2 cups shredded Cheese cheese to the dry ingredients.

Chili and Corn Muffins: Decrease the sugar to 2 tablespoons and add ½ cup chopped drained canned green chilies and 1 cup canned, frozen, or fresh corn to the dry ingredients.

Artichoke and Parmesan Muffins: Decrease the sugar to 2 tablespoons and add 1 cup chopped marinated artichoke hearts and 1 cup shredded or grated Parmesan cheese to the dry ingredients.

Greek Muffins: Decrease the sugar to 2 tablespoons and add 1 cup crumbled feta cheese, ½ cup chopped pitted Greek olives, and ¼ cup chopped sun-dried tomatoes to the dry ingredients.

Apple Streusel Muffins

3 cups unbleached all-purpose flour

1 tablespoon baking powder

½ teaspoon salt

1 teaspoon ground cinnamon

½ cup firmly packed brown sugar

2 cups coarsely chopped tart apples

2 tablespoons vegetable oil

1 cup milk

2 tablespoons butter, chilled

Makes about 12 large muffins

If you use a good, tart apple such as a Granny Smith, these muffins, topped with a buttery streusel, taste like mini–apple pies. Because I like lots of texture, I do not peel the apples for these muffins, but you may if you prefer.

1. Preheat the oven to 375°F. Grease 12 standard (7-tablespoon) muffin cups or line them with paper liners.

2. In a large bowl, whisk together the flour, baking powder, salt, cinnamon, and brown sugar until well mixed. Remove ½ cup of the mixture and set aside. Add the apples to the remaining flour mixture and toss to combine.

3. Combine the oil and the milk. Add the liquid ingredients to the dry ingredients and stir just until mixed. Take care not to overmix—the batter should be slightly lumpy.

5. Spoon the batter into the prepared muffin cups, filling them two-thirds full. If you want extra-large muffins, fill the cups to the top.

6. To make the streusel topping, cut the butter into small pieces. Add to the reserved flour mixture and using 2 knives, cut the butter into the flour until it forms rice-size pieces. Sprinkle the streusel over the top of the muffins.

7. Bake the muffins for 30 minutes, or until they are golden brown (the internal temperature should reach 190°F). Immediately remove from the pans and serve warm, or cool on a rack.

Make sure to consult the information on flour and other ingredients and on utensils (chapter 1) and the last baking class on making quick breads (chapter 12).

Almond Orange Muffins

3 cups unbleached all-purpose flour

1½ tablespoons baking powder

1 teaspoon salt

2 tablespoons sugar

8 ounces almond paste, crumbled

2 large eggs, beaten

1½ cups fresh orange juice

Makes about 12 large muffins

Almond paste gives these muffins rich, nutty flavor and smooth texture. Be sure to add the orange juice to the almond paste slowly so that the mixture becomes smooth and combines easily with the dry ingredients.

1. Preheat the oven to 400°F. Grease 12 standard (7-tablespoon) muffin cups or line with paper liners.

2. In a large bowl, whisk together the flour, baking powder, salt, and sugar until well combined.

3. Beat the almond paste with the eggs. Add the orange juice, a little at a time, stirring until smooth. Add the mixture to the dry ingredients all at once and stir just until combined. Take care not to overmix—the mixture should be slightly lumpy.

4. Spoon the batter into the prepared muffin cups so that they are two-thirds full. If you want extra-large muffins, fill the cups to the top.

5. Bake for 20 to 25 minutes, or until lightly browned (the internal temperature of the muffins should reach 190°F). Remove from the pans and serve warm, or cool on a rack.

Orange Banana Bran Muffins

1½ cups unprocessed oat bran or wheat bran

1 cup unbleached all-purpose flour

1 tablespoon baking powder

1 teaspoon baking soda

3 tablespoons firmly packed brown sugar

2 teaspoons grated orange peel

½ sunflower seeds

½ cup ripe mashed banana (about 1 banana)

1¾ cups fresh orange juice

1 tablespoon vegetable oil

1 teaspoon vanilla extract

Makes about 12 large muffins

Bran muffins can be mealy and dry if not made properly. Mix the batter until it is thick but still falls off a spoon without prodding. I call this the ploppable stage, falling in between pourable—when the batter easily pours from the bowl—and thick—when it needs to be released from a spoon with another utensil or your finger. If the batter for these muffins is ploppable, they will be moist and full flavored.

1. Preheat the oven to 375°F. Grease 12 standard (7-tablespoon) muffin cups or line them with paper liners.

2. In a large bowl, whisk together the bran, flour, baking powder, baking soda, brown sugar, orange peel, and sunflower seeds until well combined.

3. Combine the banana, orange juice, oil, and vanilla. Whisk until smooth. Add the banana mixture to the dry ingredients all at once and stir just until combined. Take care not to overmix—the mixture should be slightly lumpy.

4. Spoon the batter into the prepared muffin cups so that they are two-thirds full. If you want extra-large muffins, fill the cups to the top.

5. Bake the muffins for 20 to 25 minutes, or until golden brown (the internal temperature should reach 190°F). Immediately remove the muffins from the pans and serve warm, or cool on a rack.

Carrot Raisin Muffins

2 cups unbleached all-purpose flour

1 tablespoon baking powder

½ teaspoon salt

2 tablespoons sugar

2 cups finely grated carrots

1 cup raisins

1 cup milk

1 large egg, lightly beaten

2 tablespoons vegetable oil

Makes about 12 large muffins

One of my favorite salads is a good old-fashioned carrot and raisin salad, a flavor combination that is equally tasty in a muffin. Carrots are naturally sweet and add moisture, and everyone knows what good flavor and texture raisins provide. Store opened boxes of raisins in the refrigerator, sealed in an airtight container or a zip-style plastic bag to keep them soft.

1. Preheat the oven to 375°F. Grease 12 standard (7-tablespoon) muffin cups or line them with paper liners.

2. In a large bowl, whisk together the flour, baking powder, salt, and sugar until well combined. Add the carrots and raisins and toss to mix.

3. Combine the milk, egg, and oil. Add all at once to the dry ingredients and stir just until combined. Take care not to overmix —the mixture should be slightly lumpy.

4. Spoon the batter into the prepared pans so that they are two-thirds full. If you want extra-large muffins, fill the cups to the top.

5. Bake the muffins for 25 to 30 minutes, or until golden brown (the internal temperature should reach 190°F). Remove from the pan and serve warm, or cool on a rack.

The center of whatever you're baking should be as close to the vertical center of the oven as the racks will allow. This enhances more even baking.

Chili and Cheddar Muffins

2 cups unbleached all-purpose flour

½ cup stone-ground cornmeal

1 tablespoon baking powder

½ teaspoon salt

1½ cups shredded Cheddar cheese

1 large egg, lightly beaten

1 tablespoon vegetable oil

1 cup milk

1 (4-ounce) can green chilies, well drained and chopped

Makes about 12 large muffins

These muffins combine the flavors of Cheddar, mild green chilies, and cornmeal. The result is great any time, but I especially like them with chili con carne. If you have any leftovers, split them, spread lightly with butter, and toast under the broiler.

1. Preheat the oven to 375°F. Grease 12 standard (7-tablespoon) muffin cups or line with paper liners.

2. In a large bowl, whisk together the flour, cornmeal, baking powder, and salt until well combined. Add the cheese and toss to mix.

3. Combine the egg, oil, milk, and chilies. Add all at once to the dry ingredients and stir just until combined. Take care not to overmix—the batter should be slightly lumpy.

4. Spoon the batter into the prepared pans so that they are two-thirds full. If you want extra-large muffins, fill the cups to the top.

5. Bake the muffins for 25 to 30 minutes, or until golden brown (the internal temperature should reach 190°F). Remove from the pans and serve warm, or cool on a rack.

Quinoa Orange Muffins

¾ *cup quinoa*

3 cups unbleached all-purpose flour

1½ tablespoons baking powder

1 teaspoon salt

¼ *cup sugar*

1 tablespoon grated orange peel

2 large eggs, lightly beaten

2 tablespoons vegetable oil

1½ cups fresh orange juice

Makes about 12 large muffins

Quinoa (pronounced KEEN-wa) is an ancient grain that is a nutritional powerhouse. When toasted, as it is here, its mild, nutty flavor bursts forth and blends pleasingly with the orange. Quinoa has a bitter coating and must always be rinsed before using. It is found in most health food and specialty stores, and a number of supermarkets are beginning to carry it in their gourmet sections.

1. Put the quinoa in a strainer and rinse thoroughly under cold running water. Shake off the excess water. Put the quinoa into a dry, heavy 10-inch skillet and toast, stirring occasionally, over medium heat for about 15 minutes or until the quinoa dries and turns golden.

2. Preheat the oven to 375°F. Grease 12 standard (7-tablespoon) muffin cups or line them with paper liners.

3. In a large bowl, whisk together the quinoa, flour, baking powder, salt, sugar, and orange peel until well combined.

4. Combine the eggs, oil, and orange juice. Add the liquid ingredients all at once to the dry ingredients and stir just until combined. Take care not to overmix—the mixture should be slightly lumpy.

5. Spoon the batter into the prepared muffin cups so that they are two-thirds full. If you want extra-large muffins, fill the cups to the top.

6. Bake the muffins for 25 to 30 minutes, or until golden brown (the internal temperature should reach 190°F). Immediately remove from the pans and serve warm, or cool on a rack.

Wheat Germ and Banana Muffins

1½ cups unbleached all-purpose flour

1 cup wheat germ

1 teaspoon salt

1 tablespoon baking powder

1 teaspoon baking soda

1 cup chopped roasted peanuts

1½ cups buttermilk

1½ cups mashed bananas (about 3 bananas)

½ cup honey

2 tablespoons vegetable oil

Makes about 12 large muffins

This recipe became a favorite with my faithful recipe testers during the recipe development stage of this book. You can vary the flavor of the muffins by using very ripe bananas and toasting the wheat germ, which will give the muffins a strong banana-wheat flavor. Yellow, barely soft bananas and raw wheat germ give the muffins subtler flavor. The peanuts add crunch.

1. Preheat oven to 375°F. Grease 12 standard (7-tablespoon) muffin cups or line with paper liners.

2. In a large bowl, whisk together the flour, wheat germ, salt, baking powder, baking soda, and peanuts until well mixed.

3. Combine the buttermilk, bananas, honey, and oil. Stir well. Add the liquid mixture all at once to the dry ingredients and stir just until combined. Take care not to overmix—the mixture should be slightly lumpy.

4. Spoon the batter into the prepared cups so that they are two-thirds full. If you want extra-large muffins, fill the cups to the top.

5. Bake the muffins for 20 to 25 minutes, or until golden brown (the internal temperature should reach 190°F). Immediately remove the muffins from the pans and serve warm, or cool on a rack.

Originally buttermilk was the liquid remaining after churning butter. Today, it is skim milk mixed with a culture. Manufacturers sometimes add butter particles to imitate old-fashioned buttermilk.

Zucchini Lemon Muffins

2 cups unbleached all-purpose flour

1 tablespoon baking powder

½ teaspoon salt

1 tablespoon grated lemon peel

2 cups shredded zucchini

1 cup milk

1 large egg, lightly beaten

2 tablespoons vegetable oil

¼ cup honey

Makes about 12 large muffins

Here is a good way to use the abundant supply of end-of-summer zucchini every gardener has. Zucchini adds moisture to muffins and quick breads, much the same way that carrots do. One of my recipe testers suggested we change the name of these muffins to "How to Slip Zucchini to the Kids." They are so delicious that children wolf them down!

1. Preheat the oven to 375°F. Grease 12 standard (7-tablespoon) muffin cups or line them with paper liners.

2. In a large bowl, whisk together the flour, baking powder, salt, and lemon peel until well combined. Add the zucchini and toss to mix.

3. Combine the milk, egg, oil, and honey. Add all at once to the dry ingredients and stir just until combined. Take care not to overmix—the mixture should be slightly lumpy.

4. Spoon the batter into the prepared pans so that they are two-thirds full. If you prefer extra-large muffins, fill the cups to the top.

5. Bake the muffins for 25 to 30 minutes, or until they are golden brown (the internal temperature should reach 190°F). Immediately remove from the pans and serve warm, or cool on a rack.

Many people like to use paper liners when making muffins. I don't use the liners because I like a good crust on a muffin, not soft sides. Not only that, but the cups are messy when you peel them off. If you're at the dinner table, where do you put this messy piece of paper? When you use a good nonstick, heavyweight muffin pan, you don't need the paper.

Blueberry Buckwheat Muffins

1 cup old-fashioned rolled oats

1½ cups buckwheat flour

2 tablespoons baking powder

1 teaspoon salt

1 teaspoon ground cinnamon

½ cup firmly packed dark brown sugar

2 teaspoons grated orange peel

½ cup sunflower seeds

1½ cups blueberries, washed and drained

2 eggs, lightly beaten

1½ cups fresh orange juice

2 tablespoons vegetable oil

Makes about 12 large muffins

The buckwheat flour and cinnamon give these muffins a deep brown color that sets off the blueberries beautifully. The combination of flavors also works well in this healthful, robust muffin. Try it for breakfast or with a hearty soup for supper.

1. Preheat the oven to 375°F. Grease 12 standard (7-table-spoon) muffin cups or line them with paper liners.

2. In a large bowl, whisk together the oats, buckwheat flour, baking powder, salt, cinnamon, sugar, and orange peel until well combined. Add the sunflower seeds and blueberries. Toss until well mixed.

3. Whisk together the eggs, orange juice, and oil until smooth. Add the egg mixture all at once to the dry ingredients and stir until just combined. Take care not to overmix—the mixture should be slightly lumpy.

4. Spoon the batter into the prepared muffin cups so that they are two-thirds full. If you want extra-large muffins, fill the cups to the top.

5. Bake the muffins for 20 to 25 minutes, or until they are well browned (the internal temperature should reach 190°F). Immediately remove from the pans and serve warm, or cool on a rack.

Aloha Bread

5 cups unbleached all-
purpose flour

1½ cups sugar

2½ tablespoons baking
powder

1½ teaspoons salt

1½ cups unsweetened
shredded coconut

1 cup coarsely chopped
macadamia nuts

3 cups canned crushed
unsweetened pineapple with
juice

3 large eggs, beaten

3 tablespoons vegetable oil

**Makes two 8½ × 4½-inch
loaves, four 5 × 3½-inch
loaves, or six 15-ounce cans**

This bread captures the flavors of Hawaii. If possible, use fresh coconut or packaged unsweetened shredded coconut, not the sweetened sort destined for coconut cake. For the use of cans, see the next recipe.

1. Preheat the oven to 375°F. Grease two 8½ × 4½-inch pans, four 5 × 3½-inch pans, or six 15-ounce cans.

2. In a large bowl, whisk together the flour, sugar, baking powder, and salt until well combined. Add the coconut and macadamia nuts and stir until mixed.

3. Combine the pineapple, eggs, and oil. Add all at once to the dry ingredients and stir until just combined. Spoon the batter into the pans. If using cans, spoon the batter into them so that they are about half full.

4. Bake 8½-inch loaves for about 1 hour to 1¼ hours, 5-inch loaves for 35 to 40 minutes, 15-ounce cans for 25 to 30 minutes, or until golden brown and springy to the touch (the internal temperature should reach 190°F). Cool for 10 minutes in the pans before turning out onto a rack to cool completely.

Banana Date Nut Bread

3 cups unbleached all-purpose flour

3 teaspoons baking powder

½ teaspoon baking soda

½ teaspoon salt

¾ cup pitted dates, coarsely chopped

¾ cup pecans, coarsely chopped

¾ cup firmly packed brown sugar

¾ cup solid vegetable shortening

4 large eggs, lightly beaten

2 cups mashed bananas (about 4 bananas)

Makes two 8½ × 4½-inch loaves, four 5 × 3½-inch loaves, or six 15-ounce cans

This old-fashioned favorite never seems to go out of style. My preference is for strong banana flavor, so I use very ripe bananas with speckled dark skins. If you prefer milder flavor, use bananas that are at their peak, with skins that are still bright yellow.

For fun, I like to bake this bread in 15-ounce cans—the sort that tomato sauce comes in. Be sure to wash the cans thoroughly. Leave the bottoms attached and during baking, stand the cans upright in the oven. The bread that comes from the cans can be cut into perfectly round slices that look lovely on salad plates. This bread is delicious sliced very thin and spread with whipped cream cheese.

1. Preheat the oven to 350°F. Grease two 8½ × 4½-inch pans, four 5 × 3½-inch pans, or six 15-ounce cans.

2. In a medium bowl, whisk together the flour, baking powder, baking soda, and salt until well combined. Add the dates and pecans and toss to mix.

3. In a large bowl, cream the sugar with the shortening. Add the eggs and continue to beat until well mixed.

4. Add half the flour mixture to the creamed mixture and mix well. Add half the bananas and stir just until combined. Stir in the remaining flour and then the bananas. Spoon the batter into the prepared pans. If using cans, spoon the batter into them so that they are about half full.

5. Bake 8½-inch loaves for about 1 hour to 1¼ hours, 5-inch loaves for 35 to 40 minutes, or 15-ounce cans for 25 to 30 minutes, or until the loaves are golden brown and springy to the touch (the internal temperature should reach 190°F). Cool for 10 minutes in the pans before turning out onto racks to cool completely.

Bara Brith

3 cups dried currants

3 cups strong hot tea

5 cups unbleached all-purpose flour

2 teaspoons salt

2 tablespoons baking powder

2¼ cups firmly packed brown sugar

1½ cups milk

1½ teaspoons vanilla extract

3 large eggs, lightly beaten

Makes two 8½ × 4½-inch loaves, four 5 × 3½-inch loaves, or six 15-ounce cans

The translation of this Welsh name is "speckled bread." There are many recipes for bara brith, some with yeast, others with baking powder. Although the bread must be started a day ahead to give the currants time to macerate in the tea, the rest of the procedure is quick and the bread is tasty, perfect for teatime.

For the use of cans, see the preceding recipe.

1. The day before baking, combine the currants and the hot tea. Cover and let stand at room temperature for 24 hours.

2. When ready to bake, preheat the oven to 325°F. Grease two 8½ × 4½-inch pans, four 5 × 3½-inch pans, or six 15-ounce cans.

3. In a large bowl, whisk together the flour, salt, baking powder, and sugar until well combined.

4. Combine the milk, vanilla, eggs, currants, and any tea that has not been absorbed. Add all at once to the dry ingredients and stir just until combined. Spoon the batter into the pans. If using cans, spoon the batter into them so that they are about half full.

5. Bake 8½-inch loaves for about 1 hour to 1¼ hours, 5-inch loaves for 35 to 40 minutes, or 15-ounce cans for 25 to 30 minutes, or until the internal temperature reaches 190°F. Cool in the pans for 10 minutes before turning out onto racks to cool completely.

Fruit and Nut Cottage Cheese Bread

5½ cups unbleached all-purpose flour

1½ teaspoons salt

2 tablespoons baking powder

1¼ cups sugar

1½ cups coarsely chopped walnuts

¾ cup raisins

¾ cup coarsely chopped dried apricots

¾ cup unsweetened shredded coconut

1 tablespoon grated orange peel

1½ cups small-curd cottage cheese

1¼ cups milk

3 large eggs, beaten

⅔ cup solid vegetable shortening, melted

Makes two 8½ × 4½ inch loaves, four 5 × 3½-inch loaves, or six 15-ounce cans

I like to make this bread with coarsely chopped nuts and dried apricots, but for a more delicate tea bread, chop them fine. You can also substitute another kind of dried fruit, such as pears or apples, for the apricots. The secret to this particularly moist bread is that the hot loaves are wrapped in foil, so they cool slowly in a steamy environment.

For the use of cans, see page 391.

1. Preheat the oven to 350°F. Grease two 8½ × 4½-inch pans, four 5 × 3½-inch pans, or six 15-ounce cans.

2. In a large bowl, whisk together the flour, salt, baking powder, and sugar until well combined. Stir in the walnuts, raisins, apricots, coconut, and orange peel.

3. Beat together the cottage cheese, milk, eggs, and shortening. Add all at once to the dry ingredients and stir just until combined. Spoon the batter into the prepared pans. If using cans, spoon the batter into them so that they are about half full.

4. Bake 8½-inch loaves for about 1 hour to 1¼ hours, 5-inch loaves for 35 to 40 minutes, or 15-ounce cans for 25 to 30 minutes, or until well browned (the internal temperature should reach 190°F). Cool the loaves in the pans for 10 minutes. Turn out of the pans and wrap them in foil for about 2 hours to steam until cool.

Gingered Pear Walnut Bread

1½ cups solid vegetable shortening

1½ cups sugar

4 large eggs

5½ cups unbleached all-purpose flour

1 tablespoon baking powder

1½ teaspoons baking soda

1½ teaspoons salt

1 to 2 tablespoons finely chopped crystallized ginger

2 cups coarsely chopped walnuts

3 cups peeled, cored, and finely chopped pears (about 3 medium)

2¼ cups buttermilk

Makes two 8½ × 4½-inch loaves, four 5 × 3½-inch loaves, or six 15-ounce cans

Crystallized ginger and fresh pears are a natural flavor combination and marry well in this recipe for a sweet bread that tastes just right with chicken or duck salad. For lively flavor with an obvious gingery bite, add the full two tablespoons of crystallized ginger. Serve the bread sliced thin and spread with sweet butter or whipped cream cheese.

For the use of cans, see page 391.

1. Preheat the oven to 375°F. Grease two 8½ × 4½-inch pans, four 5 × 3½-inch pans, or six 15-ounce cans.

2. In a large bowl, beat the shortening with the sugar until light and fluffy. Add the eggs one at a time, beating well after each addition.

3. In a medium bowl, whisk together the flour, baking powder, baking soda, and salt until well combined. Stir in the ginger, walnuts, and pears.

4. Add half the dry ingredients to the creamed mixture. Add half the buttermilk and stir until combined. Add the remaining dry ingredients and then buttermilk, stirring just until combined. Spoon the batter into the prepared pans. If using cans, spoon the batter into them so that they are about half full.

5. Bake 8½-inch loaves for about 1 hour to 1¼ hours, 5-inch loaves for 35 to 40 minutes, 15-ounce cans for 25 to 30 minutes, or until they are well browned (the internal temperature should reach 190°F). Cool the bread in the pans for 10 minutes before turning them out onto a rack to cool completely.

Irish Soda Bread

2 cups unbleached all-
purpose flour, plus
additional as needed

1 teaspoon baking soda

1 teaspoon salt

1 tablespoon caraway seeds

2 tablespoons sugar

4 tablespoons (½ stick)
unsalted butter, chilled

½ cup currants or raisins

1 cup buttermilk

Makes 1 large round loaf

Soda breads are associated with Irish cooking, where they often are served with a strong cup of tea. The open-crumbed bread is equally good served with stew for dinner or made into French toast for breakfast. This one, with its mixture of caraway seeds and currants, has a sweet-and-sour flavor that is hard to beat. For nutty flavor, replace half the amount of all-purpose flour with whole wheat flour. Traditionally, soda breads are broken rather than sliced.

1. Preheat the oven to 375°F.

2. In a large bowl, whisk together the 2 cups of flour, the baking soda, salt, caraway seeds, and sugar until well combined.

3. Using a pastry blender or 2 knives, cut the butter into the dry ingredients until it forms rice-size pieces. Add the raisins and toss until combined. Add the buttermilk all at once and stir just until combined.

4. Turn the dough out onto a floured board and knead gently 8 or 9 times. Roll the dough into a ball and coat heavily with flour. Put the dough on a parchment-lined or well-greased baking sheet and flatten the ball slightly so that the loaf is about 3 inches high. Using a sharp, well-floured knife, cut a cross on the top of the loaf about ½ inch deep.

5. Bake the bread for 30 to 35 minutes, or until golden brown (the internal temperature should reach 190°F). Remove from the baking sheet and cool on a rack.

Raisin Walnut Rosemary Bread

3 cups golden raisins

3 cups scalded milk

2 cups sugar

6 tablespoons (¾ stick) unsalted butter, at room temperature

3 large eggs, at room temperature

2 teaspoons vanilla extract

4½ cups unbleached all-purpose flour

2 teaspoons salt

2 tablespoons baking powder

2 tablespoons crushed fresh rosemary leaves or 2 teaspoons crushed dried

2 cups coarsely chopped walnuts

Makes two 8½ × 4½-inch loaves, four 5 × 3½-inch loaves, or six 15-ounce cans

Rosemary is a strong-flavored, flowery herb with a heady aroma that fills the house when this bread is baking. It is the only herb I like in sweet breads and I have combined it here with golden raisins, walnuts, and sugar to make a lovely tea or dessert bread. If you have an herb garden, or if you grow rosemary on the windowsill, make this bread with fresh rosemary. I use scalded milk to soak the raisins. Scalding means to heat the liquid just until almost boiling—in fact, to 180°F. The saturated raisins stay very soft during baking.

For the use of cans, see page 391.

1. Add the raisins to the scalded milk. Cover and cool for about 30 minutes, until lukewarm.

2. Preheat the oven to 350°F. Grease two 8½ × 4½-inch pans, four 5 × 3½-inch pans, or six 15-ounce cans.

3. In a large bowl, beat the sugar with the butter. Add the cooled raisin mixture, the egg, and the vanilla and mix well.

4. In a medium bowl, whisk together the flour, salt, baking powder, rosemary, and nuts until well combined. Add to the butter mixture all at once and stir just until combined. Spoon the batter into the prepared pans. If using cans, spoon the batter into them so that they are about half full.

5. Bake 8½-inch loaves for about 1 hour to 1¼ hours, 5-inch loaves for 35 to 40 minutes, or 15-ounce cans for 25 to 30 minutes or until well browned (the internal temperature should reach 190°F). Cool for 10 minutes in the pans before turning out onto a rack to cool completely.

Sun-Dried Tomato, Scallion, and Olive Bread

3¾ cups milk

¼ cup olive oil

3 large eggs, lightly beaten

5¼ cups unbleached all-purpose flour

3 teaspoons salt

¼ cup sugar

2 tablespoons baking powder

⅔ cup coarsely chopped sun-dried tomatoes, drained if oil-packed

1½ cups thinly sliced scallions (use all the white part and about 1½ inches of green)

¾ cup thinly sliced pitted ripe black olives

Makes two 8½ × 4½-inch loaves, four 5 × 3½-inch loaves, or six 15-ounce cans

Although most quick breads are sweet, there are some excellent savory ones—this loaf being a perfect example. I serve this with cocktails or as an accompaniment to soup and salad. If you serve it as an hors d'oeuvre, spread the slices with a thin layer of butter or cream cheese to keep them from drying out.

For the use of cans, see page 391.

1. Preheat the oven to 350°F. Grease two 8½ × 4½-inch pans, four 5 × 3½-inch pans, or six 15-ounce cans.

2. In a medium bowl, whisk the milk, oil, and eggs together to combine.

3. In a large bowl, whisk together the flour, salt, sugar, and baking powder until well combined. Add the sun-dried tomatoes, scallions, and olives and toss to combine.

4. Add the liquid ingredients to the dry ingredients all at once and stir just until mixed. Spoon the batter into the pans. If using cans, spoon the batter into them so that they are half full.

5. Bake 8½-inch loaves for about 1 hour to 1¼ hours, 5-inch loaves for 35 to 40 minutes, or 15-ounce cans for 25 to 30 minutes, or until well browned (the internal temperature should reach 190°F). Cool for 10 minutes in the pans before turning out onto racks to cool completely.

Tortone

¾ cup coarsely chopped dried figs

¾ cup coarsely chopped dried apricots

¾ cup coarsely chopped pitted dates

1 tablespoon grated orange peel

¾ cup golden raisins

¾ cup currants

⅓ cup dark rum

1½ cups whole pine nuts

1½ cups whole hazelnuts (unskinned)

1½ cups whole almonds

1½ cups whole Brazil nuts

1½ cups shredded unsweetened coconut

6 ounces coarsely chopped bittersweet or semisweet chocolate

1½ teaspoons coarsely ground black pepper

1½ cups warm honey

2¼ cups unbleached all-purpose flour

Makes two 8½ × 4½-inch loaves, four 5 × 3½-inch loaves, or six 15-ounce cans

This unleavened Italian bread combines sweet fruits, nuts, and chocolate spiced with black pepper. As you read through the lengthy list of ingredients don't think you have found a mistake: there is very little liquid in the batter and no leavener at all. Not surprisingly, this is a very dense, compact bread tasting intensely of the large amount of fruit and unchopped nuts bound together by a relatively small measure of flour. Tortone is a great alternative to fruitcake at Christmas. Because the fruit must marinate, it takes 2 days to make tortone.

For the use of cans, see page 391.

1. The day before baking, combine the figs, apricots, dates, orange peel, raisins, currants, and rum in a large glass bowl. Stir to mix. Cover with plastic wrap and let stand for 24 hours.

2. When ready to bake, preheat the oven to 325°F. Grease two 8½ × 4½-inch pans, four 5 × 3½-inch pans, or six 15-ounce cans. Cut strips of parchment paper and line the bottoms of the pans (cut the paper long enough to extend up both ends of the pan and an inch above—this will give you handles to pull the finished loaves out of the pan). Grease the paper. (To line a can, cut a 5 × 10-inch strip of parchment paper. Grease both sides of the paper and insert it so that ½ inch of the paper stands above the edge of the top of the can.)

3. Add the pine nuts, hazelnuts, almonds, Brazil nuts, coconut, chocolate, and pepper to the fruit mixture. Stir to combine. Add the honey and stir until well mixed.

4. Add the flour to the fruit-nut mixture, ½ cup at a time, stirring well after each addition. Spoon the batter into the prepared pans and press down slightly to remove any air bubbles. If using cans, spoon the batter into them so that they are half full.

5. Bake 8½-inch loaves for about 1 hour to 1¼ hours, 5-inch loaves for 35 to 40 minutes, or 15-ounce cans for 25 to 30 minutes. Watch the bread carefully during the last 10 minutes to make sure it does not brown too quickly. If this happens, cover the pans loosely with aluminum foil, shiny side up.

6. Cool the loaves in the pans for 15 minutes. Slide the blade of a knife along the sides of the pans to loosen the bread before turning out onto a wire rack. Cool completely before peeling off the parchment paper. If using cans, remove the bottom of the can and push the bread out.

7. Wrap the bread so that it is airtight and store at room temperature. Tortone is best if allowed to mellow for 12 hours before serving.

Vi's Brown Bread

2¼ cups raisins

2¼ cups boiling water

1½ cups sugar

3 tablespoons unsalted butter, at room temperature

2 large eggs

2 tablespoons molasses

⅓ cup milk

1½ teaspoons vanilla extract

4¼ cups unbleached all-purpose flour

1½ teaspoons salt

1 tablespoon baking soda

¾ cup coarsely chopped walnuts

Makes two 8½ × 4½-inch loaves, four 5 × 3½-inch loaves, or six 15-ounce cans

My mother-in-law, Vi Oppenneer, shared this recipe with me for the best version of brown bread I have ever tried. It is easier than the steamed kind and just as moist and flavorful. I spread slices of this bread with cream cheese or butter and serve it with Boston baked beans, hearty chowders, or sliced cold meat.

For the use of cans, see page 391.

1. Add the raisins to the boiling water. Cover and cool for about 30 minutes, until lukewarm.

2. Preheat the oven to 350°F. Grease two 8½ × 4½-inch pans, four 5 × 3½-inch pans, or six 15-ounce cans.

3. In a large bowl, combine the sugar, butter, the raisin mixture, eggs, molasses, milk, and vanilla. Mix well.

4. In a medium bowl, whisk together the flour, salt, baking soda, and nuts. Add to the raisin mixture all at once and stir just until combined. Spoon the batter into the prepared pans. If using cans, spoon the batter into them so that they are about half full.

5. Bake 8½-inch loaves for about 1 hour to 1¼ hours, 5-inch loaves for 35 to 40 minutes, or 15-ounce cans for 25 to 30 minutes, or until the internal temperature reaches 190°F. Cool in the pans for 10 minutes. Turn out the warm loaves, wrap immediately in foil, and let steam for 2 hours until cool.

Whole Wheat–Dried Cherry Bread

2 cups dried cherries

2¼ cups milk

1½ cups granulated sugar

3 tablespoons unsalted butter, at room temperature

2 large eggs, lightly beaten

2 teaspoons almond extract

2¼ cups unbleached all-purpose flour

1½ cups whole wheat pastry flour

1½ teaspoons salt

1½ tablespoons baking powder

1½ cups coarsely chopped or slivered almonds

Makes two 8½ × 4½-inch loaves, four 5 × 3½-inch loaves, or six 15-ounce cans

Dried cherries are sensational in breads—even better than raisins. The flavor is concentrated and the texture is chewy. Look for dried cherries in specialty shops and mail order catalogues such as those listed on page 411. If you have trouble finding dried cherries, substitute dried cranberries, blueberries, or raisins. The fruit will stay soft and moist during baking, making this an excellent tea bread.

For the use of cans, see page 391.

1. Heat the milk in a saucepan over medium heat until it is scalded (tiny bubbles will appear all around the edge). Add the cherries to the scalded milk. Cover and cool for about 30 minutes, or until lukewarm.

2. Preheat the oven to 350°F. Grease two 8½ × 4½-inch pans, four 5 × 3½-inch pans, or six 15-ounce cans.

3. In a large bowl, combine the sugar, butter, the cherry mixture, the eggs, and the almond extract and stir to mix.

4. In a medium bowl, whisk together the all-purpose flour, whole wheat flour, salt, baking powder, and almonds until well combined. Add to the cherry mixture all at once and stir just until combined. Spoon the batter into the prepared pans. If using cans, spoon the batter into them so that they are about half full.

5. Bake 8½-inch loaves for about 1 hour to 1¼ hours, 5-inch loaves for 35 to 40 minutes, or 15-ounce cans for 25 to 30 minutes, or until the internal temperature reaches 190°F. Cool in the pans for 10 minutes before turning out onto wire racks to cool completely.

Troubleshooting

Every now and then even the most seasoned baker has problems with a loaf of bread: the dough won't rise, the crumb is excessively airy, the crust is burned on the bottom. These and other disasters are usually easy to remedy—if you know what to consider. Here are some of the most common problems home bakers encounter and the reasons for them.

Lumps in the dough (yeast and quick breads):

○ The dough was improperly kneaded or mixed.
○ Powdered milk was used and was not mixed with the flour or liquefied before being added.
○ The flour was old or improperly stored.

Yeast dough did not rise in the bowl, or rose very slowly:

○ The liquid was too hot and damaged or killed the yeast.
○ The liquid was too cold and did not properly activate the yeast.
○ The yeast was old, past expiration date.
○ Too much sugar in the dough makes it sluggish.
○ Too much salt in the dough inhibits yeast development.
○ Too much flour makes the dough heavy.
○ Too much fat weighs down the dough.
○ The flour was old or improperly stored.
○ The dough was made with whole grain flour and so did not rise as high as dough made with all-purpose flour.
○ The dough was improperly kneaded.
○ Insufficient rising time—if the dough is left in a cool place, it will rise but will take longer than expected. Be patient.
○ The rising place was too cool or drafty.

You don't have the correct-size loaf pan:

○ Shape the dough into a round or oval and set it on a well-greased baking sheet to rise. Just before baking, make 2 or 3 shallow slits in the top with a serrated knife. Bake according to the recipe.

❍ Use a well-greased can, such as a tomato sauce or coffee can (see pages 377 and 391 for more information on baking bread in cans).

The crust on yeast bread is too thick:

❍ Too much flour.
❍ The bread stayed in the oven too long.
❍ Insufficient rising time.
❍ Oven temperature was too low.

The crust on yeast bread separated from the loaf (called shelling):

❍ Too much yeast.
❍ The outside of the bread dried out before baking (be sure to cover the dough with a tightly woven kitchen towel).
❍ Insufficient rising time.
❍ Oven temperature was too low.

Yeast bread crumbles and is hard to slice:

❍ Dough improperly kneaded.
❍ Too much flour.
❍ Rising place was too warm.
❍ Dough allowed to rise too long before baking.
❍ Oven temperature was too low.
❍ Finished loaf should be sliced on its side with a sharp serrated knife (dull knives chew the slices).

Bread has a sour, yeasty, or gassy taste and smell:

❍ Too much yeast.
❍ Rising place was too warm.
❍ Dough allowed to rise too long before baking.

Yeast bread did not rise in the oven:

❍ Insufficient rising time.
❍ Rising place was too warm.

Yeast bread rose nicely but collapsed in the oven:

❍ Dough was allowed to rise too long before baking.

Yeast bread rose unevenly in the oven:

❍ The oven is not heating evenly. Rotate the pans in the oven after the first 10 minutes of baking.

Yeast bread has dark streaks through it:

❍ The dough was improperly kneaded.
❍ The rising bowl was greased too heavily with butter or shortening that wouldn't absorb back into the dough.
❍ The dough was exposed to too much air during rising and so developed a crust.
❍ The dough was turned out onto a floured work surface for shaping rather than a lightly oiled one.

Yeast bread has large holes:

❍ Gases (caused by the yeast) were not completely expelled before shaping.
❍ The dough was allowed to rise too quickly or left for too long before baking.
❍ Too much yeast.
❍ The dough was improperly kneaded.
❍ Cold liquid was added to the dough.
❍ If you are making French bread, rejoice! Holes are considered perfection.

Yeast bread is doughy on the bottom:

❍ The bread rose too much and fell slightly during baking.
❍ The bread was baked in shiny pans, which prevented the crust from browning properly.
❍ The flour was old or improperly stored.
❍ The bread did not bake completely.

Yeast bread has a crack on its side:

○ Too much flour.
○ The flour was old or improperly stored.
○ Oven temperature was too high.
○ Insufficient rising time.
○ The oven is not heating evenly (have it checked).
○ If freestanding loaf, the top was not slit before baking.
○ The top of the dough dried out before baking.
○ This is not necessarily a bad trait; all bread expands in the oven and sometimes this causes the crust to crack. Next time slit the dough down the middle if the crack is excessive.

Yeast bread is cracked on top:

○ Too much flour.
○ The dough was improperly kneaded.
○ The bread cooled too quickly or was in a drafty place.

Yeast bread is heavy and compact:

○ Too much flour.
○ Insufficient rising time.
○ Too much salt.
○ The flour was old or improperly stored.
○ Not enough wheat flour in the dough to form good gluten meshwork.
○ The dough was improperly kneaded.

Freestanding yeast loaf flattened too much:

○ The dough was improperly kneaded.
○ Not enough flour.
○ The loaf rose too long and collapsed in the oven.

Yeast bread wet inside and coarsely grained:

○ The bread was underbaked.
○ Insufficient rising time.
○ Not enough flour.

Yeast bread falls in oven:

○ The dough was allowed to rise too quickly or left for too long before baking.

Yeast bread is pale or does not brown on the sides:

○ The bread was baked in shiny pans, which reflect heat rays and prevent the crust from browning properly.
○ The pans were too close together or not placed in the center of the oven.
○ The oven temperature was too low.
○ The flour was old or improperly stored.
○ The dough was allowed to rise for too long before baking.
○ The bread was underbaked.
○ Do not hesitate to remove the bread from the pan and set it directly on the oven rack for 5 to 10 minutes to help it brown. It is not delicate, like a cake, and will not fall.

Yeast bread has a flat top:

○ The dough was improperly kneaded.
○ Not enough flour.
○ The flour was old or improperly stored.
○ The dough was allowed to rise for too long before baking and consequently fell in the oven.

The bottom of the loaf is overbrowned (yeast and quick breads):

○ The pans were too close together, so that there was not enough air flow—leave at least one inch between the pans and an inch between the pans and sides of the oven.
○ Oven temperature was too high.

The bread has no flavor (yeast and quick breads):

○ Not enough salt, sugar, or both.
○ The flour was old or improperly stored.
○ Other ingredients were past their prime (herbs and spices lose potency within a year).

Muffins and quick breads have large tunnels or holes:

❍ The batter was overmixed.

Muffins and quick breads have tough textures:

❍ The batter was overmixed.

Muffins have a high center peak:

❍ The oven was not hot enough.

Quick bread cracked on top:

❍ No problem! Quick breads almost always crack in the oven.

Biscuits did not rise:

❍ The leavener was old and lost its potency.
❍ The biscuit cutter was twisted when cutting the dough and therefore the sides were sealed.

Finishing Touches

Washes

Although plain, unadorned loaves of bread are appetizingly rustic and earthy, there are times when a shiny wash or a pretty glaze makes the difference between the ordinary and the special.

For shine, a little color, and sometimes a soft crust, I frequently brush washes lightly over unbaked bread just before baking. Following, listed alphabetically, are some of my favorites.

Note: Washes containing egg should be applied sparingly so they will not drip down onto the pan and cause the bread the stick.

○ Egg, for a bright golden shine: Beat 1 egg with 1 tablespoon of cold water. Just before baking the bread, brush the wash lightly over all exposed surfaces. Bake as directed.

○ Egg white, for shine without color: Beat 1 egg white with 1 tablespoon of cold water until frothy. Just before baking the bread, brush the wash lightly over all exposed surfaces. Bake as directed.

○ Egg yolk, for a deep, rich golden shine: Beat 1 egg yolk with 1 tablespoon of cold water. Just before baking the bread, brush the wash lightly over all exposed surfaces. Bake as directed. (If you use 2 yolks and 2 teaspoons of water, the shine will be even deeper and richer.)

○ Egg yolk with milk, for a dark, rich shine: Beat 1 egg yolk with 1 tablespoon of milk. Just before baking the bread, brush the wash lightly over all exposed surfaces. Bake as directed.

○ Honey, for a flat yellow shine: Combine 2 tablespoons of honey with 2 tablespoons of warm water. Just before baking the bread, brush about half the wash lightly over all exposed surfaces. Bake as directed. Five minutes before the end of baking, take the loaf from the oven and brush with the remaining wash. Return the loaf to the oven.

○ Milk, for a golden shine that is not quite as bright as an egg wash: Lightly brush about 2 tablespoons of whole, low-fat, or skim milk on all exposed surfaces. Bake as directed. The higher the fat content of the milk, the darker the finish.

❍ Milk with oil or butter, for a golden shine and a soft crust: Combine 1 tablespoon of warm whole, low-fat, or skim milk with 1 tablespoon of melted butter or vegetable oil. Brush lightly over all exposed surfaces. Bake as directed.

❍ Molasses, for a dark, flat shine: Combine 2 tablespoons of molasses (the darker the better) with 2 tablespoons of warm water. Just before baking the bread, brush about half the wash lightly over all exposed surfaces. Bake as directed. Five minutes before the end of baking, take the loaf from the oven and brush with the remaining wash. Return the loaf to the oven.

❍ Oil, for a soft crust: Brush about 2 tablespoons of vegetable oil over all exposed surfaces. Bake as directed. For a slight shine, brush oil over the bread again right after it bakes.

❍ Water, for a chewy crust: Just before baking brush about 2 tablespoons of cold water over all exposed surfaces. Bake as directed.

Glazes and Decorations

It is not often that breads need glazes, but when one is appropriate, it makes the loaf elegant and festive. I especially like to glaze shaped loaves, such as braids and wreaths. Another easy and especially appealing way to decorate a loaf of bread is with plain, ordinary flour. And all manner of ingredients such as seeds, salt, and sugars can be sprinkled over loaves before baking. Following are some ideas for decorating bread.

❍ Cornstarch glaze: While the bread is baking, combine 1 tablespoon of cornstarch with ½ cup of cold water in a small saucepan. Cook over medium heat for about 2 minutes, or until the mixture is thick and translucent. About 5 minutes before the end of baking, take the bread from the oven and paint all exposed surfaces with the cornstarch glaze. Return the bread to the oven. The glaze gives the finished loaf a translucent shine. This is particularly attractive on dark breads.

❍ Flour: Form the dough into the shape you want. I like to flour round or oval freestanding loaves, but the method works with any shape. Roll the shaped dough in flour until it is heavily coated. Set the bread on or in a pan, cover it, and let it rise. As it rises, the dough's expansion creates patterns in the flour. Bake the bread as directed. During baking, the crust lightens and the flour toasts and turns slightly yellow.

Flouring is especially dramatic on dark breads such as pumpernickel. Different kinds of flour produce different results. For example, semolina flour toasts to a more golden color than unbleached all-purpose flour, and rye flour turns a dull, dark brown in the oven.

○ Sprinkles: Use ingredients that can be sprinkled over bread in conjunction with one of the egg glazes above. Just before baking, lightly brush all exposed surfaces with egg wash and sprinkle the ingredient of your choice over the bread. The egg wash glues the sprinkle to the bread. Use any of the following or invent your own.

Caraway seeds
Coarse or kosher salt
Coarse sugar (pärlsocker is large-grained and will not dissolve in the oven)
Finely ground nuts
Finely ground onions soaked in oil to prevent scorching
Poppy seeds
Rolled grain, such as barley, oats, triticale, rye, or wheat
Sesame seeds
Sunflower seeds
Unprocessed bran
Wheat germ

Crusts

Crusts may be thin or thick, chewy and soft or nicely crisp. Following are some guidelines to producing the type of crust you like best.

○ Thin, crisp crust, method 1: Set a heavy, flat pan, such as a 7-inch cast iron skillet, on the lower oven shelf as the oven preheats. Put 1 cup of ice cubes into the hot pan when you put the bread in the oven. The ice melts and creates steam.

○ Thin, crisp crust, method 2: Put a pan of boiling water on the lower shelf in the oven with the bread. Remove it after the first 10 minutes of baking. Take care it does not slosh or spill.

○ Thin, crisp crust, method 3: During the first 10 minutes of baking, open the oven every 3 minutes and spray the bread with water or brush it with cold water. Work quickly, because every time you open the oven door, heat escapes.

○ Crisp crust: Place a baking stone in a hot oven 30 minutes before you are ready to bake the bread, and turn the oven on, to the temperature called for in the recipe. Be sure to put the stone in the section of the oven where the bread should be during baking and take into account the height of the stone. For instance, if the bread is high rising, lower the oven rack to accommodate stone and loaf. After the stone is completely heated, put the loaf directly on it, unless it is in a bread pan.

○ Chewy, crisp crust similar to that on French bread: Use both the ice cube method and baking stone method described above.

○ Thick crust: Brush the bread with water. Do this in conjunction with any of the methods described above for both effects.

○ Thin, crisp, crackly crust: Use the unglazed ceramic baking oven called a La Cloche to bake the bread. See the description on page 35 and the baking instructions on page 68.

Sources

"Perfect Bread: How to Conquer Bread Baking" is a 45-minute video featuring Betsy Oppenneer. Using close-up photography that shows mixing, kneading, and baking, the video is designed to reassure novices and help experienced bakers get even better results. Send a check or money order for $33 (includes shipping and handling) to The Breadworks, Dept. PB, RR1, Box 238A, Canaan, New Hampshire, 03741; or call 1-603-632-9171. Visa and MasterCard accepted.

"Perfect Bread: Fun with Creative Shapes" is a 45-minute video featuring Betsy Oppenneer. This video helps bakers master the art of shaping dough into an array of fanciful shapes, including braids and wreaths. The video is $33; to order see information above.

The King Arthur Flour Baker's Catalogue is a resource for baking supplies and equipment and is mentioned often in *The Bread Book*. To order the catalogue, call 1-800-827-6836; or write to The Baker's Catalogue, RR2, Box 56, Norwich, Vermont, 05055.

L'Esprit de Campagne is a great resource for dried apples, dried Montmorency cherries, dried blueberries and cranberries, and all types of sun-ripened dried Roma tomato products (these are the kind of sun-dried tomatoes I prefer in my recipes). Call 1-703-955-1014, or write to L'Esprit de Campagne, P.O. Box 3130, Winchester, Virginia, 22604, for a brochure.

Vanns Spices Ltd. carries a full line of dried herbs and spices. Buying directly from the producer assures a fresher product. Call 1-410-583-1643, or write Vanns Spices Ltd., 1238 East Joppa Road, Baltimore, Maryland, 21286, for a brochure.

Brewster River Mill is a small enterprise offering freshly ground grains and maple sugar products. Call 1-802-644-2987, or write Brewster River Mill, Mill Street, Jeffersonville, Vermont, 05464, for a brochure.

Index